Fiat Punto
Owners Workshop Manual

Martynn Randall

Models covered

(5956 - 224)

Fiat Grande Punto, Punto Evo & Punto Hatchback with 1.2 litre (1242cc) & 1.4 litre (1368cc) petrol engines

Does NOT cover 'TwinAir', 'Multiair' or 'T-Jet' petrol models, diesel models, dual-fuel models, 'Dualogic' transmission, Abarth models or Van
Does NOT cover models from earlier Punto range available through 2006 and 2007 (sometimes known as 'Punto Classic').

© Haynes Publishing 2015

ABCDE
FGHIJ
KLMNO
PQRST

A book in the **Haynes Owners Workshop Manual Series**

ISBN **978 0 85733 956 0**

British Library Cataloguing in Publication Data
A catalogue record for this book is available from the British Library.

Printed in the USA

Haynes Publishing
Sparkford, Yeovil, Somerset BA22 7JJ, England

Haynes North America, Inc
861 Lawrence Drive, Newbury Park, California 91320, USA

Haynes Publishing Nordiska AB
Box 1504, 751 45 UPPSALA, Sverige

Printed using 33-lb Resolute Book 65 4.0 from Resolute Forest Products Calhoun, TN mill. Resolute is a member of World Wildlife Fund's Climate Savers programme committed to significantly reducing GHG emissions. This paper uses 50% less wood fibre than traditional offset. The Calhoun Mill is certified to the following sustainable forest management and chain of custody standards: SFI, PEFC and FSC Controlled Wood.

Contents

LIVING WITH YOUR FIAT PUNTO

Introduction	Page	0•4
Safety first!	Page	0•5

Roadside repairs

If your car won't start	Page	0•6
Identifying leaks	Page	0•7
Towing	Page	0•7
Jump starting	Page	0•8
Wheel changing	Page	0•9

Weekly checks

Introduction	Page	0•10
Underbonnet check points	Page	0•10
Engine oil level	Page	0•11
Brake/clutch fluid level	Page	0•12
Coolant level	Page	0•12
Battery	Page	0•13
Screen/headlight washer fluid level	Page	0•13
Electrical systems	Page	0•14
Wiper blades	Page	0•14
Tyre condition and pressure	Page	0•15

Lubricants and fluids

	Page	0•16

Tyre pressures

	Page	0•16

MAINTENANCE

Routine maintenance and servicing

Servicing specifications	Page	1•2
Maintenance schedule	Page	1•3
Maintenance procedures	Page	1•5

Contents

REPAIRS AND OVERHAUL

Engine and Associated Systems

SOHC (8-valve) engine in-car repair procedures   Page   2A•1

DOHC (16-valve) 1.4L engine in-car repair procedures   Page   2B•1

General engine removal and overhaul procedures   Page   2C•1

Cooling, heating and ventilation systems   Page   3•1

Fuel and exhaust systems   Page   4A•1

Emissions control systems   Page   4B•1

Starting and charging systems   Page   5A•1

Ignition system   Page   5B•1

Transmission

Clutch   Page   6•1

Manual gearbox   Page   7•1

Driveshafts   Page   8•1

Brakes and suspension

Braking system   Page   9•1

Suspension and steering   Page   10•1

Body equipment

Bodywork and fittings   Page   11•1

Body electrical system   Page   12•1

Wiring diagrams   Page   12•20

REFERENCE

Dimensions and weights   Page   REF•1

Fuel economy   Page   REF•2

Conversion factors   Page   REF•6

Vehicle jacking and support   Page   REF•7

Buying spare parts   Page   REF•7

General repair procedures   Page   REF•8

Vehicle identification   Page   REF•9

Tools and working facilities   Page   REF•10

MOT test checks   Page   REF•12

Fault finding   Page   REF•16

Index   Page   REF•22

0•4 Introduction

The Fiat Grande Punto range covered by this manual was introduced in January 2006, on 3-door and 5-door hatchback form, with a choice petrol engines. The engines covered are the popular 1.2 litre, and 1.4 litre SOHC (8-valve) and 1.4 litre (16-valve) units, with multi-point fuel injection, and the latest emission control systems. The engines are of a well-proven design and have been used extensively in a range of Fiat vehicles.

Fully independent front suspension is fitted, with semi-independent torsion beam suspension used at the rear. Electrically operated power steering is standard equipment on all models. A five-speed manual transmission is fitted.

In November 2010, the Punto Evo was introduced, which is a facelifted version of the Grande Punto, with new lights, bumpers, and a revised interior. This was followed by a further facelifted version in August of 2012, which was simply called 'Punto'.

The Grande Punto/Evo/Punto is very well-equipped for a small car. Standard and optional equipment includes multi-airbags, trip computer, electric windows, ABS, central locking and air conditioning.

For the home mechanic, the Grande Punto/Evo/Punto is a straightforwards car to maintain, and most of the items requiring frequent attention are easily accessible.

This manual covers the following models:
1.2 litre (1242cc) and 1.4 litre (1368cc) SOHC 8-valve petrol
1.4 litre (1368cc) DOHC 16-valve petrol

This manual DOES NOT cover:
TwinAir, Multiair or T-Jet petrol models
Diesel engines
Dual-fuel models
Dualogic transmission
Abarth or Van models
Punto range available from 2006 to 2007 (sometimes known as 'Punto Classic)

Your Fiat Grande Punto/Evo/Punto manual

The aim of this Manual is to help you get the best value from your vehicle. It can do so in several ways. It can help you decide what work must be done (even should you choose to get it done by a garage). It will also provide information on routine maintenance and servicing, and give a logical course of action and diagnosis when random faults occur. However, it is hoped that you will use the manual by tackling the work yourself. On simpler jobs it may even be quicker than booking the car into a garage and going there twice, to leave and collect it. Perhaps most important, a lot of money can be saved by avoiding the costs a garage must charge to cover its labour and overheads.

The manual has drawings and descriptions to show the function of the various components so that their layout can be understood. Tasks are described and photographed in a clear step-by-step sequence. The illustrations are numbered by the Section number and paragraph number to which they relate – if there is more than one illustration per paragraph, the sequence is denoted alphabetically.

References to the "left" or "right" of the vehicle are in the sense of a person in the driver's seat, facing forwards.

Acknowledgements

Thanks are due to Draper Tools, who provided some of the workshop tools, and to all those people at Sparkford who helped in the production of this manual.

This manual is not a direct reproduction of the vehicle manufacturer's data, and its publication should not be taken as implying any technical approval by the vehicle manufacturers or importers.

We take great pride in the accuracy of information given in this manual, but vehicle manufacturers make alterations and design changes during the production run of a particular vehicle of which they do not inform us. No liability can be accepted by the authors or publishers for loss, damage or injury caused by any errors in, or omissions from, the information given.

Project vehicles

The main vehicle used in the preparation of this manual, and which appears in many of the photographic sequences, was a 1.4 L DOHC 16-valve petrol engine with manual transmission transmission.

Fiat Grande Punto 5-door

Working on your car can be dangerous. This page shows just some of the potential risks and hazards, with the aim of creating a safety-conscious attitude.

General hazards

Scalding

• Don't remove the radiator or expansion tank cap while the engine is hot.
• Engine oil, transmission fluid or power steering fluid may also be dangerously hot if the engine has recently been running.

Burning

• Beware of burns from the exhaust system and from any part of the engine. Brake discs and drums can also be extremely hot immediately after use.

Crushing

• When working under or near a raised vehicle, always supplement the jack with axle stands, or use drive-on ramps.
Never venture under a car which is only supported by a jack.
• Take care if loosening or tightening high-torque nuts when the vehicle is on stands. Initial loosening and final tightening should be done with the wheels on the ground.

Fire

• Fuel is highly flammable; fuel vapour is explosive.
• Don't let fuel spill onto a hot engine.
• Do not smoke or allow naked lights (including pilot lights) anywhere near a vehicle being worked on. Also beware of creating sparks (electrically or by use of tools).
• Fuel vapour is heavier than air, so don't work on the fuel system with the vehicle over an inspection pit.
• Another cause of fire is an electrical overload or short-circuit. Take care when repairing or modifying the vehicle wiring.
• Keep a fire extinguisher handy, of a type suitable for use on fuel and electrical fires.

Electric shock

• Ignition HT and Xenon headlight voltages can be dangerous, especially to people with heart problems or a pacemaker. Don't work on or near these systems with the engine running or the ignition switched on.

• Mains voltage is also dangerous. Make sure that any mains-operated equipment is correctly earthed. Mains power points should be protected by a residual current device (RCD) circuit breaker.

Fume or gas intoxication

• Exhaust fumes are poisonous; they can contain carbon monoxide, which is rapidly fatal if inhaled. Never run the engine in a confined space such as a garage with the doors shut.
• Fuel vapour is also poisonous, as are the vapours from some cleaning solvents and paint thinners.

Poisonous or irritant substances

• Avoid skin contact with battery acid and with any fuel, fluid or lubricant, especially antifreeze, brake hydraulic fluid and Diesel fuel. Don't syphon them by mouth. If such a substance is swallowed or gets into the eyes, seek medical advice.
• Prolonged contact with used engine oil can cause skin cancer. Wear gloves or use a barrier cream if necessary. Change out of oil-soaked clothes and do not keep oily rags in your pocket.
• Air conditioning refrigerant forms a poisonous gas if exposed to a naked flame (including a cigarette). It can also cause skin burns on contact.

Asbestos

• Asbestos dust can cause cancer if inhaled or swallowed. Asbestos may be found in gaskets and in brake and clutch linings. When dealing with such components it is safest to assume that they contain asbestos.

Special hazards

Hydrofluoric acid

• This extremely corrosive acid is formed when certain types of synthetic rubber, found in some O-rings, oil seals, fuel hoses etc, are exposed to temperatures above 4000C. The rubber changes into a charred or sticky substance containing the acid. *Once formed, the acid remains dangerous for years. If it gets onto the skin, it may be necessary to amputate the limb concerned.*
• When dealing with a vehicle which has suffered a fire, or with components salvaged from such a vehicle, wear protective gloves and discard them after use.

The battery

• Batteries contain sulphuric acid, which attacks clothing, eyes and skin. Take care when topping-up or carrying the battery.
• The hydrogen gas given off by the battery is highly explosive. Never cause a spark or allow a naked light nearby. Be careful when connecting and disconnecting battery chargers or jump leads.

Air bags

• Air bags can cause injury if they go off accidentally. Take care when removing the steering wheel and trim panels. Special storage instructions may apply.

Diesel injection equipment

• Diesel injection pumps supply fuel at very high pressure. Take care when working on the fuel injectors and fuel pipes.

 Warning: Never expose the hands, face or any other part of the body to injector spray; the fuel can penetrate the skin with potentially fatal results.

Remember...

DO

• Do use eye protection when using power tools, and when working under the vehicle.

• Do wear gloves or use barrier cream to protect your hands when necessary.

• Do get someone to check periodically that all is well when working alone on the vehicle.

• Do keep loose clothing and long hair well out of the way of moving mechanical parts.

• Do remove rings, wristwatch etc, before working on the vehicle – especially the electrical system.

• Do ensure that any lifting or jacking equipment has a safe working load rating adequate for the job.

DON'T

• Don't attempt to lift a heavy component which may be beyond your capability – get assistance.

• Don't rush to finish a job, or take unverified short cuts.

• Don't use ill-fitting tools which may slip and cause injury.

• Don't leave tools or parts lying around where someone can trip over them. Mop up oil and fuel spills at once.

• Don't allow children or pets to play in or near a vehicle being worked on.

The following pages are intended to help in dealing with common roadside emergencies and breakdowns. You will find more detailed fault finding information at the back of the manual, and repair information in the main chapters.

If your car won't start and the starter motor doesn't turn

☐ If it's a model with automatic transmission, make sure the selector is in 'P' or 'N'.
☐ Open the bonnet, and make sure the battery terminals are clean and tight.
☐ Switch on the headlights and try to start the engine. If the headlights go very dim when you're trying to start, the battery is probable flat. Get out of trouble by jump starting using a friends car.

If your car won't start even though the starter motor turns as normal

☐ Is there fuel in the tank?
☐ Is there moisture on electrical connections under the bonnet? Switch off the ignition, then wipe off any obvious dampness with a dry cloth. Spray a water-dispersant aerosol product (WD-40 or equivalent) on ignition and fuel system electrical connectors like those shown in the photos.

1 Check the condition and security of the battery connections

2 Check the security of the fuel injection system components wiring plugs

3 Check the engine management control module (ECM) wiring plugs

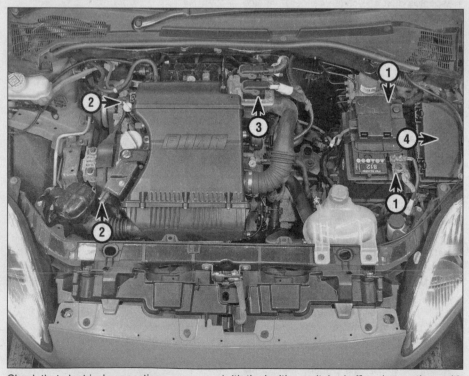

Check that electrical connections are secure (with the ignition switched off) and spray them with a water-dispersant spray like WD-40 if you suspect a problem due to damp

4 Check the engine compartment fuses

Identifying leaks

Puddles on the garage floor or drive, or obvious wetness under the bonnet or underneath the car, suggest a leak that needs Investigating. I can sometimes be difficult to decide where the leak is coming from, especially if the engine bay is very dirty already. Leaking oil of fluid can also be blown rearwards by the passage of air under the car, giving a false impression of where the problem lies.

 Warning: Most automotive oils and fluids are poisonous, Wash them off skin, and change out of contaminated clothing without delay.

 The smell of a fluid leaking from the car may provide a clue to what's leaking. Some fluids are distinctly coloured. It may help to clean the car carefully and to park it over some clean paper overnight as an aid to locating the source of the leak. Remember that some leaks may only occur while the engine is running.

Sump oil

Engine oil may leak from the drain plug...

Oil from filter

...or from the base of the oil filter.

Gearbox oil

Gearbox oil can leak from the seals at the inboard ends of the driveshafts.

Antifreeze

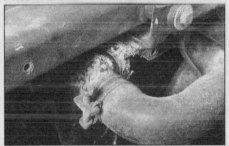

Leaking antifreeze often leaves a crystalline deposit like this.

Brake fluid

A leak occurring at a wheel is almost certainly brake fluid.

Power steering fluid

Power steering fluid may leak from the pipe connectors on the steering rack.

Towing

When all else fails, you may find yourself having to get a tow home – or of course you may be helping somebody else. Long-distance recovery should only be done by a garage or breakdown service. For shorter distances, DIY towing using another car is easy enough, but observe the following points:

☐ Use a proper tow-rope – they are not expensive. The vehicle being towed must display an ON TOW sign in its rear window.
☐ Always turn the ignition to the 'on' position when the vehicle is being towed, so that the steering lock is released, and that the direction indicator and brake lights will work.
☐ The front towing eye socket is located in the front bumper. Prise out the cap from the bumper.

☐ The rear towing eye socket cover is located in the rear bumper. Prise out the cap from the rear bumper.
☐ Before being towed, release the handbrake and make sure the transmission is in neutral.
☐ Note that greater-than-usual pedal pressure will be required to operate the brakes, since the vacuum servo unit is only operational with the engine running, and no power assistance will be available for the steering.
☐ The driver of the car being towed must keep the tow-rope taut at all times to avoid snatching.
☐ Only drive at moderate speeds, and keep the distance towed to a minimum. Drive

smoothly, and allow plenty of time for slowing down at junctions.

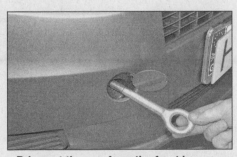

Prise out the cap from the front bumper

Jump starting

When jump-starting a car using a booster battery, observe the following precautions:

✓ Before connecting the booster battery, make sure that the ignition is switched off.
✓ Ensure that all electrical equipment (lights, heater, wipers, etc) is switched off.
✓ Take note of any special precautions printed on the battery case.
✓ Make sure that the booster battery is the same voltage as the discharged one in the vehicle.
✓ If the battery is being jump-started from the battery in another vehicle, the two vehicles MUST NOT TOUCH each other.
✓ Make sure that the transmission is in neutral (or PARK, in the case of automatic transmission)

 HAYNES HiNT *Budget jump leads can be a false economy, as they often do not pass enough current to start large capacity or diesel engines. They can also get hot.*

 HAYNES HiNT *Jump starting will get you out of trouble, but you must correct whatever made the battery go flat in the first place. There are three possibilities:*

1 *The battery has been drained by repeated attempts to start, or by leaving the lights on.*

2 *The charging system is not working properly (alternator drivebelt slack or broken, alternator wiring fault or alternator itself faulty).*

3 *The battery itself is at fault (electrolyte low, or battery worn out).*

1 Connect one end of the red jump lead to the positive (+) terminal of the flat battery

2 Connect the other end of the red lead to the positive (+) terminal of the booster battery.

3 Connect one end of the black jump lead to the negative (-) terminal of the booster battery

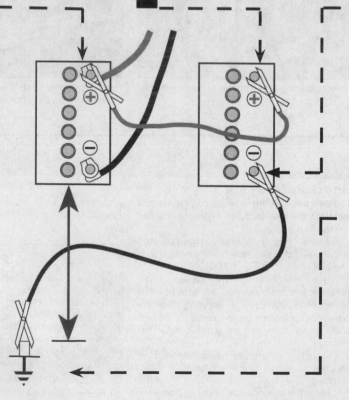

4 Connect the other end of the black jump lead to a bolt or bracket on the engine block, well away from the battery, on the vehicle to be started

5 Make sure that the jump leads will not come into contact with the fan, drive-belts or other moving parts of the engine. Start the engine using the booster battery and run it at idle speed. Switch on the lights, rear window demister and heater blower motor, then disconnect the jump leads in the reverse order of connection. Turn off the lights etc.

Wheel changing

 Warning: Do not change a wheel in a situation where you risk being hit by another vehicle. On busy roads, try to stop in a lay-by or a gateway. Be wary of passing traffic while changing the wheel – it is easy to become distracted by the job in hand.

Preparation

☐ When a puncture occurs, stop as soon as it is safe to do so.

☐ Park on firm level ground, if possible, and well out of the way of other traffic. If jacking on a slope is unavoidable, chock the wheel diagonally opposite the one to be removed on the downhill side, using the chock provided in the toolkit.

☐ Use hazard warning lights if necessary.

☐ If the ground is soft, use a flat piece of wood to spread the load under the jack.

Changing the wheel

1 The tool kit and spare wheel are located under the luggage compartment floor panel. Lift the panel, unscrew the plastic nut, then lift out the toolkit holder and spare wheel.

2 Using the wheel brace supplied, slacken the wheel bolts

3 Position the jack head beneath the jacking point (indicated by an arrow) under the sill closest to the punctured wheel. Engage the jack head with the sill flange, then smoothly raise the vehicle undo the tyre is clear of the road surface.

4 Unscrew the wheel bolts, and remove the wheel.

5 Fit the spare wheel, and screw-in the bolts. Lightly tighten the bolts with the wheelbrace, then lower the vehicle to the ground. Securely tighten the wheel bolts. Note that the wheel bolts should be slackened and retightened to the specified torque at the earliest possible opportunity.

Finally . . .

☐ Remove the wheel chocks.

☐ Stow the punctured wheel and tools back in the luggage compartment, and secure them in position.

☐ Check the tyre pressure on the tyre just fitted. If it is low, or if you don't have a pressure gauge with you, drive slowly to the next garage and inflate the tyre to the correct pressure. In the case of the narrow 'space-saver' spare wheel this pressure is much higher than for a normal tyre.

☐ Have the punctured wheel repaired as soon as possible, or another puncture will leave you stranded.

Caution: If a temporary 'space-saver' spare wheel is fitted, do not exceed 50 mph (80 kmh), and take particular care when cornering.

Introduction

There are some very simple checks which need only take a few minutes to carry out, but which could save you a lot of inconvenience and expense.

☐ These Weekly checks require no great skill or special tools, and the small amount of time they take to perform could prove to be very well spent, for example:

☐ Keeping an eye on tyre condition and pressures, will not only help to stop them wearing out prematurely, but could also save your life.

☐ Many breakdowns are caused by electrical problems. Battery-related faults are particularly common, and a quick check on a regular basis will often prevent the majority of these.

☐ If your car develops a brake fluid leak, the first time you might know about it is when your brakes don't work properly. Checking the level regularly will give advance warning of this kind of problem.

☐ If the oil or coolant levels run low, the cost of repairing any engine damage will be far greater than fixing the leak, for example.

Underbonnet check points

▲ **DOHC (16-valve) engine – SOHC (8-valve) engine similar**

A *Engine oil level dipstick*

B *Engine oil filler cap*

C *Coolant expansion tank*

D *Brake fluid reservoir*

E *Screen/headlight washer fluid reservoir*

F *Battery*

Engine oil level

Before you start
✔ Make sure that your car is on level ground
✔ Check the oil level before the car is driven, or at least 5 minutes after the engine has been switched off.

 If the oil is checked immediately after driving the vehicle, some of the oil will remain in the upper engine components, resulting in an inaccurate reading on the dipstick!

The correct oil
Modern engines place great demands on their oil. It is very important that the correct oil for your car is used (See "Lubricants and fluids").

Car care
● If you have to add oil frequently, you should check whether you have any oil leaks. Place some clean paper under the car overnight, and check for stains in the morning. If there are no leaks, the engine may be burning oil (see "Fault finding").
● Always maintain the level between the upper and lower dipstick marks. If the level is too low severe engine damage may occur. Oil seal failure may result if the engine is overfilled by adding too much oil.

1 Withdraw the dipstick. Using a clean rag or paper towel, wipe all the oil from the dipstick. Insert the clean dipstick into the tube as far as it will go, then withdraw it again.

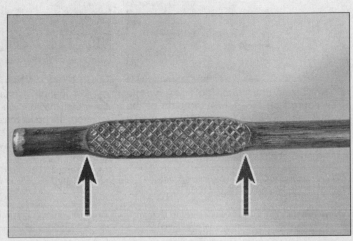

2 Note the oil level on the end of the dipstick, which should be between the upper MAX mark and the lower MIN mark.

3 Oil is added through the filler cap on top of the engine. Rotate the cap through a quarter-turn anti-clockwise and withdraw it.

4 Top-up the level. A funnel may help to reduce spillage. Add the oil slowly, checking the level on the dipstick often. Do not overfill.

Brake/clutch fluid level

 Warning: Brake fluid can harm your eyes and damage painted surfaces, so use extreme caution when handling and pouring it.
Caution: Do not use fluid that has been standing open for some time, as it absorbs moisture from the air, which can cause a dangerous loss of braking effectiveness.

Note: *The fluid level in the reservoir will drop slightly as the brake pads wear down, but the fluid level must never be allowed to drop below the "MIN" mark.*

Before you start
✔ Make sure that your car is on level ground.

Safety first!
● If the reservoir requires repeated topping-up this is an indication of a fluid leak somewhere in the system, which should be investigated immediately.

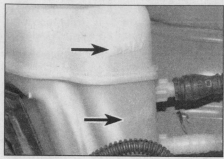

1 The brake and clutch fluid reservoir is mounted on the right-hand side of the bulkhead. The MAX and MIN level marks are indicated on the side of the reservoir and the fluid level should be maintained between these marks at all times.

2 On manual transmission models, the clutch master cylinder is supplied with fluid from the brake master cylinder reservoir.
If topping-up is necessary, wipe the area around the filler cap with a clean rag before removing the cap. It's a good idea to inspect the reservoir. The fluid should be changed if dirt is visible.

3 Carefully add fluid, avoiding spilling it on surrounding paintwork. Use only the specified hydraulic fluid; mixing different types of fluid can cause damage to the system and/or a loss of braking effectiveness. After filling to the correct level, refit the cap securely. Wipe off any spilt fluid.

Coolant level

 Warning: DO NOT attempt to remove the expansion tank pressure cap when the engine is hot, as there is a very great risk of scalding. Do not leave open containers of coolant about, as it is poisonous.

Car care
● With a sealed-type cooling system, adding coolant should not be necessary on a regular basis. If frequent topping-up is required, it is likely there is a leak. Check the radiator, all hoses and joint faces for signs of staining or wetness, and rectify as necessary.
● It is important that antifreeze is used in the cooling system all year round, not just during the winter months. Don't top-up with water alone, as the antifreeze will become too diluted.
● The coolant level varies with the temperature of the engine. When the engine is cold, the coolant level should be level with the marker bar withing the filler neck. When the engine is hot, the level will rise approximately 15 mm.

1 If topping-up is necessary, wait until the engine is cold, then slowly unscrew the expansion tank filler cap anti-clockwise, to release any pressure in the system, and remove it.

2 Add a mixture of water and antifreeze through the expansion tank filler neck ...

3 ... until the coolant is level with the MAX mark on the side of the expansion tank. Refit the cap, turning it clockwise as far as it will go until it is secure.

Battery

Caution: Before carrying out any work on the vehicle battery, read the precautions given in "Safety first" at the start of this manual.

✔ Make sure that the battery tray is in good condition, and that the clamp is tight. Corrosion on the tray, retaining clamp and the battery itself can be removed with a solution of water and baking soda. Thoroughly rinse all cleaned areas with water. Any metal parts damaged by corrosion should be covered with a zinc-based primer, then painted.

✔ Periodically (approximately every three months), check the charge condition of the battery as described in " 5 ".

✔ If the battery is flat, and you need to jump start your vehicle, see 4.

✔ The battery is located at the left-hand side of the engine compartment. The exterior of the battery should be inspected periodically for damage such as a cracked case or cover.

1 Release the clips and remove the electrostatic protection from the top of the battery (where fitted).

2 Check the tightness of the battery cable clamps to ensure good electrical connections. You should not be able to move them. Also check each cable for cracks and frayed conductors.

Battery corrosion can be kept to a minimum by applying a layer of petroleum jelly to the clamps and terminals after they are reconnected.

3 If corrosion (white, fluffy deposits) is evident, remove the cables from the battery terminals, clean them with a small wire brush, then refit them. Automotive stores sell a tool for cleaning the battery post...

4 ... as well as the battery cable clamps

Screen/headlight washer fluid level

● Screenwash additives not only keep the windscreen clean during foul weather, they also prevent the washer system freezing in cold weather – which is when you are likely to need it most. Don't top up using plain water as the screenwash will become too diluted, and will freeze during cold weather.

⚠ *Warning: On no account use coolant antifreeze in the washer system – this could discolour or damage paintwork.*

1 The reservoir for the windscreen and rear window, and headlight (where applicable) washer systems is located in the front left-hand corner of the engine compartment. If topping up is necessary, open the cap.

2 When topping-up the reservoir a screenwash additive should be added in the quantities recommended on the container.

Electrical systems

✔ Check all external lights and the horn. Refer to the appropriate Sections of Chapter 12 for details if any of the circuits are found to be inoperative.

✔ Visually check all accessible wiring connectors, harnesses and retaining clips for security, and for signs of chafing or damage.

 HAYNES HiNT *If you need to check your brake lights and indicators unaided, back up to a wall or garage door and operate the lights. The reflected light should show if they are working properly.*

1 If a single indicator light, brake light or headlight has failed, it is likely that a bulb has blown and will need to be replaced. Refer to Chapter 12 Section 6 for details. If both brake lights have failed, it is possible that the stop-light switch operated by the brake pedal has failed. Refer to Chapter 12 Section 5 for details.

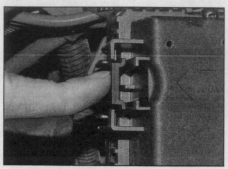

2 If more than one indicator light or headlight has failed, it is likely that either a fuse has blown or that there is a fault in the circuit (see Chapter 12). The main fusebox is located on the left-hand side of the facia, other fuseboxes are described in Chapter 12 Section 3.

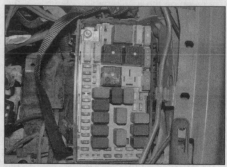

3 To replace a blown fuse, pull it out directly from the fusebox. Fit a new fuse of the same rating, available from car accessory shops. It is important that you find the reason that the fuse blew (see "Electrical fault finding" in Chapter 12 Section 2).

Wiper blades

Front wiper blades

● Set the wipers in the 'Service position' by switching on the ignition, setting the wiper switch to continuous slow wipe, then when the arms are in the vertical position, turn off the ignition.

● Fold the wiper arms away from the windscreen.

Caution: Do not attempt to fold the arms away from the windscreen when they at not at the vertical position, otherwise damage to the bonnet may result.

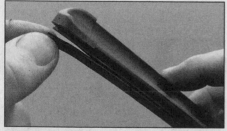

1 Check the condition of the wiper blades. If they are cracked or show any signs of deterioration, or if the glass swept area is smeared, renew them. For maximum clarity of vision, wiper blades should be renewed annually, as a matter of course.

2 Squeeze together the clips, and slide the blade from the arm

3 On rear wiper blades, pull the blade away from the screen, and pull the blade from the arm

Tyre condition and pressure

It is very important that tyres are in good condition, and at the correct pressure – having a tyre failure at any speed is highly dangerous. Tyre wear is influenced by driving style – harsh braking and acceleration, or fast cornering, will all produce more rapid tyre wear. As a general rule, the front tyres wear out faster the the rears. Interchanging the tyres from front to rear ("rotating" the tyres) may result in more even wear. However, if this is completely effective, you may have the expense of replacing all four tyres at once!

Remove any nails or stones embedded in the tread before they penetrate the tyre to cause deflation. If removal of a nail does reveal that the tyre has been punctured, refit the nail so that its point of penetration is marked. Then immediately change the wheel, and have the tyre repaired by a tyre dealer.

Regularly check the tyres for damage in the form of cuts or bulges, especially in the side walls. Periodically remove the wheels, and clean any dirt or mud from the inside and outside surfaces. Examine the wheel rims for signs of rusting, corrosion or other damage. Light alloy wheels are easily damaged by "kerbing" whilst parking; steel wheels may also become dented or buckled. A new wheel is very often the only way to overcome severe damage.

New tyres should be balanced when they are fitted, but it may become necessary to re-balance them as they ear, or if the balance weights fitted to the wheel rim should fall off. Unbalanced tyres will wear more quickly, as will the steering and suspension components. Wheel imbalance is normally signified by vibration, particularly at a certain speed (typically around 50 mph). If this vibration is felt only through the steering wheel, then it is likely that just the front wheels need balancing. If, however, the vibration is felt through the whole car, the rear wheels could be out of balance. Wheel balancing should be carried out by a tyre dealer or garage.

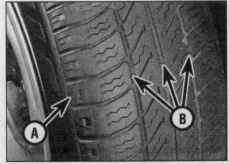

1 Tread Depth - visual check
The original tyres have tread wear safety bands (B), which will appear when the tread depth reaches approximately 1.6 mm. The band positions are indicated by a triangular mark on the tyre sidewall (A)

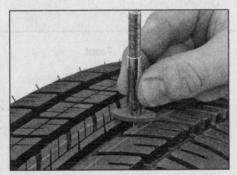

2 Tread Depth - manual check
Alternatively, tread wear can be monitored with a simple, inexpensive device known as a tread depth indicator gauge

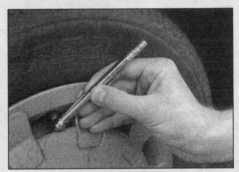

3 Tyre Pressure Check
Check the tyre pressures regularly with the tyres cold. Do not adjust the tyre pressures immediately after the vehicle has been used, or an inaccurate setting will result

Tyre tread wear patterns

Shoulder Wear

Underinflation (wear on both sides)
Under-inflation will cause overheating of the tyre, because the tyre will flex too much, and the tread will not sit correctly on the road surface. This will cause a loss of grip and excessive wear, not to mention the danger of sudden tyre failure due to heat build-up.
Check and adjust pressures
Incorrect wheel camber (wear on one side)
Repair or renew suspension parts
Hard cornering
Reduce speed!

Centre Wear

Overinflation
Over-inflation will cause rapid wear of the centre part of the tyre tread, coupled with reduced grip, harsher ride, and the danger of shock damage occurring in the tyre casing.
Check and adjust pressures

If you sometimes have to inflate your car's tyres to the higher pressures specified for maximum load or sustained high speed, don't forget to reduce the pressures to normal afterwards.

Uneven Wear

Front tyres may wear unevenly as a result of wheel misalignment. Most tyre dealers and garages can check and adjust the wheel alignment (or "tracking") for a modest charge.
Incorrect camber or castor
Repair or renew suspension parts
Malfunctioning suspension
Repair or renew suspension parts
Unbalanced wheel
Balance tyres
Incorrect toe setting
Adjust front wheel alignment
Note: *The feathered edge of the tread which typifies toe wear is best checked by feel.*

Lubricants and fluids

Engine oil:
All models . . . . 5W/40 meeting Fiat specification 9.55535-S2. Eg. Selenia KPE, Castrol Edge 5W40

Coolant . . . . Paraflu Up*

Manual gearbox . . . . SAE 75W80 API GL4-Plus. Tutela Car Technyx

Brake/clutch fluid . . . . Hydraulic fluid DOT 4 Plus

Check with dealer for latest specifications.

Tyre pressures

All models	Front	Rear
175/65 R15:		
Medium load	2.2 bar (32 psi)	2.1 bar (30 psi)
Full load	2.2 bar (32 psi)	2.2 bar (32 psi)
185/65 R15:		
Medium load	2.2 bar (32 psi)	2.0 bar (29 psi)
Full load	2.2 bar (32 psi)	2.2 bar (32 psi)
195/55 R16:		
Medium load	2.2 bar (32 psi)	2.0 bar (32 psi)
Full load	2.2 bar (32 psi)	2.2 bar (32 psi)
205/45 R17:		
Medium load	2.4 bar (35 psi)	2.2 bar (32 psi)
Full load	2.4 bar (35 psi)	2.4 bar (35 psi)

Chapter 1
Routine maintenance and servicing

Contents

Section number

Air filter element renewal	23
Antifreeze concentration check	21
Auxiliary drivebelt check and renewal	5
Brake fluid renewal	22
Brake pad check	7
Coolant renewal	29
Driveshaft gaiter check	8
Emission control system check	28
Engine management system check	19
Engine oil and filter renewal	4
Evaporative loss system check	27
Exhaust system check	11
Handbrake check and adjustment	12
Hinge and lock lubrication	13
Hose and fluid leak check	6

Section number

HT lead check	18
Introduction	2
Maintenance schedule	1
Manual transmission oil level check	25
Pollen filter renewal	20
Regular maintenance	3
Road test	14
Service indicator reset	15
Spark plug renewal	17
Steering and suspension check	9
Timing belt inspection	24
Timing belt renewal	26
Underbody sealant check	10
Valve clearance check and adjustment	16

Degrees of difficulty

Easy, suitable for novice with little experience 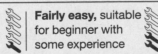	**Fairly easy,** suitable for beginner with some experience	**Fairly difficult,** suitable for competent DIY mechanic	**Difficult,** suitable for experienced DIY mechanic 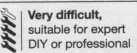	**Very difficult,** suitable for expert DIY or professional

Lubricants and fluids................................... Refer to 'Weekly checks'

Capacities

Engine oil (with filter):
    SOHC 8v engines.. 2.6 litres
    DOHC 16v engines.. 2.9 litres
Cooling system... 5.3 litres
Fuel tank 45 litres
Manual transmission:
    SOHC 8v models... 1.5 litres
    DOHC 16v models.. 1.7 litres

Cooling system

Protection at mixture of 50% anti-freeze and 50% water .... -40°C

Engine

Valve clearances (cold) – SOHC 8v engines:
    Intake .... 0.3 mm
    Exhaust... 0.4 mm
Auxiliary drivebelt tension:
    SOHC 8V models without air conditioning.................... 5.0 mm deflection midway between pulleys
    Models with air conditioning and DOHC 16v models .... Controlled by automatic tensioner

Ignition system

Ignition timing.. Refer to Chapter 5B Section 4
Spark plugs:
    SOHC 8v engines.. NGK ZKR7A-10
    DOHC 16v engines.. NGK ZKR7A-10

Braking system

Brake pad friction material minimum thickness (front and rear)....... 1.5 mm
Brake shoe friction material minimum thickness .... 2.0 mm

Torque wrench settings

	Nm	lbf ft
Engine oil drain plug:		
SOHC 8v engines	45	33
DOHC 16v	20	15
Engine oil filter cap	25	18
Manual transmission		
Drain plug	18	13
Filler plug	25	18
Roadwheel bolts	120	89
Spark plugs	18	13

1 Maintenance schedule

1 The maintenance intervals in this manual are provided with the assumption that you, not the dealer, will be carrying out the work. These are the minimum maintenance intervals recommended by us for vehicles driven daily. If you wish to keep your vehicle in peak condition at all times, you may wish to perform some of these procedures more often. We encourage frequent maintenance, because it enhances the efficiency, performance and resale value of your vehicle.
2 When the vehicle is new, it should be serviced by a factory-authorised dealer service department, in order to preserve the factory warranty.

Every 250 miles or weekly
☐ Refer to "Weekly checks' '

Every 6000 miles or 6 months, whichever occurs first
☐ Renew the engine oil and filter (Section 4).

Note: *Frequent oil and filter changes are good for the engine. We recommend changing the oil at the mileage specified here, or at least twice a year if the mileage covered is less.*

Every 12 000 miles or 12 months, whichever occurs first

In addition to the item listed in the previous service, carry out the following:

☐ Check the auxiliary drivebelt (Section 5).
☐ Hose and fluid leak check (Section 6).
☐ Check the brake pads for wear (Section 7).
☐ Check the condition of the driveshaft gaiters (Section 8).
☐ Check the steering and suspension components for condition and security (Section 9).
☐ Check the underbody and sealant for damage (Section 10).
☐ Check the condition of the exhaust system and its mountings (Section 11).
☐ Check and if necessary adjust the handbrake (Section 12).
☐ Lubricate all hinges and locks (Section 13).
☐ Road test (Section 14).
☐ Service indicator reset (Section 15).

Every 24 months or 24 000 miles, whichever occurs first
☐ Check and if necessary adjust the valve clearances – SOHC 8v engines (Section 16).
☐ Renew the spark plugs (Section 17).
☐ Check the condition of the spark plug HT leads (Section 18).
☐ Check the engine management system (Section 19).
☐ Renew the pollen filter (Section 20).
☐ Check the anti-freeze concentration (Section 21).

Every 2 years, regardless of mileage
☐ Renew the brake fluid (Section 22).

Every 36 000 miles or 3 years – whichever occurs first
☐ Renew the air filter element (Section 23).
☐ Check the condition of the timing belt (Section 24).
☐ Check and if necessary top-up the manual transmission oil level (Section 25).

Every 48 000 miles or 4 years – whichever occurs first
☐ Renew the timing belt (Section 26)*.
☐ Check the operation of the evaporative loss system (Section 27).
☐ Check the condition and operation of the crankcase emission control system (Section 28).

Note: **Although the normal interval for timing belt renewal is 72 000 miles (120 000 km), it is strongly recommended that the belt is renewed at 48 000 miles on vehicles which are subjected to intensive use, ie, mainly short journeys or a lot of stop-start driving. The actual belt renewal interval is therefore very much up to the individual owner, but bear in mind that severe engine damage will result if the belt breaks.*

Every 10 years, regardless of mileage
☐ Renew the coolant (Section 29).

Front underbody view

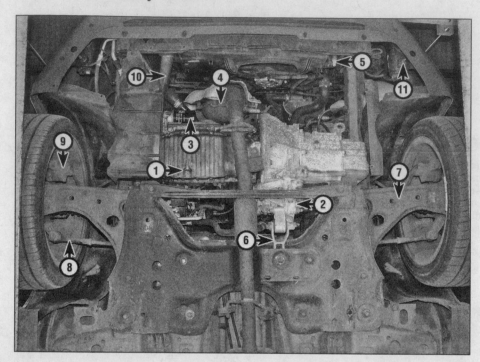

1 Engine oil drain plug
2 Transmission drain plug
3 Engine oil filter
4 Catalytic converter
5 Coolant drain plug
6 Rear engine mounting rod
7 Suspension lower arm
8 Steering track rod end
9 Brake caliper
10 Radiator lower hose
11 Fog light adjustment screw

Rear underbody view

1 Fuel tank
2 Exhaust silencer
3 Fuel filler pipe
4 Handbrake cable
5 Shock absorber
6 Coil spring
7 Rear axle

Underbonnet view – DOHC (16-valve) model shown, others similar

1 Engine oil filler cap
2 Engine oil level dipstick
3 Brake/clutch fluid reservoir
4 Air filter cover
5 Coolant expansion tank cap
6 Screenwash fluid reservoir cap
7 Engine compartment fusebox
8 Battery
9 Engine management ECU

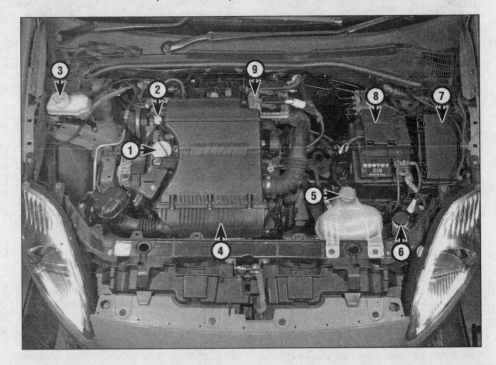

2 Introduction

1 This Chapter is designed to help the home mechanic maintain his/her vehicle for safety, economy, long life and peak performance.
2 The Chapter contains a maintenance schedule, followed by Sections dealing specifically with each task in the schedule. Visual checks, adjustments, component renewal and other helpful items are included. Refer to the accompanying illustrations of the engine compartment and the underside of the vehicle for the locations of the various components.
3 Servicing your vehicle in accordance with the above recommendations and the following Sections will provide a planned maintenance programme, which should result in a long and reliable service life. This is a comprehensive plan, so maintaining some items, but not others at the specified service intervals, will not produce the same results.
4 As you service your vehicle, you will discover that many of the procedures can – and should – be grouped together, because of the particular procedure being performed, or because of the proximity of two otherwise-unrelated components to one another. For example, if the vehicle is raised for any reason, the exhaust can be inspected at the same time as the suspension and steering components.
5 The first step in this maintenance

programme is to prepare yourself before the actual work begins. Read through all the Sections relevant to the work to be carried out, then make a list and gather all the parts and tools required. If a problem is encountered, seek advice from a parts specialist, or a dealer service department.

3 Regular maintenance

1 If, from the time the vehicle is new, the routine maintenance schedule is followed closely, and frequent checks are made of fluid levels and high-wear items, as suggested throughout this manual, the engine will be kept in relatively good running condition, and the need for additional work will be minimised.
2 It is possible that there will be times when the engine is running poorly due to the lack of regular maintenance. This is even more likely if a used vehicle, which has not received regular and frequent maintenance checks, is purchased. In such cases, additional work may need to be carried out, outside of the regular maintenance intervals.
3 If engine wear is suspected, a compression test (refer to Chapter 2A Section 2, or Chapter 2B Section 2 as applicable) will provide valuable information regarding the overall performance of the main internal components. Such a test can be used as a basis to decide on the extent of the work to be carried out. If, for example, a compression test indicates

serious internal engine wear, conventional maintenance as described in this Chapter will not greatly improve the performance of the engine, and may prove a waste of time and money, unless extensive overhaul work is carried out first.
4 The following series of operations are those most often required to improve the performance of a generally poor-running engine:

Primary operations

a) Clean, inspect and test the battery (see 'Weekly checks').
b) Check all the engine-related fluids (refer to 'Weekly checks').
c) Check the condition and tension of the auxiliary drivebelt (Section 5).
d) Check the condition of all hoses, and check for fluid leaks (Section 6).
e) Renew the spark plugs (Section 17).
f) Inspect the HT leads (Section 18).
g) Check the condition of the air filter, and renew if necessary (Section 23).
5 If the above operations do not prove fully effective, carry out the following secondary operations:

Secondary operations

6 All items listed under Primary operations, plus the following:
a) Check the charging system (Chapter 5A Section 5).
b) Check the ignition system (Chapter 5B Section 8).
c) Check the fuel system (Chapter 4A Section 8).

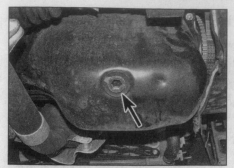

4.3a Sump drain plug – SOHC engines

4.3b Sump drain plug – DOHC engines

Keep the drain plug pressed into the sump while unscrewing it by hand the last couple of turns. As the plug releases, move it away sharply so the stream of oil issuing from the sump runs into the container, not up your sleeve.

4 Engine oil and filter renewal

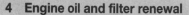

1 Frequent oil and filter changes are the most important preventative maintenance which can be undertaken by the DIY owner. As engine oil ages, it becomes diluted and contaminated, which leads to premature engine wear.

2 Before starting this procedure, gather all the necessary tools and materials. Also make sure that you have plenty of clean rags and newspapers handy to mop-up any spills. Ideally, the engine oil should be warm, as it will drain better, and any impurities suspended in the oil will be removed with it. Take care, however, not to touch the exhaust or any other hot parts of the engine when working under the vehicle. To avoid any possibility of scalding, and to protect yourself from possible skin irritants and other harmful contaminants in used engine oils, it is advisable to wear gloves when carrying out this work. Access to the underside of the vehicle will be greatly improved if it can be raised on a lift, driven onto ramps, or jacked up and supported on axle stands as described in *'Vehicle jacking and support'*. Whichever method is chosen, make sure that the vehicle remains level, or if it is at an angle, that the drain plug is at the lowest point.

3 Slacken the drain plug about half a turn using an Allen key (SOHC 8v) or socket/spanner (DOHC 16v) **(see illustrations)**. Position the draining container under the drain plug, then remove the plug completely (see **Haynes Hint**).

4 Allow some time for the old oil to drain, noting that it may be necessary to reposition the container as the oil flow slows to a trickle.

5 After all the oil has drained, wipe off the drain plug with a clean rag, then clean the area around the drain plug opening and refit the plug using a new seal **(see illustration)**. Tighten the plug to the specified torque.

6 Move the container into position under the oil filter, which is located on the front right-hand side of the engine **(see illustration)**.

7 Using an oil filter removal tool if necessary, slacken the filter initially, then unscrew it by hand the rest of the way **(see illustration)**. Empty the oil in the old filter into the container.

8 Use a clean rag to remove all oil, dirt and sludge from the filter sealing area on the engine. Check the old filter to make sure that the rubber sealing ring has not stuck to the engine. If it has, carefully remove it.

9 Apply a light coating of clean engine oil to the sealing ring on the new filter, then screw it into position on the engine **(see illustration)**. Tighten the filter firmly by hand only – do not use any tools.

10 Remove the old oil and all tools from under the car then lower it to the ground (if applicable).

11 Withdraw the dipstick, and remove the oil filler cap from the cylinder head cover. Fill the engine, using the correct grade and type of oil (see Lubricants and fluids 0 Section 5). An oil can spout or funnel may help to reduce spillage. Pour in half the specified quantity of oil first, then wait a few minutes for the oil to run to the sump. Continue adding oil a small quantity at a time until the level is up to the MAX mark on the dipstick. Refit the filler cap.

12 Start the engine and run it for a few minutes; check for leaks around the oil filter seal and the sump drain plug. Note that there may be a delay of a few seconds before the oil pressure warning light goes out when the engine is first started, as the oil circulates through the engine oil galleries and the new oil filter before the pressure builds-up.

4.5 Renew the sump plug sealing washer

4.6 The oil filter is located on the front right-hand side of the engine

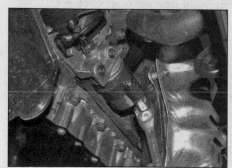

4.7 Use an oil filter removal tool to initially slacken the filter

4.9 Apply a light coating of engine oil to the filter sealing ring

13 Switch off the engine, and wait a few minutes for the oil to settle in the sump once more. With the new oil circulated and the filter completely full, recheck the level on the dipstick, and add more oil as necessary.

14 Dispose of the used engine oil and filter safely, referring to General repair procedures in the Reference Chapter. Do not discard the old filter with domestic household waste. The facility for waste oil disposal provided by many local council refuse tips generally has a filter receptacle alongside.

5.5a Alternator lower pivot bolt...

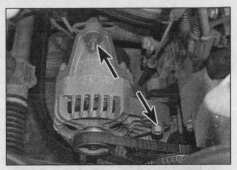

5.5b... and upper adjustment bolts

5 Auxiliary drivebelt check and renewal

Note: *On models with a manually-adjusted drivebelt (SOHC 8v engines), Fiat specify the use of a special tool to correctly set the drivebelt tension. If access to this equipment cannot be obtained, an approximate setting can be achieved using the method described below. If the method described is used, the tension should be checked using the special tool at the earliest possible opportunity.*

Check

1 Slacken the right-hand front roadwheel bolts, raise the front of the vehicle, and support it securely on axle stands, as described in 'Vehicle jacking and support'. Remove the roadwheel.

2 Undo the screws and remove the lower/front section of the wheelarch liner.

3 Using a socket on the crankshaft pulley bolt, rotate the crankshaft so that the full length of the drivebelt can be examined. Look for cracks, splitting and fraying on the surface of the belt; check also for signs of glazing (shiny patches) and separation of the belt plies. If damage or wear is visible, the belt should be renewed.

4 If the condition of the belt is satisfactory, where applicable check the drivebelt tension as described below.

Renewal

SOHC 8V models without air conditioning

5 Slacken the alternator lower pivot bolt and the upper adjustment bolts **(see illustrations)**. Swivel the alternator towards the engine and slip the drivebelt off the alternator pulley.

6 Unbolt and remove the crankshaft TDC sensor from the front of the engine (refer to Chapter 4A Section 9 if necessary).

7 Remove the drivebelt from the crankshaft pulley.

8 When renewing a drivebelt, ensure that the correct type is used. Fit the belt around the two pulleys then swivel the alternator outwards to take up any slack in the belt.

9 Refit the crankshaft TDC sensor, then adjust the drivebelt tension correctly as described below.

All other models

10 Using a socket or spanner on the drivebelt tensioner pulley retaining bolt, rotate the tensioner against spring-pressure to release the tension from the belt **(see illustrations)**. Hold the tensioner in this position using a suitable pin/rod and slip the drivebelt off the alternator and air conditioning compressor pulleys. Allow the tensioner to return to the released position.

11 Remove the drivebelt from the crankshaft pulley.

12 When renewing a drivebelt, ensure that the correct type is used.

13 Fit the belt around the pulleys, then rotate the tensioner until the bolt can be clipped into place over the tensioner pulley.

14 Release the tensioner to allow the spring loaded arm to automatically tension the belt.

15 Refit the wheel arch liner panel and roadwheel, then lower the car to the ground.

Tensioning

16 Correct tensioning of the belt will ensure that it has a long life. A belt which is too slack will slip and perhaps squeal. Beware, however, of overtightening, as this can cause wear in the alternator bearings. On models equipped with air conditioning, and DOHC 16v engines, the correct belt tension is maintained automatically by means of the spring-loaded tensioning mechanism. On all other models, the tension must be adjusted manually as follows.

17 The belt should be tensioned so that, under firm thumb pressure, there is approximately 5.0 mm of free movement at the mid-point between the pulleys. To adjust the drivebelt, slacken the alternator pivot and adjustment bolts (if not already done) then swivel the alternator outwards until the belt tension is correct. Hold the alternator in this position and fully tighten the adjustment bolts followed by the pivot bolt.

18 Refit the wheel arch liner panel and roadwheel, then lower the car to the ground.

6 Hose and fluid leak check

1 Visually inspect the engine joint faces, gaskets and seals for any signs of water or oil leaks. Pay particular attention to the areas around the camshaft cover, cylinder head, oil filter and sump joint faces. Bear in mind that, over a period of time, some very slight seepage from these areas is to be expected – what you are really looking for is any indication of a serious leak. Should a leak be found, renew the offending gasket or oil seal by referring to the appropriate Chapters in this manual.

2 Also check the security and condition of all the engine-related pipes and hoses. Ensure that all cable-ties or securing clips are in place and in good condition. Clips that are broken or missing can lead to chafing of the hoses, pipes or wiring, which could cause more serious problems in the future.

5.10a Rotate the tensioner against the spring pressure...

5.10b... and lock it in place using a rod/pin

A leak in the cooling system will usually show up as white-or antifreeze coloured deposits on the area adjoining the leak.

3 Carefully check the radiator hoses and heater hoses along their entire length. Renew any hose which is cracked, swollen or deteriorated. Cracks will show up better if the hose is squeezed. Pay close attention to the hose clips that secure the hoses to the cooling system components. Hose clips can pinch and puncture hoses, resulting in cooling system leaks.

4 Inspect all the cooling system components (hoses, joint faces, etc) for leaks. A leak in the cooling system will usually show up as white- or antifreeze-coloured deposits on the area adjoining the leak (see **Haynes Hint**). Where any problems of this nature are found on system components, renew the component or gasket with reference to Chapter 3.

5 With the vehicle raised, inspect the fuel tank and filler neck for punctures, cracks and other damage. The connection between the filler neck and tank is especially critical. Sometimes a rubber filler neck or connecting hose will leak due to loose retaining clamps or deteriorated rubber.

6 Carefully check all rubber hoses and metal fuel lines leading away from the petrol tank. Check for loose connections, deteriorated hoses, crimped lines, and other damage. Pay particular attention to the vent pipes and hoses, which often loop up around the filler neck and can become blocked or crimped. Follow the lines to the front of the vehicle,

carefully inspecting them all the way. Renew damaged sections as necessary.

7 Closely inspect the metal brake pipes, which run along the vehicle underbody. If they show signs of excessive corrosion or damage they must be renewed.

8 From within the engine compartment, check the security of all fuel hose attachments and pipe unions, and inspect the fuel hoses and vacuum hoses for kinks, chafing and deterioration.

7 Brake pad check

1 Brake discs are fitted to the front of all models, and also to the rear of 1.4 litre 16v Sport models.

2 Raise the front, or rear, of the vehicle (as applicable), and support it securely on axle stands as described in *'Vehicle jacking and support'*. Remove the appropriate roadwheels.

3 Using a steel rule, measure the thickness of the friction material of the brake pads on both front, or rear brakes. This must not be less than 1.5 mm. Check the thickness of the pad friction material through the hole on the caliper **(see illustration)**.

4 For a comprehensive check, the brake pads should be removed and cleaned. The operation of the caliper can then also be checked, and the condition of the brake disc itself can be fully examined on both sides. Refer to Chapter 9 for further information.

5 If any pad's friction material is worn to the specified thickness or less, all four pads on the front, or rear axle must be renewed as a set. Refer to Chapter 9.

6 On completion refit the roadwheels and lower the car to the ground.

8 Driveshaft gaiter check

1 With the car raised and securely supported on stands (see *'Vehicle jacking and support'*), turn the steering onto full lock, then slowly rotate the roadwheel. Inspect the condition of

the outer constant velocity (CV) joint rubber gaiters, squeezing the gaiters to open out the folds. Check for signs of cracking, splits or deterioration of the rubber, which may allow the grease to escape, and lead to water and grit entry into the joint. Also check the security and condition of the retaining clips. Repeat these checks on the inner CV joints **(see illustration)**. If any damage or deterioration is found, the gaiters should be renewed (see Chapter 8 Section 3).

2 At the same time, check the general condition of the CV joints themselves by first holding the driveshaft and attempting to rotate the wheel. Repeat this check by holding the inner joint and attempting to rotate the driveshaft. Any appreciable movement indicates wear in the joints, wear in the driveshaft splines, or a loose driveshaft retaining nut.

9 Steering and suspension check

Front suspension and steering

1 Raise the front of the vehicle and support it securely on axle stands, as described in *'Vehicle jacking and support'*.

2 Inspect the balljoint dust covers and the steering rack and pinion gaiters for splits, chafing or deterioration. Any wear of these will cause loss of lubricant, together with dirt and water entry, resulting in rapid deterioration of the balljoints or steering gear.

3 Grasp the roadwheel at the 12 o'clock and 6 o'clock positions, and try to rock it **(see illustration)**. Very slight free play may be felt, but if the movement is appreciable, further investigation is necessary to determine the source. Continue rocking the wheel while an assistant depresses the footbrake. If the movement is now eliminated or significantly reduced, it is likely that the hub bearings are at fault. If the free play is still evident with the footbrake depressed, then there is wear in the suspension joints or mountings.

4 Now grasp the wheel at the 9 o'clock and 3 o'clock positions, and try to rock it as before. Any movement felt now may again be caused

7.3 Check the thickness of the pad friction material through the hole in the caliper

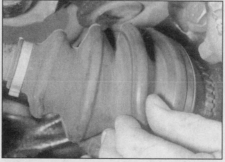

8.1 Check the condition of the driveshaft gaiter

9.3 Rock a roadwheel to check for wear in the steering/suspension components

by wear in the hub bearings or the steering track rod balljoints. If the inner or outer balljoint is worn, the visual movement will be obvious.

5 Using a large screwdriver or flat bar, check for wear in the suspension mounting bushes by levering between the relevant suspension component and its attachment point. Some movement is to be expected as the mountings are made of rubber, but excessive wear should be obvious. Also check the condition of any visible rubber bushes, looking for splits, cracks or contamination of the rubber.

6 With the car standing on its wheels, have an assistant turn the steering wheel back-and-forth about an eighth of a turn each way. There should be very little, if any, lost movement between the steering wheel and roadwheels. If this is not the case, closely observe the joints and mountings previously described, but in addition check the steering column universal joints for wear, and the rack and pinion steering gear itself.

Strut/shock absorber check

7 Check for any signs of fluid leakage around the suspension strut/shock absorber body, or from the rubber gaiter around the piston rod. Should any fluid be noticed, the suspension strut/shock absorber is defective internally, and should be renewed.
Note: *Suspension struts/shock absorbers should always be renewed in pairs on the same axle.*

8 The efficiency of the suspension strut/shock absorber may be checked by bouncing the vehicle at each corner. Generally speaking, the body will return to its normal position and stop after being depressed. If it rises and returns on a rebound, the suspension strut/shock absorber is probably suspect. Examine also the suspension strut/shock absorber upper and lower mountings for any signs of wear.

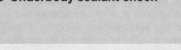

10 Underbody sealant check

1 Jack up the front and rear of the car and support it securely on axle stands, as described in 'Vehicle jacking and support'. Alternatively position the car over an inspection pit.

2 Check the underbody, wheel housings and side sills for rust and/or damage to the underbody sealant. If evident, repair as necessary.

11 Exhaust system check

1 With the engine cold (at least an hour after the vehicle has been driven), check the complete exhaust system from the engine to

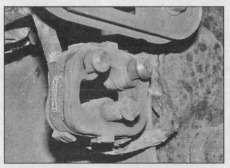

11.2 Check the condition of the exhaust rubber mountings

the end of the tailpipe. The exhaust system is most easily checked with the car raised on a hoist, or suitably supported on axle stands, as described in 'Vehicle jacking and support', so that the exhaust components are readily visible and accessible.

2 Check the exhaust pipes and connections for evidence of leaks, severe corrosion and damage. Make sure that all brackets and mountings are in good condition, and that all relevant nuts and bolts are tight **(see illustration)**. Leakage at any of the joints or in other parts of the system will usually show up as a black sooty stain in the vicinity of the leak.

3 Rattles and other noises can often be traced to the exhaust system, especially the brackets and mountings. Try to move the pipes and silencers. If the components are able to come into contact with the body or suspension parts, secure the system with new mountings. Otherwise separate the joints (if possible) and twist the pipes as necessary to provide additional clearance.

12 Handbrake check and adjustment

1 Apply the handbrake by pulling it through a maximum of five clicks of the ratchet mechanism and check that this locks the rear wheels, holding the vehicle stationary on an incline. In this position, there should be sufficient reserve travel in the handbrake lever to allow for brake shoe/pad wear and cable stretching. If not, the handbrake mechanism should be adjusted as described in Chapter 9 Section 15.

13 Hinge and lock lubrication

1 Lubricate the hinges of the bonnet, doors and tailgate with a light general-purpose oil. Similarly, lubricate all latches, locks and lock strikers. At the same time, check the security and operation of all the locks.

2 Lightly lubricate the bonnet release mechanism with a suitable grease.

14 Road test

Instruments and electrical equipment

1 Check the operation of all instruments and electrical equipment.

2 Make sure that all instruments read correctly, and switch on all electrical equipment in turn, to check that it functions properly.

Steering and suspension

3 Check for any abnormalities in the steering, suspension, handling or road feel.

4 Drive the vehicle, and check that there are no unusual vibrations or noises.

5 Check that the steering feels positive, with no excessive sloppiness, or roughness, and check for any suspension noises when cornering and driving over bumps.

Drivetrain

6 Check the performance of the engine, clutch, transmission and driveshafts.

7 Listen for any unusual noises from the engine, clutch and gearbox/transmission.

8 Make sure that the engine runs smoothly when idling, and that there is no hesitation when accelerating.

9 Check that the clutch action is smooth and progressive, that the drive is taken up smoothly, and that the pedal travel is not excessive. Also listen for any noises when the clutch pedal is depressed.

10 Check that all gears can be engaged smoothly without noise, and that the gear lever action is smooth and not abnormally vague or notchy.

11 Listen for a metallic clicking sound from the front of the vehicle, as the vehicle is driven slowly in a circle with the steering on full lock. Carry out this check in both directions. If a clicking noise is heard, this indicates wear in a driveshaft joint, in which case renew the joint if necessary.

Braking system

12 Make sure that the vehicle does not pull to one side when braking, and that the wheels do not lock when braking hard.

13 Check that there is no vibration through the steering when braking.

14 Check that the handbrake operates correctly without excessive movement of the lever, and that it holds the vehicle stationary on a slope.

15 Test the operation of the brake servo unit as follows. With the engine off, depress the footbrake four or five times to exhaust the vacuum. Hold the brake pedal depressed, then start the engine. As the engine starts, there should be a noticeable give in the brake pedal as vacuum builds-up. Allow the engine to run for at least two minutes, and then

16.7 Check the valve clearance with a feeler blade

16.11 Using a modified C-spanner and a screwdriver to remove a shim

16.13 Shim thickness is marked on the lower face (here 4.20 mm)

switch it off. If the brake pedal is depressed now, it should be possible to detect a hiss from the servo as the pedal is depressed. After about four or five applications, no further hissing should be heard, and the pedal should feel considerably harder.

15 Service indicator reset

1 Once the service has been completed, the Service indicator will need to be reset. This can only be done using Fiat diagnostic equipment (Examiner or equivalent). Consequently, we recommend this task be entrusted to a Fiat dealer or suitably equipped specialist.

16 Valve clearance check and adjustment

Note: *The following procedure is not applicable to DOHC (16-valve) engines which utilise self-adjusting hydraulic tappets.*

1 The importance of having the valve clearances correctly adjusted cannot be overstressed, as they vitally affect the performance of the engine. Adjustment should only be necessary when the valve gear has become noisy, after engine overhaul, or when trying to trace the cause of power loss. The clearances are checked as follows. The engine must be cold for the check to be accurate.

2 Apply the handbrake then jack up the right-hand front of the car and support on an axle stand, as described in *'Vehicle jacking and support'*. Engage top gear. The engine can now be rotated by turning the right-hand front roadwheel.

3 Remove all spark plugs as described in Section 17.

4 Remove the camshaft cover as described in Chapter 2A Section 7.

5 Each valve clearance must be checked when the high point of the cam lobe is pointing directly upward away from the cam follower.

6 Check the clearances in the firing order

1–3–4–2, No 1 cylinder being at the timing belt end of the engine. This will minimise the amount of crankshaft rotation required.

7 Insert the appropriate feeler blade between the heel of the cam and the cam follower shim of the first valve **(see illustration)**. If necessary alter the thickness of the feeler blade until it is a stiff, sliding fit. Record the thickness, which will, of course, represent the valve clearance for this particular valve.

8 Turn the engine, check the second valve clearance and record it.

9 Repeat the operations on all the remaining valves, recording their respective clearances.

10 Remember that the clearance for intake and exhaust valves differs – see Specifications. Counting from the timing belt end of the engine, the valve sequence is:

Intake 2-4-5-7

Exhaust 1-3-6-8

11 Where clearances are incorrect, the particular shim will have to be changed. To remove the shim, turn the crankshaft until the high point of the cam is pointing directly upward. The cam follower will now have to be depressed so that the shim can be extracted. Special tools are commercially available to do the job, otherwise you will have to make up a forked lever to locate on the rim of the cam follower. This must allow room for the shim to be prised out by means of the cut-outs provided in the cam follower rim **(see illustration)**.

12 Once the shim is extracted, establish its thickness and change it for a thicker or thinner one to bring the previously recorded clearance within specification. For example, if the measured valve clearance was 1.27 mm too great, a shim thicker by this amount will be required. Conversely, if the clearance was 1.27 mm too small, a shim thinner by this amount will be required.

13 Shims have their thickness (mm) engraved on them; although the engraved side should be fitted so as not to be visible, wear still occurs and often obliterates the number. In this case, measuring their thickness with a metric micrometer is the only method to establish their thickness **(see illustration)**.

14 In practice, if several shims have to be

changed, they can often be interchanged, so avoiding the necessity of having to buy more new shims than is necessary, but do not turn the engine with any shims missing.

15 If more than two or three valve clearances are found to be incorrect, it will be more convenient to remove the camshaft for easier removal of the shims.

16 Where no clearance can be measured, even with the thinnest available shim in position, the valve will have to be removed and the end of its stem ground off squarely. This will reduce its overall length by the minimum amount to provide a clearance. This job should be entrusted to an engine reconditioning specialist as it is important to keep the end of the valve stem square.

17 On completion, refit the camshaft cover as described in Chapter 2A Section 7, and the spark plugs as described in Section 17.

18 Lower the vehicle to the ground.

17 Spark plug renewal

1 The correct functioning of the spark plugs is vital for the correct running and efficiency of the engine. It is essential that the plugs fitted are appropriate for the engine (a suitable type is specified at the beginning of this Chapter). If this type is used and the engine is in good condition, the spark plugs should not need attention between scheduled replacement intervals. Spark plug cleaning is rarely necessary, and should not be attempted unless specialised equipment is available, as damage can easily be caused to the firing ends.

SOHC 8v engines

2 Remove the air cleaner assembly as described in Chapter 4A Section 2.

3 If the marks on the original-equipment spark plug (HT) leads cannot be seen, mark the leads 1 to 4, to correspond to the cylinder the lead serves (No 1 cylinder is at the timing belt end of the engine). Pull the leads from the plugs by gripping the end fitting, not the

17.3 Grip the HT lead end fitting, not the lead

17.6 Remove the spark plugs using a deep socket and extension bar

HAYNES HINT

It is very often difficult to insert spark plugs into their holes without cross-threading them. To avoid this possibility, fit a short length of 8 mm internal diameter rubber hose over the end of the spark plug. The flexible hose acts as a universal joint to help align the plug with the plug hole. Should the plug begin to cross-thread, the hose will slip on the spark plug, preventing thread damage to the cylinder head.

lead, otherwise the lead connection may be fractured **(see illustration)**.

DOHC 16v engines

4 Remove the ignition coils as described in Chapter 5B Section 3.

All engines

5 It is advisable to remove the dirt from the spark plug recesses using a clean brush, vacuum cleaner or compressed air before removing the plugs, to prevent dirt dropping into the cylinders.

6 Unscrew the plugs using a spark plug spanner, suitable box spanner or a deep socket and extension bar **(see illustration)** Keep the socket aligned with the spark plug – if it is forcibly moved to one side, the ceramic insulator may be broken off. As each plug is removed, examine it as follows.

7 Examination of the spark plugs will give a good indication of the condition of the engine. If the insulator nose of the spark plug is clean and white, with no deposits, this is indicative of a weak mixture or too hot a plug (a hot plug transfers heat away from the electrode slowly, a cold plug transfers heat away quickly).

8 If the tip and insulator nose are covered with hard black-looking deposits, this indicates that the mixture is too rich. If the plug is black and oily, then it is likely that the engine is fairly worn, as well as the mixture being too rich.

9 If the insulator nose is covered with light tan to greyish-brown deposits, then the mixture is correct and it is likely that the engine is in good condition.

10 Note that the electrode gap on the recommended spark plugs is pre-set, and requires no adjustment.

11 Before fitting the spark plugs, check that the threaded connector sleeves are tight, and that the plug exterior surfaces and threads are clean (see **Haynes Hint**).

12 Remove the rubber hose (if used), and tighten the plug to the specified torque using the spark plug socket and a torque wrench. Refit the remaining spark plugs in the same manner.

13 The remainder of refitting is a reversal of removal.

18 HT lead check

⚠ *Warning: Due to the high voltages produced by the electronic ignition system, extreme care must be taken when working on the system with the ignition switched on. Persons with surgically-implanted cardiac pacemaker devices should keep well clear of the ignition circuits, components and test equipment.*

Note: *This procedure only applies to SOHC 8v engines*

1 The spark plug (HT) leads should be checked whenever new spark plugs are fitted.

2 Remove the air cleaner assembly as described in Chapter 4A Section 2.

3 Pull the leads from the plugs by gripping the end fitting, not the lead, otherwise the lead connection may be fractured.

4 Check inside the end fitting for signs of corrosion, which will look like a white crusty powder. Push the end fitting back onto the spark plug, ensuring that it is a tight fit on the plug. If not, remove the lead again and use pliers to carefully crimp the metal connector inside the end fitting until it fits securely on the end of the spark plug.

5 Using a clean rag, wipe the entire length of the lead to remove any built-up dirt and grease. Once the lead is clean, check for burns, cracks and other damage. Do not bend the lead excessively, nor pull the lead lengthways – the conductor inside might break.

6 Disconnect the other end of the lead from the ignition coil. Again, pull only on the end fitting. Check for corrosion and a tight fit in the same manner as the spark plug end. Refit the lead securely on completion.

7 Check the remaining leads one at a time, in the same way.

8 If new spark plug (HT) leads are required, purchase a set for your specific car and engine.

9 Refit the air cleaner assembly on completion of the checks.

10 Even with the ignition system in first-class condition, some engines may still occasionally experience poor starting attributable to damp ignition components. To disperse moisture, a water-dispersant aerosol should be liberally applied.

19 Engine management system check

1 This check is part of the manufacturer's maintenance schedule, and involves testing the engine management system using special dedicated test equipment. Such testing will allow the test equipment to read any fault codes stored in the electronic control unit memory.

2 Unless a fault is suspected, this test is not essential, although it should be noted that it is recommended by the manufacturers.

3 If access to suitable test equipment is not possible, make a thorough check of all ignition, fuel and emission control system components, hoses, and wiring, for security and obvious signs of damage. Further details of the fuel system, emission control system and ignition system can be found in the relevant parts of Chapter 4A, 4B and Chapter 5B.

20 Pollen filter renewal

1 Remove the passengers glovebox as described in Chapter 11 Section 25.

2 Carefully prise the rear edge of the passengers side centre console front trim

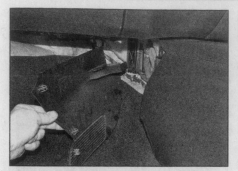

20.2 Pull out the rear edge, and slide the trim panel rearwards

20.3 Undo the screw and pull the cover from the housing

20.4 Slide the pollen filter from the housing

panel outwards, and manoeuvre it rearwards from place **(see illustration)**.

3 Undo the retaining screw and remove the pollen filter cover **(see illustration)**.

4 Withdraw the filter from its housing **(see illustration)**.

5 Wipe clean the housing, then fit the new filter, noting the arrows on the filter element must point rearwards **(see illustration)**.

6 Refit the centre console panel and glovebox.

21 Antifreeze concentration check

1 The cooling system should be filled with the recommended antifreeze and corrosion protection fluid. Over a period of time, the concentration of fluid may be reduced due to topping-up (this can be avoided by topping-up with the correct antifreeze mixture) or fluid loss. If loss of coolant has been evident, it is important to make the necessary repair before adding fresh fluid. The exact mixture of antifreeze-to-water which you should use depends on the relative weather conditions. The mixture should contain at least 40% anti-freeze, but not more than 70%. Consult the mixture ratio chart on the antifreeze container before adding coolant. Use antifreeze which meets the car manufacturer's specifications.

2 With the engine cold, carefully remove the cap from the expansion tank. If the engine is not completely cold, place a cloth rag over the cap before removing it, and remove it slowly to allow any pressure to escape.

3 Antifreeze checkers are available from car accessory shops. Draw some coolant from the expansion tank and observe how many plastic balls are floating in the checker. Usually, 2 or 3 balls must be floating for the correct concentration of antifreeze, but follow the manufacturer's instructions.

4 If the concentration is incorrect, it will be necessary to either withdraw some coolant and add antifreeze, or alternatively drain the old coolant and add fresh coolant of the correct concentration.

22 Brake fluid renewal

⚠️ *Warning: Brake hydraulic fluid can harm your eyes and damage painted surfaces, so use extreme caution when handling and pouring it. Do not use fluid that has been standing open for some time, as it absorbs moisture from the air. Excess moisture can cause a dangerous loss of braking effectiveness.*

1 The procedure is similar to that for the bleeding of the hydraulic system as described in Chapter 9 Section 2, except that the brake fluid reservoir should be emptied by syphoning, using a clean poultry baster or similar before starting, and allowance should be made for the old fluid to be expelled when bleeding a section of the circuit.

2 Working as described in Chapter 9 Section 2, open the first bleed screw in the sequence, and pump the brake pedal gently

until nearly all the old fluid has been emptied from the master cylinder reservoir.

3 Top-up to the MAX level with new fluid, and continue pumping until only the new fluid remains in the reservoir, and new fluid can be seen emerging from the bleed screw. Tighten the screw, and top the reservoir level up to the MAX level line.

4 Work through all the remaining bleed screws in the sequence until new fluid can be seen at all of them. Be careful to keep the master cylinder reservoir topped-up to above the MIN level at all times, or air may enter the system and greatly increase the length of the task.

5 When the operation is complete, check that all bleed screws are securely tightened, and that their dust caps are refitted. Wash off all traces of spilt fluid, and recheck the master cylinder reservoir fluid level.

6 Check the operation of the brakes before taking the car on the road.

23 Air filter element renewal

SOHC 8v models

1 Undo the retaining screws, and remove the filter cover **(see illustration)**.

2 Lift the filter element from the cover **(see illustration)**.

3 Remove any debris that may have collected inside the air cleaner and wipe the inner surfaces clean.

20.5 The arrows on the filter must point rearwards

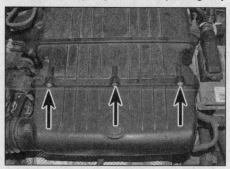

23.1 Undo the 3 screws above and below the cover

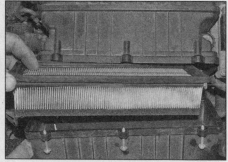

23.2 Note the orientation of the filter element

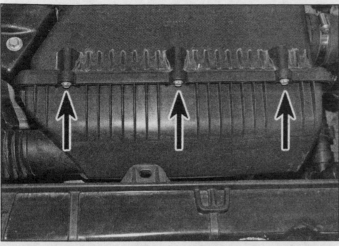

23.6 Undo the screws and open the filter cover

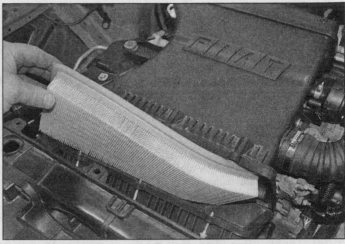

23.9 Locate the new filter element in the housing

4 Fit a new air filter element in position, ensuring that the edges are securely seated.
5 Refit the cover and securely tighten the retaining screws.

DOHC 16v models

6 Undo the retaining screws, and open the filter cover **(see illustration)**.
7 Lift the filter element from place.
8 Remove any debris that may have collected inside the air cleaner and wipe the inner surfaces clean.
9 Fit a new filter element in position, ensuring the edges are securely seated **(see illustration)**.
10 Refit the cover and tighten the retaining screws securely.

24 Timing belt inspection

1 The function of the timing belt is to drive the camshaft and coolant pump. Should the belt slip or break in service, the valve timing will be disturbed and piston-to-valve contact will occur, resulting in serious engine damage. It is therefore vitally important that the condition of the belt and surrounding components should be checked very carefully.

25.2 Transmission filler/level plug

2 To gain access to the belt, remove the upper timing belt cover as described in Chapter 2A Section 4 or Chapter 2B Section 4.
3 With the covers removed, inspect the timing belt for any signs of uneven wear, splitting, or oil contamination. Pay particular attention to the roots of the teeth. To enable the full length of the belt to be examined, turn the crankshaft using a spanner or socket on the crankshaft sprocket centre bolt.
4 Check for any signs of coolant leakage from the coolant pump or oil leakage from the crankshaft right-hand oil seal. If there is any doubt about the condition of the belt, it should be renewed as described in Chapter 2A Section 5 or Chapter 2B Section 5. If any coolant or oil leakage is evident, trace the source of the leak and rectify it before fitting the new timing belt.
5 On completion of the inspection, refit the timing belt covers.

25 Manual transmission oil level check

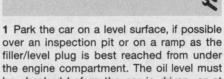

1 Park the car on a level surface, if possible over an inspection pit or on a ramp as the filler/level plug is best reached from under the engine compartment. The oil level must be checked before the car is driven, or at least 5 minutes after the engine has been switched off. If the oil is checked immediately after driving the car, some of the oil will remain distributed around the transmission components, resulting in an inaccurate level reading.
2 Wipe clean the area around the filler/level plug, which is situated on the front of the transmission **(see illustration)**. Using an Allen key, unscrew the plug and clean it.
3 The oil level should reach the lower edge of the filler/level hole. A certain amount of oil will have gathered behind the filler/level plug, and will trickle out when it is removed;

this does not necessarily indicate that the level is correct. To ensure that a true level is established, wait until the initial trickle has stopped, then add oil as necessary until a trickle of new oil can be seen emerging. The level will be correct when the flow ceases; use only good-quality oil of the specified type. Make sure that the vehicle is completely level when checking the level and do not overfill.
4 When the level is correct refit and tighten the plug and wipe away any spilt oil.

26 Timing belt renewal

1 Refer to Chapter 2A Section 5 or Chapter 2B Section 5 as applicable.

27 Evaporative loss system check

1 Refer to Chapter 4B Section 1 and check that all wiring and hoses are correctly connected to the evaporative loss system components.

28 Emission control system check

1 Refer to Chapter 4B. A full check of the emissions control systems must be made by a Fiat dealer.

29 Coolant renewal

 Warning: Wait until the engine is cold before starting this procedure. Do not allow

anti-freeze to come into contact with your skin, or with the painted surfaces of the vehicle. Rinse off spills immediately with plenty of water. Never leave antifreeze lying around in an open container, or in a puddle in the driveway or on the garage floor. Children and pets are attracted by its sweet smell, but antifreeze can be fatal if ingested.

Coolant system draining

1 With the engine completely cold, cover the expansion tank cap with a wad of rag, and slowly turn the cap anti-clockwise to relieve the pressure in the cooling system (a hissing sound will normally be heard). Wait until any pressure remaining in the system is released, then continue to turn the cap until it can be removed.

2 Place a suitable container beneath the drain tap at the left-hand end of the radiator, then open the drain tap and allow the coolant to drain **(see illustration)**.

3 The cooling system bleed screw should be opened to aid the draining process and help prevent airlocks. The screw is located at the top right-hand edge of the radiator **(see illustration)**. If the coolant has been drained for a reason other than renewal, then provided it is clean and less than two years old, it can be re-used, though this is not recommended.

4 When the coolant has finished draining, close the drain tap and remove the container.

Cooling system flushing

5 If coolant renewal has been neglected, or if the antifreeze mixture has become diluted, then in time, the cooling system may gradually lose efficiency, as the coolant passages become restricted due to rust, scale deposits, and other sediment. The cooling system efficiency can be restored by flushing the system clean.

6 The radiator should be flushed independently of the engine, to avoid contamination.

Radiator flushing

7 To flush the radiator disconnect the top and bottom hoses and any other relevant hoses from the radiator, with reference to Chapter 3.

8 Insert a garden hose into the radiator top inlet. Direct a flow of clean water through the radiator, and continue flushing until clean water emerges from the radiator bottom outlet.

9 If after a reasonable period, the water still does not run clear, the radiator can be flushed with a good proprietary cooling system cleaning agent. It is important that

29.2 Radiator drain tap

their manufacturer's instructions are followed carefully. If the contamination is particularly bad, insert the hose in the radiator bottom outlet, and reverse-flush the radiator.

Engine flushing

10 To flush the engine, remove the thermostat housing as described in Chapter 3 Section 4.

11 With the top and bottom hoses disconnected from the radiator, insert a garden hose into the radiator bottom hose. Direct a clean flow of water through the engine, and continue flushing until clean water emerges from the thermostat housing opening in the cylinder head.

12 On completion of flushing, refit the thermostat housing and reconnect the hoses with reference to Chapter 3 Section 4.

Cooling system filling

13 Before attempting to fill the cooling system, make sure that all hoses and clips are in good condition, and that the clips are tight. Note that an antifreeze mixture must be used all year round, to prevent corrosion of the engine components (see below).

14 Remove the expansion tank filler cap, and fill the system by slowly pouring the coolant into the expansion tank to prevent airlocks from forming. Ensure that the bleed screw is open.

15 If the coolant is being renewed, begin by pouring in a couple of litres of water, followed by the correct quantity of antifreeze, then top-up with more water. Periodically squeeze the radiator top and bottom hoses to help expel any trapped air in the system.

16 Continue adding coolant until it is seen to emerge from the bleed screw. Close the bleed screw as the coolant emerges.

17 Top-up the coolant level to the MAX mark and refit the expansion tank cap. Ensure that the bleed screw is closed.

18 Start the engine and run it at idling speed

29.3 The coolant bleed screw is at the right-hand corner – access is limited

for two to three minutes. Allow the engine to continue running until the electric cooling fan operates, but during this time periodically increase the engine speed gradually to 2000 to 3000 rpm.

19 Stop the engine and allow it to cool down completely.

20 Check for leaks, particularly around disturbed components. Check the coolant level in the expansion tank, and top-up if necessary. Note that the system must be cold before an accurate level is indicated in the expansion tank.

Anti-freeze mixture

21 The antifreeze should always be renewed at the specified intervals. This is necessary not only to maintain the antifreeze properties, but also to prevent corrosion which would otherwise occur as the corrosion inhibitors become progressively less effective.

22 Always use a monoethylene-glycol based antifreeze of the specified type (see Lubricants and fluids). The quantity of antifreeze and levels of protection are indicated in the Specifications.

23 Before adding antifreeze, the cooling system should be completely drained, preferably flushed, and all hoses checked for condition and security.

24 After filling with antifreeze, a label should be attached to the expansion tank, stating the type and concentration of antifreeze used, and the date installed. Any subsequent topping-up should be made with the same type and concentration of antifreeze.

25 Do not use engine antifreeze in the windscreen/tailgate washer system, as it will cause damage to the vehicle paintwork. A screenwash additive should be added to the washer system in the quantities stated on the bottle.

Chapter 2 Part A
SOHC (8-valve) in-car repair procedures

Contents

Section number

Camshaft and followers – removal, inspection and refitting 10
Camshaft cover – removal and refitting 7
Camshaft oil seal – renewal 8
Compression test – description and interpretation 2
Crankshaft oil seals – renewal 9
Cylinder head – removal and refitting........................ 11
Engine assembly/valve timing settings – general information
  and usage... 3
Engine mountings – inspection and renewal 13

Section number

Engine pressure warning light switch – removal and refitting 16
Flywheel – removal, inspection and refitting 12
General information 1
Oil pump and pick-up tube – removal, inspection and refitting..... 15
Sump – removal and refitting................................ 14
Timing belt – general information, removal and refitting 5
Timing belt covers – removal and refitting 4
Timing belt tensioner and sprockets – removal, inspection
  and refitting... 6

Degrees of difficulty

Easy, suitable for novice with little experience	Fairly easy, suitable for beginner with some experience	Fairly difficult, suitable for competent DIY mechanic	Difficult, suitable for experienced DIY mechanic	Very difficult, suitable for expert DIY or professional

Specifications

General

Engine type:
1.2 L	4-cylinder in-line petrol single overhead camshaft (SOHC) 8v
1.4 L	4-cylinder in-line petrol single overhead camshaft (SOHC) 8v with variable valve timing

Engine code:
1.2 L Euro 4 emissions level	199A4000
1.2 L Euro 5 emissions level/ECO	169A4000
1.4 L	350A1000

Bore:
1.2 L	70.8 mm
1.4 L	72.0 mm

Stroke:
1.2 L	78.86 mm
1.4 L	84.0 mm

Capacity:
1.2 L	1242 cc
1.4 L	1368 cc

Firing order: 1-3-4-2
No. 1 cylinder location: Timing (right-hand) end of the engine
Direction of crankshaft rotation: Clockwise (seen from the right-hand side of the vehicle)
Compression ratio: 11 : 1

Output:
Maximum power:
1.2 L Euro 4	48 kW @ 5500 rpm
1.2 L Euro 5	51 kW @ 5500 rpm
1.4 L	57 kW @ 6000 rpm

Maximum torque:
1.2 L	102 Nm @ 3000 rpm
1.4 L	115 Nm @ 3000 rpm

Lubrication system

Minimum system pressure:
 At idle speed.. 0.9 bar
 At 4000 rpm:
  1.2 L... 3.5 bar
  1.4 L... 4.2 bar
Pump outer rotor-to-housing clearance........................... 0.080 to 0.186 mm
Rotor axial clearance .... 0.025 to 0.056 mm

Torque wrench settings

	Nm	lbf ft
Camshaft bearing cap bolts	20	15
Camshaft cover bolts	10	7
Camshaft sprocket bolt:		
1.2 L	70	52
1.4 L:		
Bolt:		
Stage 1	20	15
Stage 2	Angle-tighten a further 55°	
Threaded cap	28	21
Connecting rod bolts*:		
Stage 1	20	15
Stage 2	Angle-tighten a further 40°	
Crankshaft pulley bolts (M8)	25	17
Crankshaft sprocket bolt:		
Stage 1	20	15
Stage 2	Angle-tighten a further 90°	
Crankshaft left-hand oil seal housing bolts	10	7
Cylinder block-to-transmission support bracket bolts:		
M8	25	17
M10	40	30
M12	55	41
Cylinder head bolts*:		
Stage 1	30	22
Stage 2	Angle-tighten a further 90°	
Stage 3	Angle-tighten a further 90°	
Engine/transmission mountings:		
Right-hand side mounting-to-body	60	45
Right-hand side mounting-to-support bracket	80	59
Right-hand side mounting support bracket-to-engine:		
1.2 L	60	45
1.4 L	50	37
Left-hand side mounting-to-body	90	66
Left-hand side mounting-to-support bracket	95	70
Rear mounting rod-to-subframe:		
Stage 1	55	41
Stage 2	Angle-tighten a further 90°	
Rear mounting rod-to-transmission bracket	95	70
Flywheel bolts*	45	33
Main bearing cap bolts:		
Stage 1	20	15
Stage 2	Angle-tighten a further 90°	
Oil pump bolts	10	7
Oil pressure warning switch	30	22
Sump drain plug	45	33
Sump:		
M6 nuts	10	7
M8 bolts	25	17
Timing belt tensioner nut	28	21

*Do not re-use

1 General information

How to use this Chapter

1 This Part of Chapter 2 is devoted to in-car repair procedures for Single OverHead Camshaft (SOHC) 8v 1.2 litre and 1.4 litre petrol engines. Similar information covering the 1.4 litre Double OverHead Camshaft (DOHC) 16v engines will be found in Part B of this Chapter. Part C covers the removal of the engine/transmission as a unit, and describes the engine dismantling and overhaul procedures.

2 In Parts A and B, the assumption is made that the engine is installed in the car, with all ancillaries connected. If the engine has been removed for overhaul, the preliminary dismantling information which precedes each operation may be ignored.

3 Note that whilst it may be possible physically to overhaul items such as the piston/ connecting rod assemblies with the engine in the vehicle, such tasks are not usually carried out as separate operations and usually require the execution of several additional procedures (not to mention the cleaning of components and of oilways). For this reason, all such tasks are classed as major overhaul procedures and are described in Chapter 2C.

Engine description

4 The engine covered in this Part of Chapter 2 is a water-cooled, single overhead camshaft (SOHC), in-line four-cylinder unit, with cast iron cylinder block and aluminium-alloy cylinder head. The engine is mounted transversely at the front of the car, with the transmission bolted to the left-hand end.

5 The cylinder head carries the camshaft which is driven by a toothed timing belt and runs in three bearings. It also houses the inlet and exhaust valves, which are closed by single coil springs, and which run in guides pressed into the cylinder head. The camshaft actuates the valves directly via cam followers mounted in the cylinder head. Adjustment of the valve clearances is by means of shims located on top of the followers. The cylinder head contains integral oilways which supply and lubricate the followers (tappets).

6 The crankshaft is supported by five main bearings, and endfloat is controlled by a thrust bearing fitted to the upper section of the centre main bearing.

7 Engine coolant is circulated by a pump, driven by the timing belt. For details of the cooling system, refer to Chapter 3.

8 Lubricant is circulated under pressure by a pump, driven from the front of the crankshaft. Oil is drawn from the sump through a strainer, and then forced through an externally-mounted, renewable screw-on filter. From there, it is distributed to the cylinder head,
where it lubricates the camshaft journals and tappets, and also to the crankcase, where it lubricates the main bearings, connecting rod big and small-ends, gudgeon pins and cylinder bores.

Repair operations possible with the engine in the car

9 The following operations can be carried out with the engine in the car:
a) Compression pressure – testing
b) Valve clearances – checking and adjustment
c) Camshaft cover – removal and refitting.
d) Timing belt covers – removal and refitting
e) Timing belt – removal, refitting and adjustment
f) Camshaft and cam followers – removal, inspection and refitting.
g) Cylinder head – removal and refitting.
h) Cylinder head and pistons* – decarbonising.
i) Sump – removal and refitting.
j) Oil pump – removal and refitting.
k) Crankshaft oil seals – renewal.
l) Camshaft oil seal – renewal
m) Engine mountings – inspection and renewal.
n) Flywheel – inspection and renewal.
Note: *Although it is possible to remove these components with the engine in place, for reasons of access and cleanliness it is recommended that the engine be removed.

2 Compression test – description and interpretation

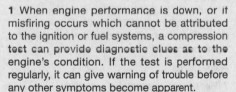

1 When engine performance is down, or if misfiring occurs which cannot be attributed to the ignition or fuel systems, a compression test can provide diagnostic clues as to the engine's condition. If the test is performed regularly, it can give warning of trouble before any other symptoms become apparent.

2 The engine must be fully warmed-up to normal operating temperature, the battery must be fully-charged, and all the spark plugs must be removed (see Chapter 1 Section 17). The aid of an assistant will also be required.

3 Disable the ignition and fuel injection systems by disconnecting the wiring multi-plug connectors at the engine management ECU, referring to Chapter 4A Section 9 for further information.

4 Fit a compression tester to the No 1 cylinder spark plug hole – the type of tester which screws into the plug thread is to be preferred.

5 Crank the engine on the starter motor; after one or two revolutions, the compression pressure should build-up to a maximum figure, and then stabilise. Record the highest reading obtained.

6 Repeat the test on the remaining cylinders, recording the pressure in each.

7 All cylinders should produce very similar
pressures; a difference of more than 2 bars between any two cylinders indicates a fault. Note that the compression should build-up quickly in a healthy engine; low compression on the first stroke, followed by gradually-increasing pressure on successive strokes, indicates worn piston rings. A low compression reading on the first stroke, which does not build-up during successive strokes, indicates leaking valves or a blown head gasket (a cracked head could also be the cause). Deposits on the undersides of the valve heads can also cause low compression.

8 Although Fiat do not specify exact compression pressures, as a guide, any cylinder pressure of below 10 bars can be considered as less than healthy. Refer to a Fiat dealer or other specialist if in doubt as to whether a particular pressure reading is acceptable.

9 If the pressure in any cylinder is low, carry out the following test to isolate the cause. Introduce a teaspoonful of clean oil into that cylinder through its spark plug hole, and repeat the test.

10 If the addition of oil temporarily improves the compression pressure, this indicates that bore or piston wear is responsible for the pressure loss. No improvement suggests that leaking or burnt valves, or a blown head gasket, may be to blame.

11 A low reading from two adjacent cylinders is almost certainly due to the head gasket having blown between them; the presence of coolant in the engine oil will confirm this.

12 If the compression reading is unusually high, the combustion chambers are probably coated with carbon deposits. If this is the case, the cylinder head should be removed and decarbonised.

13 On completion of the test, refit the spark plugs and reconnect the engine management ECU wiring connectors.

3 Engine assembly/valve timing settings – general information and usage

General information

1 The camshaft is driven by the crankshaft, by means of a timing belt and sprockets. Both sprockets rotate in phase with each other and this provides the correct valve timing as the engine rotates. When the timing belt is removed during servicing or repair, it is possible for the camshaft and crankshaft to rotate independently of each other and the correct valve timing is then lost.

2 The design of the engine is such that potentially damaging piston-to-valve contact may occur if the camshaft is rotated when any of the pistons are stationary at, or near, the top of their stroke.

3 For this reason it is important that the correct phasing between the camshaft and crankshaft is preserved whilst the timing belt

is off the engine. This is achieved by setting the engine in a reference position (known as Top Dead Centre or TDC) before the timing belt is removed and then preventing the camshaft and crankshaft from rotating until the belt is refitted. Similarly, if the engine has been dismantled for overhaul, the engine can be set to TDC during reassembly to ensure that the correct shaft phasing is restored.

4 TDC is the highest point in the cylinder that each piston reaches as the crankshaft turns. Each piston reaches TDC at the end of the compression stroke and again at the end of the exhaust stroke. However, for the purpose of timing the engine, TDC refers to the position of No 1 piston at the end of its compression stroke. On all engines in this manual, No 1 piston (and cylinder) is at the timing belt end of the engine.

Usage

Note: *Fiat special tools 2.000.004.400 and 2.000.004.500 (or equivalents) will be required for this procedure.*

5 These engines are not equipped with conventional timing marks and it is therefore necessary to use special tools to determine TDC for No 1 piston, and the correct corresponding position for the camshaft.

6 Remove the air cleaner housing as described in Chapter 4A Section 2.

7 Remove the engine management ECU as described in Chapter, 4A Section 9 then undo the fasteners and remove the ECU support bracket.

8 Remove the ignition coils as described in Chapter 5B Section 3.

9 Remove the timing belt upper cover as described in Section 4.

10 Remove the camshaft cover as described in Section 7.

11 Remove the timing belt lower cover as described in Section 4.

12 Remove the spark plugs as described in Chapter 1 Section 17.

13 Turn the engine by means of the crankshaft sprocket until the Fiat tool No. 2.000.004.400 located correctly in the slot at the left-hand end of the camshaft, and the upper mating surface of the cylinder head. Secure the tool to the cylinder head using the bolt(s) provided **(see illustration)**. Note that after-market equivalents of these tools may be available (try www.asttools.co.uk).

14 With the camshaft locked in place it must be possible to locate the crankshaft locking tool (No. 2.000.004.500) over the end of the crankshaft, and secure it to the engine block as shown **(see illustration)**.

4 Timing belt covers – removal and refitting

Removal

Upper cover

1 If both the upper and lower timing belt covers are to be removed, firmly apply the handbrake, then jack up the front of the car and support it securely on axle stands as described in *'Vehicle jacking and support'*. Remove the right-hand front roadwheel, then undo the fasteners and remove the engine undershield (where fitted).

2 Undo the bolts and remove the upper cover **(see illustration)**.

Lower cover

3 Remove the upper cover as previously described in this Section.

4 Remove the auxiliary drivebelt as described in Chapter 1 Section 5.

5 Undo the bolts and remove the crankshaft pulley from the sprocket.

6 Undo the retaining bolts and remove the lower timing belt cover.

Refitting

7 Refitting is a reversal of removal.

8 If a new crankshaft pulley has been fitted, it must be initialised as follows:

a) Turn on the ignition and start the engine. If the injection warning light flashes, the initialisation procedure must be carried out.

b) Allow the engine to idle until normal operating temperature is reached – do not press the accelerator during this process.

c) Carry out three engine speed accelerations, reaching 6000 rpm. After each acceleration, allow the engine to idle.

d) If the injection warning light continues to flash, the initialisation is not complete. Repeat the procedure.

e) Turn the ignition off, and wait at least 1 minute for the information to be stored in the ECU memory.

5 Timing belt – general information, removal and refitting

General information

1 The function of the timing belt is to drive the camshaft and coolant pump. Should the belt slip or break in service, the valve timing will be disturbed and piston-to-valve contact will occur, resulting in serious engine damage.

2 The timing belt should be renewed at the specified intervals (see Chapter 1 Section 1) or earlier if it is contaminated with oil, or if it is at all noisy in operation (a scraping noise due to uneven wear).

3 If the timing belt is being removed, it is a wise precaution to check the condition of the coolant pump at the same time (check for signs of coolant leakage). This may avoid the need to remove the timing belt again at a later stage, should the coolant pump fail.

Removal

4 Set the engine at TDC for No 1 piston as described in Section 3.

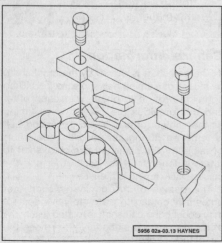

3.13 With the special tool located in the camshaft slot, bolt the tool to the cylinder head

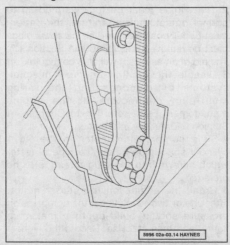

3.14 Fit the special tool to the crankshaft and bolt it to the engine block

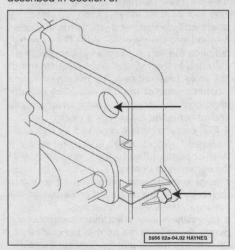

4.2 Timing belt upper cover bolts

5.6 Right-hand engine mounting assembly retaining bolts

5.8 Timing belt tensioner nut

5 Position a workshop jack under the engine, with a block of wood at the jack head to prevent damage, then take the weight of the engine.

6 Undo the retaining bolts and remove the right-hand engine mounting assembly (see illustration).

7 Undo the retaining bolts and remove the right-hand engine mounting support bracket.

8 Release the nut on the timing belt tensioner, move the tensioner pulley away from the belt and retighten the nut to hold the pulley in the retracted position (see illustration).

9 If the timing belt is to be re-used, use white paint or chalk to mark the direction of rotation on the belt (if markings do not already exist), then slip the belt off the sprockets. Note

TOOL TiP

To make a camshaft sprocket holding tool, obtain two lengths of steel strip about 6 mm thick by 30 mm wide or similar, one 600 mm long, then other 200 mm long (all dimensions are approximate). bolt the two strips together to form a forked end, leaving the bolt slack so that the shorter strip can pivot freely. At the end of each 'prong' of the fork, secure a bolt with a nut and a locknut, to act as the fulcrums; these will engage with the cut-outs in the sprocket, and should protrude about 30 mm.

that the crankshaft and camshaft must not be rotated whilst the belt is removed.

10 Check the timing belt carefully for any signs of uneven wear, splitting, or oil contamination. Pay particular attention to the roots of the teeth. Renew it if there is the slightest doubt about its condition. If the engine is undergoing an overhaul, renew the belt as a matter of course, regardless of its apparent condition. The cost of a new belt is nothing compared with the cost of repairs should the belt break in service. If signs of oil contamination are found, trace the source of the oil leak and rectify it. Wash down the engine timing belt area and all related components, to remove all traces of oil.

Refitting

11 Before refitting, thoroughly clean the timing belt sprockets. Check that the tensioner pulley rotates freely, without any sign of roughness. If necessary, renew the tensioner pulley as described in Section 6.

12 Referring to Section 3, make sure that the crankshaft and camshaft are still set at their correct TDC positions and the camshaft and

crankshaft are locked in the correct positions using the special tools.

1.2 L models

13 Slacken the camshaft sprocket retaining bolt, while holding the sprocket stationary using a suitable tool (see Tool Tip).

1.4 L models

14 Unscrew the threaded cap, then slacken the camshaft sprocket retaining bolt (see illustration). Use an open-ended spanner on the hexagonal section of the camshaft to prevent the sprocket from rotating.

All models

15 With the arrows on the timing belt pointing in the direction of engine rotation, engage the timing belt with the crankshaft sprocket first, then place it around the coolant pump sprocket and the camshaft sprocket. Finally slip the belt around the tensioner pulley.

16 Release the tensioner nut and insert the jaws of a pair of right-angled circlip pliers (or similar) into the two holes on the front face of the tensioner pulley. Rotate the pulley anti-clockwise to the stop – the pulley is now in the maximum tension position (see illustration).

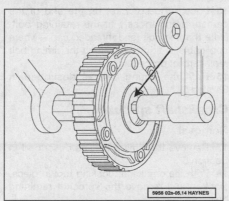

5.14 Use a spanner on the camshaft hexagonal section, undo the cap and bolt

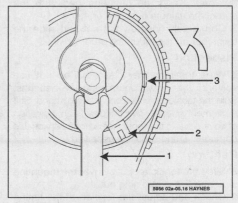

5.16 Using pliers (or similar) (1) rotate the pulley anti-clockwise unit the front fork (2) contacts the stop (3)

1.2 L models

17 Tighten the camshaft sprocket retaining bolt to the specified torque, while holding the sprocket stationary using the method described previously.

1.4 L models

18 Disconnect the upper oxygen sensor wiring plug, then remove the exhaust manifold heatshield.

19 Undo the 2 retaining bolts and remove the timing belt side cover **(see illustration)**.

20 In order to prevent the camshaft sprocket from rotating, fit Fiat tool No. 2000 004 200 to the underside of the sprocket and tighten the retaining bolt **(see illustration)**.

21 Tighten the camshaft sprocket retaining bolt to the specified torque.

22 Refit the cap to the centre of the camshaft sprocket and tighten it to the specified torque.

All models

23 Remove the camshaft and crankshaft locking tools.

24 Turn the engine clockwise through two complete revolutions, then hold the tensioner pulley stationary, slacken the tensioner nut, and rotate the pulley until the tensioner front fork is aligned with the rear fork. Tighten the tensioner nut to the specified torque.

25 With the engine positioned again at TDC, check that the camshaft and crankshaft locking tools can be fitted. If not, repeat the complete tensioning procedure.

26 The remainder of refitting is a reversal of removal.

---

6 Timing belt tensioner and sprockets – removal, inspection and refitting

Timing belt tensioner

Removal

1 Set the engine at TDC for No 1 piston as described in Section 3.

2 Loosen the nut on the timing belt tensioner and move the tensioner pulley away from the belt. Keep the belt engaged with the sprockets using a cable-tie or string.

3 Completely unscrew the nut and slide the tensioner off the mounting stud.

Inspection

4 Wipe the tensioner clean but do not use solvents that may contaminate the bearings. Spin the tensioner pulley on its hub by hand. Stiff movement or excessive freeplay is an indication of severe wear; the tensioner is not a serviceable component, and should be renewed.

Refitting

5 Slide the tensioner pulley over the mounting stud and fit the retaining nut.

6 Check and adjust the tension of the timing belt as described in Section 5.

7 The remainder of refitting is a reversal of removal.

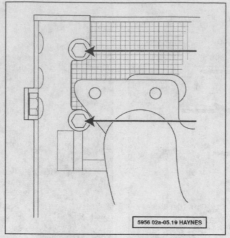

5.19 Side cover retaining bolts

Camshaft sprocket

Removal

8 Remove the timing belt as described in Section 5.

1.2 L models

9 Slacken the camshaft sprocket retaining bolt while holding the sprocket stationary with a suitable tool as described in Section 5.

1.4 L models

10 Unscrew the threaded cap, then remove the camshaft sprocket retaining bolt as described in Section 5.

All models

11 Remove the sprocket from the end of the camshaft.

Inspection

12 With the sprocket removed, examine the camshaft oil seal for signs of leaking. If necessary, refer to Section 8 and renew it.

13 Check the sprocket teeth for damage.

14 Wipe clean the sprocket and camshaft mating surfaces.

Refitting

15 Locate the sprocket on the end of the camshaft and loosely fit the retaining bolt. Note that the bolt (and threaded cap – where applicable) is tightened during the timing belt replacement procedure.

16 Refit the timing belt as described in Section 5.

Crankshaft sprocket

Removal

17 Remove the timing belt as described in Section 5.

18 With the crankshaft locking tool in place, slacken and remove the sprocket retaining bolt.

19 Remove the crankshaft locking tool.

20 Slide the sprocket from the end of the crankshaft.

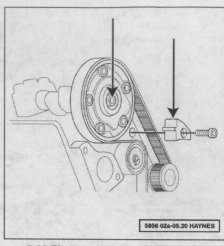

5.20 Fit the special tool to hold the sprocket, then tighten the retaining bolt

Inspection

21 With the sprocket removed, examine the crankshaft oil seal for signs of leaking. If necessary renew the seal as described in Section 9.

22 Check the sprocket teeth for damage.

23 Wipe clean the sprocket and crankshaft mating surfaces.

Refitting

24 Slide the sprocket onto the crankshaft making sure the integral key engages with the slot on the end of the crankshaft.

25 Refit the crankshaft locking tool.

26 Refit the sprocket retaining bolt and tighten it to the specified torque.

27 Refit the timing belt as described in Section 5.

---

7 Camshaft cover – removal and refitting

Removal

1 Remove the air cleaner assembly as described in Chapter 4A Section 2.

2 Remove the engine management ECU as described in Chapter 4A Section 9, then remove the ECU support bracket.

3 Remove the ignition coils as described in Chapter 5B Section 3.

4 Remove the timing belt upper cover as described in Section 4.

5 Undo the bolt and detach the earth lead from the camshaft cover.

6 Disconnect the wiring plug, undo the retaining bolt and remove the camshaft position sensor.

7 On 1.4 L models, disconnect the variable valve timing solenoid wiring plug.

8 Progressively unscrew the mounting bolts from the top of the camshaft cover and lift off the cover – note the location of any supports on the bolts. If it sticks, do not attempt to lever

it off – instead free it by working around the cover and tapping it lightly with a soft-faced mallet.

9 Recover the camshaft cover gasket. Inspect the gasket carefully, and renew it if damage or deterioration is evident.

10 Clean the mating surfaces of the cylinder head and camshaft cover thoroughly, removing all traces of oil and old gasket – take care to avoid damaging the surfaces as you do this.

Refitting

11 Locate a new gasket on the camshaft cover and make sure it is correctly seated (see illustration).

1.2 L models

12 Lower the cover onto the cylinder head, making sure the gasket is not displaced. Ensure the cover is flush with the cylinder head at the left-hand end.

13 Insert the cover retaining bolts and tighten them progressively to the specified torque.

1.4 L models

14 Apply a little silicone sealant to the four corners of the camshaft cover, and refit the gasket.

15 Position the cover on the cylinder head, then attach Fiat tool No. 2000 004 300 (template) to the left-hand end of the cylinder head (see illustration). This tool correctly positions the camshaft cover in relation to the cylinder head.

16 Progressively tighten the camshaft cover bolt to the specified torque.

All models

17 The remainder of refitting is a reversal of removal.

7.11 Ensure the gasket is correctly seated

pull on the screw with pliers to extract the seal.

4 Clean the seal housing, and polish off any burrs or raised edges, which may have caused the seal to fail in the first place.

5 Lubricate the lips of the new seal with clean engine oil, and drive it into position until it seats on its locating shoulder. Use a suitable tubular drift, such as a socket, which bears only on the hard outer edge of the seal. Take care not to damage the seal lips during fitting. Note that the seal lips should face inwards.

6 Refit the camshaft front bearing cap, and tighten the bolts to the specified torque.

7 Refit the camshaft sprocket as described in Section 6.

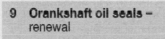
9 Crankshaft oil seals – renewal

Right-hand side oil seal

1 The seal is located in the oil pump casing on the right-hand end of the crankshaft. Remove the crankshaft sprocket as described in Section 6.

2 Using a small screwdriver, carefully prise the oil seal from the oil pump casing, taking care not to damage the surface of the crankshaft (see illustration).

3 Clean the seating in the housing and the surface of the crankshaft. To prevent damage to the new oil seal as it is being fitted, wrap

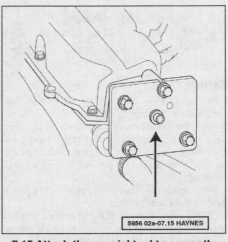
7.15 Attach the special tool to correctly position the camshaft cover

some adhesive tape around the end of the crankshaft and lightly oil it.

4 Lubricate the oil seal lip with clean engine oil then offer it up to the oil pump casing. Ensure that the sealing lip is facing inwards (see illustration).

5 Using a suitable tubular drift, drive the oil seal squarely into the casing (see illustration). Remove the adhesive tape.

6 Refit the crankshaft sprocket as described in Section 6.

Left-hand side oil seal

Note: The left-hand side oil seal is integral with the oil seal housing.

7 Remove the flywheel as described in Section 12.

8 Remove the sump as described in Section 14.

9 Undo the retaining bolts and remove the housing complete with integral seal.

10 Clean the cylinder block mating face, and the seal contact face on the crankshaft.

11 Lubricate the lip of the new seal, then located the seal housing on the cylinder block. Refit the housing retaining bolts and tighten them to the specified torque.

12 Refit the sump as described in Section 14.

13 Refit the flywheel as described in Section 12.

8 Camshaft oil seal – renewal

1 Remove the camshaft sprocket as described in Section 6.

2 Undo the bolts and remove the camshaft front bearing cap.

3 Punch or drill a small hole in the oil seal. Screw a self-tapping screw into the hole, and

9.2 Carefully prise the oil seal from the casing

9.4 Lubricate the seal lip and offer it into place

9.5 Drive the seal squarely into the casing

10 Camshaft and followers
– removal, inspection and refitting

Removal

1 Remove the camshaft sprocket as described in Section 6.

2 Mark the positions of the camshaft bearing caps, numbering them from the timing belt end. Where applicable, remove the camshaft locking tool from the left-hand end of the camshaft.

3 Progressively unscrew the bolts and remove the bearing caps.

4 Lift the camshaft carefully from the cylinder head, checking that the valve clearance shims and cam followers are not withdrawn by the adhesion of the oil. Recover the oil seal from the end of the camshaft.

5 Remove the shims and cam followers, but keep them in their originally fitted order.

Inspection

6 Inspect the camshaft for wear on the surfaces of the lobes and journals. Normally their surfaces should be smooth and have a dull shine; look for scoring and pitting. Accelerated wear will occur once the hardened exterior of the camshaft has been damaged.

7 Examine the bearing cap and journal surfaces for signs of wear.

8 To measure the camshaft endfloat, temporarily refit the camshaft then push the camshaft to one end of the cylinder head as far as it will travel. Attach a dial test indicator to the cylinder head and zero it, then push the camshaft as far as it will go to the other end of the cylinder head and record the gauge reading. Verify the reading by pushing the camshaft back to its original position and checking that the gauge indicates zero again.

9 Where the camshaft and bearings are worn excessively, consider renewing the complete cylinder head, together with camshaft and cam followers. A reconditioned head may be available from engine overhaul specialists.

Refitting

10 Lubricate the cam followers and locate them in their correct positions in the cylinder head. Locate the shims in the cam followers making sure they are in their original positions.

11 Lubricate the journals then locate the camshaft in the cylinder head with the cam lobes of No 1 cylinder facing upwards (ie, No 1 piston at TDC).

12 Refit the bearing caps in their correct positions then refit the bearing cap retaining bolts. Progressively tighten the bolts to the specified torque.

13 Lubricate the lips of the new seal with clean engine oil, and drive it into position until it seats on its locating shoulder. Use a suitable tubular drift, such as a socket, which bears only on the hard outer edge of the seal. Take care not to damage the seal lips during fitting. Note that the seal lips should face inwards. Where applicable, refit the oil seal retaining cap at the right-hand end of the camshaft **(see illustration)**.

14 The remainder of refitting is a reversal of removal, noting the following points:

a) *Check and if necessary, adjust the valve clearances as described in Chapter 1, then refit the camshaft cover as described in Section 7.*

b) *On 1.4 L models, if the camshaft has been renewed, the self-learning feature must be completed by starting the engine without pressing the accelerator pedal, and allowing the engine to idle for at least ten seconds.*

c) *Tighten all fasteners to their specified torque.*

11 Cylinder head –
removal and refitting

Removal

1 Disconnect the battery negative lead as described in Chapter 5A Section 4.

2 Remove the timing belt as described in Section 5.

3 Remove the exhaust manifold as described in Chapter 4A Section 12.

4 Drain the engine coolant as described in Chapter 1 Section 29.

5 Carefully prise the check valve from the brake servo.

6 Disconnect the following wiring plugs:

a) *Absolute pressure sensor.*

b) *Air temperature/pressure sensor.*

c) *Throttle body.*

d) *Injector wiring loom.*

e) *Fuel vapour solenoid (purge) valve.*

f) *Coolant temperature sensor.*

7 Disconnect the fuel supply pipe, and the vapour pipe.

8 Disconnect the various coolant hoses from the cylinder head.

9 Unscrew the cylinder head bolts half a turn at a time in the reverse order to that specified for tightening **(see illustration 11.23)**. When the bolts are free, remove them with their washers.

10 Lift the cylinder head from the block. If it is stuck tight insert pieces of wood into the exhaust ports, and use them as levers to rock the head off the block. On no account drive levers into the gasket joint, or attempt to tap the head sideways, as it is located on positioning dowels.

11 Remove and discard the cylinder head gasket.

12 If required, remove the intake manifold from the cylinder head as described in Chapter 4A Section 11.

13 The cylinder head can be dismantled as described in Chapter 2C after removing the camshaft and cam followers as described in Section 10.

Preparation for refitting

14 The mating faces of the cylinder head and cylinder block must be perfectly clean before refitting the head. Use a hard plastic or wooden scraper to remove all traces of gasket and carbon; also clean the piston crowns.

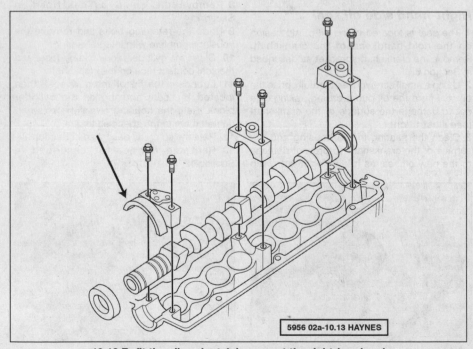

10.13 Refit the oil seal retaining cap at the right-hand end

5956 02a-10.13 HAYNES

Take particular care when cleaning the piston crowns as the soft aluminium alloy is easily damaged. Make sure that the carbon is not allowed to enter the oil and water passages – this is particularly important for the lubrication system, as carbon could block the oil supply to the engine's components. Using adhesive tape and paper, seal the water, oil and bolt holes in the cylinder block. To prevent carbon entering the gap between the pistons and bores, smear a little grease in the gap. After cleaning each piston, use a small brush to remove all traces of grease and carbon from the gap, then wipe away the remainder with a clean rag. Clean all the pistons in the same way.

15 Check the mating surfaces of the cylinder block and the cylinder head for nicks, deep scratches and other damage. If slight, they may be removed carefully with a file, but if excessive, machining may be the only alternative to renewal. If warpage of the cylinder head gasket surface is suspected, use a straight-edge to check it for distortion as described in Chapter 2C Section 7.

16 Check the condition of the cylinder head bolts, and particularly their threads, whenever they are removed. Wash the bolts in a suitable solvent, and wipe them dry. Check each bolt for any sign of visible wear or damage, renewing them if necessary. Although Fiat do not specify that the bolts must be renewed, it is strongly recommended that the bolts should be renewed as a complete set whenever they are disturbed.

17 Refit the camshaft and followers as described in Section 10, then adjust the valve clearances as described in Chapter 1 Section 16 before refitting the cylinder head to the block.

Refitting

18 Before refitting the assembled cylinder head, make sure that the head and block mating surfaces are perfectly clean, and that the bolt holes in the cylinder block have been mopped out to clear any oil.

19 Referring to Section 3, make sure that the crankshaft and camshaft are still set at their correct TDC positions and the camshaft is locked in the correct position using the special tool.

20 The new gasket should not be removed from its nylon cover until required for use. Fit the gasket dry, and make sure that the mating surfaces on the head and block are perfectly clean.

21 Place the gasket on the cylinder block so that the word ALTO can be read from above **(see illustration)**.

22 Lower the cylinder head onto the block so that it locates on the positioning dowels.

23 The cylinder head bolt threads must be clean and lightly lubricated. Screw the bolts in finger-tight then working progressively and in the sequence shown, tighten all the cylinder head bolts to the Stage 1 torque setting given in the Specifications, using a torque wrench and a suitable socket **(see illustration)**. With

11.21 Place the cylinder head gasket so the work ALTO can be read from above

all the bolts tightened to their Stage 1 setting, working again in the specified sequence, first angle-tighten the bolts through the specified Stage 2 angle, then again through the Stage 3 angle, using a socket and extension bar. It is recommended that an angle-measuring gauge is used during this stage of tightening, to ensure accuracy.

24 Where applicable, refit the intake and exhaust manifolds with reference to Chapter 4A.

25 The remainder of refitting is a reversal of removal, noting the following points:

a) Tighten all fasteners to their specified torque where given.

b) Refill the cooling system as described in Chapter 1 Section 29.

c) Reconnect the battery negative lead as described in Chapter 5A Section 4.

d) On 1.4 L models, if the cylinder head has been renewed, the self-learning feature must be completed by starting the engine without pressing the accelerator pedal, and allowing the engine to idle for at least ten seconds.

12 Flywheel – removal, inspection and refitting

Removal

1 Remove the clutch assembly as described in Chapter 6 Section 5.

2 The flywheel must now be held stationary while the bolts are loosened. A home-made locking tool may be fabricated from a piece of scrap metal and used to lock the ring gear (see **Tool Tip**). Bolt the tool to one of the transmission bellhousing mounting bolt holes on the cylinder block.

HAYNES HiNT *A flywheel ring gear locking tool can be made from a short strip of steel bent to form a right-angle. Cut a slot in the upper part and bend this part up to engage with the ring gear teeth. File the edges to form a tooth profile. Drill a hole in the lower part to enable the tool to be bolted to the bellhousing flange.*

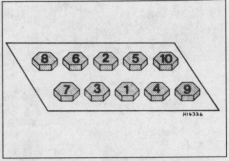

11.23 Cylinder head bolts tightening sequence

3 Mark the position of the flywheel with respect to the crankshaft using a dab of paint. Unscrew and remove the mounting bolts together with the spacer plate, then lift off the flywheel. Discard the flywheel bolts; new ones must be used on refitting.

Inspection

4 If the flywheel's clutch mating surface is deeply scored, cracked or otherwise damaged, the flywheel must be renewed. However, it may be possible to have it surface-ground; seek the advice of a Fiat dealer or engine reconditioning specialist.

5 If the ring gear is badly worn or has missing teeth, the flywheel must be renewed.

Refitting

6 Clean the mating surfaces of the flywheel and crankshaft. Remove any remaining locking compound from the threads of the crankshaft holes, using the correct-size tap, if available.

7 If the new retaining bolts are not supplied with their threads already precoated, apply a suitable thread-locking compound to the threads of each bolt.

8 Offer up the flywheel to the crankshaft, using the alignment marks made during removal, and fit the new retaining bolts together with the spacer plate.

9 Lock the flywheel using the method employed on removal, and tighten the retaining bolts to the specified torque.

10 Refit the clutch as described in Chapter 6 Section 5.

13 Engine mountings – inspection and renewal

Inspection

1 Firmly apply the handbrake, then jack up the front of the car and support it securely on axle stands as described in 'Vehicle jacking and support'.

2 Check the mounting rubbers to see if they are cracked, hardened or separated from the metal at any point; renew the mounting if any such damage or deterioration is evident.

3 Check that all the mounting's fasteners are securely tightened; use a torque wrench to check if possible.

13.10 Left-hand mounting retaining bolts

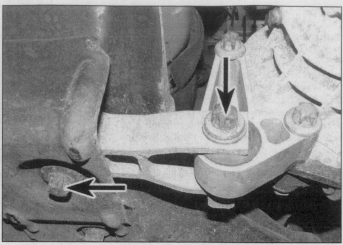

13.14 Rear mounting rod bolts

4 Using a large screwdriver or a crowbar, check for wear in the mounting by carefully levering against it to check for free play. Where this is not possible enlist the aid of an assistant to move the engine/transmission back-and-forth, or from side-to-side, while you watch the mounting. While some free play is to be expected, even from new components, excessive wear should be obvious. If excessive free play is found, check first that the fasteners are correctly secured, then renew any worn components as described below.

Renewal

Right-hand mounting

5 Place a trolley jack beneath the right-hand side of the engine, with a block of wood on the jack head. Raise the jack until it is supporting the weight of the engine.
6 Undo the bolts securing the mounting to the vehicle body, and the bolts securing the mounting to the support bracket (see illustration 5.6). Remove the mounting.
7 Refitting is a reversal of removal, tightening the retaining bolts to the specified torque.

14.4 Subframe crossbrace retaining bolts

Left-hand mounting

8 Remove the battery and battery tray as described in Chapter 5A Section 4.
9 Place a trolley jack beneath the transmission, with a block of wood on the jack head. Raise the jack until it is supporting the weight of the engine/transmission.
10 Undo the retaining bolts securing the mounting to the vehicle body and support bracket, and remove the mounting (see illustration).
11 Refitting is a reversal of removal, tightening the retaining bolts to their specified torque.

Rear mounting

12 Raise the front of the vehicle and support it securely on axle stands, as described in 'Vehicle jacking and support'.
13 Undo the nuts securing the front exhaust pipe to the catalytic converter, then undo the bolt securing the pipe support bracket clamp.
14 Undo the bolts and manoeuvre the rear mounting rod from place (see illustration).
15 Refitting is a reversal of removal, tightening the retaining bolts to their specified torque.

14 Sump – removal and refitting

Removal

1 Firmly apply the handbrake, then jack up the front of the car and support it securely on axle stands as described in 'Vehicle jacking and support'.
2 Drain the engine oil as described in Chapter 1 Section 4.
3 Undo the retaining bolts and remove the support bracket between the transmission and engine cylinder block.

4 Undo the bolts and remove the crossbrace from the front subframe (see illustration).
5 Disconnect the front exhaust pipe at the joining flange, release the flexible mounting and move the pipe to one side.
6 Undo the retaining bolts and remove the flywheel guard.
7 Unscrew the sump securing bolts and nuts then cut through as much of the joint sealant as possible using a sharp knife. Pull the sump downwards to release it from the remaining sealant and remove it from under the car.
8 Thoroughly clean the sump and the cylinder block mating surfaces ensuring that all traces of old sealant are removed.

Refitting

9 Apply a 3.0 mm bead of RTV silicone sealant to the sump flange, then locate the sump in position. Refit the retaining bolts and nuts and tighten to the specified torque.
10 The remainder of refitting is a reversal of removal.
11 Lower the car to the ground and wait at least 1 hour before filling the engine with oil as described in Chapter 1 Section 4.

15 Oil pump and pick-up tube – removal, inspection and refitting

Removal

1 Remove the crankshaft sprocket as described in Section 6.
2 Drain the engine oil and remove the oil filter as described in Chapter 1 Section 4.
3 Remove the sump as described in Section 14.
4 Remove the coolant pump as described in Chapter 3 Section 7.
5 Disconnect the wiring connector from the oil pressure switch on the side of the pump casing.

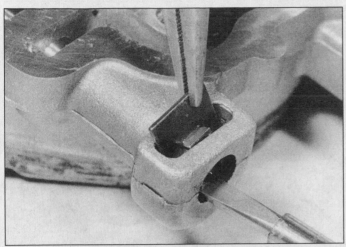

15.8a Remove the oil pump pressure relief valve keeper plate

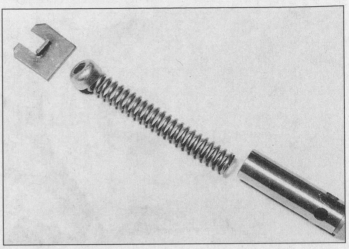

15.8b Oil pump pressure relief valve components

6 Undo the oil pump retaining bolts, noting the location of the longer bolt, and withdraw the pump assembly from the front of the engine. Recover the gasket.

Inspection

7 With the pump on the bench, undo the two bolts and remove the pick-up tube. Using a small screwdriver or similar tool, hook out the pick-up tube sealing O-ring from the pump body.

8 The pressure relief valve components can be removed for examination by depressing the spring and pulling out the keeper plate **(see illustrations)**.

9 If pump wear is suspected, check the rotors in the following way. Extract the fixing screws and remove the rear cover plate. The screws are very tight, and will probably require the use of an impact screwdriver **(see illustration)**.

10 Inspect the pump rotors, pump casing and cover for any signs of wear or damage. If satisfactory, refit the rotors to the pump casing ensuring that the orientation marks are facing upwards.

11 Check the clearance between the outer rotor and the pump casing using feeler blades. Check the rotor endfloat by placing a straight-edge across the pump casing, and checking the gap between the straight-edge and rotor face **(see illustrations)**. If the clearances are outside the specified tolerance, renew the oil pump complete.

12 If the pump is unworn, lubricate the rotors with clean engine oil then place the cover plate in position. Apply thread locking compound to the retaining screws and tighten the screws securely.

13 Locate a new O-ring in the pump casing then refit the pick-up tube. Secure the tube with the two bolts tightened securely.

14 Lubricate the pressure relief valve

15.9 Use an impact screwdriver to remove the oil pump rear cover plate screws

components then refit the valve, spring and end cap, securing the assembly with the keeper plate.

15 Lever out the crankshaft oil seal and drive a new one squarely into the oil pump casing

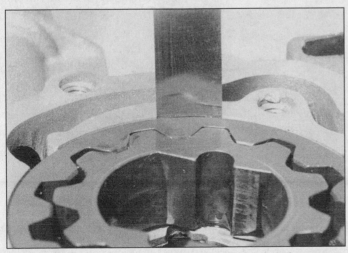

15.11a Measure the oil pump rotor-to-pump casing clearance

15.11b Measure the oil pump rotor endfloat

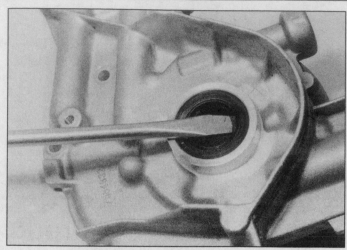

15.15a Prise out the oil pump seal

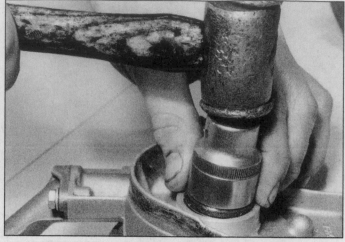

15.15b Use a socket to fit a new seal to the oil pump

(see illustrations). Lubricate the oil seal lips with clean engine oil.

16 Prior to refitting, prime the pump by pouring clean engine oil into its inlet duct, while at the same time turning the oil pump inner rotor.

Refitting

17 Ensure that the oil pump and cylinder block mating faces are clean, then place a new gasket on the pump casing. Retain the gasket in position by inserting two of the pump retaining bolts.

18 Locate the pump on the cylinder block, insert the retaining bolts and tighten them progressively to the specified torque.

19 The remainder of refitting is a reversal of removal.

16 Engine pressure warning light switch – removal and refitting

1 Raise the front of the vehicle and support it securely on axle stands as described in 'Vehicle jacking and support'.

2 Disconnect the wiring plug from the switch, then unscrew it from the housing (see illustration). Be prepared for oil spillage.

3 Screw the new switch into the housing and tighten it to the specified torque.

4 Reconnect the wiring plug and lower the vehicle to the ground. Check the engine oil level as described in 'Weekly checks'.

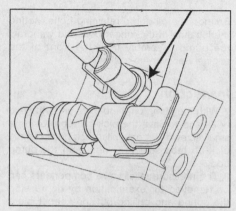

16.2 The oil pressure warning light switch is located on the oil filter housing at the front of the engine

Chapter 2 Part B
DOHC (16-valve) 1.4L in-car repair procedures

Contents

Section number

Camshaft and followers – removal, inspection and refitting 10
Camshaft housing – removal and refitting 9
Camshaft oil seal – renewal 7
Compression test – description and interpretation 2
Crankshaft oil seals – renewal 8
Cylinder head – removal and refitting. 11
Engine assembly/valve timing settings – general information
    and usage. 3
Engine mountings – inspection and renewal 13

Section number

Engine pressure warning light switch – removal and refitting 16
Flywheel – removal, inspection and refitting 12
General information 1
Oil pump and pick-up tube – removal, inspection and refitting. . . . 15
Sump – removal and refitting. 14
Timing belt – general information, removal and refitting 5
Timing belt covers – removal and refitting 4
Timing belt tensioner and sprockets – removal, inspection
    and refitting. 6

Degrees of difficulty

Easy, suitable for novice with little experience	**Fairly easy,** suitable for beginner with some experience	**Fairly difficult,** suitable for competent DIY mechanic	**Difficult,** suitable for experienced DIY mechanic	**Very difficult,** suitable for expert DIY or professional

Specifications

General

Engine type:
1.4 L	4-cylinder in-line petrol double overhead camshaft (DOHC) 16v variable valve timing
Engine code	199A6000
Bore	72.0 mm
Stroke	84.0 mm
Capacity	1368 cc
Firing order.	1-3-4-2
No. 1 cylinder location	Timing (right-hand) end of the engine
Direction of crankshaft rotation	Clockwise (seen from the right-hand side of the vehicle)
Compression ratio	10.8 : 1

Output:
Maximum power.	70 kW @ 6000 rpm
Maximum torque	125 Nm @ 4500 rpm

Lubrication system

Minimum system pressure:
At idle speed.	0.7 bar
At 4000 rpm	4.0 bar
Pump outer rotor-to-housing clearance.	0.100 to 0.210 mm
Rotor axial clearance	0.025 to 0.070 mm

Torque wrench settings

	Nm	lbf ft
Camshaft drive gear bolts	120	89
Camshaft housing-to-cylinder head bolts	15	11
Camshaft housing bolt caps	15	11
Camshaft housing timing plugs	15	11
Camshaft sprocket bolt	120	89
Connecting rod bolts*:		
Stage 1	20	15
Stage 2	Angle-tighten a further 40°	
Crankshaft pulley bolts (M8)	25	17
Crankshaft sprocket bolt:		
Stage 1	20	15
Stage 2	Angle-tighten a further 110°	
Crankshaft left-hand oil seal housing bolts	10	7
Cylinder head bolts*:		
Stage 1	30	22
Stage 2	Angle-tighten a further 90°	
Stage 3	Angle-tighten a further 90°	
Engine/transmission mountings:		
Right-hand side mounting-to-body	60	45
Right-hand side mounting-to-support bracket	80	59
Right-hand side mounting support bracket-to-engine	60	45
Left-hand side mounting-to-body	90	66
Left-hand side mounting-to-support bracket	95	70
Rear mounting rod-to-subframe:		
Stage 1	55	41
Stage 2	Angle-tighten a further 90°	
Rear mounting rod-to-transmission bracket	95	70
Flywheel bolts:*		
Stage 1	15	11
Stage 2	Angle-tighten a further 45°	
Lower crankcase/Main bearing cap bolts:		
M8	30	22
M10:		
Stage 1	20	15
Stage 2	Angle-tighten a further 90°	
Oil pump bolts	10	7
Oil pressure warning switch	30	22
Oil spray jet	10	7
Sump drain plug	20	15
Sump:		
Sump-to-transmission bolts	40	30
M6 nuts	10	7
M6 bolts	10	7
M8 bolts	25	17
M10 bolt	70	52
Timing belt tensioner nut	25	17

*Do not re-use

1 General information

How to use this Chapter

1 This Part of Chapter 2 is devoted to in-car repair procedures for the 1.4 litre Double OverHead Camshaft (DOHC) 16v petrol engine. Similar information covering the 1.2 and 1.4 litre Single OverHead Camshaft (SOHC) 8v engines will be found in Part A of this Chapter. Part C covers the removal of the engine/transmission as a unit, and describes the engine dismantling and overhaul procedures.

2 In Parts A and B, the assumption is made that the engine is installed in the car, with all ancillaries connected. If the engine has been removed for overhaul, the preliminary dismantling information which precedes each operation may be ignored.

3 Note that whilst it may be possible physically to overhaul items such as the piston/ connecting rod assemblies with the engine in the vehicle, such tasks are not usually carried out as separate operations and usually require the execution of several additional procedures (not to mention the cleaning of components and of oilways). For this reason, all such tasks are classed as major overhaul procedures and are described in Chapter 2C.

Engine description

4 The engine covered in this Part of Chapter 2 is a water-cooled, double overhead camshaft (DOHC), in-line four-cylinder unit, with cast iron cylinder block and aluminium-alloy cylinder head. The engine is mounted transversely at the front of the car, with the transmission bolted to the left-hand end.

5 The intake and exhaust camshafts rotate in a separate aluminum housing bolted to the top of the cylinder head, and act directly onto their respective valves/followers. The valve followers incorporate hydraulic compensation elements, which maintain the correct clearance at all times, and are 'maintenance free'. A toothed rubber timing belt, driven by crankshaft sprocket, rotates the exhaust camshaft via a 'phase transformer' which varies the position of the camshafts in relation to the crankshaft. This variable valve timing results in increased output/driveability, and reduced exhaust emissions. The operation of the phase transformer is actuated by engine oil pressure, controlled by an electrically operated solenoid valve, itself controlled by the engine management ECU.The cylinder head houses the inlet and exhaust valves, which are closed by coil springs, and run in guides pressed into the cylinder head. The camshafts are fitted with gears at their left-hand ends which are in constant mesh – i.e. the exhaust camshaft drives the intake camshaft.

6 The cylinder head contains integral oilways which supply and lubricate the followers (hydraulic tappets).

7 The crankshaft is supported by five main bearings, and endfloat is controlled by a thrust bearing fitted to the upper section of the centre main bearing.

8 Engine coolant is circulated by a pump, driven by the timing belt. For details of the cooling system, refer to Chapter 3.

9 Lubricant is circulated under pressure by a pump, driven from the front of the crankshaft. Oil is drawn from the sump through a strainer, and then forced through an externally-mounted, renewable screw-on filter. From there, it is distributed to the cylinder head, where it lubricates the camshaft journals and tappets, and also to the crankcase, where it lubricates the main bearings, connecting rod big and small-ends, gudgeon pins and cylinder bores.

Repair operations possible with the engine in the car

10 The following operations can be carried out with the engine in the car:
a) Compression pressure – testing
b) Camshaft housing – removal and refitting.
c) Timing belt covers – removal and refitting.
d) Timing belt – removal, refitting and adjustment
e) Camshafts and followers – removal, inspection and refitting.
f) Cylinder head – removal and refitting.
g) Cylinder head and pistons* – decarbonising.
h) Sump – removal and refitting.
i) Oil pump – removal and refitting.
j) Crankshaft oil seals – renewal.

k) Camshaft oil seal – renewal
l) Engine mountings – inspection and renewal.
m) Flywheel – inspection and renewal.
Note:* *Although it is possible to remove these components with the engine in place, for reasons of access and cleanliness it is recommended that the engine be removed.*

2 Compression test – description and interpretation

1 When engine performance is down, or if misfiring occurs which cannot be attributed to the ignition or fuel systems, a compression test can provide diagnostic clues as to the engine's condition. If the test is performed regularly, it can give warning of trouble before any other symptoms become apparent.

2 The engine must be fully warmed-up to normal operating temperature, the battery must be fully-charged, and all the spark plugs must be removed (see Chapter 1 Section 17). The aid of an assistant will also be required.

3 Disable the ignition and fuel injection systems by disconnecting the wiring multi-plug connectors at the engine management ECU, referring to Chapter 4A Section 10 for further information.

4 Fit a compression tester to the No 1 cylinder spark plug hole – the type of tester which screws into the plug thread is to be preferred.

5 Crank the engine on the starter motor with the accelerator pedal fully depressed; after one or two revolutions, the compression pressure should build-up to a maximum figure, and then stabilise. Record the highest reading obtained.

6 Repeat the test on the remaining cylinders, recording the pressure in each.

7 All cylinders should produce very similar pressures; a difference of more than 2 bars between any two cylinders indicates a fault. Note that the compression should build-up quickly in a healthy engine; low compression on the first stroke, followed by gradually-increasing pressure on successive strokes, indicates worn piston rings. A low compression reading on the first stroke, which does not build-up during successive strokes, indicates leaking valves or a blown head gasket (a cracked head could also be the cause). Deposits on the undersides of the valve heads can also cause low compression.

8 Although Fiat do not specify exact compression pressures, as a guide, any cylinder pressure of below 10 bars can be considered as less than healthy. Refer to a Fiat dealer or other specialist if in doubt as to whether a particular pressure reading is acceptable.

9 If the pressure in any cylinder is low, carry out the following test to isolate the cause. Introduce a teaspoonful of clean oil into that

cylinder through its spark plug hole, and repeat the test.

10 If the addition of oil temporarily improves the compression pressure, this indicates that bore or piston wear is responsible for the pressure loss. No improvement suggests that leaking or burnt valves, or a blown head gasket, may be to blame.

11 A low reading from two adjacent cylinders is almost certainly due to the head gasket having blown between them; the presence of coolant in the engine oil will confirm this.

12 If the compression reading is unusually high, the combustion chambers are probably coated with carbon deposits. If this is the case, the cylinder head should be removed and decarbonised.

13 On completion of the test, refit the spark plugs and reconnect the engine management ECU wiring connectors.

3 Engine assembly/valve timing settings – general information and usage

Caution: Do not attempt to rotate the engine whilst the camshafts are locked in position. If the engine is to be left in this state for a long period of time, it is a good idea to place suitable warning notices inside the car, and in the engine compartment. This will reduce the possibility of the engine being accidentally cranked on the starter motor, which is likely to cause damage with the locking tools in place.

1 To accurately set the valve timing for all operations requiring removal and refitting of the timing belt, timing holes are drilled in the camshafts and cylinder head extension. The holes are used in conjunction with camshaft locking tools and crankshaft positioning rods to lock the camshafts when all the pistons are positioned at the mid-point of their stroke. This arrangement prevents the possibility of the valves contacting the pistons when refitting the cylinder head or timing belt, and also ensures that the correct valve timing can be obtained. The design of the engine is such that there are no conventional timing marks on the crankshaft or camshaft sprockets to indicate the normal TDC position. Therefore, for any work on the timing belt, camshafts or cylinder head the locking and positioning tools must be used.

2 The special Fiat tools for setting the camshafts and pistons consist of two rods which slide in sleeves that are screwed into No 1 and No 2 cylinder spark plug holes. The rods are pushed down to contact the pistons, and the crankshaft is then turned until both rods protrude from their sleeves by the same amount. With the crankshaft correctly set, two camshaft locking pins are used, one for the inlet camshaft and one for the exhaust camshaft. The pins are screwed into holes

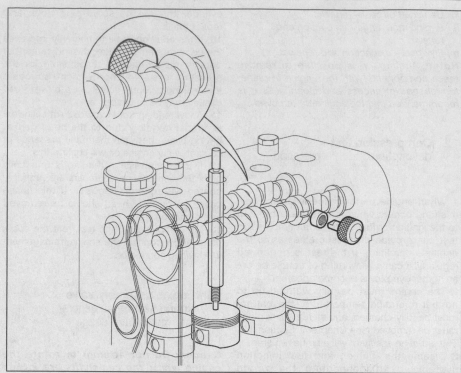

3.2a Arrangement of Fiat special tools for setting the piston position and locking the camshafts

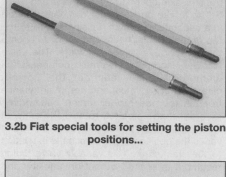

3.2b Fiat special tools for setting the piston positions...

3.2c... and locking the camshafts

on each side of the cylinder head extension so that they engage with slots machined in the camshafts. The arrangement of the Fiat special tools are shown **(see illustrations)**. The tool numbers are as follows:
a) Camshaft locking tools
   Tool No 1860985000
b) Piston positioning tool
   Tool No 1860992000
3 Although the special Fiat tools are relatively inexpensive and should be readily available from Fiat dealers (or automotive tool specialists), it is possible to fabricate suitable alternatives, with the help of a local machine shop, as described below. Once the tools have been made up, their usage is described in the relevant Sections of this Chapter where the tools are required.

Camshaft locking tools

4 Remove the fuel rail, complete with injectors as described in Chapter 4A Section 10.
5 Unscrew the sealing plug from the front face and rear face of the cylinder head extension.
6 Using the sealing plugs as a pattern, obtain a length of threaded dowel rod or two suitable bolts to screw into the sealing plug hole. With the help of a machine shop or engineering works, make up the camshaft locking tools by having the dowel rod or bolts machined **(see illustrations)**. Note that two will be needed, one for each camshaft.

Crankshaft setting tool

7 To make the crankshaft setting tools, four old spark plugs will be required, together with four lengths of dowel rod. The length of each dowel rod is not critical, but it must be long enough to protrude about 100 mm above the top of the cylinder head extension when resting on top of a piston located half-way down its bore. What is critical, however, is that all four dowel rods must be exactly the same length.
8 Break off the ceramic upper section of each plug and remove the centre electrode and earth tip. The easiest way to do this is to mount each spark plug in a vice (after removing the ceramic upper plug section) and drill a hole down through the centre of the plug. The diameter of the drill bit should be the same as the diameter of the dowel rod to be used. When finished you should have four spark plug bodies and four equal length dowel rods which will slide through the centre of the spark plugs.

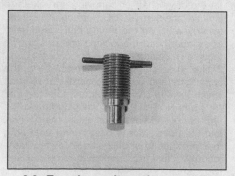

3.6a To make an alternative camshaft locking tool...

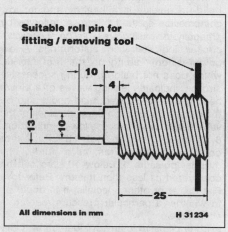

Suitable roll pin for fitting / removing tool

10
4
13
10
25

All dimensions in mm   H 31234

3.6b... have suitable dowel rods or bolts machined to the dimensions shown

4   Timing belt covers –
   removal and refitting

Removal

Upper cover

1 Undo the retaining bolts and manoeuvre

the timing belt upper cover from place (see illustration).

Lower cover

2 Remove the timing belt upper cover as described previously in this Section.
3 Remove the auxiliary drivebelt as described in Chapter 1 Section 5.
4 Undo the 3 bolts and remove the crankshaft pulley from the sprocket (see illustration).
5 Undo the retaining bolt in the centre of the lower cover (see illustration).
6 Release the crankshaft position sensor and oil pressure switch wiring from the periphery of the cover, and manoeuvre the cover from place (see illustration).

Refitting

7 Refitting is a reversal of removal.

---

5 Timing belt – general information, removal and refitting

General information

1 The function of the timing belt is to drive the camshaft and coolant pump. Should the belt slip or break in service, the valve timing will be disturbed and piston-to-valve contact will occur, resulting in serious engine damage.
2 The timing belt should be renewed at the specified intervals (see Chapter 1 Section 1) or earlier if it is contaminated with oil, or if it is at all noisy in operation (a scraping noise due to uneven wear).
3 If the timing belt is being removed, it is a wise precaution to check the condition of the coolant pump at the same time (check for signs of coolant leakage). This may avoid the need to remove the timing belt again at a later stage, should the coolant pump fail.
4 Before carrying out this procedure, it will be necessary to obtain or fabricate suitable camshaft locking tools and piston positioning tools as described in Section 3. The procedures contained in this Section depict the use of the home-made alternative tools described in Section 3, which were fabricated in the Haynes workshop. If the manufacturer's tools are being used instead, the procedures

4.1 Timing belt upper cover retaining bolts

4.5 Timing belt lower cover retaining bolt

are virtually identical. Do not attempt to remove the timing belt unless the special tools or their alternatives are available.
5 Additionally, the exhaust camshaft sprocket must be locked in place whilst the its retaining bolt is slackend, and re-tightened. Fiat special tool No. 2000 015 800 is available for this task, although an equivalent tool may be available from automotive tool specialists.

Removal

6 Remove the air filter assembly as described in Chapter 4A Section 2.
7 Remove the fuel rail, complete with injectors as described in Chapter 4A Section 10.
8 Remove the upper, and lower timing belt covers as described in Section 4.
9 Remove the spark plugs as described in Chapter 1 Section 17.

4.4 Undo the 3 outer bolts to remove the crankshaft pulley

4.6 Release the wiring from the cover

10 Unscrew the 2 sealing plugs from the front and rear of the camshaft housing to enable the camshaft locking tools to be inserted.
11 Screw the spark plug bodies of the home-made piston positioning tools into each spark plug hole and insert the dowel rods into each body. To keep the dowel rods vertical, locate a suitable washer or similar over the rod and into the recess at the top of the spark plug hole. In the Haynes' workshop, an old valve stem oil seal housing was used but anything similar will suffice (see illustrations).
12 Using a socket on the crankshaft sprocket centre bolt, turn the crankshaft in the normal direction of rotation until all four dowel rods are protruding from the top of the cylinder head extension by the same amount. As the engine is turned, two of the rods will move up and two will move down until the position is reached

5.11a Screw the spark plug bodies of the home-made piston positioning tools into each spark plug hole...

5.11b... place a suitable washer or similar into the recess to keep the dowel rod vertical...

5.11c... then insert the dowel rods

5.12 Place a straight-edge along the top of the rods and turn the crankshaft until the straight-edge contacts all four rods

5.14a Screw the camshaft locking tools into the timing holes in the front...

5.14b... and rear of the cylinder head extension

5.14c The tools engage in the camshaft slots when fitted (shown removed for clarity)

where they are all at the same height. The best way to check this is to place a straight-edge along the top of the rods and turn the crankshaft very slowly until the straight-edge contacts all four rods **(see illustration)**.

13 When all four rods are at the same height, all the pistons will be at the mid-point of their stroke. Using a screwdriver or similar inserted into the front timing hole in the cylinder head extension, check that the timing slot in the exhaust camshaft is approximately aligned with the timing hole. If the camshaft slot cannot be felt, turn the crankshaft through one complete revolution and realign the dowel rods using the straight-edge. Check again

for the camshaft slot. Note that although the pistons can be at the mid-point of their stroke twice for each cycle of the engine, the camshaft slots will only be positioned correctly once per cycle. In this position the dowel on the crankshaft pulley will be 180° from the crankshaft position sensor.

14 With the pistons correctly set, it should now be possible to screw in the camshaft locking tools into the timing holes in the cylinder head extension. To provide the necessary degree of timing accuracy, the machined end of the locking tools are a very close fit in the slots machined in the camshafts **(see illustrations)**. To allow the tools to be screwed fully into

engagement, it may be necessary to move the crankshaft in one direction or another very slightly until the tools are felt to engage fully.

15 Place a trolley jack under the right-hand side of the engine, with a block of wood on the jack head. Raise the jack until it is supporting the weight of the engine.

16 Undo the retaining bolts, and remove the right-hand engine mounting **(see illustration 13.6)**.

17 Undo the retaining bolts and remove the engine mounting support bracket from the cylinder head.

18 Release the nut on the timing belt tensioner to release the tension on the belt **(see illustration)**.

19 If the timing belt is to be re-used, use white paint or chalk to mark the direction of rotation on the belt (if markings do not already exist), then slip the belt off the sprockets. Note that the crankshaft must not be rotated whilst the belt is removed.

20 Check the timing belt carefully for any signs of uneven wear, splitting, or oil contamination. Pay particular attention to the roots of the teeth. Renew it if there is the slightest doubt about its condition. If the engine is undergoing an overhaul, renew the belt as a matter of course, regardless of its apparent condition. The cost of a new belt is nothing compared with the cost of repairs should the belt break in service. If signs of oil contamination are found, trace the source of the oil leak and rectify it. Wash down the engine timing belt area and all related components to remove all traces of oil.

Refitting

21 Before refitting, thoroughly clean the timing belt sprockets. Check that the tensioner pulley rotates freely, without any sign of roughness. If necessary, renew the tensioner pulley as described in Section 6.

22 The camshaft sprocket must now be locked in place whilst the centre bolt is slackened. Engage Fiat tool No. 2000 015 800 (or equivalent) with the camshaft sprocket teeth, and bolt it securely to the cylinder head **(see illustration)**.

23 With the camshaft sprocket held, use

5.18 Release the nut on the timing belt tensioner

5.22 The Fiat tool bolts to the cylinder head, and lock the camshaft sprocket

5.23a Unscrew the plug...

5.23b... and slacken the centre bolt

5.27 Use right-angle circlip pliers to turn the pulley clockwise until it reaches the stop

suitable Torx bits/keys to remove the plug, and slacken the centre bolt (see illustrations).

24 Remove the camshaft sprocket holding tool.

25 Check that the pistons are still correctly positioned at the mid-point of their stroke and that the camshafts are locked with the locking tools.

26 Ensuring that the direction markings (where present) on the timing belt point in the normal direction of engine rotation, engage the timing belt with the crankshaft sprocket first, then place it around the coolant pump sprocket and the camshaft sprocket. Finally slip the belt around the tensioner pulley.

27 Insert the jaws of a pair of right-angled circlip pliers (or similar) into the two holes on the front face of the tensioner pulley. Rotate the pulley anti-clockwise until the indicator fork touches the stop. Maintain the effort applied to the tensioner pulley, then tighten the pulley retaining nut (see illustration).

28 Refit the sprocket holding tool, then tighten the sprocket retaining bolt to the specified torque.

29 Remove the sprocket holding tool.

30 Remove the piston positioning tools and camshaft locking tools and turn the crankshaft through two complete turns in the normal direction of rotation.

31 Slacken the tensioner pulley retaining nut and reposition the tensioner so that the mobile indicator is aligned with the fixed reference

mark (see illustration). Hold the pulley in this position and tighten the retaining nut to the specified torque.

32 Turn the crankshaft through a further two complete turns in the normal direction of rotation. Check that the timing is correct by refitting the piston positioning tools and camshaft locking tools as described previously.

33 When all is correct, remove the setting and locking tools and refit the sealing plugs to the cylinder head extension, using new O-rings if necessary. Tighten the plugs to the specified torque..

34 The remainder of refitting is a reversal of removal.

6 Timing belt tensioner and sprockets – removal, inspection and refitting

Timing belt tensioner
Removal

1 Remove the timing belt as described in Section 5.

2 Completely unscrew the retaining nut and slide the tensioner from the mounting stud.

Inspection

3 Wipe the tensioner clean but do not use solvents that may contaminate the bearings. Spin the tensioner pulley on its hub by hand. Stiff

movement or excessive freeplay is an indication of severe wear; the tensioner is not a serviceable component, and should be renewed.

Refitting

4 Slide the tensioner pulley onto the mounting stud, and fit the retaining nut.

5 Refit the timing belt as described in Section 5.

Camshaft sprocket
Removal

6 Remove the timing belt as described in Section 5.

7 Unscrew the plug and bolt, then slide the sprocket from the end of the camshaft.

Inspection

8 With the sprocket removed, examine the camshaft oil seal for signs of leaking. If necessary, refer to Section 7 and renew it.

9 Check the sprocket teeth for damage.

10 Wipe clean the sprocket and camshaft mating surfaces.

11 No inspection or repair procedures for the variable valve/phase transformer elements are given by Fiat. If a fault is suspected, consult a Fiat dealer or specialist.

Refitting

12 Locate the sprocket on the end of the camshaft, then refit the retaining bolt finger tight only at this stage.

13 Refit the timing belt as described in Section 5.

Crankshaft sprocket
Removal

14 Remove the timing belt as described in Section 5.

15 Working underneath the vehicle, prise out the cap at the front and undo the bolt securing the flywheel cover.

16 Engage Fiat tool No. 1781 000 400 with the flywheel teeth, and use the cover bolt to secure the tool.

17 In addition to the flywheel being locked, the crankshaft sprocket must also be locked to prevent damage to the internal locating pin. Fit Fiat tool No. 2000 004 500 to the crankshaft sprocket using the pulley bolts, and secure it to the cylinder block using the bolt supplied (see illustration).

18 Using a suitable socket and extension bar, unscrew the crankshaft sprocket retaining bolt.

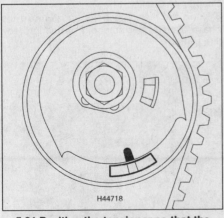

5.31 Position the tensioner so that the mobile indicator is aligned with the fixed reference mark

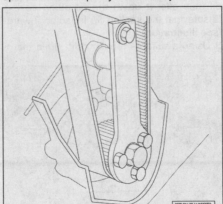

6.17 Bolt the special tool to the sprocket and cylinder block

7.4 Use a socket to drive the oil seal squarely into place

8.2 Carefully prise the crankshaft right-hand oil seal from the oil pump casing

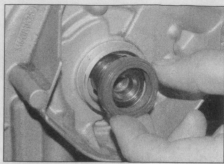

8.4 Locate the new oil seal on the oil pump casing with the sealing lips facing inwards

19 Remove the locking tool and slide the sprocket from place.

Inspection

20 With the sprocket removed, examine the crankshaft oil seal for signs of leaking. If necessary, refer to Section 8 and renew it.
21 Check the sprocket teeth for damage.
22 Wipe clean the sprocket and crankshaft mating surfaces.

Refitting

23 Slide the sprocket into place on the end of the crankshaft.
24 Fit the crankshaft sprocket locking tool, then refit the sprocket retaining bolt and tighten it to the specified torque.
25 Remove the sprocket and flywheel locking tools.
26 Refit the flywheel cover bolt, and refit the cap.
27 Refit the timing belt as described in Section 5.

7 Camshaft oil seal – renewal

1 Remove the camshaft sprocket as described in Section 6.
2 Punch or drill a small hole in the oil seal. Screw a self-tapping screw into the hole, and pull on the screw with pliers to extract the seal.
3 Clean the seal housing, and polish off any burrs or raised edges, which may have caused the seal to fail in the first place.

4 Lubricate the lips of the new seal with clean engine oil, and drive it into position until it seats on its locating shoulder (see illustration). Use a suitable tubular drift, such as a socket, which bears only on the hard outer edge of the seal. Take care not to damage the seal lips during fitting. Note that the seal lips should face inwards.
5 Refit the camshaft sprocket as described in Section 6.

8 Crankshaft oil seals – renewal

Right-hand side oil seal

1 The seal is located in the oil pump casing on the right-hand end of the crankshaft. Remove the crankshaft sprocket as described in Section 6.
2 Using a small screwdriver, carefully prise the oil seal from the oil pump casing, taking care not to damage the surface of the crankshaft (see illustration).
3 Clean the seating in the housing and the surface of the crankshaft. To prevent damage to the new oil seal as it is being fitted, wrap some adhesive tape around the end of the crankshaft and lightly oil it.
4 Lubricate the oil seal lip with clean engine oil then offer it up to the oil pump casing. Ensure that the sealing lip is facing inwards (see illustration).
5 Using a suitable tubular drift, drive the oil

seal squarely into the casing (see illustration). Remove the adhesive tape.
6 Refit the crankshaft sprocket as described in Section 6.

Left-hand side oil seal

Note: *The left-hand side oil seal is integral with the oil seal housing.*
7 Remove the flywheel as described in Section 12.
8 Remove the sump as described in Section 14.
9 Undo the retaining bolts and remove the housing complete with integral seal (see illustration).
10 Clean the cylinder block mating face, and the seal contact face on the crankshaft.
11 Lubricate the lip of the new seal, then located the seal housing on the cylinder block. Refit the housing retaining bolts and tighten them to the specified torque.
12 Refit the sump as described in Section 14.
13 Refit the flywheel as described in Section 12.

9 Camshaft housing – removal and refitting

Removal

1 Remove the camshaft sprocket as described in Section 6.
2 Remove the intake manifold as described in Chapter 4A Section 11.
3 Undo the retaining bolts and remove the phase transformer solenoid protection (see illustration).

8.5 Using a suitable tubular drift, drive the oil seal squarely into the casing

8.9 Oil seal/housing retaining bolts

9.3 Remove the phase transformer solenoid protection

4 Disconnect the phase transformer solenoid wiring plug.

5 Disconnect the camshaft sensor wiring plug, then undo the nuts and remove the wiring loom bracket from the left-hand end of the cylinder head.

6 Undo the fasteners and remove the oil vapour separator **(see illustration)**.

7 Unscrew the protective caps covering the camshaft housing retaining bolts **(see illustration)**.

8 To retain the cam followers in place as the cylinder head extension is removed, Fiat special tool No 1860988000 will be required. This tool consists of two strips of suitably-slotted thin metal angle which slip between the cylinder head extension and cylinder head mating faces as the extension is lifted off. The tool holds the cam followers in place in the extension allowing the assembly to be withdrawn without fouling the inlet and exhaust valves. The tools are relatively inexpensive and readily available from Fiat dealers. Suitable alternatives can be fabricated, if desired, using thin metal angle strip **(see Tool tip)**.

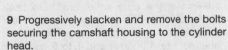

9.6 Oil separator retaining bolt/nut

9.7 Unscrew the protective caps

9 Progressively slacken and remove the bolts securing the camshaft housing to the cylinder head.

10 Lift the camshaft housing up very slightly, keeping it square to the cylinder head. Slip the tools in place to hold the cam followers, then lift the housing off the cylinder head **(see illustrations)**. Recover the gasket between the two assemblies.

11 Dismantling and inspection procedures

for the housing and camshafts are given in Section 10.

Refitting

12 Ensure that the mating faces of the cylinder head and housing are thoroughly cleaned, with all traces of old gasket removed, then locate a new gasket on the cylinder head **(see illustration)**.

13 Check that the pistons are still correctly

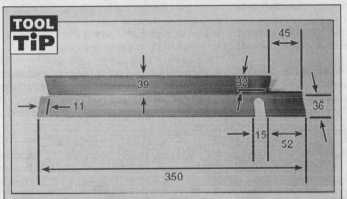

TOOL TiP

To make a cam follower retaining tool, obtain two lengths of thin metal angle and cut both to the dimensions shown (in mm).

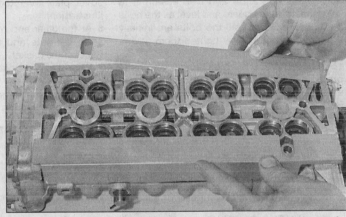

9.10a Lift the cylinder head extension slightly and insert the tools (shown with the cylinder head removed for clarity)...

9.10b... then remove the cylinder head extension

9.12 Locate a new gasket on the cylinder head

9.15 Renew the protective caps O-ring seals

positioned at the mid-point of their stroke and that the camshafts are locked with the locking tools. Locate the cam follower retaining tools in position and carefully lower the extension assembly over the valves and onto the cylinder head. When all the cam followers have engaged their respective valves, remove the tools.

14 Refit the retaining bolts and tighten them progressively to pull the housing down onto the cylinder head. Do this slowly and carefully as the valve springs will be compressed during this operation and it is essential to keep the housing square and level as the bolts are tightened. Once all the bolts are initially tightened, progressively tighten them further to the specified torque.

15 If necessary renew the O-ring seals on the protective caps covering the cylinder head extension retaining bolts **(see illustration)**. Refit the caps and tighten them securely.

16 The remainder of refitting is a reversal of removal.

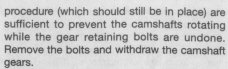

10 Camshaft and followers
– removal, inspection and refitting

Removal

1 Remove the camshaft housing as described in Section 9.
2 Place the assembly upside-down on a bench and lift off the cam follower retaining tools.
3 Remove the cam followers from their locations in the cylinder head extension and place them in an oil-tight compartmented box labelled 1 to 8 (intake) and 1 to 8 (exhaust) **(see illustration)**. Alternatively, place them into individual storage jars or containers suitably marked. Fill the box or the jars with clean engine oil until each cam follower is just submerged.
4 Remove the camshaft sprocket as described in Section 6.
5 Undo the two bolts and remove the cover plate over the intake camshaft **(see illustration)**.
6 At the other end of the camshaft housing, undo the nuts and remove the end cover. Recover the gasket.
7 Undo the two bolts securing the camshaft drivegears to the intake and exhaust camshafts **(see illustration)**. The camshaft locking tools used in the timing belt removal

procedure (which should still be in place) are sufficient to prevent the camshafts rotating while the gear retaining bolts are undone. Remove the bolts and withdraw the camshaft gears.
8 Remove the camshaft locking tools.
9 Carefully remove the intake camshaft from the camshaft housing **(see illustration)**. Suitably mark the camshaft IN to avoid confusion when refitting.
10 Punch or drill a small hole in the exhaust camshaft oil seal. Screw a self-tapping screw into the hole, and pull on the screw with pliers to extract the seal **(see illustration)**.
11 Carefully remove the exhaust camshaft from the camshaft housing **(see illustration)**. Suitably mark the camshaft EX to avoid confusion when refitting.

Inspection

12 Examine the camshaft bearing surfaces and cam lobes for signs of wear ridges and scoring. Renew the camshaft if any of these conditions are apparent. Examine the condition of the bearing surfaces, both on the camshaft journals and in the camshaft housing. If the housing bearing surfaces are worn excessively, the housing will need to be renewed. If suitable measuring equipment is available, camshaft bearing journal wear can be checked by direct measurement.
13 Examine the cam follower bearing surfaces which contact the camshaft lobes for wear ridges and scoring. Renew any follower on which these conditions are apparent. If a follower bearing surface is badly scored,

10.3 Lift out the camshaft followers

10.5 Remove the intake camshaft cover plate

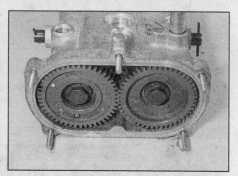

10.7 Undo the 2 bolts securing the camshaft drive gears

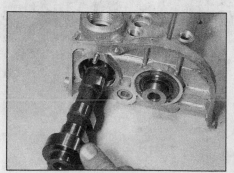

10.9 Carefully remove the intake camshaft

10.10 Extract the camshaft oil seal...

10.11... and remove the exhaust camshaft

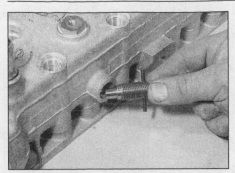

10.15 Refit the camshaft locking tools

10.16 Lubricate the oil seal lip and drive it squarely into place

10.17a Tighten the intake camshaft drivegear retaining bolt to the specified torque

10.17b Refit the exhaust drivegear whilst aligning the anti-backlash inner gear teeth

10.18a Locate a new gasket on the end cover...

10.18b... then wrap round the protruding tangs to retain the gasket

also examine the corresponding lobe on the camshaft for wear, as it is likely that both will be worn. Renew worn components as necessary.

Refitting

14 Liberally lubricate the camshaft journals and camshaft housing bearings, then locate both camshafts in position. Note that the exhaust camshaft is nearest to the front facing side of the engine.

15 With the camshafts in position, rotate them as necessary until the camshaft locking tools can be re-inserted **(see illustration)**.

16 Lubricate the lips of a new exhaust camshaft oil seal with clean engine oil, and drive it into position until it seats on its locating shoulder **(see illustration)**. Use a suitable tubular drift, such as a socket, which bears

only on the hard outer edge of the seal. Take care not to damage the seal lips during fitting. Note that the seal lips should face inwards.

17 Refit the intake camshaft drive gear, then fit the exhaust gear, aligning the (inner and outer) teeth, then tighten the bolts to the specified torque **(see illustrations)**.

18 Locate a new gasket on the camshaft housing end cover, then wrap round the protruding tangs on the gasket to retain it in position **(see illustrations)**.

19 Locate the end cover on the camshaft housing and secure with the retaining nuts securely tightened.

20 Locate a new O-ring on the inlet camshaft cover plate, then apply RTV gasket sealant to the cover plate contact face. Fit the cover plate and secure with the two bolts securely tightened.

21 Refit the camshaft sprocket and secure with the retaining bolt tightened finger tight only at this stage.

22 Liberally lubricate the cam followers and place them in position in their respective cylinder head extension bores **(see illustration)**.

23 Locate the cam follower retaining tools in position and refit the camshaft housing as described in Section 9.

11 Cylinder head – removal and refitting

Removal

Note: *The cylinder head bolts are of special splined design and a Fiat tool should be obtained to unscrew them. A Torx key will not fit, although in practice it was found that a close-fitting Allen key could be used as an alternative.*

1 Disconnect the battery negative lead as described in Chapter 5A Section 4.

2 Remove the timing belt as described in Section 2.

3 Remove the camshaft housing as described in Section 9.

4 Remove the exhaust manifold as described in Chapter 4A Section 12.

5 Drain the engine coolant as described in Chapter 1 Section 29.

6 Undo the retaining bolt and remove the timing belt inner guard **(see illustration)**.

10.22 Lubricate the cam followers and place them in position in their respective bores

11.6 Remove the belt inner gaurd

11.7 Disconnect the coolant temperature sensor wiring plug as the left-hand end of the cylinder head

11.18 Place the gasket so the words ALTO/TOP can be read from above

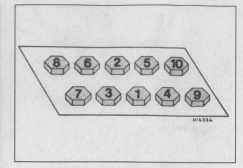

11.20 Cylinder head bolt tightening sequence

7 Disconnect the wiring plug from the coolant temperature sensor **(see illustration)**.

8 Release the clamps and disconnect the coolant hoses from the left-hand end of the cylinder head.

9 Check that nothing remains attached to the cylinder head likely to impede removal, then unscrew the cylinder head bolts half a turn at a time in the reverse order to the tightening sequence **(see illustration 11.20)**. When the bolts are free, remove them from their locations.

10 Lift the cylinder head from the block. If it is stuck tight insert pieces of wood into the exhaust ports, and use them as levers to rock the head off the block. On no account drive levers into the gasket joint, or attempt to tap the head sideways, as it is located on positioning dowels.

11 Remove and discard the cylinder head gasket.

12 Refer to Chapter 2C, Section 8 for cylinder head dismantling and inspection procedures.

Preparation for refitting

13 The mating faces of the cylinder head and cylinder block must be perfectly clean before refitting the head. Use a hard plastic or wooden scraper to remove all traces of gasket and carbon; also clean the piston crowns. Take particular care when cleaning the piston crowns as the soft aluminium alloy is easily damaged. Make sure that the carbon is not allowed to enter the oil and water passages – this is particularly important for the lubrication system, as carbon could block the oil supply to the engine's components. Using adhesive tape and paper, seal the water, oil and bolt holes in the cylinder block. To prevent carbon entering the gap between the pistons and bores, smear a little grease in the gap. After cleaning each piston, use a small brush to remove all traces of grease and carbon from the gap, then wipe away the remainder with a clean rag. Clean all the pistons in the same way.

14 Check the mating surfaces of the cylinder block and the cylinder head for nicks, deep scratches and other damage. If slight, they may be removed carefully with a file, but if excessive, machining may be the only alternative to renewal. If warpage of the cylinder head gasket surface is suspected,

use a straight-edge to check it for distortion as described in Chapter 2C Section 7.

15 Check the condition of the cylinder head bolts, and particularly their threads, whenever they are removed. Wash the bolts in a suitable solvent, and wipe them dry. Check each bolt for any sign of visible wear or damage, renewing them if necessary. Although Fiat do not specify that the bolts must be renewed, it is strongly recommended that the bolts should be renewed as a complete set whenever they are disturbed.

Refitting

16 Before refitting the assembled cylinder head, make sure that the head and block mating surfaces are perfectly clean, and that the bolt holes in the cylinder block have been mopped out to clear any oil.

17 The new gasket should not be removed from its nylon cover until required for use. Fit the gasket dry, and make sure that the mating surfaces on the head and block are perfectly clean.

18 Place the gasket on the cylinder block so that the word ALTO can be read from above **(see illustration)**.

19 Lower the cylinder head onto the block so that it locates on the positioning dowels.

20 The cylinder head bolt threads must be clean and lightly lubricated. Screw the bolts in finger-tight then working progressively and in the sequence shown, tighten all the cylinder head bolts to the Stage 1 torque setting given in the Specifications, using a torque wrench and a suitable socket **(see illustration)**. With all the bolts tightened to their Stage 1 setting, working again in the specified sequence, first angle-tighten the bolts through the specified Stage 2 angle, then again through the Stage 3 angle, using a socket and extension bar. It is recommended that an angle-measuring gauge is used during this stage of tightening, to ensure accuracy.

21 The remainder of refitting is a reversal of removal, noting the following points:

a) *Tighten all fasteners to their specified torque where given.*

b) *Refill the cooling system as described in Chapter 1 Section 29.*

c) *Reconnect the battery negative lead as described in Chapter 5A Section 4.*

12 Flywheel – removal, inspection and refitting

Removal

1 Remove the clutch assembly as described in Chapter 6 Section 5.

2 The flywheel must now be held stationary while the bolts are loosened. A home-made locking tool may be fabricated from a piece of scrap metal and used to lock the ring gear **(see illustration)**. Bolt the tool to one of the transmission bellhousing mounting bolt holes on the cylinder block.

3 Mark the position of the flywheel with respect to the crankshaft using a dab of paint. Unscrew and remove the mounting bolts together with the spacer plate, then lift off the flywheel. Discard the flywheel bolts; new ones must be used on refitting.

Inspection

4 If the flywheel's clutch mating surface is deeply scored, cracked or otherwise damaged, the flywheel must be renewed. However, it may be possible to have it surface-ground; seek the advice of a Fiat dealer or engine reconditioning specialist.

5 If the ring gear is badly worn or has missing teeth, the flywheel must be renewed.

Refitting

6 Clean the mating surfaces of the flywheel and crankshaft. Remove any remaining

12.2 Make up a tool to lock the flywheel

13.6 Undo the bolts and remove the mounting and bracket

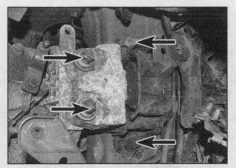

13.10 Left-hand mounting/bracket retaining bolts

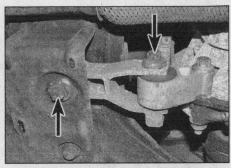

13.14 Rear mounting link rod bolts

locking compound from the threads of the crankshaft holes, using the correct-size tap, if available.

7 If the new retaining bolts are not supplied with their threads already precoated, apply a suitable thread-locking compound to the threads of each bolt.

8 Offer up the flywheel to the crankshaft, using the alignment marks made during removal, and fit the new retaining bolts together with the spacer plate.

9 Lock the flywheel using the method employed on removal, and tighten the retaining bolts to the specified torque.

10 Refit the clutch as described in Chapter 6 Section 5.

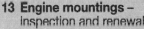

13 Engine mountings – inspection and renewal

Inspection

1 Firmly apply the handbrake, then jack up the front of the car and support it securely on axle stands as described in 'Vehicle jacking and support'.

2 Check the mounting rubbers to see if they are cracked, hardened or separated from the metal at any point; renew the mounting if any such damage or deterioration is evident.

3 Check that all the mounting's fasteners are securely tightened; use a torque wrench to check if possible.

4 Using a large screwdriver or a crowbar, check for wear in the mounting by carefully

14.3 Subframe crossbrace retaining bolts

levering against it to check for free play. Where this is not possible enlist the aid of an assistant to move the engine/transmission back-and-forth, or from side-to-side, while you watch the mounting. While some free play is to be expected, even from new components, excessive wear should be obvious. If excessive free play is found, check first that the fasteners are correctly secured, then renew any worn components as described below.

Renewal

Right-hand mounting

5 Place a trolley jack beneath the right-hand side of the engine, with a block of wood on the jack head. Raise the jack until it is supporting the weight of the engine.

6 Undo the bolts securing the mounting to the vehicle body, and the bolts securing the mounting to the support bracket (see illustration). Remove the mounting.

7 Refitting is a reversal of removal, tightening the retaining bolts to the specified torque.

Left-hand mounting

8 Remove the battery and battery tray as described in Chapter 5A Section 4.

9 Place a trolley jack beneath the transmission, with a block of wood on the jack head. Raise the jack until it is supporting the weight of the engine/transmission.

10 Undo the retaining bolts securing the mounting to the vehicle body and support bracket, and remove the mounting (see illustration).

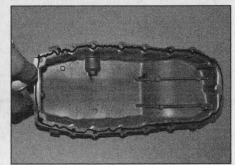

14.10 Apply a thin bead of sealant to the sump flange

11 Refitting is a reversal of removal, tightening the retaining bolts to their specified torque.

Rear mounting

12 Raise the front of the vehicle and support it securely on axle stands, as described in 'Vehicle jacking and support'.

13 Undo the nuts securing the front exhaust pipe to the catalytic converter, then undo the bolt securing the pipe support bracket clamp.

14 Undo the bolts and manoeuvre the rear mounting link rod from place (see illustration).

15 Refitting is a reversal of removal, tightening the retaining bolts to their specified torque.

14 Sump – removal and refitting

Removal

1 Firmly apply the handbrake, then jack up the front of the car and support it securely on axle stands as described in 'Vehicle jacking and support'.

2 Drain the engine oil as described in Chapter 1 Section 4.

3 Undo the bolts and remove the crossbrace from the front subframe (see illustration).

4 Disconnect the front exhaust pipe at the joining flange, release the flexible mounting and move the pipe to one side.

5 Remove the bolts securing the sump to the transmission casing.

6 Undo the nuts/bolts securing the sump to the lower crankcase.

7 Undo the side bolts securing the lower flywheel guard to the transmission.

8 Cut through as much of the joint sealant as possible using a sharp knife. Pull the sump downwards to release it from the remaining sealant and remove it from under the car.

9 Thoroughly clean the sump and the cylinder block mating surfaces ensuring that all traces of old sealant are removed.

Refitting

10 Apply a 3.0 mm bead of RTV silicone sealant to the sump flange, then locate the sump in position (see illustration). Refit the

15.7a Unbolt and remove the oil pump pick-up tube...

15.7b... then hook out the pick-up tube O-ring seal

15.8a Unscrew the oil pressure relief valve plug...

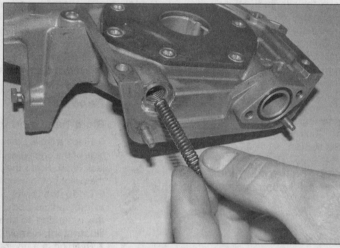

15.8b... withdraw the spring...

bolts securing the sump to the transmission casing, and tighten them to the specified torque.

11 Refit the remaining sump retaining bolts/nuts and tighten them to the specified torque.

12 The remainder of refitting is a reversal of removal.

13 Lower the car to the ground and wait at least 1 hour before filling the engine with oil as described in Chapter 1 Section 4.

15 Oil pump and pick-up tube
– removal, inspection and refitting

Removal

1 Remove the crankshaft sprocket as described in Section 6.

2 Drain the engine oil and remove the oil filter as described in Chapter 1 Section 4.

3 Remove the sump as described in Section 14.

4 Remove the coolant pump as described in Chapter 3 Section 7.

5 Disconnect the wiring connector from the oil pressure switch on the side of the pump casing.

6 Undo the oil pump retaining bolts, noting the location of the longer bolt, and withdraw the pump assembly from the front of the engine. Recover the gasket.

Inspection

7 With the pump on the bench, undo the two bolts and remove the pick-up tube (see illustrations). Using a small screwdriver or

15.8c... and plunger

similar tool, hook out the pick-up tube sealing O-ring from the pump body.

8 The pressure relief valve components can be removed for examination by unscrewing the end plug and withdrawing the spring and plunger (see illustrations).

9 If pump wear is suspected, check the rotors in the following way. Extract the fixing screws and remove the rear cover plate. The screws are very tight, and will probably require the use of an impact screwdriver (see illustration).

15.9 Undo the screws and remove the oil pump rear cover plate

15.10 Refit the pump rotors with the orientation marks facing upwards

15.11a Check the oil pump outer rotor-to-pump casing clearance

15.11b Check the oil pump rotor endfloat

16.2 Unscrew the oil pressure warning light switch

10 Inspect the pump rotors, pump casing and cover for any signs of wear or damage. If satisfactory, refit the rotors to the pump casing ensuring that the orientation marks are facing upwards (see illustration).

11 Check the clearance between the outer rotor and the pump casing using feeler blades. Check the rotor endfloat by placing a straight-edge across the pump casing, and checking the gap between the straight-edge and rotor face (see illustrations). If the clearances are outside the specified tolerance, renew the oil pump complete.

12 If the pump is unworn, lubricate the rotors with clean engine oil then place the cover plate in position. Apply thread locking compound to the retaining screws and tighten the screws securely.

13 Locate a new O-ring in the pump casing

then refit the pick-up tube. Secure the tube with the two bolts tightened securely.

14 Lubricate the pressure relief valve plunger then refit the plunger and spring. Apply thread-locking compound to the end plug then refit and securely tighten the plug.

15 Lever out the crankshaft oil seal and drive a new one squarely into the oil pump casing. Lubricate the oil seal lips with clean engine oil.

16 Prior to refitting, prime the pump by pouring clean engine oil into its inlet duct, while at the same time turning the oil pump inner rotor.

Refitting

17 Ensure that the oil pump and cylinder block mating faces are clean, then place a new gasket on the pump casing. Retain the gasket in position by inserting two of the pump retaining bolts.

18 Locate the pump on the cylinder block,

insert the retaining bolts and tighten them progressively to the specified torque.

19 The remainder of refitting is a reversal of removal.

16 Engine pressure warning light switch – removal and refitting

1 Raise the front of the vehicle and support it securely on axle stands as described in 'Vehicle jacking and support'.

2 Disconnect the wiring plug from the switch, then unscrew it from the housing (see illustration). Be prepared for oil spillage.

3 Screw the new switch into the housing and tighten it to the specified torque.

4 Reconnect the wiring plug and lower the vehicle to the ground. Check the engine oil level as described in 'Weekly checks'.

Notes

Chapter 2 Part C
General engine removal and overhaul procedures

Contents

Section number

Crankshaft – bearing selection and refitting 17
Crankshaft – inspection 13
Crankshaft – removal 10
Cylinder block/crankcase – cleaning and inspection 11
Cylinder head – dismantling 6
Cylinder head – reassembly 8
Cylinder head and valves – cleaning and inspection 7
Engine – initial start-up after overhaul 19
Engine and transmission – removal, separation and refitting 4
Engine overhaul – dismantling sequence 5

Section number

Engine overhaul – general information 2
Engine overhaul – reassembly sequence 15
Engine removal – methods and precautions 3
General information 1
Main and big-end bearings – inspection 14
Piston rings – refitting 16
Piston/connecting rod assembly – bearing selection and refitting . . 18
Piston/connecting rod assembly – cleaning and inspection 12
Piston/connecting rod assembly – removal 9

Degrees of difficulty

Easy, suitable for novice with little experience	**Fairly easy,** suitable for beginner with some experience	**Fairly difficult,** suitable for competent DIY mechanic	**Difficult,** suitable for experienced DIY mechanic	**Very difficult,** suitable for expert DIY or professional

Specifications

Note: *At the time of writing, some specifications for certain engines were not available. Where the relevant specifications are not given here, refer to your Fiat dealer for further information.*

Cylinder head

Maximum gasket face distortion . . . . 0.1 mm
Cylinder head height:
  SOHC 8v engines . . . . 125.5 ± 0.1 mm minimum
  DOHC 16v engines . . . . 77.0 ± 0.2 mm (factory value)

Valves

	Intake	Exhaust
Valve stem diameter:		
SOHC 8v engines	4.982 to 5.000 mm	4.974 to 4.992 mm
DOHC 16v engines	5.982 to 6.000 mm	5.974 to 5.992 mm mm
Valve head diameter:		
SOHC 8v engines	33.10 to 33.30 mm	27.80 to 28.10 mm
DOHC 16v engines	27.02 to 27.05 mm	22.52 to 22.55 mm
Valve clearance:		
SOHC 8v engines	0.3 mm	0.4 mm
DOHC 16v engines	Hydraulic adjustment	

Crankshaft

Endfloat:
  SOHC 8v engines . . . . 0.055 to 0.265 mm
  DOHC 16v engines . . . . 0.155 to 0.355 mm

Pistons

Ring end gap:	1.2L 8v engines	1.4L 8v engines	1.4L 16v engines
1st compression ring	0.20 to 0.40 mm	0.20 to 0.40 mm	0.20 to 0.40 mm
2nd compression ring	0.25 to 0.70 mm	0.50 to 0.70 mm	0.25 to 0.45 mm
Oil control ring	0.20 to 0.45 mm	0.20 to 0.40 mm	0.20 to 0.40 mm

1 General information

1 Included in this Part of Chapter 2 are details of removing the engine from the car and general overhaul procedures for the cylinder head, cylinder block/crankcase and all other engine internal components.

2 The information given ranges from advice concerning preparation for an overhaul and the purchase of parts, to detailed step-by-step procedures covering removal, inspection, renovation and refitting of engine internal components.

2 Engine overhaul –
general information

1 It is not always easy to determine when, or if, an engine should be completely overhauled, as a number of factors must be considered.

2 High mileage is not necessarily an indication that an overhaul is needed, while low mileage does not preclude the need for an overhaul. Frequency of servicing is probably the most important consideration. An engine which has had regular and frequent oil and filter changes, as well as other required maintenance, should give many thousands of miles of reliable service. Conversely, a neglected engine may require an overhaul very early in its life.

3 Excessive oil consumption is an indication that piston rings, valve seals and/or valve guides are in need of attention. Make sure that oil leaks are not responsible before deciding that the rings and/or guides are worn. Perform a compression test, as described in Part A or B of this Chapter (as applicable), to determine the likely cause of the problem.

4 Check the oil pressure with a gauge fitted in place of the oil pressure switch, and compare it with that specified in Part A or B. If it is extremely low, the main and big-end bearings, and/or the oil pump, are probably worn out.

5 Loss of power, rough running, knocking or metallic engine noises, excessive valve gear noise, and high fuel consumption may also point to the need for an overhaul, especially if they are all present at the same time. If a complete service does not remedy the situation, major mechanical work is the only solution.

6 A full engine overhaul involves restoring all internal parts to the specification of a new engine. During a complete overhaul, the pistons and the piston rings are renewed, and the cylinder bores are reconditioned. New main and big-end bearings are generally fitted; if necessary, the crankshaft may be reground, to compensate for wear in the journals. The valves are also serviced as well, since they are usually in less-than-perfect condition at this point. Always pay careful attention to the condition of the oil pump when overhauling the engine, and renew it if there is any doubt as to its serviceability. The end result should be an as-new engine that will give many trouble-free miles.

Note: *Critical cooling system components such as the hoses, thermostat and coolant pump should be renewed when an engine is overhauled. The radiator should be checked carefully, to ensure that it is not clogged or leaking. Also, it is a good idea to renew the oil pump whenever the engine is overhauled.*

7 Before beginning the engine overhaul, read through the entire procedure, to familiarise yourself with the scope and requirements of the job. Overhauling an engine is not difficult if you follow carefully all of the instructions, have the necessary tools and equipment, and pay close attention to all specifications. It can, however, be time-consuming. Plan on the car being off the road for a minimum of two weeks, especially if parts must be taken to an engineering works for repair or reconditioning. Check on the availability of parts and make sure that any necessary special tools and equipment are obtained in advance. Most work can be done with typical hand tools, although a number of precision measuring tools are required for inspecting parts to determine if they must be renewed. Often the engineering works will handle the inspection of parts and offer advice concerning reconditioning and renewal.

Note: *Always wait until the engine has been completely dismantled, and until all components (especially the cylinder block/crankcase and the crankshaft) have been inspected, before deciding what service and repair operations must be performed by an engineering works. The condition of these components will be the major factor to consider when determining whether to overhaul the original engine, or to buy a reconditioned unit. Do not, therefore, purchase parts or have overhaul work done on other components until they have been thoroughly inspected. As a general rule, time is the primary cost of an overhaul, so it does not pay to fit worn or sub-standard parts.*

8 As a final note, to ensure maximum life and minimum trouble from a reconditioned engine, everything must be assembled with care, in a spotlessly-clean environment.

3 Engine removal –
methods and precautions

1 If you have decided that the engine must be removed for overhaul or major repair work, several preliminary steps should be taken.

2 Locating a suitable place to work is extremely important. Adequate workspace, along with storage space for the car, will be needed. If a workshop or garage is not available, at the very least, a flat, level, clean work surface is required.

3 Cleaning the engine compartment and engine/transmission before beginning the removal procedure will help keep tools clean and organised.

4 An engine hoist will also be necessary. Make sure the equipment is rated in excess of the weight of the engine (and transmission if both are being removed). Safety is of primary importance, considering the potential hazards involved in lifting the engine out of the car.

5 If this is the first time you have removed an engine, an assistant should ideally be available. Advice and aid from someone more experienced would also be helpful. There are many instances when one person cannot simultaneously perform all of the operations required when lifting the engine out of the vehicle.

6 Plan the operation ahead of time. Before starting work, arrange for the hire of or obtain all of the tools and equipment you will need. Some of the equipment necessary to perform engine removal and installation safely and with relative ease (in addition to an engine hoist) is as follows: a heavy duty trolley jack, complete sets of spanners and sockets (see *Tools and working facilities*), wooden blocks, and plenty of rags and cleaning solvent for mopping-up spilled oil, coolant and fuel. If the hoist must be hired, make sure that you arrange for it in advance, and perform all of the operations possible without it beforehand. This will save you money and time.

7 Plan for the car to be out of use for quite a while. An engineering works will be required to perform some of the work, which the do-it-yourselfer cannot accomplish without special equipment. These places often have a busy schedule, so it would be a good idea to consult them before removing the engine, in order to accurately estimate the amount of time required to rebuild or repair components that may need work.

8 During the engine/transmission removal procedure, it is advisable to make notes of the locations of all brackets, cable ties, earthing points, etc, as well as how the wiring harnesses, hoses and electrical connections are attached and routed around the engine and engine compartment. An effective way of doing this is to take a series of photographs of the various components before they are disconnected or removed; the resulting photographs will prove invaluable when the engine/transmission is refitted.

9 Always be extremely careful when removing and refitting the engine. Serious injury can result from careless actions. Plan ahead and take your time, and a job of this nature, although major, can be accomplished successfully.

10 The engine and transmission assembly is removed downwards from the engine compartment on all models described in this manual.

4.6 Front subframe crossbrace bolts

4.8 Remove the heatshield around the exhaust manifold

4.12 Disconnect the coolant hoses from the expansion tank

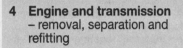

4 Engine and transmission – removal, separation and refitting

Note: *The engine is lowered from the engine compartment as a complete unit with the transmission; the two are then separated for overhaul.*

Removal

1 On models with air conditioning, have the refrigerant circuit evacuated by a Fiat dealer or suitably equipped repairer. The system will need to be recharged upon completion.
2 Remove the battery and battery tray as described in Chapter 5A Section 4.
3 Remove the air cleaner assembly as described in Chapter 4A Section 2.
4 Slacken the front roadwheel bolts, raise the front of the vehicle and support it securely on axle stands as described in *'Vehicle jacking and support'*.
5 Drain the coolant system as described in Chapter 1 Section 29.
6 Undo the bolts and remove the front subframe crossbrace **(see illustration)**.
7 Remove the engine rear/lower mounting link rod as described in Chapter 2A Section 13 or Chapter 2B Section 13.
8 Remove the exhaust manifold heat shield **(see illustration)**.
9 On DOHC 16v models, remove the exhaust manifold as described in Chapter 4A Section 12.

10 On SOHC 8v models, disconnect the front exhaust pipe from the flange, and move it to one side.
11 Release the clamps then disconnect the upper and lower coolant hoses from the radiator.
12 Release the clamps and disconnect the coolant hoses from the coolant expansion tank **(see illustration)**.
13 Prise out the wire clips and disconnect the heater hoses at the engine compartment bulkhead **(see illustration)**.
14 Disconnect the reversing light switch wiring plug at the top/front of the transmission casing.
15 Undo the retaining bolts and move the clutch slave cylinder to one side. Ensure the clutch pedal is not depressed until the slave cylinder is bolted back into place.

16 Undo the retaining nut and disconnect the earth lead on the transmission casing **(see illustration)**.
17 Undo the nut and disconnect the starter motor supply lead from the circuit board.
18 Disconnect the gear change cables from the transmission as described in Chapter 7 Section 3.
19 Disconnect the wiring plugs from the engine management ECU **(see illustration)**.
20 On DOHC 16V models, release the clamp and disconnect the air intake hose from the throttle body.
21 Disconnect the engine wiring loom plug at the left-hand end of the cylinder head **(see illustration)**.
22 Carefully disconnect the vacuum pipe from the intake manifold **(see illustration)**.
23 Depress the release button and

4.13 Prise out the clip a little and pull the heater hoses from the connections

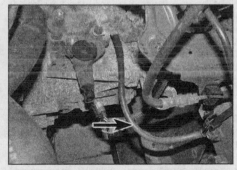

4.16 Disconnect the earth lead from the transmission casing

4.19 Fold over the locking lever and disconnect the ECU wiring plugs

4.21 Prise out the yellow catch, and slide up the grey lock to disconnect the plug

4.22 Disconnect the vacuum pipe from the manifold

4.23 Depress the catch and disconnect the fuel supply pipe

4.24 Squeeze together the clips and disconnect the vapour pipe

disconnect the fuel feed pipe from the fuel rail **(see illustration)**. Plug the openings to prevent contamination. Be prepared for fluid spillage.

24 Depress the release button and disconnect the EVAP vapour pipe from the manifold **(see illustration)**.

25 With reference to Chapter 9 Section 21, remove the ABS wheel speed sensor from the front hub carrier each side. There's no need to disconnect the sensor wiring plug.

26 Remove both driveshafts as described in Chapter 8 Section 2.

27 Where applicable, depress the release button each side and disconnect the air conditioning feed (right-hand side of the condenser) and return (central engine compartment bulkhead) pipes at the quick-release connectors **(see illustrations)**. Plug the openings to prevent contamination.

28 Attach a suitable hoist to the engine right-hand lifting eye and the left-hand lifting eye on the transmission. To prevent the engine/transmission assembly tipping backward during removal, a third lifting eye, fabricated from scrap metal or similar should be secured to a suitable location in the vicinity of the alternator/compressor. Attach the hoist to the additional eye and evenly take the weight of the engine/transmission.

29 With the engine supported, undo the bolts securing the right-hand engine mounting to the support bracket on the engine.

30 Undo the bolts securing the left-hand side engine/transmission mounting to the support bracket on the transmission casing.

31 Make a final check to ensure all wiring/hoses have been disconnected the make prevent the engine/transmission assembly from being removed.

32 Carefully lower the engine/transmission from the engine compartment taking care not to damage the surrounding components. Ideally lower the unit onto a low trolley so that it may be withdrawn from under the car. Disconnect the hoist from the engine/transmission assembly.

Separation

33 Rest the engine/transmission assembly on a firm, flat surface, and use wooden blocks as wedges to keep the unit steady.

34 Disconnect all the individual wiring connectors from the various components on the engine and transmission to enable the main engine wiring harness to be removed. Make notes or attach labels to each connector to aid reconnection.

35 Detach the wiring harness support brackets and plastic ducting mountings, release the relevant cable ties and remove the complete harness assembly from the engine/transmission.

36 Remove the starter motor as described in Chapter 5A Section 8.

37 Where applicable, undo the bolts and remove the support brace linking the transmission to the cylinder block.

38 Unbolt and remove the cover plate from the base of the transmission casing.

39 Ensure that both engine and transmission are individually supported, then remove the

remaining bolts securing the transmission bellhousing to the engine. Note the correct fitted positions of each bolt (and the relevant brackets) to aid refitting.

40 Withdraw the transmission from the engine, ensuring that the weight of the transmission is not allowed to hang on the input shaft while it is engaged with the clutch friction plate.

41 If they are loose, remove the locating dowels from the engine or transmission.

Connection

42 If the engine and transmission have not been separated, proceed to paragraph 50.

43 Ensure the transmission input shaft splines are clean and free from any debris. Fiat do not recommend applying any form of lubricant to the splines of the shaft.

44 Ensure that the locating dowels are correctly positioned in the engine or transmission, and that the release bearing is correctly engaged with the fork.

45 Carefully offer the transmission to the engine, until the locating dowels are engaged. Ensure that the weight of the transmission is not allowed to hang on the input shaft as it is engaged with the clutch friction plate.

46 Refit the engine-to-transmission bolts, ensuring that all the necessary brackets are correctly positioned, and tighten them to the specified torque.

47 Refit the cover plate to the base of the transmission bellhousing.

48 Where applicable, locate the support brace linking the transmission to the cylinder block, then insert the bolts hand-tight. With all the bolts inserted, tighten them securely.

49 Refit the starter motor as described in Chapter 5A Section 8.

50 Refit and reconnect the wiring harness to the components on the engine/transmission assembly, making sure it is correctly routed.

Refitting

51 Locate the engine/transmission assembly beneath the engine compartment and attach the hoist to the lifting eyes.

52 Carefully lift the assembly up into the engine compartment taking care not to damage the surrounding components.

53 Align the left-hand engine/transmission mounting with the bracket, insert the bolts, but only finger-tighten them at this stage.

54 Alight the right-hand engine mounting with the support bracket, refit the bolts, and tighten them to the specified torque.

55 Now tighten the left-hand mounting bolts to their specified torque.

56 Working beneath the vehicle, refit the rear engine mounting and tighten the bolts to the specified torque.

57 Disconnect the hoist from the engine and transmission lifting eyes and remove the hoist from under the vehicle.

58 The remainder of the refitting procedure is the direct reverse of the removal procedure, noting the following points:

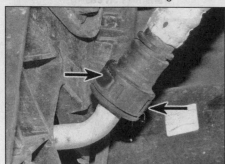

4.27a Depress the button each side, and disconnect the refrigerant pipe from the right-hand side of the condenser...

4.27b... and behind the engine (viewed from beneath)

a) Ensure that all hoses are correctly routed and are secured with the correct hose clips, where applicable. If the hose clips cannot be used again; proprietary worm-drive clips should be fitted in their place.
b) Refill the coolant system as described in Chapter 1 Section 29.
c) Where applicable, have the refrigerant circuit recharged by a Fiat dealer or suitably equipped repairer.
d) Tighten all fasteners to their specified torque where given.
e) When the engine is started for the first time, check for air, coolant, lubricant and fuel leaks from manifolds, hoses, etc. If the engine has been overhauled, read the notes in Section 19 before attempting to start it.

5 Engine overhaul – dismantling sequence

1 It is preferable to dismantle and work on the engine with it mounted on a portable engine stand. These stands can generally be hired from a tool hire shop. Before the engine is mounted on a stand, the flywheel/driveplate should be removed, so that the stand bolts can be tightened into the end of the cylinder block.
2 If a stand is not available, it is possible to dismantle the engine with it blocked up on a sturdy workbench, or on the floor. Be extra careful not to tip or drop the engine when working without a stand.
3 If a reconditioned engine is to be obtained, or if the original engine is to be overhauled, the external components in the following list must be removed first. These components can then be transferred to the reconditioned engine, or refitted to the existing engine after overhaul.
a) Alternator (including mounting brackets, where fitted) (Chapter 5A Section 6).
b) Engine mounting brackets.

c) The ignition system and HT components including all sensors, etc. (Chapter 5B).
d) The fuel injection system components (Chapter 4A).
e) Intake manifold (Chapter 4A Section 11).
f) All remaining electrical switches, actuators, sensors and the engine wiring harness.
g) Engine oil level dipstick.
h) Oil filter (Chapter 1 Section 4).
i) Cooling system components (Chapter 3).
j) Flywheel (Chapter 2A Section 12 or Chapter 2B Section 12).
k) Clutch components (Chapter 6 Section 5).
Note: When removing the external components from the engine, pay close attention to details that may be helpful or important during refitting. Note the fitted position of gaskets, seals, spacers, pins, washers, bolts, and other small components.
4 If a 'short' engine is to be obtained (cylinder block, crankshaft, pistons and connecting rods all assembled), then the cylinder head, sump, oil pump, timing belt, sprockets and tensioner will have to be removed also.
5 If a complete overhaul of the existing engine is being undertaken, the engine can be dismantled, in the order given below.
a) Flywheel.
b) Timing belt, sprockets and tensioner.
c) Intake manifold.
d) Cylinder head.
e) Sump.
f) Oil pump.
g) Pistons/connecting rods.
h) Crankshaft.

6 Cylinder head – dismantling

Note: New and reconditioned cylinder heads are available from the manufacturer, and from engine reconditioning specialists. Some specialist tools are required for dismantling and inspection, and new components may not be readily available. It may therefore be

6.1 Keep groups of components together in labelled bags or boxes

more practical and economical to obtain a reconditioned head, rather than overhaul the original head.
1 During dismantling, it is essential that each valve is stored together with its collets, retainer, spring, and spring seat. The valves should also be kept in their correct sequence, unless they are so badly worn that they are to be renewed. If they are going to be kept and used again, place each valve assembly in a labelled polythene bag or similar small container **(see illustration)**. Number the bags or containers 1 to 8, or 1 to 8 inlet, and 1 to 8 exhaust, as applicable. Note that No 1 valve is at the timing belt end of the engine.
2 Remove the cylinder head as described in Part A or B of this Chapter (as applicable).
3 Undo the retaining nut and slide the timing belt tensioner off the mounting stud.
4 Undo the bolts and remove the thermostat housing from the left-hand end of the cylinder head. Recover the housing gasket.
5 On SOHC (8-valve) engines, if not already done, remove the camshaft and cam followers as described in Chapter 2A Section 10, and the spark plugs as described in Chapter 1 Section 17.
6 Starting with valve No 1, compress the valve spring using a spring compressor and extract the two split collets from the top of the valve stem **(see illustrations)**. It may be

6.6a Compress the valve springs using a valve spring compressor...

6.6b... and extract the two split collets from the top of the valve stem

6.7a Release the compressor, and remove the spring retainer...

6.7b... and valve spring

necessary to tap the jaw of the compressor, directly over the spring, with a light hammer to free the spring retainer.

7 Release the compressor, and remove the spring retainer and spring (see illustrations).

8 Using pliers, if necessary, extract the valve stem oil seal from the top of the guide, then lift off the spring seat (see illustrations).

9 Withdraw the valve through the combustion chamber, then remove all the remaining valves in the same way.

7 Cylinder head and valves – cleaning and inspection

1 Thorough cleaning of the cylinder head and valve components, followed by a detailed inspection, will enable you to decide how much valve service work must be carried out during the engine overhaul. Note: If the engine has been severely overheated, it is best to assume that the cylinder head is warped – check carefully for signs of this.

Cleaning

2 Scrape away all traces of old gasket material from the cylinder head.

3 Scrape away the carbon from the combustion chambers and ports, then wash the cylinder head thoroughly with paraffin or a suitable solvent.

4 Scrape off any heavy carbon deposits that may have formed on the valves, then use a power-operated wire brush to remove deposits from the valve heads and stems.

Inspection

Note: Be sure to perform all the following inspection procedures before concluding that the services of a machine shop or engine overhaul specialist are required. Make a list of all items that require attention.

Cylinder head

5 Inspect the head very carefully for cracks, evidence of coolant leakage, and other damage. If cracks are found, a new cylinder head should be obtained.

6 Use a straight-edge and feeler blade to check that the cylinder head gasket surface is not distorted. If it is, it may be possible to have it machined, provided that the cylinder head is not reduced to less than the specified height.

7 Examine the valve seats in each of the combustion chambers. If they are severely pitted, cracked, or burned, they will need to be renewed or recut by an engine overhaul specialist. If they are only slightly pitted, this can be removed by grinding-in the valve heads and seats with fine valve-grinding compound, as described later in this Section.

8 Check the valve guides for wear by inserting the relevant valve, and checking for side-to-side motion of the valve. A very small amount of movement is acceptable. If the movement seems excessive, remove the valve. Measure the valve stem diameter (see later in this Section), and renew the valve if it

is worn. If the valve stem is not worn, the wear must be in the valve guide, and the guide must be renewed. The renewal of new valve guides should be entrusted to a Fiat dealer or engine overhaul specialist, who will have the necessary tools available.

9 If renewing the valve guides, the valve seats should be recut or reground only after the guides have been fitted.

10 Examine the camshaft bearing surfaces in the cylinder head and the bearing caps for signs of wear or damage. If the bearings are excessively worn, consult a Fiat dealer, or an engine overhaul specialist for further advice.

Valves

11 Examine the head of each valve for pitting, burning, cracks, and general wear. Check the valve stem for scoring and wear ridges. Rotate the valve, and check for any obvious indication that it is bent. Look for pits or excessive wear on the tip of each valve stem. Renew any valve that shows any such signs of wear or damage.

12 If the valve appears satisfactory at this stage, measure the valve stem diameter at several points using a micrometer. Any significant difference in the readings obtained indicates wear of the valve stem. Should any of these conditions be apparent, the valve(s) must be renewed.

13 If the valves are in satisfactory condition, they should be ground (lapped) into their respective seats, to ensure a smooth, gas-tight seal. If the seat is only lightly pitted, or if it has been recut, fine grinding compound should be used to produce the required finish. Coarse valve-grinding compound should not be used, unless a seat is badly burned or deeply pitted. If this is the case, the cylinder head and valves should be inspected, to decide whether seat recutting, or even the renewal of the valve or seat insert (where possible) is required.

14 Valve grinding is carried out as follows. Place the cylinder head upside-down on a bench.

15 Smear a trace of (the appropriate grade of) valve-grinding compound on the seat face, and press a suction grinding tool onto the valve head (see illustration). With a semi-rotary action, grind the valve head

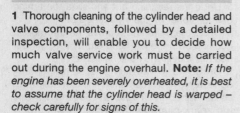

6.8a Extract the valve stem oil seal from the top of the guide...

6.8b... then lift off the spring seat

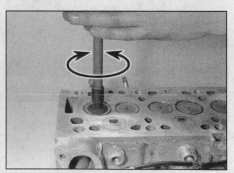

7.15 Grinding-in a valve

to its seat, lifting the valve occasionally to redistribute the grinding compound. A light spring placed under the valve head will greatly ease this operation.

16 If coarse grinding compound is being used, work only until a dull, matt even surface is produced on both the valve seat and the valve, then wipe off the used compound, and repeat the process with fine compound. When a smooth unbroken ring of light grey matt finish is produced on both the valve and seat, the grinding operation is complete. Do not grind-in the valves any further than absolutely necessary, or the seat will be prematurely sunk into the cylinder head.

17 When all the valves have been ground-in, carefully wash off all traces of grinding compound using paraffin or a suitable solvent, before reassembling the cylinder head.

Valve components

18 Examine the valve springs for signs of damage and discoloration. Compare the length of the valve springs with that of a new component, where possible, and if necessary renew the springs.

19 Stand each spring on a flat surface, and check it for squareness. If any of the springs are damaged, distorted or have lost their tension, obtain a complete new set of springs. It is normal to renew the valve springs as a matter of course if a major overhaul is being carried out.

20 Renew the valve stem oil seals regardless of their apparent condition.

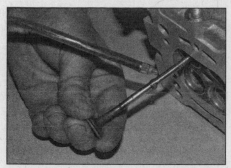

8.1 Lubricate the valve stems, and insert the valves into their original locations

8.3 Use a suitable socket or metal tube to press the valve stem oil seal firmly onto the guide

compressor, then repeat the procedure on the remaining valves.

6 With all the valves installed, support the cylinder head on blocks of wood and, using a hammer and interposed block of wood, tap the end of each valve stem to settle the components.

7 Refit the thermostat housing as described in Chapter 3 Section 4.

8 Located the timing belt tensioner on the mounting stud and refit the retaining nut.

9 On SOHC 8v engines, refit the camshaft and cam followers as described in Chapter 2A Section 10, and the spark plugs as described in Chapter 1 Section 17.

10 Refit the cylinder head as described in Chapter 2A Section 11 or Chapter 2B Section 11 as applicable.

---

8 Cylinder head – reassembly

1 Lubricate the stems of the valves, and insert the valves into their original locations **(see illustration)**. If new valves are being fitted, insert them into the locations to which they have been ground.

2 Refit the spring seat.

3 Working on the first valve, dip the new valve stem seal in fresh engine oil. New seals are normally supplied with protective sleeves, which should be fitted to the tops of the valve stems to prevent the collet grooves from damaging the oil seals. If no sleeves are supplied, wind a little thin tape round the top of the valve stems to protect the seals. Carefully locate the seal over the valve and onto the guide. Take care not to damage the seal as it is passed over the valve stem. Use a suitable socket or tube to press the seal firmly onto the guide **(see illustration)**. Remove the sleeve from the valve stem.

4 Locate the valve spring on top of the seat, then refit the spring cap. On engines where the spring is tapered, make sure that the large diameter end of the spring locates on the seat.

5 Fit the compressor tool, then compress the valve spring and locate the split collets in the recess in the valve stem. Release the

---

9 Piston/connecting rod assembly – removal

1 Remove the sump and cylinder head as described in Chapter 2A or Chapter 2B as applicable.

2 Undo the bolts and remove the oil pump pick-up tube.

3 If there is a pronounced wear ridge at the top of any bore, it may be necessary to remove it with a scraper or ridge reamer, to avoid piston damage during removal. Such a ridge indicates excess bore wear.

4 Check to see if the big-end caps and connecting rods are numbered **(see**

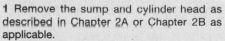

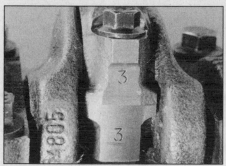

9.4 Connecting rod and big-end cap identification numbers

illustration). If no numbers are visible, use quick-drying paint, or similar, to mark each connecting rod and big-end cap with its respective cylinder number on the flat machined surface provided. Note that No 1 cylinder is at the timing belt end of the engine.

5 Turn the crankshaft to bring pistons 1 and 4 to BDC (bottom dead centre).

6 Unscrew the bolts from No 1 piston big-end bearing cap, and remove the big-end cap and bearing shell **(see illustration)**. If the bearing shells are to be re-used, tape the cap and the shell together.

7 Using a hammer handle, push the piston up through the bore, and remove it from the top of the cylinder block. Recover the bearing shell, and tape it to the connecting rod for safe-keeping.

8 Loosely refit the big-end cap to the connecting rod, and secure with the bolts – this will help to keep the components in their correct order.

9 Remove No. 4 assembly in the same way.

10 Turn the crankshaft 180° to bring pistons 2 and 3 to BDC (bottom dead centre), and remove them in the same way.

---

10 Crankshaft – removal

1 Remove the sump, oil pump/pick-up tube, and flywheel as described in Chapter 2A or Chapter 2B as applicable.

2 Remove the pistons and connecting rods,

9.6 Unscrew the retaining bolts and remove the big-end cap and bearing shell

10.5 Main bearing cap identification markings – SOHC (8-valve) engines

10.7 Thrustwashers located on the centre main bearing shell – SOHC (8-valve) engines

10.10 Remove the lower crankcase from the cylinder block – DOHC (16-valve) engines

as described in Section 9. If no work is to be done on the pistons and connecting rods there is no need to remove the cylinder head, or to push the pistons out of the cylinder bores. The pistons should just be pushed far enough up the bores that they are positioned clear of the crankshaft journals.

3 Unbolt the crankshaft oil seal housing from the cylinder block and recover the gasket, where fitted.

4 Check the crankshaft endfloat as described in Section 13, then proceed as follows.

SOHC 8v engines

5 Note the identification markings on the main bearing caps which should be as follows. One line on the cap nearest the timing belt end, two on the second cap, C on the centre cap, then three and four lines on the remaining caps (see illustration). If no markings are visible, mark them using quick-drying paint.

6 Slacken and remove the main bearing cap retaining bolts, and lift off each bearing cap. Recover the lower bearing shells, and tape them to their respective caps for safe-keeping.

7 Lift the crankshaft from the crankcase and remove the upper bearing shells from the crankcase. Note that the centre main bearing shell incorporates thrustwashers to control crankshaft endfloat (see illustration). If the shells are to be used again, keep them identified for position.

DOHC 16v engines

8 Working in the reverse of the tightening sequence (see illustration 17.16a), progressively slacken and remove the ten outer bolts securing the lower crankcase to the cylinder block.

9 Again, working in the reverse of the tightening sequence, progressively slacken and remove the ten inner (main bearing) bolts.

10 With all the retaining bolts removed, tap around the outer periphery of the lower crankcase using a mallet to break the seal between the lower crankcase and cylinder block. Once the seal is released and the crankcase is clear of the locating dowels, lift it up and off the crankshaft and cylinder block (see illustration). Recover the lower main bearing shells, and tape them to their

respective locations in the lower crankcase. If the two locating dowels are a loose fit, remove them and store them with the lower crankcase.

11 Lift out the crankshaft, recover the upper main bearing shells, and store them along with the relevant lower bearing shells. Note that the centre main bearing shell incorporates thrustwashers to control crankshaft endfloat.

11 Cylinder block/crankcase – cleaning and inspection

Cleaning

1 Remove all external components, brackets and electrical switches/sensors from the block. Note the position of any mounting brackets before removal. For complete cleaning, the core plugs should ideally be removed. Drill a small hole in the plugs, and then insert a self-tapping screw into the hole. Pull out the plugs by pulling on the screw with a pair of grips, or by using a slide hammer.

2 Where applicable, undo the retaining bolts and remove the piston oil jet spray tubes from inside the cylinder block.

3 Remove all traces of gasket/sealant from the cylinder block, and from the lower crankcase on DOHC (16-valve) engines, taking care not to damage the gasket/sealing surfaces.

4 Remove all oil gallery plugs (where fitted). The plugs are usually very tight – they may have to be drilled out, and the holes

11.8 Clean the cylinder block threads using a correct-sized tap

retapped. Use new plugs when the engine is reassembled.

5 If the castings are extremely dirty, they should be steam-cleaned.

6 After the castings have been steam-cleaned, clean all oil holes and oil galleries one more time. Flush all internal passages with warm water until the water runs clear. Dry thoroughly, and apply a light film of oil to all mating surfaces, to prevent rusting. Also oil the cylinder bores. If you have access to compressed air, use it to speed up the drying process, and to blow out all the oil holes and galleries.

 Warning: Wear eye protection when using compressed air.

7 If the castings are not very dirty, you can do an adequate cleaning job with hot (as hot as you can stand!), soapy water and a stiff brush. Take plenty of time, and do a thorough job. Regardless of the cleaning method used, be sure to clean all oil holes and galleries very thoroughly, and to dry all components well. Protect the cylinder bores as described above, to prevent rusting.

8 All threaded holes must be clean, to ensure accurate torque readings during reassembly. To clean the threads, run the correct-size tap into each of the holes to remove rust, corrosion, thread sealant or sludge, and to restore damaged threads (see illustration). If possible, use compressed air to clear the holes of debris produced by this operation.

9 Ensure that all threaded holes in the cylinder block are dry.

10 After coating the mating surfaces of the new core plugs with suitable sealant, fit them to the cylinder block. Make sure that they are driven in straight and seated correctly, or leakage could result.

11 Where applicable, fit the new oil gallery plugs.

12 If the engine is not going to be reassembled right away, cover it with a large plastic bag to keep it clean; protect all mating surfaces and the cylinder bores as described above, to prevent rusting.

Inspection

13 Visually check the castings for cracks and corrosion. Look for stripped threads in the

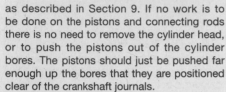

threaded holes. If there has been any history of internal water leakage, it may be worthwhile having an engine reconditioning specialist check the cylinder block with special equipment. If defects are found, have them repaired if possible, or renew the assembly.

14 Check each cylinder bore for scuffing and scoring. Check for signs of a wear ridge at the top of the cylinder, indicating that the bore is excessively worn.

15 Accurate measuring of the cylinder bores requires specialised equipment and experience. We recommend having the bores measured by an engine reconditioning specialist who will also be able to supply appropriate pistons should a rebore be necessary.

16 If the cylinder bores and pistons are in reasonably good condition, and not worn beyond the specified limits, and if the piston-to-bore clearances can be maintained, then it will only be necessary to renew the piston rings. If this is the case, the cylinder bores must be honed to allow the new piston rings to bed-in correctly and provide the best possible seal. An engine reconditioning specialist will carry out this work at moderate cost.

17 If the engine is not going to be reassembled right away, cover it with a large plastic bag to keep it clean and prevent rusting. If the engine is ready for reassembly Apply suitable sealant to the new oil gallery plugs, and insert them into the holes in the block. Tighten the plugs securely

18 Where applicable, refit the piston oil jet spray tubes to the cylinder block, and securely tighten the retaining bolts. Bend over the tabs to lock the bolts.

19 Refit all the external components and electrical switches/sensors removed prior to cleaning.

12 Piston/connecting rod assembly – cleaning and inspection

1 Before the inspection process can begin, the piston/connecting rod assemblies must be cleaned, and the original piston rings removed from the pistons.

Note: *Always use new piston rings when the engine is reassembled.*

2 Carefully expand the old rings over the top of the pistons. The use of two or three old feeler blades will be helpful in preventing the rings dropping into empty grooves. Be careful not to scratch the piston with the ends of the ring. The rings are brittle, and will snap if they are spread too far. They are also very sharp – protect your hands and fingers.

3 Scrape away all traces of carbon from the top of the piston. A hand-held wire brush (or a piece of fine emery cloth) can be used, once the majority of the deposits have been scraped away.

4 Remove the carbon from the ring grooves in the piston, using an old ring. Break the ring

in half to do this (be careful not to cut your fingers – piston rings are sharp). Be careful to remove only the carbon deposits – do not remove any metal, and do not nick or scratch the sides of the ring grooves.

5 Once the deposits have been removed, clean the piston/connecting rod assembly with paraffin or a suitable solvent, and dry thoroughly. Make sure that the oil return holes in the ring grooves are clear.

6 If the pistons and cylinder bores are not damaged or worn excessively, and if the cylinder block does not need to be rebored, the original pistons can be refitted. Normal piston wear shows up as even vertical wear on the piston thrust surfaces, and slight looseness of the top ring in its groove. New piston rings, however, should always be used when the engine is reassembled.

7 Carefully inspect each piston for cracks around the skirt, around the gudgeon pin holes, and at the piston ring lands (between the ring grooves).

8 Look for scoring and scuffing on the piston skirt, holes in the piston crown, and burned areas at the edge of the crown. If the skirt is scored or scuffed, the engine may have been suffering from overheating, and/or abnormal combustion which caused excessively high operating temperatures. The cooling and lubrication systems should be checked thoroughly. Scorch marks on the sides of the pistons show that blow-by has occurred. A hole in the piston crown, or burned areas at the edge of the piston crown, indicates that abnormal combustion has been occurring. If any of the above problems exist, the causes must be investigated and corrected, or the damage will occur again.

9 Corrosion of the piston, in the form of pitting, indicates that coolant has been leaking into the combustion chamber and/or the crankcase. Again, the cause must be corrected, or the problem may persist in the rebuilt engine.

10 Examine each connecting rod carefully for signs of damage, such as cracks around the big-end and small-end bearings. Check that the rod is not bent or distorted. Damage is highly unlikely, unless the engine has been seized or badly overheated. Detailed checking of the connecting rod assembly can only

13.2 Using a dial gauge to check the crankshaft endfloat

be carried out by an engine reconditioning specialist with the necessary equipment.

11 On all engines, the gudgeon pins are an interference fit in the connecting rod small-end bearing. Therefore, piston and/or connecting rod renewal should be entrusted to an engine reconditioning specialist who will have the necessary tooling to remove and install the gudgeon pins.

12 Although not specified by Fiat, it is highly recommended that the big-end cap bolts are renewed as a complete set prior to refitting.

13 Crankshaft – inspection

Checking endfloat

1 If the crankshaft endfloat is to be checked, this must be done when the crankshaft is still installed in the cylinder block/crankcase, but is free to move.

2 Check the endfloat using a dial gauge in contact with the end of the crankshaft. Push the crankshaft fully one way, and then zero the gauge. Push the crankshaft fully the other way, and check the endfloat. The result can be compared with the figures given in the Specifications, and will give an indication as to whether new thrustwashers are required (see illustration).

3 If a dial gauge is not available, feeler blades can be used. First push the crankshaft fully towards the flywheel end of the engine, then use feeler blades to measure the gap between the crankpin web and the main bearing thrustwasher.

Inspection

4 Clean the crankshaft using paraffin or a suitable solvent, and dry it, preferably with compressed air if available. Be sure to clean the oil holes with a pipe cleaner or similar probe, to ensure that they are not obstructed.

5 Check the main and big-end bearing journals for uneven wear, scoring, pitting and cracking.

6 Big-end bearing wear is accompanied by distinct metallic knocking when the engine is running (particularly noticeable when the engine is pulling from low speed) and some loss of oil pressure.

7 Main bearing wear is accompanied by severe engine vibration and rumble – getting progressively worse as engine speed increases – and again by loss of oil pressure.

8 Check the bearing journal for roughness by running a finger lightly over the bearing surface. Any roughness (which will be accompanied by obvious bearing wear) indicates that the crankshaft requires regrinding (where possible) or renewal.

9 If the crankshaft has been reground, check for burrs around the crankshaft oil holes (the holes are usually chamfered, so burrs should not be a problem unless regrinding has been

carried out carelessly). Remove any burrs with a fine file or scraper, and thoroughly clean the oil holes.

10 Have the crankshaft inspected and measured by a Fiat dealer or engine reconditioning specialist. They will be able to advise of any reconditioning work needed, and supply the appropriate replacement bearings etc.

14 Main and big-end bearings – inspection

Inspection

1 Even though the main and big-end bearings should be renewed during the engine overhaul, the old bearings should be retained for close examination, as they may reveal valuable information about the condition of the engine. Main and big-end bearings are available in standard sizes and a range of undersizes to suit reground crankshafts. The engine reconditioner will select the correct bearing shells for a standard or machined crankshaft.

2 Bearing failure can occur due to lack of lubrication, the presence of dirt or other foreign particles, overloading the engine, or corrosion. Regardless of the cause of bearing failure, the cause must be corrected (where applicable) before the engine is reassembled, to prevent it from happening again **(see illustration)**.

3 When examining the bearing shells, remove them from the cylinder block/crankcase, the main bearing caps, the connecting rods and the connecting rod big-end caps. Lay them out on a clean surface in the same general position as their location in the engine. This will enable you to match any bearing problems

FATIGUE FAILURE
CRATERS OR POCKETS

IMPROPER SEATING
BRIGHT (POLISHED) SECTIONS

SCRATCHED BY DIRT
DIRT EMBEDDED INTO BEARING MATERIAL

LACK OF OIL
OVERLAY WIPED OUT

EXCESSIVE WEAR
OVERLAY WIPED OUT

TAPERED JOURNAL
RADIUS RIDE

H 28395

14.2 Typical bearing failures

with the corresponding crankshaft journal. Do not touch any shell's bearing surface with your fingers while checking it.

4 Dirt and other foreign matter gets into the engine in a variety of ways. It may be left in the engine during assembly, or it may pass through filters or the crankcase ventilation system. It may get into the oil, and from there into the bearings. Metal chips from machining operations and normal engine wear are often present. Abrasives are sometimes left in engine components after reconditioning, especially when parts are not thoroughly cleaned using the proper cleaning methods. Whatever the source, these foreign objects often end up embedded in the soft bearing material, and are easily recognised. Large particles will not embed in the bearing, and will score or gouge the bearing and journal. The best prevention for this cause of bearing failure is to clean all parts thoroughly, and keep everything spotlessly-clean during engine assembly. Frequent and regular engine oil and filter changes are also recommended.

5 Lack of lubrication (or lubrication breakdown) has a number of interrelated causes. Excessive heat (which thins the oil), overloading (which squeezes the oil from the bearing face) and oil leakage (from excessive bearing clearances, worn oil pump or high engine speeds) all contribute to lubrication breakdown. Blocked oil passages, which can be the result of misaligned oil holes in a bearing shell, will also oil-starve a bearing, and destroy it. When lack of lubrication is the cause of bearing failure, the bearing material is wiped or extruded from the steel backing of the bearing. Temperatures may increase to the point where the steel backing turns blue from overheating.

6 Driving habits can have a definite effect on bearing life. Full-throttle, low-speed operation (labouring the engine) puts very high loads on bearings, tending to squeeze out the oil film. These loads cause the bearings to flex, which produces fine cracks in the bearing face (fatigue failure). Eventually, the bearing material will loosen in pieces, and tear away from the steel backing.

7 Short-distance driving leads to corrosion of bearings, because insufficient engine heat is produced to drive off the condensed water and corrosive gases. These products collect in the engine oil, forming acid and sludge. As the oil is carried to the engine bearings, the acid attacks and corrodes the bearing material.

8 Incorrect bearing installation during engine assembly will lead to bearing failure as well. Tight-fitting bearings leave insufficient bearing running clearance, and will result in oil starvation. Dirt or foreign particles trapped behind a bearing shell result in high spots on the bearing, which lead to failure.

9 Do not touch any shell's bearing surface with your fingers during reassembly; there is a risk of scratching the delicate surface, or of depositing particles of dirt on it.

10 As mentioned at the beginning of this

Section, the bearing shells should be renewed as a matter of course during engine overhaul; to do otherwise is false economy.

15 Engine overhaul – reassembly sequence

1 Before reassembly begins, ensure that all new parts have been obtained, and that all necessary tools are available. Read through the entire procedure to familiarise yourself with the work involved, and to ensure that all items necessary for reassembly of the engine are at hand. In addition to all normal tools and materials, thread-locking compound will be needed. A suitable tube of sealant will also be required for the joint faces that are fitted without gaskets. It is recommended that Fiat's own products are used, which are specially formulated for this purpose.

2 In order to save time and avoid problems, engine reassembly can be carried out in the following order:

a) *Crankshaft.*
b) *Piston/connecting rod assemblies.*
c) *Oil pump.*
d) *Sump.*
e) *Flywheel.*
f) *Cylinder head.*
g) *Coolant pump.*
h) *Timing belt tensioner, sprockets and timing belt.*
i) *Engine external components.*

3 At this stage, all engine components should be absolutely clean and dry, with all faults repaired. The components should be laid out on a completely clean work surface.

16 Piston rings – refitting

1 Before fitting new piston rings, the ring end gaps must be checked as follows.

2 Lay out the piston/connecting rod assemblies and the new piston ring sets, so that the ring sets will be matched with the same piston and cylinder during the end gap measurement and subsequent engine reassembly.

3 Insert the top ring into the first cylinder, and push it down the bore using the top of the piston. This will ensure that the ring remains square with the cylinder walls. Position the ring near the bottom of the cylinder bore, at the lower limit of ring travel. Note that the top and second compression rings are different. The second ring is easily identified by the step on its lower surface, and by the fact that its outer face is tapered.

4 Measure the end gap using feeler blades.

5 Repeat the procedure with the ring at the top of the cylinder bore, at the upper limit of its travel and compare the measurements with the figures given in the Specifications.

6 If the gap is too small (unlikely if reputable parts are used), it must be enlarged, or the ring ends may contact each other during engine operation, causing serious damage. Ideally, new piston rings providing the correct end gap should be fitted. As a last resort, the end gap can be increased by filing the ring ends very carefully with a fine file. Mount the file in a vice equipped with soft jaws, slip the ring over the file with the ends contacting the file face, and slowly move the ring to remove material from the ends. Take care, as piston rings are sharp, and are easily broken.

7 With new piston rings, it is unlikely that the end gap will be too large. If the gaps are too large, check that you have the correct rings for the engine and for the cylinder bore size.

8 Repeat the checking procedure for each ring in the first cylinder, and then for the rings in the remaining cylinders. Remember to keep rings, pistons and cylinders matched up.

9 Once the ring end gaps have been checked and if necessary corrected, the rings can be fitted to the pistons.

Note: *Always follow any instructions supplied with the new piston ring sets – different manufacturers may specify different procedures. Do not mix up the top and second compression rings, as they have different cross-sections.*

10 Fit the piston rings using the same technique as for removal. Fit the bottom (oil control) ring first, and work up. Ensure that the second compression ring is fitted the correct way up, with its identification mark (either a dot of paint or the word TOP stamped on the ring surface) at the top.

11 Position the rings so that the end gaps are 180° apart and are offset from the gudgeon pin centreline.

17 Crankshaft – bearing selection and refitting

Bearing selection

1 Main bearings for the engines described in this Chapter are available in standard sizes and a range of undersizes to suit reground crankshafts. Refer to your Fiat dealer or engine reconditioning specialist for details.

Refitting

2 Clean the backs of the bearing shells, and the bearing locations in both the cylinder block and the main bearing caps or lower crankcase.

3 Press the bearing shells into their locations, ensuring that the tab on each shell engages in the notch in the cylinder block or bearing cap/lower crankcase. Note that the bearing shell incorporating the thrustwashers is fitted to the centre main bearing shell location in the cylinder block. Take care not to touch any shell's bearing surface with your fingers.

4 Wipe dry the shells with a lint-free cloth,

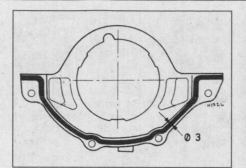

17.11 Application area for sealant on the crankshaft oil seal housing

then liberally lubricate each bearing shell in the cylinder block with clean engine oil.

5 Lower the crankshaft into position so that Nos 2 and 3 cylinder crankpins are at TDC; Nos 1 and 4 cylinder crankpins will be at BDC, ready for fitting No 1 piston. Proceed as follows according to engine type.

SOHC 8v engines

6 Lubricate the lower bearing shells in the main bearing caps with clean engine oil.

7 Fit the main bearing caps to their correct locations, ensuring that they are fitted the correct way round (the bearing shell tab recesses in the block and caps must be on the same side). Insert the bolts loosely.

8 Tighten the main bearing cap bolts to the specified Stage 1 torque wrench setting. Once all the bolts have been tightened to the Stage 1 setting, angle-tighten the bolts through the specified Stage 2 angle, using a socket and extension bar. It is recommended that an angle-measuring gauge is used during this stage of the tightening, to ensure accuracy.

9 Check that the crankshaft rotates freely.

10 Prise out the crankshaft oil seal and fit a new seal to the housing (Chapter 2A Section 9).

11 Lubricate the oil seal lips then carefully locate the oil seal housing into position, using a new gasket. If the oil seal housing was originally fitted without a gasket, apply

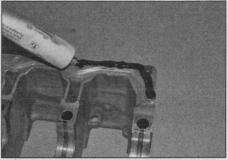

17.13 Apply a 2.0 mm bead of sealant to the lower crankcase mating surface

a 3.0 mm bead of RTV silicone sealant to the housing flange **(see illustration)**. Refit the retaining bolts and tighten them securely.

12 Continue with engine reassembly in the sequence given in Section 15.

DOHC 16v engines

13 Thoroughly degrease the mating surfaces of the cylinder block and the lower crankcase. Apply a 2.0 mm bead of RTV silicone sealant to the lower crankcase mating surface **(see illustration)**.

14 Lubricate the lower bearing shells with clean engine oil, then refit the lower crankcase, ensuring that the shells are not displaced, and that the locating dowels engage correctly.

15 Install the ten inner (main bearing) bolts, and the ten outer bolts securing the lower crankcase to the cylinder block. Screw all the bolts in until they are just making contact with the lower crankcase.

16 Working in sequence, tighten the ten inner (main bearing) bolts to the Stage 1 torque setting given in the Specifications. Once all the ten inner bolts have been tightened to the Stage 1 setting, angle-tighten the bolts through the specified Stage 2 angle, using a socket and extension bar. It is recommended that an angle-measuring gauge is used during this stage of the tightening, to ensure accuracy **(see illustrations)**.

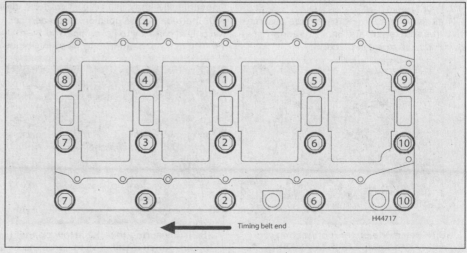

17.16a Lower crankcase retaining bolt tightening sequence

17.16b Tighten the 10 inner lower crankcase bolts to the Stage 1 torque setting using torque wrench...

17.16c... then through the Stage 2 angle using an angle-measuring gauge

17 Working in the same sequence as for the inner (main bearing) bolts, tighten the ten outer bolts to the specified torque.

18 With the lower crankcase in place, check that the crankshaft rotates freely.

19 Fit a new left-hand crankshaft oil seal as described in Chapter 2B Section 8.

20 Continue with engine reassembly in the sequence given in Section 15.

18 Piston/connecting rod assembly – bearing selection and refitting

Bearing selection

1 Big-end bearings for the engines described in this Chapter are available in standard sizes and a range of undersizes to suit reground crankshafts. Refer to your Fiat dealer or engine reconditioning specialist for details.

Refitting

2 Clean the backs of the bearing shells, and the bearing locations in both the connecting rods and bearing caps.

3 Press the bearing shells into their locations, ensuring that the tab on each shell engages in the notch in the connecting rod and cap. Take care not to touch any shell's bearing surface with your fingers.

4 Note that the following procedure assumes that the crankshaft and main bearing caps/lower crankcase are in place.

5 Lubricate the cylinder bores, the pistons, and piston rings, then lay out each piston/connecting rod assembly in its respective position.

6 Start with assembly No 1. Position the piston ring gaps as described in Section 16, then clamp them in position with a piston ring compressor.

7 Insert the piston/connecting rod assembly into the top of cylinder No 1, ensuring that the arrow on the piston crown is pointing towards the timing belt end of the engine (see illustrations).

8 Using a block of wood or hammer handle against the piston crown, tap the assembly into the cylinder until the piston crown is flush with the top of the cylinder (see illustration).

9 Ensure that the bearing shell is still correctly installed. Liberally lubricate the crankpin and both bearing shells. Taking care not to mark the cylinder bores, tap the piston/connecting rod assembly down the bore and onto the crankpin.

10 Refit the big-end bearing cap, tightening its retaining bolts finger-tight at first. Note that the faces with the identification marks must match (which means that the bearing shell locating tabs abut each other). On DOHC 16v engines, the connecting rod caps are 'fractured' from the rods during production. Consequently, they will only align correctly with the rods in one position, and each cap will only fit correctly to its' original rod.

11 Tighten the bearing cap retaining bolts

evenly and progressively to the Stage 1 torque setting, then angle-tighten them to the specified Stage 2 angle using an angle-measuring gauge.

12 Once the bearing cap retaining bolts have been correctly tightened, rotate the crankshaft. Check that it turns freely; some stiffness is to be expected if new components have been fitted, but there should be no signs of binding or tight spots.

13 Refit the remaining piston/connecting rod assemblies in the same way.

14 Continue with the engine reassembly in the sequence given in Section 15.

19 Engine – initial start-up after overhaul

1 With the engine refitted in the car, double-check the engine oil and coolant levels. Make a final check that everything has been reconnected, and that there are no tools or rags left in the engine compartment.

2 Start the engine, noting that this may take a little longer than usual, due to the fuel system components having been disturbed. Make sure that the oil pressure warning light goes out then allow the engine to idle.

3 While the engine is idling, check for fuel, water and oil leaks. Don't be alarmed if there are some odd smells and smoke from parts getting hot and burning off oil deposits.

4 Assuming all is well, keep the engine idling until hot water is felt circulating through the top hose, then switch off the engine.

5 After a few minutes, recheck the oil and coolant levels as described in 'Weekly checks', and top-up as necessary.

6 Note that there is no need to retighten the cylinder head bolts once the engine has first run after reassembly.

7 If new pistons, rings or crankshaft bearings have been fitted, the engine must be treated as new, and run-in for the first 500 miles (800 km). Do not operate the engine at full-throttle, or allow it to labour at low engine speeds in any gear. It is recommended that the oil and filter be changed at the end of this period.

18.7a Insert the piston/connecting rod assembly into the top of the cylinder No 1...

18.7b... ensuring that the arrow on the piston crown is pointing towards the timing belt end of the engine

18.8 Tap the assembly into the cylinder using block of wood or hammer handle

Chapter 3
Cooling, heating and ventilation systems

Contents

Section number

Air conditioning system – general information and
  precautions. 9
Air conditioning system components – removal and refitting 10
Coolant pump -removal, inspection and refitting. 7
Cooling system hoses – disconnection and renewal 2
Electric cooling fan assembly – testing, removal and refitting 5

Section number

Engine coolant temperature sensor (ECT) –
  testing, removal and refitting 6
General information and precautions. 1
Heating and ventilation system components – removal and refitting 8
Radiator – removal, inspection and refitting. 3
Thermostat – removal, testing and refitting 4

Degrees of difficulty

Easy, suitable for novice with little experience 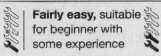	**Fairly easy,** suitable for beginner with some experience	**Fairly difficult,** suitable for competent DIY mechanic	**Difficult,** suitable for experienced DIY mechanic	**Very difficult,** suitable for expert DIY or professional

Specifications

System
Type . . . . Pressurised, pump-assisted with front mounted radiator and ECM controlled cooling fan

Thermostat
Type . . . . Wax

Operating temperatures

	Starts to open	Fully open
All engines	85 to 89° C	100° C

Expansion tank
Cap pressure . . . . 0.98 bar

Air conditioning system
Refrigerant R134a
Refrigerant charge quantity . . . . 500 ± 40g
Lubricating oil. . . . . ND 8

Torque wrench settings

	Nm	lbf ft
Compressor mounting bolts.	25	17
Coolant pump.	10	7
Engine coolant temperature sensor	18	13
Facia crossmember to vehicle body	20	15
Pressure sensor	8	5
Thermostat housing bolts.	10	7

1 General information and precautions

General information

1 The engine cooling system is of pressurised type, comprising of a coolant pump driven by the timing belt, a crossflow radiator, a coolant expansion tank, an electric cooling fan, a thermostat, heater matrix, and all associated hoses and switches.

2 The system functions as follows: the coolant pump circulates cold water around the cylinder block and head passages, and through the intake manifold, heater matrix and throttle body to the thermostat housing.

3 When the engine is cold, the thermostat remains closed and prevents coolant from circulating through the radiator. When the coolant reaches a predetermined temperature, the thermostat opens, and the coolant passed through the top hose to the radiator. As the coolant circulates through the radiator, it is cooled by the in-rush of air when the car is in forward motion. the airflow is supplemented by the action of the electric cooling fan, when necessary.

4 When the engine is at normal operating temperature, the coolant expands, and some if it is displaced in to the expansion tank. Coolant collects in the tank, and is returned to the radiator when the system cools.

5 The three-speed electric cooling fan is mounted at the rear of the radiator and controlled by the engine management electronic control unit, in conjunction with the engine coolant temperature sensor.

Precautions

⚠️ **Warning: Do not attempt to remove the pressure cap, or disturb any part of the cooling system, while the engine is hot, as there is a high risk of scalding. If the pressure cap must be removed before the engine and radiator have fully cooled (even though this is not recommended), the pressure in the cooling system must first be relieved. Cover the cap with a thick layer of cloth, to avoid scalding, and slowly unscrew the pressure cap until a hissing sound is heard (be prepared to refit the cap quickly if bubbling noises are heard and hot coolant starts to come out). When the hissing stops, indicating that the pressure has reduced, slowly unscrew the pressure cap until it can be removed; if more hissing sounds are heard, wait until they have stopped before unscrewing the cap completely. At all times, keep your face well away from the pressure cap opening, and protect your hands.**

⚠️ **Warning: Do not allow antifreeze to come into contact with your skin, or with the painted surfaces of the vehicle. Rinse off spills immediately with plenty of water. Never leave antifreeze lying around in an open container, or in a puddle in the driveway or on the garage floor. Children and pets are attracted by its sweet smell, but antifreeze can be fatal if ingested.**

⚠️ **Warning: The cooling fan could cut in even if the engine is not running (if the ignition is on). Be careful to keep your hands, hair, and any loose clothing well clear when working in the engine compartments.**

2 Cooling system hoses – disconnection and renewal

⚠️ **Warning: Never work on the cooling system when it is hot. Release any pressure from the system by loosening the expansion tank cap, having first covered it with a cloth to avoid any possibility of scalding.**

1 The number, routing and pattern of hoses will vary according to model, but the same basic procedure applies. Before commencing work, make sure that the new hoses are to hand, along with new hose clips if needed. It is good practice to renew the hose clips at the same time as the hoses.

2 Drain the cooling system as described in Chapter 1 Section 29, saving the coolant if it is fit for re-use. Squirt a little penetrating oil onto the hose clips if they are corroded.

3 Release the hose clips from the hose concerned. Three types of clip are used; worm-drive, spring, and crimped. The worm-drive clip is released by turning its screw anti-clockwise. The spring clip is released by squeezing its tags together with pliers, at the same time working the clip away from the hose stub. The crimped clips are not re-usable, and are best cut off with snips or side-cutters.

4 Unclip any wires, cables or other hoses, which may be attached to the hose being removed. Make notes for reference when reassembling, if necessary.

5 Release the hose from its stubs with a twisting motion. Be careful not to damage the stubs on delicate components such as the radiator, or thermostat housings. If the hose is stuck fast, the best course is often to cut it off using a sharp knife, but again be careful not to damage the stubs.

6 Before fitting the new hose, smear the stubs with washing-up liquid or a suitable rubber lubricant to aid fitting. Do not use oil or grease, which may attack the rubber.

7 Fit the hose clips over the ends of the hose, and then fit the hose over its stubs. Work the hose into position. When satisfied, locate and tighten the hose clips.

8 Refill the cooling system as described in Chapter 1 Section 29. Run the engine, and check that there are no leaks.

9 Recheck the tightness of the hose clips on any new hoses after a few hundred miles.

10 Top-up the coolant level if necessary, as described in 'Weekly checks'.

3 Radiator – removal, inspection and refitting

Note: *If leakage is the reason for removing the radiator, bear in mind that minor leaks can often be cured using proprietary radiator sealing compound, with the radiator in situ.*

Removal

1 Raise the front of the vehicle and support it securely on axle stands, as described in 'Vehicle jacking and support'.

2 Undo the fasteners and remove the engine undershield (where fitted).

3 Disconnect the battery negative lead as described in Chapter 5A Section 4.

4 Remove both headlights as described in Chapter 12 Section 8.

5 Remove the front bumper as described in Chapter 11 Section 6.

6 Undo the retaining bolt and move the horn to one side **(see illustration)**. Release the wiring harness from the front wing crossmember.

7 Undo the retaining bolts and manoeuvre the front wing crossmember from place **(see illustration)**.

8 With reference to Chapter 1 Section 29, drain the cooling system.

3.6 Horn retaining bolt

3.7 Undo the bolts and remove the front wing crossmember – left-hand bolts arrowed

9 Undo the bolts and move the coolant expansion tank to one side **(see illustration)**.
10 Disconnect the electric cooling fan wiring plug.
11 Slacken the clamps, then disconnect the upper and lower coolant hoses from the radiator **(see illustrations)**.
12 Undo the 2 retaining bolts (Ribe size 7) at the upper edge, and manoeuvre the radiator, complete with cooling fan/shroud, from place **(see illustration)**.
13 If required, release the catches and detach the cooling fan shroud from the radiator **(see illustration 5.9)**.

Inspection

14 If the radiator was removed because of clogging (causing overheating) then try reverse flushing using a garden hose or, in severe cases, use a radiator cleanser strictly in accordance with the manufacturer's instructions.
15 If necessary, a radiator specialist can perform a flow test on the radiator, to establish whether an internal blockage exists.
16 A leaking radiator must be referred to a specialist for permanent repair. Do not attempt to weld or solder a leaking radiator, as damage to the plastic components may result.
17 Inspect the radiator rubber mounting grommets, and renew them if necessary.

Refitting

18 Refitting is a reversal of removal, bearing in mind the following points:
a) *Ensure the radiator lower lugs engage correctly with the lower mounting grommets.*
b) *On completion, refill the cooling system as described in Chapter 1 Section 29.*

---

4 Thermostat
removal, testing and refitting

Note: *The thermostat housing is bolted to the left-hand end of the cylinder head. The thermostat itself cannot be separated from the housing and can only be renewed as part of a complete assembly.*

3.9 Coolant tank retaining bolts

3.11b... and upper coolant hose

3.11a Slacken the clamp and disconnect the lower coolant hose...

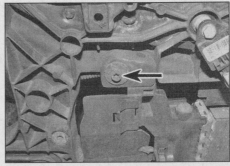

3.12 Remove the bolt at the upper corners of the radiator

Removal

1 Drain the cooling system as described in Chapter 1 Section 29.
2 Disconnect the battery negative lead as described in Chapter 5A Section 4.
3 Disconnect the hoses from the thermostat housing **(see illustration)**.
4 Disconnect the wiring plug from the engine coolant temperature sensor.
5 Undo the retaining bolts and remove the thermostat housing **(see illustrations)**. Renew the housing gasket.

Testing

6 A rough test of the thermostat may be made by suspending it with a piece of string in a container full of water. Heat the water to bring it to the boil and observe the movement of the valve shaft through the inlet port.
7 The thermostat valve must be fully open

by the time the water boils. If not, renew the complete thermostat/housing assembly.
8 If a thermometer is available, the precise opening temperature of the thermostat may be determined; compare with the figures given in the Specifications. The opening temperature is also marked on the thermostat housing.
9 Note that a thermostat which fails to close completely as the water cools must also be renewed.

Refitting

10 Ensure that the cylinder head and thermostat housing mating surfaces are completely clean and free from all traces of the old gasket material.
11 Lay a new gasket in position on the cylinder head, then fit the thermostat housing and insert retaining bolts. Tighten the bolts to the specified torque.

4.3 Disconnect the thermostat housing hoses

4.5a Undo the thermostat housing bolts

4.5b The thermostat is integral with the housing

12 Reconnect the coolant hoses to the thermostat housing, and secure them with the clamps where applicable.
13 Reconnect the engine coolant temperature sensor wiring plug.
14 Reconnect the battery negative lead as described in Chapter 5A Section 4.
15 Refill the cooling system as described in Chapter 1 Section 29.

5 Electric cooling fan assembly – testing, removal and refitting

Testing

1 Detailed fault diagnosis should be carried out by a Fiat dealer or suitably equipped repairer using dedicated test equipment, but basic diagnosis can be carried out as follows.
2 If the fan does not appear to work, run the engine until normal operating temperature is reached, then allow it to idle. The fan should cut in within a few minutes (before the warning light illuminates, or the temperature gauge needle enters the red section). If not, switch off the engine and disconnect the cooling fan motor wiring connector.
3 The motor can be tested by disconnecting it from the wiring loom, and connecting a 12 volt supply directly to it. The motor should operate – if not, the motor, or the motor wiring, is faulty.
4 If the motor operates when tested as described, the fault is likely to be in one of the cooling fan relays, the relay fuse, or the engine wiring harness. If these components are satisfactory any further fault diagnosis should be referred to a suitably-equipped Fiat dealer or repairer – do not attempt to test the engine management electronic control unit.

Removal

5 Disconnect the battery negative lead as described in Chapter 5A Section 4.
6 Undo the retaining bolts and move the coolant expansion tank to one side (see illustration 3.9).
7 Disconnect the electric cooling fan wiring plug (see illustration).
8 Where applicable, disconnect the wiring plug from the fan motor resistor.
9 Release the catches, and manoeuvre the

5.7 Slide out the yellow locking tab, press the clip and disconnect the wiring plug

coolant fan/shroud assembly from place (see illustration).

Refitting

10 Refitting is a reversal of removal.

6 Engine coolant temperature sensor (ECT) – testing, removal and refitting

Testing

1 The engine coolant temperature sensor is fitted into the thermostat housing at the left-hand end of the cylinder head (see illustration).
2 The unit contains a thermistor – an electronic component whose electrical resistance decreases at a predetermined rate as its temperature rises.
3 The engine management ECU supplies the sensor with a set voltage and then, by measuring the current flowing in the sensor circuit, it determines the engine temperature. This information is then used, in conjunction with other inputs, to control the engine management system and associated components. The sensor signal is also used to operate the temperature gauge and/or warning light on the instrument panel.
4 If the sensor circuit should fail to provide plausible information, the ECU back-up facility will override the sensor signal. In this event, the ECU assumes a predetermined setting which will allow the engine management system to operate, albeit at

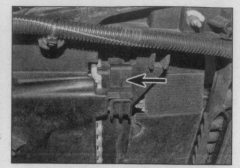

5.9 Push-in the catch each side and remove the cooling fan shroud

reduced efficiency. When this occurs, the engine warning light on the instrument panel will illuminate, and the advice of a Fiat dealer or repairer should be sought. The sensor itself can be tested by removing it, and checking the resistances at various temperatures using an ohmmeter (heat the sensor in a container of water, and monitor the temperature with a thermometer). The resistance values are given in the Specifications.

Removal

5 Disconnect the battery negative lead as described in Chapter 5A Section 4.
6 Disconnect the wiring plug from the coolant temperature sensor, located on the thermostat housing at the left-hand end of the cylinder head.
7 Partially drain the cooling system to just below the level of the sensor (see Chapter 1, Section 29). Alternatively, have ready a suitable bung to plug the aperture in the housing when the sensor is removed.
8 Carefully unscrew the sensor and recover the sealing ring. If the system has not been drained, plug the sensor aperture to prevent further coolant loss.

Refitting

9 Check the condition of the sealing ring and renew it if necessary.
10 Refitting is a reversal of removal, tightening the sensor to the specified torque. Refill (or top-up) the cooling system as described in Chapter or 'Weekly checks'.
11 On completion, start the engine and run it until it reaches normal operating temperature. Continue to run the engine until the cooling fan cuts in and out correctly.

7 Coolant pump – removal, inspection and refitting

Removal

1 Drain the cooling system as described in Chapter 1 Section 29.
2 Remove the timing belt as described in Chapter 2A Section 5 or Chapter 2B Section 5.
3 Unscrew the retaining bolts and withdraw the coolant pump (see illustration). If the

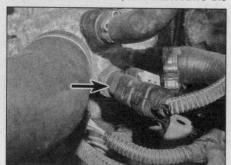

6.1 Engine coolant temperature sensor

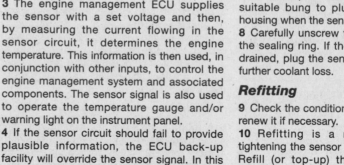

7.3 Coolant pump retaining nut (A) and bolts (B)

7.6 Apply a continuous bead of sealant to the coolant pump mating face

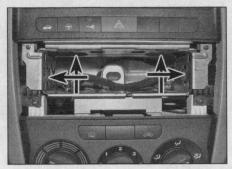

8.2 Audio unit support frame screws

8.4 Prise down the cover beneath the heater control panel

pump is stuck, tap it gently using a soft-faced mallet – do not lever between the pump and cylinder block mating faces.

Inspection

4 Check the pump body and impeller for signs of excessive corrosion or evidence of coolant leakage. Turn the impeller, and check for stiffness due to corrosion, or roughness due to excessive end play. If any of these conditions are apparent, the pump must be renewed as a complete assembly.

Refitting

5 Commence refitting by thoroughly cleaning all traces of sealant from the mating faces of the pump and cylinder block.
6 Apply a continuous bead of RTV sealant to the cylinder block mating face of the pump, taking care not to apply excessive

sealant, which may enter the pump itself (see illustration).
7 Place the pump in position in the cylinder block, then refit and tighten the bolts to the specified torque.
8 The remainder of refitting is a reversal of removal.

8 Heating and ventilation system components – removal and refitting

Heater control panel

Removal

1 Remove the facia-mounted audio unit as described in Chapter 12 Section 16.
2 On models upto 2012 model year, undo retaining screws, and pull the audio unit

casing or support frame (as applicable) from the facia (see illustration).
3 On Punto Evo/Punto (2012 model year-on) models, remove the facia panel centre frame as described in Chapter 11 Section 25.
4 Carefully prise the cover under the control panel from the facia (see illustration). Take care not to mark the facia.

Manual heater/air conditioning

5 Undo the control unit retaining screws (2 below, and 2 above), and pull it away from the facia a little (see illustrations).
6 Disconnect the wiring plugs from the control panel.
7 Note the fitted positions, then undo the control cables outer fixing clamp bolts, and detach the inner fitting from the control panel levers.
8 Pull the illumination bulb holders from the control panel, and unclip the wiring harness.
9 If required, the bulbs can be removed by pulling them from the bulbholders.

Automatic air conditioning/climate control

10 Undo the 2 retaining screws under the control panel, and the 2 screws above, then manoeuvre the panel rearwards from the facia, and disconnect the wiring plugs as they become accessible (see illustrations).

Refitting

11 Refitting is a reversal of removal.
12 Check that the operating levers on the heater assembly move through their full range

8.5a Remove the screws above...

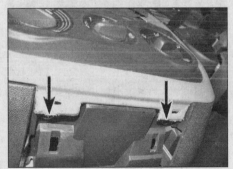

8.5b... and below the control panel

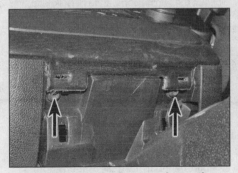

8.10a Remove the 2 screws beneath...

8.10b... and the 2 screws above...

8.10c... then manoeuvre the panel rearwards

8.13 Remove the footwell air duct

8.14 Heater blower motor wiring plug

8.15 Variator retaining screws

of travel when moving the respective knobs on the control unit. If necessary, reposition the outer cables in their clips or clamps as required.

Heater blower motor

Removal

13 Working under the passengers side of the facia, undo the retaining screw and remove the footwell air duct **(see illustration)**.
14 Disconnect the blower motor wiring plug **(see illustration)**.
15 On models with automatic climate control, disconnect the wiring plug, undo the 2 retaining screws and remove the fan 'variator' **(see illustration)**.
16 Undo the retaining screws, and remove the blower motor.

Refitting

17 Refitting is a reversal of removal.

Heater blower motor resistor

Removal

Models with manual heater/air conditioning

18 Remove the blower motor as described previously in this Section.
19 Disconnect the wiring plug, undo the retaining screw and withdraw the resistor from the casing.

Models with automatic air conditioning/climate control

20 Working under the drivers side of the facia, undo the retaining screw, and remove the footwell air duct.

21 Disconnect the wiring plugs, undo the 2 retaining screws and withdraw the resistor/variator from the blower motor casing **(see illustration 8.15)**.

Refitting

22 Refitting is a reversal of removal.

Heater matrix

Removal

23 Drain the cooling system as described in Chapter 1 Section 29, or apply clamps to the hoses where they connect with the heater matrix pipes at the engine compartment bulkhead.
24 Pull out the rear edge, then slide the front side section of the passengers side centre console rearwards.
25 Working underneath the facia, release the clamps and disconnect the coolant pipes from the matrix **(see illustration)**. Renew the pipe seals.
26 Slide the heater matrix from the housing **(see illustration)**.

Refitting

27 Refitting is a reversal of removal.

Heater housing

Removal

28 On models with air conditioning, have the refrigerant circuit evacuated by a Fiat dealer or suitably equipped repairer.
29 Drain the cooling system as described in Chapter 1 Section 29, or apply clamps to the hoses where they connect with the heater matrix pipes at the engine compartment bulkhead.
30 On models with air conditioning, undo the retaining bolt and disconnect the refrigerant pipes at the engine compartment bulkhead **(see illustration)**. Plug the openings to prevent contamination. Renew the pipes seals.
31 Remove the centre console as described in Chapter 11 Section 24.
32 Remove the complete facia as described in Chapter 11 Section 25.
33 Release the clamps and disconnect the heater coolant pipes at the engine compartment bulkhead **(see illustration)**.
34 Remove the passengers side airbag as described in Chapter 12 Section 20.

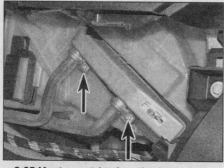

8.25 Heater matrix pipe clamps screws

8.26 Slide the matrix from place

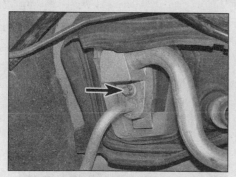

8.30 Undo the bolt and detach the refrigerant pipes

8.33 Prise out the wire clip a little, and pull the heater hoses from the bulkhead connections

8.36 Footwell air duct retaining screw

8.37 Unclip the diagnostic socket from the drivers end of the facia

35 Remove both front doors as described in Chapter 11 Section 14.

36 Undo the retaining screws and remove the footwell air duct each side **(see illustration)**.

37 Unclip the diagnostic socket **(see illustration)**.

38 Disconnect the wiring plugs from the rear of the body computer **(see illustration)**.

39 Undo the 2 retaining bolts, open the wiring multistrip, pull the body computer rearwards a little and disconnect the front wiring plugs.

40 Disconnect the wiring plug, release the clips and remove the transponder around the ignition switch **(see illustration)**.

41 Remove the steering column as described in Chapter 10 Section 13.

42 Undo the retaining bolts/nuts and remove the support bracket each side of the facia crossmember centre section **(see illustration)**.

43 Undo the bolts securing the facia crossmember to the heater casing.

44 Unclip the rear heater ducts **(see illustration)**.

45 Unclip any wiring harnesses attached to the facia crossmember, then undo the 2 bolts at each end, and with the help of an assistant, manoeuvre the facia crossmember from place.

46 Note their fitted positions, disconnect the wiring plugs from the heater casing.

47 On models with air conditioning, disconnect the drain hose from the base of the heater/air conditioning housing **(see illustration)**.

48 With the help of an assistant, manoeuvre the heater casing from the cabin. Be prepared for fluid spillage.

Refitting

49 Check the condition of the seals between the heater/air conditioning housing and the vehicle body. Renew where necessary.

50 Refitting is a reversal of removal, noting the following points:

a) *Tighten all fasteners to their specified torque where given.*

b) *Top up the cooling system as described in Chapter 1 Section 29.*

c) *Have the air conditioning refrigerant circuit recharged by a Fiat dealer or suitably equipped specialist.*

9 Air conditioning system – general information and precautions

1 An air conditioning system is fitted as standard equipment on high-specification models, and was available as an optional extra

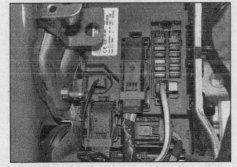

8.38 Disconnect the body computer wiring plugs

8.40 Unclip the transponder from the ignition switch

8.42 Remove the support bracket each side

8.44 Unclip the rear heater ducts

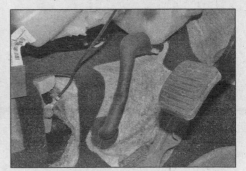

8.47 Disconnect the drain hose from the base of the housing

on lower-specification models. In conjunction with the heater, the system enables any reasonable air temperature to be achieved inside the car, it also reduces the humidity of the incoming air, aiding demisting even when cooling is not required.

2 The refrigeration circuit of the air conditioning system functions in a similar way to a domestic refrigerator. A compressor, belt-driven from the crankshaft pulley, draws refrigerant in its gaseous state from an evaporator. The refrigerant heats up as a result of being compressed, but is then passed through a condenser (mounted in front of the engine radiator) where it loses heat and enters its liquid state. After dehydration, the refrigerant is passed through an evaporator (mounted alongside the heater/ventilation unit) where it is allowed to expand and reverts to being gas. This change of state has the effect of absorbing heat from the air passing over the evaporator fins, reducing its temperature. This cool air is mixed with warm air from the heater unit to achieve the desired cabin temperature. The refrigerant is directed back to the compressor and the cycle is then repeated.

3 Various subsidiary controls and sensors protect the system against excessive temperature and pressures. Additionally, engine idle speed is increased when the system is in use to compensate for the additional load imposed by the compressor. Electronic sensors detect the rotational speed differential between the engine and the compressor – if this becomes too great (due to a malfunctioning compressor), the compressor clutch is disengaged, to preserve the drivebelt.

4 The air conditioning refrigerant service ports are located in the right-hand corner of the engine compartment **(see illustration)**.

Note: *The air conditioning electronic control system can only be tested using dedicated equipment. For this reason, it is recommended that problems with the operation of the air conditioning system are referred to a Fiat dealer or suitably equipped repairer for diagnosis.*

⚠ *Warning: The refrigeration circuit contains pressurised liquid refrigerant. The refrigerant is*

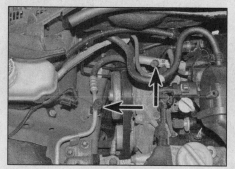

9.4 Air conditioning refrigerant circuit service ports

potentially dangerous, and should only be handled by qualified persons. Refrigerant that is allowed to come into contact with the skin will cause severe frostbite. It is not itself poisonous, but in the presence of a naked flame (including inhalation through a lighted cigarette), it forms a poisonous gas. Uncontrolled discharging of the refrigerant is dangerous and is also extremely damaging to the environment. For these reasons, disconnection of any part of the system without specialised knowledge and equipment is not recommended.
Caution: Do not allow refrigerant lines to be exposed to temperatures in excess of 110°C, for example during welding or paint-drying operations.
Caution: Do not operate the air conditioning system if it is known to be short of refrigerant, or component damage may result.

10 Air conditioning system components – removal and refitting

⚠ *Warning: Refer to the previous Section before proceeding. Before carrying out any of the procedures detailed below, the air conditioning system MUST be professionally discharged by a garage or air conditioning specialist.*
Note: *The car may be driven once the system has been discharged, but the air conditioning system should NOT be switched on, as this will cause damage to the compressor. The safest option is to have the system discharged where the car is to be worked on, and not move the car until the system has been recharged. With air conditioning becoming an increasingly common fitment, mobile air conditioning specialists are becoming more widespread.*

Evaporator

Removal

1 Remove the heater housing as described in Section 8.
2 Disconnect the wiring plug, undo the

retaining bolt, then release the clip and rotate the air intake assembly clockwise and detach it from the heater housing.
3 Undo the clamp bracket bolt, release the retainer and remove the coolant pipes from the heater housing.
4 Undo the 2 retaining bolts, release the clips around the circumference, and remove the cover from the heater housing. Note that the evaporator is integral with the cover.
5 If required, undo the 2 bolts and detach the expansion valve from the refrigerant pipes. Renew the O-ring seals.

Refitting

6 Refitting is a reversal of removal, noting the following points:
a) *Renew the refrigerant circuit O-ring seals.*
b) *Apply a little refrigerant oil to the seals prior to reassembly.*
c) *Have the refrigerant circuit recharged and leak tested by a Fiat dealer or suitably equipped specialist.*

Receiver/drier

Note: *On models to emissions level EURO 5, the receiver/drier is integral with the condenser and cannot be renewed separately.*

Removal

7 Have the air conditioning refrigerant circuit evacuated by a Fiat dealer or suitably equipped repairer.
8 Remove the front bumper as described in Chapter 11 Section 6.
9 Undo the fasteners and remove the engine undershield where fitted.
10 Release the condenser lower, left-hand side retaining clip.
11 Remove the circlip, then screw-in a M5 bolt and pull the receiver/drier from the condenser **(see illustration)**. Plug the openings to prevent contamination.

Refitting

12 Refitting is a reversal of removal.

Condenser

Removal

13 Have the air conditioning refrigerant circuit evacuated by a Fiat dealer or suitably equipped repairer.
14 Raise the front of the vehicle and support it securely on axle stands as described in *'Vehicle jacking and support'*.
15 Remove the front bumper as described in Chapter 11 Section 6.
16 Undo the fasteners and remove the engine undershield.
17 Undo the bolt and disconnect the refrigerant pipes from the condenser **(see illustration)**. Plug the openings to prevent contamination. Renew the pipe seals.
18 Release the fasteners and lift the condenser from place **(see illustrations)**.

10.11 Remove the receiver/drier circlip

10.17 Undo the bolt and disconnect the refrigerant pipes

10.18a Squeeze together the clips at the right-hand end...

10.18b... and lift the clip at the left-hand end of the condenser

Refitting

19 Refitting is a reversal of removal, noting the following points:
a) *Renew the pipe O-ring seals, and smear a little refrigerant oil on the seals prior to reassembly.*
b) *Have the refrigerant circuit recharged by a Fiat dealer or suitably equipped repairer.*

Compressor

Removal

20 Have the air conditioning refrigerant circuit evacuated by a Fiat dealer or suitably equipped repairer.
21 Remove the air cleaner assembly as described in Chapter 4A Section 2.
22 Remove the auxiliary drivebelt as described in Chapter 1 Section 5.
23 Undo the retaining bolts and remove the compressor drivebelt guard.
24 Undo the retaining bolts and disconnect the refrigerant pipes from the compressor **(see illustration)**. Plug the openings to prevent contamination. Renew the pipes O-ring seals.
25 Disconnect the wiring plug from the compressor.
26 Undo the mounting bolts and manoeuvre the compressor from place.

Refitting

27 Manoeuvre the compressor into position,

insert the mounting bolts and tighten them to the specified torque.
28 The remainder of refitting is a reversal of removal, noting the following points:
a) *Renew the pipe O-ring seals, and smear a little refrigerant oil on them prior to reassembly.*
b) *Have the refrigerant circuit recharged by a Fiat dealer or suitably equipped repairer.*

Sunlight sensor

29 Carefully prise the sensor from the facia, releasing the front and rear retaining clip **(see illustration)**.
30 Disconnect the sensor wiring plug as it becomes accessible.
31 Refitting is a reversal of removal.

Expansion valve

Removal

32 Have the air conditioning refrigerant circuit evacuated by a Fiat dealer or suitably equipped repairer.
33 Remove the air cleaner assembly as described in Chapter 4A Section 2.
34 Undo the bolt and disconnect the refrigerant pipes from the expansion valve at the engine compartment bulkhead **(see illustration 8.30)**. Plug the openings to

prevent contamination. Renew the pipe O-ring seals.
35 Undo the 2 retaining bolts and manoeuvre the expansion valve from place. Plug the openings to prevent contamination. Renew the valve O-ring seals.

Refitting

36 Refitting is a reversal of removal, noting the following points:
a) *Renew the pipe/valve O-ring seals, and smear a little refrigerant oil on the seals prior to reassembly.*
b) *Have the refrigerant circuit recharged by a Fiat dealer or suitably equipped repairer.*

Pressure sensor

37 Have the air conditioning refrigerant circuit evacuated by a Fiat dealer or suitably equipped repairer.
38 The pressure sensor is located in the refrigerant pipe on the right-hand side of the engine compartment. Disconnect the wiring plug from the sensor.
39 Unscrew the sensor from the pipe. Plug the openings to prevent contamination.
40 Refit the sensor and tighten it to the specified torque.
41 Reconnect the wiring plug.
42 Have the refrigerant circuit recharged by a Fiat dealer or suitably equipped repairer.

10.24 Refrigerant pipes connections bolts, and compressor retaining bolts

10.29 Prise the sunlight sensor from the facia

Notes

Chapter 4 Part A
Fuel and exhaust systems

Contents

Section number

Accelerator pedal – removal and refitting. 3
Air cleaner assembly – removal and refitting 2
Exhaust manifold – removal and refitting. 12
Exhaust system – general information and component renewal 13
Fuel injection components (DOHC 16v engines) –
  removal and refitting. 10
Fuel injection components (SOHC 8v engines) –
  removal and refitting. 9

Section number

Fuel injection system – testing and adjustment 8
Fuel pipes and fittings – general information and disconnection. . . . 5
Fuel pump and fuel level sensor unit – removal and refitting. 6
Fuel system – depressurisation 4
Fuel tank – removal and refitting 7
General information and precautions. 1
Intake manifold – removal and refitting 11

Degrees of difficulty

Easy, suitable for novice with little experience		Fairly easy, suitable for beginner with some experience		Fairly difficult, suitable for competent DIY mechanic		Difficult, suitable for experienced DIY mechanic		Very difficult, suitable for expert DIY or professional	

Specifications

General
System type:
SOHC 8v models	Magneti Marelli IAW 5SF3.M1 multi-point sequential fuel injection/ignition
SOHC 8v 1.4L models	Magneti Marelli IAW 5SF3.M2 multi-point sequential fuel injection/ignition
DOHC 16v models	Bosch ME 7.6.3 multi-point sequential fuel injection/ignition
Fuel pressure at idle speed (all models)	3.5 bar
Fuel pump type	Electric, immersed in the fuel tank
Fuel pump delivery rate	110 litres/hour minimum
Crankshaft position sensor resistance @ 20°C	1134 to 1386 ohms

Injector electrical resistance:
SOHC 8v engines.	13.8 to 15.2 ohms
DOHC 16v engines.	14.0 to 15.0 ohms
Minimum octane rating.	95 RON unleaded

Torque wrench settings

	Nm	lbf ft
Camshaft position sensor	10	7
Crankshaft position sensor	10	7
ECU retaining nuts	8	6
Exhaust manifold-to-cylinder head: *		
Stage 1	15	10
Stage 2	Angle-tighten a further 30°	
Fuel tank level sensor/pump cover retaining ring	70	52
Intake manifold:		
SOHC 8v engines.	25	18
DOHC 16v engines.	15	10

*Do not re-use

1 General information and precautions

General information

1 The fuel supply system consists of a fuel tank (which is mounted under the centre of the car, with an electric fuel pump immersed in it) and fuel feed line. The fuel pump supplies fuel to the fuel rail, which acts as a reservoir for the four fuel injectors which inject fuel into the inlet tracts.

2 The fuel injection and ignition functions are combined into a single engine management system. The systems fitted are manufactured by Magneti-Marelli and Bosch, and are very similar in terms of construction and operation. The only significant differences being in the software contained in the system Electronic Control Unit (ECU), and certain specific component variations according to engine type. Each system incorporates a closed-loop catalytic converter and an evaporative emission control system, and complies with the latest emission control standards. Refer to Chapter 5B for information on the ignition side of each system; the fuel side of the system operates as follows.

3 The fuel pump supplies fuel from the tank to the fuel rail (mounted directly above the fuel injectors) by means of a 'returnless' system. With this arrangement, the fuel filter and fuel pressure regulator are an integral part of the fuel pump assembly located in the fuel tank. The regulator maintains a constant fuel pressure in the supply line to the fuel rail and allows excess fuel to recirculate in the fuel tank, by means of a bypass channel, if the regulated fuel pressure is exceeded. As the fuel filter is an integral part of the pump assembly, fuel filter renewal is no longer necessary as part of the maintenance and servicing schedule.

4 The fuel injectors are electromagnetic pintle valves which spray atomised fuel into the combustion chambers under the control of the ECU. There are four injectors, one per cylinder, mounted in the inlet manifold close to the cylinder head. Each injector is mounted at an angle that allows it to spray fuel directly onto the back of the inlet valve(s). The ECU controls the volume of fuel injected by varying the length of time for which each injector is held open. The fuel injection systems are of the sequential type, whereby each injector operates individually in cylinder sequence.

5 The electrical control system consists of the ECU, along with the following sensors:

a) *Accelerator pedal position sensor –
informs the ECU of the pedal position and
rate-of-change.*

b) *Engine coolant temperature sensor –
informs the ECU of the engine temperature
(Chapter 3 Section 6).*

c) *Intake air temperature/pressure sensor –
informs the ECU of intake air temperature*
and load on the engine (expressed in terms of inlet manifold vacuum).

d) *Ambient air pressure sensor – informs the
ECU of the ambient air pressure, to allow
for fueling corrections in relation to altitude
– DOHC 16v engines only.*

e) *Lambda sensors – inform the ECU of
the oxygen content of the exhaust gases
(explained in greater detail in Part B of this
Chapter).*

f) *Crankshaft position sensor – informs the
ECU of engine speed and crankshaft
angular position.*

g) *Knock sensor – informs the ECU of
pre-ignition (detonation) within the
cylinders (refer to Chapter 5B Section 5).*

h) *Camshaft position sensor – informs the
ECU of the camshaft position.*

i) *Wheel speed sensors – informs the ECU of
the vehicle speed.*

6 Signals from each of the sensors are compared by the ECU and, based on this information, the ECU selects the response appropriate to those values, and controls the fuel injectors (varying the pulse width – the length of time the injectors are held open – to provide a richer or weaker air/fuel mixture, as appropriate). The air/fuel mixture is constantly varied by the ECU, to provide the best settings for cranking, starting (with either a hot or cold engine) and engine warm-up, idle, cruising and acceleration.

7 The ECU also has full control over the engine idle speed, via the motorised throttle body. The ECU also carries out 'fine tuning' of the idle speed by varying the ignition timing to increase or reduce the torque of the engine as it is idling. This helps to stabilise the idle speed when electrical or mechanical loads (such as headlights, air conditioning, etc) are switched on and off. The accelerator pedal position sensor informs the ECU of accelerator pedal position and from this data, the ECU controls the motorised throttle body so that a corresponding throttle opening can be obtained. This arrangement is often termed 'drive-by-wire' as there is no direct accelerator cable connection between the accelerator pedal and throttle valve.

8 On 1.4L models, the ECU also varies the camshaft timing via an electrically operated solenoid valve, which controls the flow of pressurised engine oil to the phase transformer integral with the camshaft sprocket. The ECU adjusts the timing of the camshafts during various engine load conditions to improve driveabilty, engine output, and to reduce emissions.

9 The exhaust and evaporative loss emission control systems are described in more detail in Chapter 4B.

10 If there is any abnormality in any of the readings obtained from the main engine sensors, the ECU enters its 'back-up' mode. If this happens, the erroneous sensor signal is overridden, and the ECU assumes a preprogrammed 'back-up' value, which will allow the engine to continue running, albeit at reduced efficiency. If the ECU enters this mode, the warning lamp on the instrument panel will be illuminated, and the relevant fault code will be stored in the ECU memory.

11 If the warning light illuminates, the vehicle should be taken to a Fiat dealer or suitably equipped repairer at the earliest opportunity. Once there, a complete test of the engine management system can be carried out, using a special electronic diagnostic test unit which is plugged into the system's diagnostic connector **(see illustration)**.

12 Note that if a collision should occur, the fuel inertia cut-off switch will operate and disconnect the electrical supply to the fuel pump. The switch is located behind the drivers side lower A-pillar trim panel **(see illustration)**. Should it be necessary, re-activate the switch by depressing the button on the top.

Precautions

⚠️ *Warning: Many of the procedures in this Chapter require the removal of fuel lines and connections, which may result in some fuel spillage. Before carrying out any operation on the fuel system, refer to the precautions given in 'Safety first!' at the beginning of this manual, and follow them implicitly. Petrol is a highly dangerous and volatile liquid, and the precautions necessary when handling it cannot be*

**1.11 Pull the storage compartment/
cover rearwards to access the diagnostic
connector**

1.12 Fuel inertia cut-off switch

2.1 Undo the bolts and lift the air cleaner assembly

2.5 Release the clip each side securing the cold air intake hose

overstressed. *Note that residual pressure
will remain in the fuel lines long after the
vehicle was last used. When disconnecting
any fuel line, first depressurise the fuel
system as described in Section 4.*

2 Air cleaner assembly –
   removal and refitting

Removal

SOHC 8v engines

1 Undo the retaining bolts and lift the air
cleaner assembly (see illustration).
2 Slacken the clamp then disconnect the
engine breather hose, followed by the vacuum
hose from the air cleaner assembly underside.
3 Manoeuvre the air cleaner from place.
4 Recover the sealing ring. Check the ring for
condition and renew it if necessary.

DOHC 16v engines

5 Release the clips and disconnect the cold
air intake hose from the air cleaner (see
illustration).
6 Release the clamp and disconnect the air
outlet hose (see illustration).
7 Undo the retaining bolts and manoeuvre
the air cleaner assembly from place (see
illustration).

Refitting

8 Refitting is a reversal of removal.

3 Accelerator pedal –
   removal and refitting

Removal

1 Disconnect the battery negative lead as
described in Chapter 5A Section 4.
2 Working under the drivers side of the facia,

2.6 Release the air outlet hose clamp

undo the retaining bolt, and unclip the footwell
air duct.
3 Undo the 2 retaining bolts, lower the
accelerator pedal assembly and disconnect
the sensor wiring plug (see illustration).

Refitting

4 Refitting is a reversal of removal.

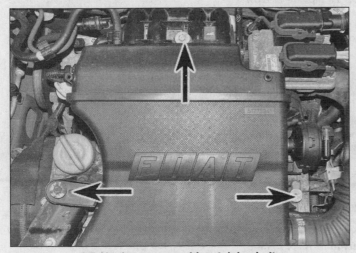

2.7 Air cleaner assembly retaining bolts

3.3 Pull out the red locking catch to disconnect the wiring plug,
then undo the pedal assembly retaining bolts

4.4a Fuel pressure relief valve – SOHC engines

4.4b Fuel pressure relief valve – DOHC engines

4 Fuel system – depressurisation

Note: *Refer to the warning given in Section 1 before proceeding.*

⚠ *Warning: The following procedure will merely relieve the pressure in the fuel system – remember that fuel will still be present in the system components and take precautions accordingly before disconnecting any of them.*

1 The fuel system referred to in this Section is defined as the tank-mounted fuel pump, the fuel rail, the fuel injectors, and the metal pipes and flexible hoses of the fuel lines between these components. All these contain fuel which will be under pressure while the engine is running and/or while the ignition is switched on. The pressure will remain for some time after the ignition has been switched off, and must be relieved before any of these components are disturbed for servicing work.

2 Disconnect the battery negative lead as described in Chapter 5A Section 4.

3 Remove the air cleaner assembly as described in Section 2.

4 Locate the pressure relief (Schrader) valve situated at the right-hand end of the fuel rail **(see illustrations)**. The valve works like a tyre valve whereby on depressing the central plunger, the system fuel pressure will be released.

5 Unscrew the protective plastic cap from the top of the valve.

6 Place an absorbent rag around the valve then, using a small screwdriver, slowly depress the central plunger to allow the pressure to be released. Ensure that the rag completely covers the valve to catch the fuel spray which will be expelled.

7 On completion of the operations for which system depressurisation was necessary, refit the Schrader valve cap and reconnect the battery negative terminal. Refit the air cleaner assembly as described in Section 2.

5 Fuel pipes and fittings – general information and disconnection

1 Depressurise the fuel system (see Section 4) and disconnect the cable from the negative battery terminal (see Chapter 5A Section 4) before proceeding.

2 The fuel supply pipe connects the fuel pump in the fuel tank to the fuel rail on the engine.

3 Whenever you're working under the vehicle, be sure to inspect all fuel and evaporative emission pipes for leaks, kinks, dents and other damage. Always replace a damaged fuel pipe immediately.

4 If you find signs of dirt in the pipes during disassembly, disconnect all pipes and blow them out with compressed air. Inspect the fuel strainer on the fuel pump pick-up unit for damage and deterioration.

Steel tubing

5 It is critical that the fuel pipes be replaced with pipes of equivalent type and specification.

6 Some steel fuel pipes have threaded fittings. When loosening these fittings, hold the stationary fitting with a spanner while turning the union nut.

Plastic tubing

⚠ *Warning: When removing or installing plastic fuel tubing, be careful not to bend or twist it too much, which can damage it. Also, plastic fuel tubing is NOT heat resistant, so keep it away from excessive heat.*

7 When replacing fuel system plastic tubing, use only original equipment replacement plastic tubing.

Flexible hoses

8 When replacing fuel system flexible hoses, use original equipment replacements, or hose to the same specification.

9 Don't route fuel hoses (or metal pipes) within 100 mm of the exhaust system or within 280 mm of the catalytic converter. Make sure that no rubber hoses are installed directly against the vehicle, particularly in places where there is any vibration. If allowed to touch some vibrating part of the vehicle, a hose can easily become chafed and it might start leaking. A good rule of thumb is to maintain a minimum of 8.0 mm clearance around a hose (or metal pipe) to prevent contact with the vehicle underbody.

Disconnecting fuel pipe fittings

10 Typical fuel pipe fittings:

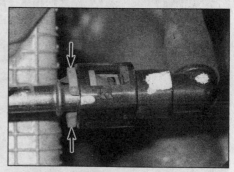

5.10a Two-tab type fitting; depress both tabs with your fingers, then pull the fuel pipe and the fitting apart

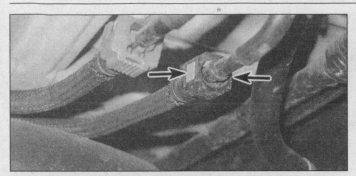

5.10b On this type of fitting, depress the two buttons on opposite sides of the fitting, then pull it off the fuel pipe

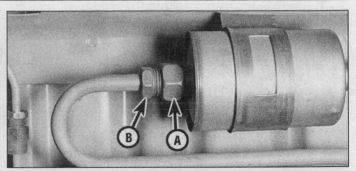

5.10c Threaded fuel pipe fitting; hold the stationary portion of the pipe or component (A) while loosening the union nut (B) with a flare-nut spanner

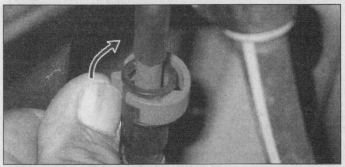

5.10d Plastic collar-type fitting; rotate the outer part of the fitting

5.10e Metal collar quick-connect fitting; pull the end of the retainer off the fuel pipe and disengage the other end from the female side of the fitting...

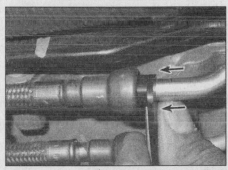

5.10f ... insert a fuel pipe separator tool into the female side of the fitting, push it into the fitting and pull the fuel pipe off the pipe

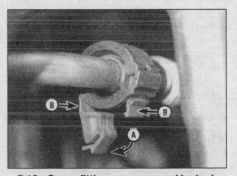

5.10g Some fittings are secured by lock tabs. Release the lock tab (A) and rotate it to the fully-opened position, squeeze the two smaller lock tabs (B)...

5.10h ... then push the retainer out and pull the fuel pipe off the pipe

5.10i Spring-lock coupling; remove the safety cover, install a coupling release tool and close the tool around the coupling...

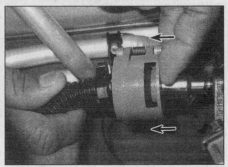

5.10j ... push the tool into the fitting, then pull the two pipes apart

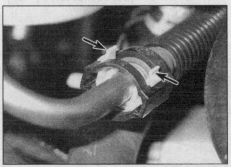

5.10k Hairpin clip type fitting: push the legs of the retainer clip together, then push the clip down all the way until it stops and pull the fuel pipe off the pipe

6.5 Prise up the cover from the floor panel

6.8a Use two strips of steel, bolted together to unscrew the locking ring...

6.8b... or use a commercially available tool

6 Fuel pump and fuel level sensor unit – removal and refitting

1 Refer to the warning given in Section 1 before proceeding.

Removal

2 Disconnect the battery negative lead as described in Chapter 5A Section 4.

3 Depressurise the fuel system as described in Section 4.

4 Remove the rear seat cushion as described in Chapter 11 Section 21.

5 Prise up and lift the cover from the aperture in the floor panel (see illustration).

6 Release the locking catch and disconnect the wiring connector from the top of the fuel pump.

7 Disconnect the fuel supply line quick-release fitting from the pump unit by pressing the tabs each side. Plug the end of the supply line or cover it with adhesive tape.

8 Unscrew the large locking ring and remove it from the tank. This is best accomplished by using a commercially available tool, or making up a simple tool from two strips of metal, suitably drilled and bolted together with two lengths of threaded bar and locknuts. Engage the tool with the ribs of the locking ring, and turn the ring anti-clockwise until it can be unscrewed by hand (see illustrations).

9 Lift the fuel pump and sensor unit assembly out of the fuel tank, taking great care not to damage the float arm. Recover the sealing O-ring and discard it – a new one must be used on refitting (see illustrations).

10 To remove the fuel level sensor, disconnect the wiring plug, then press-in the retaining tabs and slide the sensor assembly upwards from the pump assembly (see illustrations).

11 If desired, connect an ohmmeter to the sensor connector terminals and measure the circuit resistance at full, and zero deflection (see illustration):

a) Full deflection (full tank) = 40 ohms.
b) Zero deflection (empty tank) = 300 ohms.

Refitting

12 Fit the new seal to the tank aperture.

13 Manoeuvre the pump/sensor assembly into place, aligning the arrow on the pump cover with the reference mark on the tank (see illustration).

14 Tighten the locking ring securely. If suitable tools are available, tighten the locking ring to the specified torque.

6.9a Lift the pump/sensor assembly from the tank

6.9b Renew the sealing O-ring

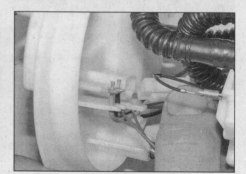

6.10a Disconnect the sensor wiring plug...

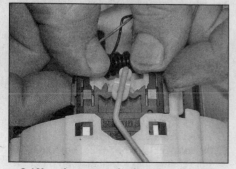

6.10b... then press-in the tabs slide the sensor from place

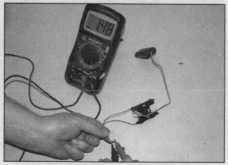

6.11 Measure the sensor resistance

6.13 Align the arrow on the pump cover with the mark on the tank

15 The remainder of refitting is a reversal of removal. Prior to refitting the access cover, reconnect the battery, start the engine and check the fuel pipe for signs of leakage.

7 Fuel tank – removal and refitting

Note: *Refer to the warning given in Section 1 before proceeding.*

Removal

1 Before removing the fuel tank, all fuel must be drained from the tank. Since a fuel tank drain plug is not provided, it is therefore preferable to carry out the removal operation when the tank is nearly empty. Before proceeding, disconnect the battery negative terminal (Chapter 5A Section 4), and syphon or hand-pump the remaining fuel from the tank.
2 Working as described in Section 6, disconnect the fuel pump wiring connector and the fuel supply line from the top of the pump.
3 Slacken the right-hand rear roadwheel bolts, raise the rear of the vehicle and support it securely on axle stands as described in *'Vehicle jacking and support'*. Remove the roadwheel, then undo the fasteners and remove the right-hand rear wheelarch liner.
4 Working underneath the vehicle, release the rear silencer from the front and rear rubber mountings, then undo the fasteners and remove the exhaust heatshield from the fuel tank.
5 Release the clamp and disconnect the fuel 'back-flow' pipe from the filler pipe.
6 Disconnect the fuel vapour pipe from the charcoal canister **(see illustration)**.
7 Slacken the clamp and disconnect the fuel filler pipe from the tank.
8 Unclip the brake pipes from the sides of the fuel tank.
9 Place a trolley jack with an interposed block of wood beneath the tank, then raise the jack until it is supporting the weight of the tank.
10 Undo the four fuel tank mounting strap bolts, then carefully lower the tank from its location. Move the exhaust system as far as possible to one side to provide the necessary clearance for removal.

7.6 Depress the release button and disconnect the vapour pipe

11 If the tank is contaminated with sediment or water, remove the fuel pump/fuel level sensor unit as described in Section 6, and swill the tank out with clean fuel. The tank is injection-moulded from a synthetic material – if seriously damaged, it should be renewed. However, in certain cases, it may be possible to have small leaks or minor damage repaired. Seek the advice of a specialist before attempting to repair the fuel tank.

Refitting

12 Refitting is a reversal of removal, noting the following points:
a) *Ensure that all pipes hoses are correctly routed and securely reconnected.*
b) *Clip the brake pipes securely into their retaining brackets.*

8 Fuel injection system – testing and adjustment

Testing

1 If a fault appears in the fuel injection/engine management system, first ensure that all the system wiring connectors are securely connected and free of corrosion. Ensure that the fault is not due to poor maintenance; ie, check that the air cleaner filter element is clean, the spark plugs are in good condition and correctly gapped, the valve clearances are correctly adjusted (where applicable), the cylinder compression pressures are correct, and that the engine breather hoses are clear and undamaged, referring to the relevant Parts of Chapter 2A and Chapter 2B for further information.
2 If these checks fail to reveal the cause of the problem, the vehicle should be taken to a Fiat dealer or suitably-equipped garage for testing. A diagnostic socket is located below the drivers side of the facia in which a fault code reader or other suitable test equipment can be connected. By using the code reader or test equipment, the engine management ECU (and the various other vehicle system ECUs) can be interrogated, and any stored fault codes can be retrieved. This will allow the fault to be quickly and simply traced, alleviating the need to test all the system components individually, which is a time-consuming operation that carries a risk of damaging the ECU.

Adjustment

3 Experienced home mechanics with a considerable amount of skill and equipment (including a tachometer and an accurately calibrated exhaust gas analyser) may be able to check the exhaust CO level and the idle speed. However, if these are found to be outside the specified tolerance, the car must be taken to a suitably-equipped garage for further testing. Neither the mixture adjustment (exhaust gas CO level) nor the idle

speed are adjustable, and should either be incorrect, a fault may be present in the engine management system.
4 Note that the engine management ECU has a 'self-learning' capability. If a component has been renewed, allow at least 15 minutes of driving time for the ECU to adapt to the characteristics of the new component.

9 Fuel injection components (SOHC 8v engines) – removal and refitting

1 Refer to the warning given in Section 1 before proceeding.
2 Before attempting any of the following procedures, disconnect the battery negative lead as described in Chapter 5A Section 4.

Throttle body assembly

Removal

3 Remove the air cleaner assembly as described in Section 2.
4 Disconnect the wiring plug from the throttle body.
5 Undo the bolts and remove the throttle body. Renew the O-ring seal.

Refitting

6 Refitting is a reversal of removal.

Fuel rail and injectors

Removal

7 Remove the air cleaner as described in Section 2.
8 Depressurise the fuel system as described in Section 4.
9 Disconnect the injector wiring harness plug.
10 Disconnect the fuel supply pipe at the quick-release connector on the left-hand end of the fuel rail.
11 Unscrew the 2 bolts securing the fuel rail assembly to the inlet manifold, then carefully pull the injectors from their manifold locations. Remove the assembly from the engine and remove the injector lower O-ring seals.
12 Disconnect the wiring plug from each injector.
13 The injectors can be removed individually from the fuel rail by extracting the relevant metal clip and easing the injector out of the rail. Remove the injector upper O-ring seals.
14 Check the electrical resistance of the injector using a multimeter and compare it with the Specifications.
Note: *If a faulty injector is suspected, before condemning the injector it is worth trying the effect of one of the proprietary injector-cleaning treatments.*

Refitting

15 Refitting is a reversal of the removal procedure, bearing in mind the following points:
a) *Renew the injector O-ring seals, and smear them with a little petroleum jelly before assembling. Take care when fitting*

the injectors to the fuel rail and do not press them in further than required to fit the retaining clip otherwise the O-ring seal may be damaged.
b) Ensure that the injector retaining clips are securely seated.
c) On completion check the fuel rail and injectors for fuel leaks.

Intake air temperature/pressure sensor

Removal

16 Disconnect the wiring plug from the sensor, located on the right-hand end of the intake manifold (see illustration).
17 Undo the retaining bolt and remove the sensor.

Refitting

18 Refitting is a reversal of removal.

Coolant temperature sensor

19 Refer to Chapter 3 Section 6.

Oxygen sensors

20 Refer to Chapter 4B Section 2.

Crankshaft position sensor

Removal

21 The crankshaft position sensor is located adjacent to the front facing side of the crankshaft pulley (see illustration).
22 Remove the timing belt lower cover as described in Chapter 2A Section 4.
23 Undo the bolt securing the sensor to the oil pump casing and remove the sensor from its location. Disconnect the wiring plug as the sensor is withdrawn.

Refitting

24 Locate the sensor in position, secure with the retaining bolt, then reconnect the wiring plug.
25 Refit the timing belt covers as described in Chapter 2A Section 4.
26 If a new crankshaft position sensor has been fitted, it must be initialised as follows:

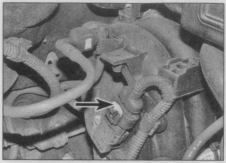

9.16 Pull out the yellow tab, depress the clip and disconnect the intake air temperature/pressure sensor

a) Start the engine. If the injection warning light flashes, the initialisation procedure must be carried out.
b) Allow the engine to idle until it reaches normal operating temperature. Do not press the accelerator pedal during this process.
c) Carry out 3 engine speed accelerations, reaching 6000 rpm each time. Allow the engine to idle between each acceleration.
d) If the injection warning light now extinguishes, the procedure is complete. If not, repeat the procedure.
e) Switch off the ignition and wait at least 1 minute for the information to be stored in the ECU memory.

Knock sensor

27 Refer to Chapter 5B Section 5.

Camshaft position sensor

Removal

28 Disconnect the wiring connector from the camshaft position sensor located at the timing belt end of the camshaft cover (see illustration).
29 Undo the retaining bolt and withdraw the sensor from the camshaft cover.

9.21 Crankshaft position sensor

Refitting

30 Refitting is a reversal of removal.

Electronic control unit (ECU)

Removal

31 Depress the clips, pivot over the locking catches to disconnect the wiring plugs from the ECU (see illustration).
32 Undo the retaining nuts and remove the ECU.
33 If required, unclip the wiring harness, undo the nut/bolts and remove the ECU support bracket.

Refitting

34 Refitting is a reversal of removal, tightening the retaining nuts to their specified torque.
35 If a new ECU has been fitted, it must be initialised as follows:
a) Start the engine. If the injection warning light flashes, the initialisation procedure must be carried out.
b) Allow the engine to idle until it reaches normal operating temperature. Do not depress the accelerator during this procedure.
c) Carry out 3 engine speed accelerations,

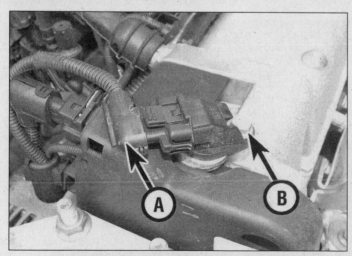

9.28 Camshaft position sensor wiring plug (A) and retaining bolt (B)

9.31 Depress the clips, and pivot over the locking catches

reaching 6000 rpm each time. Allow the
engine to idle between each acceleration.

d) *If the injection warning light now
extinguishes, the initialisation is complete.
If not, repeat the procedure.*

e) *Turn off the ignition, and wait at least 1
minute for the information to be stored in
the ECU memory.*

Inertia safety switch

Removal

36 Working under the facia on the right-hand
side, move away the floor covering and side
trim for access to the switch.

37 Disconnect the wiring plug, undo the 2
bolts and remove the switch **(see illustration
1.12)**.

Refitting

38 Refitting is a reversal of removal.

10 Fuel injection components (DOHC 16v engines) – removal and refitting

1 Refer to the warning given in Section 1
before proceeding.

2 Before attempting any of the following
procedures, disconnect the battery negative
lead as described in Chapter 5A Section 4.

Throttle body assembly

Remove

3 Release the clamps and remove the air
hose from the air cleaner assembly to the
throttle body.

4 Disconnect the throttle body wiring plug.

5 Undo the bolts and move the engine
management ECU and mounting bracket to
one side **(see illustration)**.

6 Undo the remaining bolt and remove the
throttle body. Renew the throttle body seal.

Refitting

7 Refitting is a reversal of the removal

10.5 ECU mounting bracket/throttle body bolts

procedure, bearing in mind the following
points:

a) *Ensure the throttle body and inlet manifold
mating surfaces are clean and dry, then fit
the throttle body with a new O-ring, and
securely tighten the retaining bolts.*

b) *Refit the air hose, and check for leaks.*

Fuel rail and injectors

Removal

8 Remove the air cleaner assembly as
described in Section 2.

9 Depressurise the fuel system as described
in Section 4.

10 Disconnect the fuel supply pipe at the
quick-release connector **(see illustration)**.

11 Disconnect the wiring connectors at the
fuel injectors. Release the injector wiring
harness from the retaining clips on the fuel
rail and move the harness to one side **(see
illustration)**.

12 Unscrew the two bolts securing the
fuel rail assembly to the inlet manifold, then
carefully pull the injectors from their manifold
locations **(see illustration)**. Remove the
assembly from the engine and remove the
injector lower O-ring seals.

13 The injectors can be removed individually
from the fuel rail by extracting the relevant
metal clip and easing the injector out of the

10.10 Depress the clip and disconnect the fuel supply pipe

rail. Remove the injector upper O-ring seals.

14 Check the electrical resistance of the
injector using a multimeter and compare it
with the Specifications.

Note: *If a faulty injector is suspected,
before condemning the injector it is worth
trying the effect of one of the proprietary
injector-cleaning treatments.*

Refitting

15 Refitting is a reversal of the removal
procedure, bearing in mind the following
points:

a) *Renew the injector O-ring seals, and
smear them with a little petroleum jelly
before assembling. Take care when fitting
the injectors to the fuel rail and do not
press them in further than required to fit
the retaining clip otherwise the O-ring seal
may be damaged.*

b) *Ensure that the injector retaining clips are
securely seated.*

c) *On completion check the fuel rail and
injectors for fuel leaks.*

Intake air temperature/pressure sensor

Removal

16 Disconnect the wiring connector, then
undo the retaining bolt and remove the sensor

10.11 Press-in the wire clips and disconnect the injector wiring plugs

10.12 Fuel rail retaining bolts

10.16 Intake air temperature/pressure sensor

10.19 Absolute air pressure sensor retaining bolt

10.23 Crankshaft position sensor retaining bolt

from the right-hand end of the inlet manifold (see illustration).

Refitting

17 Refitting is a reversal of removal.

Absolute air pressure sensor

Removal

18 Remove the air cleaner assembly as described in Section 2.
19 Disconnect the wiring plug, undo the retaining bolt and remove the sensor (see illustration).

Refitting

20 Refitting is a reversal of removal.

Coolant temperature sensor

21 Refer to Chapter 3 Section 6.

Oxygen sensor

22 Refer to Chapter 4B Section 2.

Crankshaft position sensor

Removal

23 The crankshaft position sensor is located adjacent to the front facing side of the crankshaft pulley (see illustration).
24 Disconnect the sensor wiring plug, undo the retaining bolt and remove the sensor.

Refitting

25 Refitting is a reversal of removal, tightening the retaining bolt to the specified torque.

Knock sensor

26 Refer to Chapter 5B Section 5.

Camshaft position sensor

Removal

27 The camshaft position sensor is located at the left-hand end of the camshaft housing (see illustration).
28 Disconnect the wiring plug, undo the retaining bolt and withdraw the sensor from position.

Refitting

29 Refitting is a reversal of removal.

Electronic control unit (ECU)

Removal

30 The ECU is located on the throttle body. Disconnect the ECU wiring plugs (see illustration).
31 Undo the nut and detach the earth connection from the ECU (see illustration).
32 Undo the 4 retaining nuts and withdraw the ECU.
33 If required, disconnect the air intake hose from the throttle body, undo the bolts and remove the ECU support bracket.

Refitting

34 Refitting is a reversal of removal. If a new ECU has been fitted, carry out the following 'self-learning' procedure:
a) Turn on the ignition (don't start the engine or press the accelerator pedal), and wait at least 29 seconds. Engine temperature must be between 5 and 100°C.
b) On models with climate control, turn on the climate control system, and set the

blower speed to position 2 for at least 15 seconds.
c) On models with cruise control, activate the system fro a few seconds by turning the switch on the control lever to ON.

Inertia safety switch

35 Refer to Section 9.

11 Intake manifold – removal and refitting

SOHC 8v engines

Removal

1 Remove the air cleaner assembly as described in Section 2.
2 Remove the fuel rail and injectors as described in Section 9.
3 Remove the throttle body as described in Section 9.
4 Disconnect the wiring plugs from the intake air pressure/temperature sensor, and the EVAP purge valve solenoid.
5 Release the clamp and disconnect the servo vacuum hose from the manifold.
6 Depress the tabs and disconnect the EVAP vapour hose from the manifold.
7 Note their fitted positions and disconnect the HT leads from the ignition coils and spark plugs.
8 Undo the manifold retaining nuts/bolts, and remove the manifold from the cylinder head.

10.27 Camshaft position sensor retaining bolt

10.30 Fold open the locking catches to disconnect the wiring plugs

10.31 Disconnect the earth lead

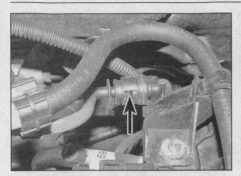

11.14 Depress the tab each side, and disconnect the vapour hose

11.16 Engine oil level dipstick guide tube bolt

11.20 Remove the manifold-to-camshaft housing bolt

Remove the sealing rings and obtain new rings for refitting.

Refitting

9 Refitting is a reverse of the removal procedure, noting the following points:
a) Ensure that the manifold and cylinder head mating surfaces are clean and dry, and fit new manifold sealing rings. Refit the manifold and tighten the fasteners to their specified torque.
b) Ensure all relevant hoses and wiring are reconnected to their original positions and are securely held (where necessary) by the retaining clips.
c) Refit the fuel rail and injectors, and the throttle body assembly with reference to Section 9.

DOHC 16v engines

Removal

10 Release the clamps and disconnect the air duct from the air cleaner to the intake manifold.
11 Remove the air cleaner assembly as described in Section 2.
12 Remove the fuel rail and injectors as described in Section 10.
13 Remove the starter motor as described in Chapter 5A Section 8.
14 Disconnect the EVAP fuel vapour hose at the quick-release connection **(see illustration)**.
15 Disconnect the air intake temperature/pressure sensor wiring plug.

16 Undo engine oil level dipstick guide tube retaining bolt **(see illustration)**.
17 Disconnect the absolute pressure sensor wiring plug **(see illustration 10.19)**.
18 Release the clamp and disconnect the engine breather hose from the manifold.
19 Release the clamp and disconnect the servo vacuum hose from the manifold.
20 Undo the bolt securing the manifold to the camshaft housing **(see illustration)**.
21 Disconnect the purge valve wiring plug.
22 Remove the engine management ECU as described in Section 10.
23 Disconnect the wiring plugs from the throttle body, and manifold variable geometry solenoid valve and sensor.
24 Release the clips and move the engine wiring duct to one side.
25 Undo the bolts securing the manifold to the cylinder head, and manoeuvre it from position. Discard the seal – a new one must be fitted **(see illustration)**.

Refitting

26 Refitting is a reverse of the removal procedure, noting the following points:
a) Ensure that the manifold and cylinder head mating surfaces are clean and dry, and fit new manifold seals. Refit the manifold and tighten its retaining bolts to the specified torque.
b) On models with air conditioning, insert the lower, right-hand retaining bolt before positioning the manifold on the cylinder head **(see illustration)**.
c) Ensure all relevant hoses and wiring are

reconnected to their original positions and are securely held (where necessary) by the retaining clips.

12 Exhaust manifold – removal and refitting

Removal

1 Raise the front of the vehicle and support it securely on axle stands, as described in 'Vehicle jacking and support'.
2 Remove the air cleaner as described in Section 2.
3 Undo the retaining nuts and remove the exhaust manifold heat shield.
4 Unscrew the nuts and disconnect the exhaust system front pipe flange from the manifold downpipe. Recover the gasket.
5 Release the exhaust pipe from the rubber mountings and move it to one side.
6 Trace the wiring back from the oxygen sensor(s), and disconnect the wiring plug(s).
7 Undo the retaining nuts and manoeuvre the exhaust manifold assembly from position **(see illustration)**. Discard the gasket.

Refitting

8 Refitting is a reversal of the removal procedure but use a new manifold gasket, and new front pipe flange gasket. Tighten all fasteners to the specified torque where given.

11.25 Renew the intake manifold seal

11.26 Insert the lower, right-hand retaining bolt before positioning the manifold

12.7 Undo the nuts and remove the exhaust manifold

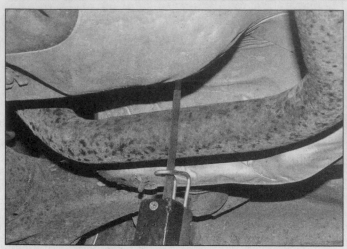

13.6 Measure from the pipe flange, and cut-through using a hacksaw

13.7 Undo the flange nuts and detach the manifold from the pipe

13 Exhaust system – general information and component renewal

General information

1 A one-piece exhaust system is fitted comprising a front pipe, intermediate silencer and rear silencer. The front pipe is connected to the exhaust manifold downpipe by means of a flange joint, and contains a flexible section to cater for engine movement. A catalytic converter is fitted to all models, and is an integral part of the exhaust manifold.

2 The system is suspended throughout its entire length by rubber mountings.

3 The intermediate and rear silencers can be individually renewed by cutting the original system at a specified distance from the front pipe flange joint. The new section is then secured by a clamping sleeve which is supplied as part of the new front or rear section.

Component renewal

Exhaust manifold and catalytic converter

4 Refer to Section 12.

Intermediate and rear silencers

5 Raise the front and rear of the vehicle, and support it securely on axle stands, as described in *'Vehicle jacking and support'*.

6 Using a tape measure, measure rearwards from the flat surface of the front pipe-to-manifold downpipe flange, and suitably mark the system 2258 mm (SOHC 8v engines) or 2201 mm (DOHC 16v engines) from the flange **(see illustration)**. This will be the cutting point for renewal of the intermediate or rear silencer.

7 Unscrew the nuts and disconnect the front pipe flange from the manifold downpipe **(see illustration)**. Recover the gasket.

8 Undo the bolt securing the rear exhaust system mounting bracket to the underbody and release the front rubber mounting. Lower the system and suitably support it.

9 Using a pipe cutter or hacksaw, cut through the system at the point previously marked, then remove the front pipe and intermediate silencer or the tailpipe and rear silencer, as applicable.

10 Remove any burrs from the remaining section at the cutting point, then slide the clamping sleeve into position. Locate the new section in place in the clamping sleeve.

11 Refit the bolt securing the rear mounting bracket and refit the rubber mounting.

12 Reconnect the front pipe flange to the manifold downpipe using a new gasket, and tighten the nuts securely.

13 Align the two exhaust system sections so that there is adequate clearance between the system and vehicle underbody, then securely tighten the clamping sleeve nut.

14 On completion, lower the vehicle to the ground.

Heat shields

15 Undo the bolts securing the front and rear exhaust system mounting brackets to the underbody. Lower the system and suitably support it.

16 The heat shields are secured to the underbody by an assortment of nuts, bolts and retaining clips. Remove the relevant attachments and withdraw the heat shield(s) from their location.

17 Refit the heat shield(s), and exhaust system mounting brackets, tightening the bracket retaining bolts securely.

Chapter 4 Part B
Emission control systems

Contents

Section number

Catalytic converter – general information and precautions 3
Engine emission control systems – component renewal 2

Section number

General information 1

Degrees of difficulty

Easy, suitable for novice with little experience	Fairly easy, suitable for beginner with some experience	Fairly difficult, suitable for competent DIY mechanic	Difficult, suitable for experienced DIY mechanic	Very difficult, suitable for expert DIY or professional

Specifications

Torque wrench setting	Nm	lbf ft
Oxygen sensors	44	32

1 General information

1 All models use unleaded petrol and are controlled by engine management systems that are 'tuned' to give the best compromise between driveability, fuel consumption and exhaust emission production. In addition, a number of systems are fitted that help to minimise other harmful emissions: a crankcase emission-control system that reduces the release of pollutants from the crankcase, an evaporative loss emission control system to reduce the release of hydrocarbons from the fuel tank; and a catalytic converter to reduce exhaust gas pollutants.

Crankcase emission control

2 To reduce the emission of unburned hydrocarbons from the crankcase into the atmosphere, the engine is sealed and the blow-by gases and oil vapour are drawn from inside the crankcase, into the inlet tract to be burned by the engine during normal combustion. Under conditions of high manifold depression (idling, deceleration) the gases will by sucked positively out of the crankcase. Under conditions of low manifold depression (acceleration, full-throttle running) the gases are forced out of the crankcase by the (relatively) higher crankcase pressure; if the engine is worn, the raised crankcase pressure (due to increased blow-by) will cause some of the flow to return under all manifold conditions.

Exhaust emission control

3 To minimise the amount of pollutants which escape into the atmosphere, a catalytic converter is fitted integrally into the exhaust manifold. The fuel system is of the closed-loop type; in which two lambda (or oxygen) sensors in the exhaust system provide the engine management system ECU with constant feedback, enabling the ECU to adjust the air/fuel mixture to optimise combustion. One lambda sensor is fitted 'upstream' of the catalytic converter, and the second sensor is fitted 'downstream' of the converter. The ECU compares the voltage signals from the two sensors to obtain the optimum inlet air/fuel ratio.

4 The lambda sensors have a heating element built-in that is controlled by the ECU to quickly bring the sensor's tip to its optimum operating temperature. The sensor's tip is sensitive to oxygen and provides a voltage signal to the ECU that varies according on the amount of oxygen in the exhaust gas. If the inlet air/fuel mixture is too rich, the exhaust gases are low in oxygen so the sensor sends a low-voltage signal, the voltage rising as the mixture weakens and the amount of oxygen rises in the exhaust gases. Peak conversion efficiency of all major pollutants occurs if the inlet air/fuel mixture is maintained at the chemically-correct ratio for the complete combustion of petrol of 14.7 parts (by weight) of air to 1 part of fuel (the stoichiometric ratio). The sensor output voltage alters in a large step at this point, the ECU using the signal change as a reference point and correcting the inlet air/fuel mixture accordingly by altering the fuel injector pulse width.

Evaporative emission control

5 To minimise the escape of unburned hydrocarbons into the atmosphere, an evaporative loss emission control system is fitted. The fuel tank filler cap is sealed and a charcoal canister is mounted underneath the right-hand wheel arch to collect the petrol vapours released from the fuel contained in the fuel tank. It stores them until they can be drawn from the canister (under the control of the engine management system ECU) via the evaporative emission control solenoid (purge) valve into the inlet tract, where they are then burned by the engine during normal combustion.

2 Engine emission control systems – component renewal

Crankcase emission control

1 The crankcase emission control system consists of a hose from the camshaft cover/camshaft housing to the air cleaner (or inlet duct).

2 The system requires no attention other than to check at regular intervals that the hose is free of blockages and undamaged.

Evaporative emission control (EVAP)

3 The evaporative loss emission control system consists of the control solenoid, the activated charcoal filter canister and connecting fuel vapour hoses.

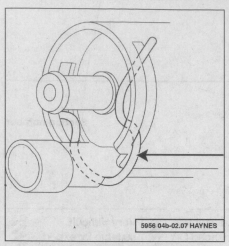

2.7 Purge valve retaining clip

Control solenoid (purge) valve

SOHC 8v engines

4 Disconnect the battery negative lead as described in Chapter 5A Section 4.
5 Depress the release tabs and disconnect the vapour pipe from the control solenoid (purge) valve. The valve is located on the underside of the intake manifold.
6 Disconnect the wiring plug from the valve.
7 Prise out the retaining clip and pull the valve from place **(see illustration)**.

DOHC 16v engines

8 Disconnect the battery negative lead as described in Chapter 5A Section 4.
9 Depress the release tabs and disconnect the vapour pipe from the control solenoid (purge) valve **(see illustration)**.
10 Disconnect the wiring plug, undo the 2 retaining screws and remove the valve.

All models

11 Refitting is a reversal of removal.

Charcoal canister

12 Slacken the right-hand rear roadwheel bolts, raise the rear of the vehicle and support

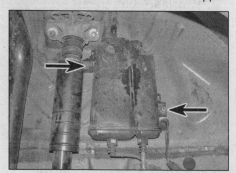

2.14 Charcoal canister retaining nuts

2.9 Depress the tab each side and disconnect the vapour pipe

it securely on axle stands, as described in *'Vehicle jacking and support'*.
13 Remove the right-hand rear roadwheel, and wheel arch liner.
14 Undo the retaining nuts securing the charcoal canister guard to the wheelarch **(see illustration)**.
15 Disconnect the vapour hoses and remove the canister.
16 Refitting is a reversal of removal.

Exhaust emission control

Catalytic converter renewal

17 The catalytic converter is an integral part of the exhaust manifold. Refer to Chapter 4A Section 12 for exhaust manifold removal and refitting procedures.

Oxygen (lambda) sensors renewal

Caution: The oxygen sensors are delicate and will not work if dropped or knocked, if their power supply is disrupted, or if any cleaning materials are used on them.
18 The two sensors are threaded into the exhaust manifold – one 'upstream' and one 'downstream' of the catalytic converter.
19 Disconnect the battery negative lead as described in Chapter 5A Section 4.
20 Trace the wiring from the sensor, and disconnect the wiring plug **(see illustration)**.
21 Unscrew the sensor, taking care to avoid damaging the sensor probe as it is removed.
Note: *As a flying lead remains connected to*

2.20 Trace the oxygen sensor wiring back to the plugs

the sensor after it has been disconnected, if the correct spanner is not available, a slotted socket will be required to remove the sensor.
22 Apply a little anti-seize grease to the sensor threads – avoid contaminating the probe tip.
23 Refit the sensor, tightening it to the specified torque. Reconnect the wiring connector.
24 Reconnect the battery as described in Chapter 5A Section 4.

3 Catalytic converter – general information and precautions

1 The catalytic converter is a reliable and simple device which needs no maintenance in itself, but there are some facts of which an owner should be aware if the converter is to function properly for its full service life.

a) *DO NOT use leaded petrol or LRP in a car equipped with a catalytic converter – the lead will coat the precious metals, reducing their converting efficiency and will eventually destroy the converter.*

b) *Always keep the ignition and fuel systems well-maintained in accordance with the manufacturer's schedule.*

c) *If the engine develops a misfire, do not drive the car at all (or at least as little as possible) until the fault is cured.*

d) *DO NOT push- or tow-start the car – this will soak the catalytic converter in unburned fuel, causing it to overheat when the engine does start.*

e) *DO NOT switch off the ignition at high engine speeds.*

f) *DO NOT use fuel or engine oil additives – these may contain substances harmful to the catalytic converter.*

g) *DO NOT continue to use the car if the engine burns oil to the extent of leaving a visible trail of blue smoke.*

h) *Remember that the catalytic converter operates at very high temperatures. DO NOT, therefore, park the car in dry undergrowth, over long grass or piles of dead leaves after a long run.*

i) *Remember that the catalytic converter is FRAGILE – do not strike it with tools during servicing work.*

j) *In some cases a sulphurous smell (like that of rotten eggs) may be noticed from the exhaust. This is common to many catalytic converter-equipped cars and once the car has covered a fewthousand miles the problem should disappear.*

k) *The catalytic converter, used on a well-maintained and well-driven car, should last for between 50-000 and100-000 miles – if the converter is no longer effective it must be renewed.*

Chapter 5 Part A
Starting and charging systems

Contents

Section number

Alternator – testing, removal and refitting 6
Battery – testing and charging 3
Battery and battery tray – disconnection, removal and refitting 4
Charging system – testing 5
Electrical fault finding – general information 2

Section number

General information and precautions 1
Ignition switch and lock barrel – removal and refitting 10
Starter motor – removal and refitting 8
Starter motor – testing and overhaul 9
Starting system – testing 7

Degrees of difficulty

Easy, suitable for novice with little experience	Fairly easy, suitable for beginner with some experience	Fairly difficult, suitable for competent DIY mechanic	Difficult, suitable for experienced DIY mechanic	Very difficult, suitable for expert DIY or professional

Specifications

System type . . . . 12-volt, negative earth

Alternator 70A

Starter motor:
Models without stop-start system . . . . Hitachi J68 1.0 kW
Models with stop-start system . . . . Bosch S74M 1.65 kW

Battery:
SOHC 8v engines without air conditioning . . . . 40 Ah
DOHC 16v engines, and models with air conditioning . . . . 50 Ah
Models with stop-start system . . . . 63 Ah

Battery charge condition:
Poor . . . . 12.5 volts
Normal . . . . 12.6 volts
Good . . . . 12.7 volts

Torque wrench settings

	Nm	lbf ft
Alternator:		
M10 nuts/bolts	50	37
M8 nuts/bolts	25	19
Starter motor bolts	25	19

1 General information and precautions

General information

1 The engine electrical system consists mainly of the charging and starting systems. Because of their engine-related functions, these components are covered separately from the body electrical devices such as the lights, instruments, etc (which are covered in Chapter 12). Information on the ignition system is covered in Part B of this Chapter.

2 The electrical system is of 12 volt negative earth type.

3 The battery fitted as original equipment is of maintenance-free (sealed for life) type and is charged by the alternator, which is belt-driven from the crankshaft pulley. If a non-original battery is fitted it may be of standard or low maintenance type.

4 The starter motor is of the pre-engaged type incorporating an integral solenoid. On starting, the solenoid moves the drive pinion into engagement with the flywheel ring gear before the starter motor is energised. Once the engine has started, a one-way clutch prevents the motor armature being driven by the engine until the pinion disengages from the flywheel.

Precautions

5 Further details of the various systems are given in the relevant Sections of this Chapter. While some repair procedures are given, the usual course of action is to renew the component concerned. The owner whose interest extends beyond mere component renewal should obtain a copy of the Automotive Electrical & Electronic Systems Manual, available from the publishers of this manual.

6 It is necessary to take extra care when working on the electrical system to avoid damage to semi-conductor devices (diodes and transistors), and to avoid the risk of personal injury. In addition to the precautions given in Safety first! at the beginning of this manual, observe the following when working on the system:

● Always remove rings, watches, etc before working on the electrical system. Even with the battery disconnected, capacitive discharge could occur if a component's live terminal is earthed through a metal object. This could cause a shock or nasty burn.

● Do not reverse the battery connections. Components such as the alternator, electronic control units, or any other components having semi-conductor circuitry could be irreparably damaged.

● If the engine is being started using jump leads and a slave battery, connect the batteries positive-to-positive and negative-to-negative (see 'Jump starting'). This also applies when connecting a battery charger but in this case both of the battery terminals should first be disconnected.

● Never disconnect the battery terminals, the alternator, any electrical wiring or any test instruments when the engine is running.

● Do not allow the engine to turn the alternator when the alternator is not connected.

● Never test for alternator output by flashing the output lead to earth.

● Never use an ohmmeter of the type incorporating a hand-cranked generator for circuit or continuity testing.

● Always ensure that the battery negative lead is disconnected when working on the electrical system.

● Before using electric-arc welding equipment on the car, disconnect the battery, alternator and components such as the fuel injection/ignition electronic control unit to protect them from the risk of damage.

2 Electrical fault finding – general information

1 Refer to Chapter 12 Section 2.

3 Battery – testing and charging

Standard and low maintenance battery – testing

1 If the vehicle covers a small annual mileage, it is worthwhile checking the specific gravity of the electrolyte every three months to determine the state of charge of the battery. Use a hydrometer to make the check and compare the results with the following table. Note that the specific gravity readings assume an electrolyte temperature of 15°C (60°F); for every 10°C (18°F) below 15°C (60°F) subtract 0.007. For every 10°C (18°F) above 15°C (60°F) add 0.007.

Ambient temperature	Above 25°C (77°F)	Below 25°C (77°F)
Fully charged	1.210 to 1.230	1.270 to 1.290
70% charged	1.17 to 1.190	1.230 to 1.250
Discharged	1.050 to 1.070	1.110 to 1.130

2 If the battery condition is suspect, first check the specific gravity of electrolyte in each cell. A variation of 0.040 or more between any cells indicates loss of electrolyte or deterioration of the internal plates.

3 If the specific gravity variation is 0.040 or more, the battery should be renewed. If the cell variation is satisfactory but the battery is discharged, it should be charged as described later in this Section.

Maintenance-free battery – testing

4 In cases where a "sealed for life" maintenance-free battery is fitted, topping-up and testing of the electrolyte in each cell is not possible. The condition of the battery can therefore only be tested using a battery condition indicator or a voltmeter.

5 Models may be fitted with a "Delco" type maintenance-free battery, with a built-in charge condition indicator. The indicator is located in the top of the battery casing, and indicates the condition of the battery from its colour. If the indicator shows green, then the battery is in a good state of charge. If the indicator turns darker, eventually to black, then the battery requires charging, as described later in this Section. If the indicator shows clear/yellow, then the electrolyte level in the battery is too low to allow further use, and the battery should be renewed. Do not attempt to charge, load or jump start a battery when the indicator shows clear/yellow.

6 If testing the battery using a voltmeter, connect the voltmeter across the battery and compare the result with those given in the Specifications under "charge condition". The test is only accurate if the battery has not been subjected to any kind of charge for the previous six hours. If this is not the case, switch on the headlights for 30 seconds, then wait four to five minutes before testing the battery after switching off the headlights. All other electrical circuits must be switched off, so check that the doors and tailgate are fully shut when making the test.

7 If the voltage reading is less than 12.2 volts, then the battery is discharged, whilst a reading of 12.2 to 12.4 volts indicates a partially discharged condition.

8 If the battery is to be charged, remove it from the vehicle (Section 4) and charge it as described later in this Section.

Standard and low maintenance battery – charging

Note: *The following is intended as a guide only. Always refer to the manufacturer's recommendations (often printed on a label attached to the battery) before charging a battery.*

9 Charge the battery at a rate of 3.5 to 4 amps and continue to charge the battery at this rate until no further rise in specific gravity is noted over a four hour period.

10 Alternatively, a trickle charger charging at the rate of 1.5 amps can safely be used overnight.

11 Specially rapid "boost" charges which are claimed to restore the power of the battery in 1 to 2 hours are not recommended, as they can cause serious damage to the battery plates through overheating.

12 While charging the battery, note that the temperature of the electrolyte should never exceed 37.8°C (100°F).

Maintenance-free battery – charging

Note: *The following is intended as a guide only. Always refer to the manufacturer's recommendations (often printed on a label attached to the battery) before charging a battery.*

13 This battery type takes considerably longer to fully recharge than the standard type, the time taken being dependent on the extent of discharge, but it can take anything up to three days.

14 A constant voltage type charger is required, to be set, when connected, to 13.9 to 14.9 volts with a charger current below 25 amps. Using this method, the battery should be usable within three hours, giving a voltage reading of 12.5 volts, but this is for a partially discharged battery and, as mentioned, full charging can take considerably longer.

15 If the battery is to be charged from a fully discharged state (condition reading less than 12.2 volts), have it recharged by your Mercedes Benz dealer or local automotive electrician, as the charge rate is higher and constant supervision during charging is necessary.

Caution: Do not charge AGM batteries above 14.8 volts, or the battery may be damaged.

4 Battery and battery tray – disconnection, removal and refitting

Battery

Disconnection

1 Open the bonnet, fold-out the locking lever from the battery negative terminal clap, and disconnect the negative lead **(see illustration)**.

Models upto 10/2008

2 Release the clips and remove the supply box cover from above the battery positive terminal **(see illustration)**.

3 Slacken the clamp nut, disconnect the positive lead from the battery and position the supply box to one side **(see illustration)**.

4.1 Fold out the locking lever and disconnect the negative lead

Models from 10/2008, or with Stop-start system

4 Pull up the plastic cover over the battery positive terminal.

5 Slacken the clamp and pull the positive lead clamp from the battery terminal.

Removal

6 Disconnect the battery as described previously in this Section.

7 Unscrew the nut or bolt (as applicable) and remove the battery retaining strap, then lift the battery out of the engine compartment **(see illustration)**. Disconnect the vent pipe (where fitted) as the battery is withdrawn.

Refitting

8 Models equipped with a stop-start system, are fitted with a battery condition sensor incorporated into the negative terminal. Fiat state that if the battery charge is less than 80%, it must be charged before using the vehicle.

9 Refitting is a reversal of removal, but smear petroleum jelly on the terminals after reconnecting the leads, and always reconnect the positive lead first, and the negative lead last.

Battery tray

Removal

10 Remove the battery as described previously in this Section.

11 Where applicable, on models with Stop-start system, prise up the retaining stud and remove the support bracket above the battery tray fastener.

12 Undo the retaining bolts, release any

4.2 Release the clips and remove the cover

wiring and remove the battery tray **(see illustration)**.

Refitting

13 Refitting is a reversal of removal

5 Charging system – testing

Note: *Refer to the warnings given in 'Safety first!' and in Section 1 of this Chapter before starting work.*

1 If the ignition warning light fails to illuminate when the ignition is switched on, first check the alternator wiring connections for security. If satisfactory, check that the warning light bulb has not blown, and that the bulbholder is secure in its location in the instrument panel. If the light still fails to illuminate, check the continuity of the warning light feed wire from the alternator to the bulbholder. If all is satisfactory, the alternator is at fault and should be renewed or taken to an auto-electrician for testing and repair.

2 If the ignition warning light illuminates when the engine is running, stop the engine and check that the drivebelt is correctly tensioned (see Chapter 1 Section 5) and that the alternator connections are secure. If all is so far satisfactory, have the alternator checked by an auto-electrician.

3 If the alternator output is suspect even though the warning light functions correctly, the regulated voltage may be checked as follows.

4.3 Slacken the nut and pull the positive clamp from the battery terminal

4.7 Battery retaining strap bolt/nut

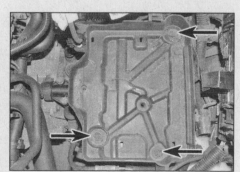
4.12 Battery tray retaining bolts

4 Connect a voltmeter across the battery terminals and start the engine.

5 Increase the engine speed until the voltmeter reading remains steady; the reading should be approximately 12 to 13 volts, and no more than 14 volts.

6 Switch on as many electrical accessories (eg, the headlights, heated rear window and heater blower) as possible, and check that the alternator maintains the regulated voltage at around 13 to 14 volts.

7 If the regulated voltage is not as stated, the fault may be due to worn brushes, weak brush springs, a faulty voltage regulator, a faulty diode, a severed phase winding or worn or damaged slip-rings. The alternator should be renewed or taken to an auto-electrician for testing and repair.

6 Alternator – testing, removal and refitting

Testing

1 If the alternator is thought to be faulty, it should be removed from the vehicle and taken to an auto-electrician for testing. However, check the cost of repairs before proceeding, as it may prove more economical to obtain a new or exchange alternator. If the brushes/regulator pack is at fault, renew it as described in Section.

Removal

2 On models with air conditioning, have the refrigerant circuit evacuated by a Fiat dealer or suitably equipped repairer.

3 Disconnect the battery negative lead as described in Section 4.

4 Remove the auxiliary drivebelt as described in Chapter 1 Section 5.

5 On models with air conditioning, undo the bolts and disconnect the refrigerant pipes from the compressor **(see illustration)**. Disconnection of the pipes is necessary to

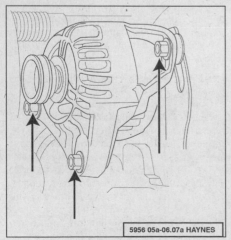

6.7a Alternator mounting bolts – non-air conditioned models

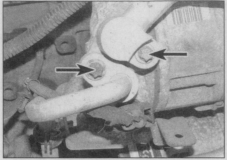

6.5 Undo the bolts and disconnect the refrigerant pipes

access the alternator upper mounting bolt. Plug the openings to prevent contamination.
6 Release the cover, and disconnect the wiring from the alternator **(see illustration)**.
7 Undo the retaining nut/bolts, and manoeuvre the alternator from place **(see illustrations)**.

Refitting

8 Refitting is a reversal of removal, noting the following points:
a) Refit the auxiliary drivebelt as described in Chapter 1 Section 5.
b) Tighten all fasteners to their specified torque where given.

7 Starting system – testing

Note: *Refer to the precautions given in Safety first! and in Section 1 of this Chapter before starting work.*

1 If the starter motor fails to operate when the ignition key is turned to the appropriate position, the following possible causes may be responsible.
a) The battery is faulty.
b) The electrical connections between the switch, solenoid, battery and starter motor are somewhere failing to pass the necessary current from the battery through the starter to earth.
c) The solenoid is faulty.
d) The starter motor is mechanically or electrically defective.

6.7b Alternator mounting bolts – air conditioned models

6.6 Undo the nuts and disconnect the alternator wiring

2 To check the battery, switch on the headlights. If they dim after a few seconds, this indicates that the battery is discharged – recharge (see Section 3) or renew the battery. If the headlights glow brightly, operate the ignition switch and observe the lights. If they dim, then this indicates that current is reaching the starter motor; therefore the fault must lie in the starter motor. If the lights continue to glow brightly (and no clicking sound can be heard from the starter motor solenoid), this indicates that there is a fault in the circuit or solenoid – see following paragraphs. If the starter motor turns slowly when operated, but the battery is in good condition, then this indicates that either the starter motor is faulty, or there is considerable resistance somewhere in the circuit.

3 If a fault in the circuit is suspected, disconnect the battery leads (including the earth connection to the body), the starter/solenoid wiring and the engine/transmission earth strap. Thoroughly clean the connections, and reconnect the leads and wiring, then use a voltmeter or test lamp to check that full battery voltage is available at the battery positive lead connection to the solenoid, and that the earth is sound. Smear petroleum jelly around the battery terminals to prevent corrosion – corroded connections are amongst the most frequent causes of electrical system faults

4 If the battery and all connections are in good condition, check the circuit by disconnecting the trigger wire from the solenoid terminal. Connect a voltmeter or test lamp between the wire end and a good earth (such as the battery negative terminal), and check that the wire is live when the ignition switch is turned to the 'start' position. If it is, then the circuit is sound – if not the circuit wiring can be checked as described in Chapter 12 Section 2.

5 The solenoid contacts can be checked by connecting a voltmeter or test lamp between the battery positive feed connection on the starter side of the solenoid and earth. When the ignition switch is turned to the 'start' position, there should be a reading or lighted bulb, as applicable. If there is no reading or lighted bulb, the solenoid is faulty and should be renewed.

6 If the circuit and solenoid are proved sound, the fault must lie in the starter motor. Begin

8.3 Starter motor upper mounting bolt

8.4a Unclip the plastic cover...

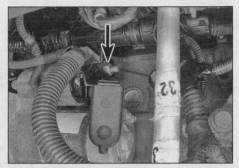

8.4b... undo the nut...

8.4c... pull out the main supply cable...

8.4d... remove the plastic moulding...

8.4e... and disconnect the remaining cable

checking the starter motor by removing it and having the brushes checked. If the fault does not lie in the brushes, the motor windings must be faulty. In this event, it may be possible to have the starter motor overhauled by a specialist, but check on the availability and cost of spares before proceeding, as it may prove more economical to obtain a new or exchange motor.

8 Starter motor – removal and refitting

Removal

1 Raise the front of the vehicle and support it securely on axle stands, as described in 'Vehicle jacking and support'.

2 Disconnect the battery negative lead as described in Section 4.
3 Unscrew and remove the starter motor upper mounting bolt located at the top of the transmission bellhousing (see illustration).
4 Open the plastic cover, undo the nut, pull the main supply cable from the stud, then remove the plastic cover/moulding, and disconnect the wiring from the solenoid terminal stud (see illustrations).
5 Unscrew the lower mounting bolt(s), then withdraw the starter motor from the transmission (see illustration).

Refitting

6 Refitting is a reversal of removal, tightening the starter motor retaining bolts to the specified torque.

9 Starter motor – testing and overhaul

1 If the starter motor is thought to be suspect, it should be removed from the vehicle and taken to an auto-electrician for testing. Most auto-electricians will be able to supply and fit brushes at a reasonable cost. However, check on the cost of repairs before proceeding as it may prove more economical to obtain a new or exchange motor.

10 Ignition switch and lock barrel – removal and refitting

Ignition switch assembly

Removal

1 Remove the steering column assembly as described in Chapter 10 Section 13.
Caution: The steering column shafts must not be rotated during this procedure.
2 The ignition switch/steering column lock assembly is secured to the steering column using 'shear' bolts. Drill-out the shear bolts, or unscrew them using a sharp chisel and hammer (see illustration). Obtain replacement shear bolts.
3 Remove the collar, followed by the ignition switch/steering lock assembly.

8.5 Starter motor lower mounting bolt

10.2 Ignition switch/steering column lock assembly shear bolts

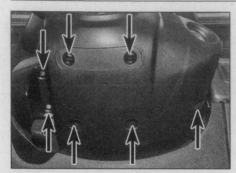

10.7 Lower steering column shroud retaining screws

10.8a Unclip the switch stalk trim panel

10.8b Upper shroud retaining bolts

Refitting

4 Position the ignition switch/steering lock assembly, insert the new shear bolts, and tighten them until their heads shear off.

5 The remainder of refitting is a reversal of removal.

Ignition switch contact assembly

Removal

6 Remove the steering wheel as described in Chapter 10 Section 12.

7 Undo the retaining screws, and unclip the steering column lower shroud **(see illustration)**.

10.18a Depress the retaining lug...

8 Unclip the steering column switch stalk trim panel, then undo the 2 retaining bolts and lift the steering column upper shroud from place **(see illustrations)**. There's no need to completely remove the shroud.

9 Insert the ignition key into the lock barrel, and turn it to the 'On' position.

10 Disconnect the wiring plug, undo the 2 retaining screws, and remove the ignition switch contact assembly.

Refitting

11 Position the contact assembly on the switch housing, and tighten the retaining screws securely.

10.18b... and withdraw the lock barrel assembly

12 Reconnect the switch wiring plug.

13 Turn the ignition key to the 'Off' position and withdraw it from the lock barrel.

14 The remainder of refitting is a reversal of removal.

Ignition key lock barrel

Removal

15 Disconnect the battery negative lead as described in Section 4.

16 Move the steering column adjustment lever to its lowest position, then remove the steering column lower shroud as described earlier in this Section.

17 Insert the ignition key into the barrel, and turn it to position 'On'.

18 Using a small screwdriver, depress the retaining lug, and withdraw the barrel assembly from the housing **(see illustrations)**.

19 Remove the circlip from the rear of the barrel assembly.

20 Depress the retaining tab, and turn the ignition key so the barrel lug aligns with the slot in the housing.

21 Carefully withdraw the barrel from the housing.

Refitting

22 Refitting is a reversal of removal, but check the operation of the barrel/lock before refitting the steering column shrouds.

Chapter 5 Part B
Ignition system

Contents

Section number

General information 1
Ignition coils – removal, testing and refitting 3
Ignition system – testing. 2

Section number

Ignition timing – checking and adjustment. 4
Knock sensor – removal and refitting. 5

Degrees of difficulty

Easy, suitable for novice with little experience	**Fairly easy,** suitable for beginner with some experience	**Fairly difficult,** suitable for competent DIY mechanic	**Difficult,** suitable for experienced DIY mechanic	**Very difficult,** suitable for expert DIY or professional

Specifications

General

System type:
SOHC 8v models	Digital (distributorless) ignition system controlled by the engine management ECU. Single BAE 940A coil assembly.
DOHC 16v models	Digital (distributorless) ignition system controlled by the engine management ECU. 4 Fedral Mogul pencil coils.
Firing order	1-3-4-2
Spark plugs	See Chapter 1 specifications
Ignition timing.	Controlled by the engine management ECU

Ignition coil(s):
SOHC 8v engines:
Primary resistance (at 23°C)	0.5 ohms ± 10%
Secondary resistance (at 23°C)	6000 ohms ± 10%

DOHC 16v engines:
Primary resistance (at 23°C)	0.5 ohms ± 10%
Secondary resistance (at 23°C)	6300 ohms ± 10%

Torque wrench setting	**Nm**	**lbf ft**
Knock sensor retaining bolt	25	18

1 General information

1 The ignition system is integrated with the fuel injection system to form a combined engine management system under the control of one ECU (see Chapter 4A for further information).

SOHC 8v models

2 The ignition side of the system is of the digital (distributorless) type, consisting of a coil assembly bolted to the top of the cylinder head cover. The ECU uses its inputs from the various sensors to calculate the required ignition advance setting and coil charging time depending on engine temperature, load and speed.

DOHC 16v models

3 The ignition side of the system is of the digital (distributorless) type, consisting of 4 'pencil' coils – each fitted directly above the spark plugs. The engine management ECU uses the inputs from the various sensors to

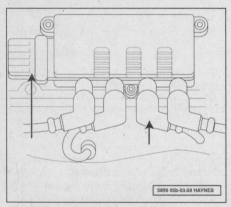

3.3 Disconnect the LT wiring plug (1) and HT leads (2)

calculate the required ignition advance setting and coil charging time depending on engine temperature, load and speed.

All models

4 A knock sensor is also incorporated into the ignition system. Mounted onto the cylinder block, the sensor detects the high-frequency vibrations caused when the engine starts to pre-ignite, or 'pink'. Under these conditions, the knock sensor sends an electrical signal to the ECU which in turn retards the ignition advance setting in small steps until the 'pinking' ceases.

2 Ignition system – testing

⚠️ **Warning: Due to the high voltages produced by the electronic ignition system, extreme care must be taken when working on the system with the ignition switched on. Persons with surgically-implanted cardiac pacemaker devices should keep well clear of the ignition circuits, components and test equipment.**

1 If a fault appears in the engine management (fuel injection/ignition) system first ensure that the fault is not due to a poor electrical connection or poor maintenance; ie, check that the air cleaner filter element is clean, the spark plugs are in good condition, that the engine breather hoses are clear and undamaged, referring to Chapter for further information. If the engine is running very roughly, check the compression pressures and the valve clearances as described in Chapter 2A Section 2, Chapter 2B Section 2 and Chapter 1 Section 16.

2 If these checks fail to reveal the cause of the problem, the vehicle should be taken to a Fiat dealer or suitably equipped repairer for testing. A diagnostic connector

is incorporated in the engine management wiring circuit into which a special electronic diagnostic tester can be plugged (Chapter 4A Section 8). The tester will locate the fault quickly and simply alleviating the need to test all the system components individually which is a time-consuming operation that carries a high risk of damaging the ECU.

3 The only ignition system checks which can be carried out by the home mechanic are those described in Chapter 1 Section 17, relating to the spark plugs, and the ignition coil test described in this Section 3. If necessary, the system wiring and wiring connectors can be checked as described in Chapter, ensuring that the ECU wiring connectors have first been disconnected.

3 Ignition coils – removal, testing and refitting

Removal

1 Remove the air cleaner assembly as described in Chapter 4A Section 2.
2 Disconnect the battery negative lead as described in Chapter 5A Section 4.

SOHC 8V models

3 Disconnect the LT wiring plug from the top of the ignition coil **(see illustration)**.
4 Identify the HT leads for position then disconnect them from the coil HT terminals.
5 Undo the retaining bolts and remove the coil assembly.

DOHC 16v models

6 Disconnect the wiring plug from the absolute pressure sensor on the top of the camshaft housing, and from the individual coils **(see illustrations)**.
7 Undo the bolt securing the wiring harness duct to the camshaft housing.
8 Undo the bolt and pull the relevant coil

3.6a Disconnect the absolute pressure sensor wiring plug

3.6b Prise out the yellow catch and depress the black clip to disconnect the wiring plugs

3.8 Undo the bolt and pull the coil(s) upwards

5.4 Knock sensor retaining bolt

upwards from the spark plug location (see illustration).

Testing

9 Testing of the coil consists of using a multimeter set to its resistance function, to check the primary and secondary windings for continuity and resistance. Compare the results obtained to those given in the Specifications at the start of this Chapter. Note the resistance of the coil windings varies slightly according to the coil temperature and the figures in the Specifications are values for the coil at 23°C.

10 Check that there is no continuity between the HT lead terminals and the coil body/mounting bracket.

11 If faulty, the coil should be renewed.

Refitting

12 Refitting is a reversal of removal, ensuring the HT leads (where applicable) are correctly reconnected.

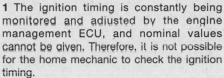

4 Ignition timing –
checking and adjustment

1 The ignition timing is constantly being monitored and adjusted by the engine management ECU, and nominal values cannot be given. Therefore, it is not possible for the home mechanic to check the ignition timing.

2 The only way in which the timing can be checked is using special electronic test equipment, connected to the engine management system diagnostic connector (refer to Chapter 4A Section 8 for further information).

5 Knock sensor –
removal and refitting

Removal

1 The knock sensor is located on the rear face of the cylinder block.

2 Raise the front of the vehicle and support it securely on axle stands, as described in 'Vehicle jacking and support'.

3 Trace the wiring back from the sensor to its wiring plug, and disconnect it from the main harness.

4 Undo the sensor retaining bolt and manoeuvre it from position (see illustration).

Refitting

5 Refitting is a reversal of removal, tightening the retaining bolt to the specified torque.

Notes

Chapter 6
Clutch

Contents

	Section number		Section number
Clutch assembly – removal, inspection and refitting	5	Clutch release mechanism – removal, inspection and refitting	6
Clutch hydraulic system – bleeding	2	Clutch slave cylinder – removal, inspection and refitting	4
Clutch master cylinder – removal and refitting	3	General information	1

Degrees of difficulty

Easy, suitable for novice with little experience	**Fairly easy,** suitable for beginner with some experience	**Fairly difficult,** suitable for competent DIY mechanic	**Difficult,** suitable for experienced DIY mechanic	**Very difficult,** suitable for expert DIY or professional

Specifications

Type	Single dry plate with diaphragm spring, hydraulically-operated
Friction plate diameter	200 mm

Torque wrench settings	Nm	lbf ft
Master cylinder retaining bolts	25	18
Pressure plate retaining bolts*	15	10
Slave cylinder mounting bolts	20	15

*Do not re-use

1 General Information

1 The clutch assembly consists of a friction plate, a pressure plate, a release bearing and release fork; all of these components are contained in the large cast-aluminium alloy bellhousing, sandwiched between the engine and the transmission. The release mechanism is hydraulic, utilising a master cylinder and slave cylinder.

2 The friction plate is fitted between the engine flywheel and the clutch pressure plate, and is allowed to slide on the transmission input shaft splines.

3 The pressure plate assembly is bolted to the engine flywheel. When the engine is running, drive is transmitted from the crankshaft, via the flywheel, to the friction plate (these components being clamped securely together by the pressure plate assembly) and from the friction plate to the transmission input shaft.

4 To interrupt the drive, the spring pressure must be relaxed. This is done by means of the clutch release bearing, fitted concentrically around the transmission input shaft. The bearing is pushed onto the pressure plate assembly by means of the release fork actuated by the slave cylinder pushrod.

5 The clutch pedal is connected to the clutch master cylinder by a short pushrod. The master cylinder is mounted on the engine side of the bulkhead in front of the driver and receives its hydraulic fluid supply from the brake master cylinder reservoir. Depressing the clutch pedal moves the piston in the master cylinder forwards, so forcing hydraulic fluid through the clutch hydraulic pipe to the slave cylinder. The piston in the slave cylinder moves forward on the entry of the fluid and actuates the clutch release fork by means of a short pushrod. The release fork pivots on its mountings, and the other end of the fork then presses the release bearing against the pressure plate spring fingers. This causes the springs to deform and releases the clamping force on the pressure plate.

6 The clutch operating mechanism is self-adjusting, and no manual adjustment is required.

2 Clutch hydraulic system – bleeding

 Warning: Hydraulic fluid is poisonous; thoroughly wash off spills from bare skin without delay. Seek immediate medical advice if any fluid is swallowed or gets into the eyes. Certain types of hydraulic fluid are inflammable and may ignite when brought into contact with hot components; when servicing any hydraulic system, it is safest to assume that the fluid IS inflammable, and to take precautions against the risk of fire as though it were petrol that was being handled. Hydraulic fluid is an effective paint stripper and will also attack many plastics. If spillage occurs onto painted bodywork or fittings it should be washed off immediately, using copious quantities of fresh water. It is also hygroscopic – it can absorb moisture from the air, which then renders it useless. Old fluid may have suffered contamination, and should never

be re-used. *When topping-up or renewing the fluid, always use the recommended grade, and ensure that it comes from a new sealed container.*

General information

1 Whenever the clutch hydraulic lines are disconnected for service or repair, a certain amount of air will enter the system. The presence of air in any hydraulic system will introduce a degree of elasticity, and in the clutch system this will translate into poor pedal feel and reduced travel, leading to inefficient gearchanges and even clutch system failure. For this reason, after reconnection of the hydraulic lines, the system must be topped-up and bled to remove any air bubbles.

2 The most effective way of bleeding the clutch hydraulic system is to use a pressure brake bleeding kit. These are readily available in motor accessories shops and are extremely effective. The following procedure describes bleeding the clutch system using such a kit. The alternative method is to bleed the system by depressing the clutch pedal – refer to the brake hydraulic system bleeding procedures contained in Chapter 9 Section 2 for details of this method.

Bleeding

3 Remove the protective cap from the slave cylinder bleed nipple **(see illustration)**. Connect a length of clear plastic hose over the nipple and insert the other end into a clean container. Pour hydraulic fluid into the container, such that the end of the hose is covered.

4 Following the manufacturer's instructions, pour hydraulic fluid into the bleeding kit vessel.

5 Unscrew the brake fluid reservoir filler cap, then connect the bleeding kit fluid supply hose to the reservoir.

6 Connect the pressure hose to a supply of compressed air – a spare tyre is a convenient source.

Caution: Check that the pressure in the tyre does not exceed the maximum supply pressure quoted by the kit manufacturer, let some air escape to reduce the pressure,

2.3 Slave cylinder bleed nipple protective cap

if necessary. Gently open the air valve and allow the air and fluid pressures to equalise. Check that there are no leaks before proceeding

7 Slacken the nipple approximately half a turn.

8 Allow the hydraulic fluid to flow from the slave cylinder, through the plastic hose and into the container. Maintain a steady flow until the emerging fluid is free of air bubbles; keep a watchful eye on the level of fluid in the bleeding kit vessel and the brake fluid reservoir – if it is allowed to drop too low, air may be forced into the system, defeating the object of the exercise. To refill the vessel, turn off the compressed air supply, remove the lid and pour in an appropriate quantity of fresh fluid – do not re-use the fluid collected in the receiving container. Repeat as necessary until the ejected fluid is bubble-free.

9 When clean hydraulic fluid, free from air bubbles, emerges from the plastic hose, tighten the slave cylinder bleed nipple.

10 Pump the clutch pedal several times to assess its feel and travel. If firm, constant pedal resistance is not felt throughout the pedal stroke, it is probable that air is still present in the system – repeat the bleeding procedure until the pedal feel is restored.

11 Depressurise the bleeding kit and remove the kit, plastic hose and receiving container from the vehicle. Refit the protective cap to the bleed nipple. Discard the fluid expelled from the hydraulic system as it will be

contaminated with moisture, air and dirt, making it unfit for further use.

12 Check the fluid level in the reservoir. At this point, the reservoir may be over-full; the excess should be removed using a clean pipette to reduce the level to the MAX mark.

13 Refit the battery tray and battery as described in Chapter 5A Section 4.

14 Finally, road test the vehicle and check the operation of the clutch system whilst changing up and down through the gears, whilst pulling away from a standstill and from a hill start.

3 Clutch master cylinder – removal and refitting

Note: *Refer to the precautions given in Section 2 regarding the use of hydraulic fluid.*

Removal

1 To minimise hydraulic fluid loss, remove the brake master cylinder reservoir filler cap, then tighten it down onto a piece of polythene to obtain an airtight seal. Alternatively, fit a brake hose clamp to the hose between the hydraulic fluid reservoir and the clutch mastercylinder.

2 Disconnect the fluid supply hose at the master cylinder, then extract the retaining clip and disconnect the hydraulic pipe from the cylinder outlet **(see illustration)**. Be prepared for fluid spillage.

3 Working under the facia, remove the retaining clip and slide out the master cylinder pushrod clevis pin from the pedal **(see illustration)**.

4 Undo the retaining bolts and manoeuvre the master cylinder from under the facia **(see illustration)**.

5 It is not possible to obtain an overhaul kit from Fiat, however some motor factors may be able to supply one. Follow the instructions with the repair kit if obtained.

Refitting

6 Refitting is a reversal of removal, but bleed the clutch hydraulic system as described in Section 2.

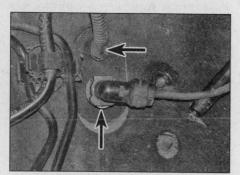

3.2 Disconnect the supply hose, the prise out the clip a little and disconnect the hydraulic pipe

3.3 Prise up the edge and slide off the clevis pin clip

3.4 Clutch master cylinder retaining bolts

4.4 Slave cylinder hose retaining clip and mounting bolts

5.3 Use a Ribe 7 bit to unscrew the pressure plate bolts

4 Clutch slave cylinder – removal, inspection and refitting

Removal

1 Remove the battery and battery tray as described in Chapter 5A Section 4.

2 To minimise hydraulic fluid loss, remove the brake master cylinder reservoir filler cap, then tighten it down onto a piece of polythene to obtain an airtight seal.

3 Place absorbent rags around the slave cylinder, and be prepared for hydraulic fluid loss.

4 Prise out the retaining clip a little, and disconnect the hydraulic hose from the slave cylinder **(see illustration)**.

5 Unscrew the slave cylinder mounting bolts, release the cylinder pushrod from the release arm on the transmission, then remove the unit from the engine compartment.

6 It is not possible to obtain an overhaul kit from Fiat, however some motor factors may be able to supply one. Follow the instructions with the repair kit if obtained.

Refitting

7 Refitting is a reversal of removal, but bleed the clutch hydraulic system as described in Section 2.

5 Clutch assembly – removal, inspection and refitting

 Warning: Dust created by clutch wear and deposited on the clutch components may contain asbestos, which is a health hazard. DO NOT blow it out with compressed air, or inhale any of it. DO NOT use petrol or petroleum-based solvents to clean off the dust. Brake system cleaner or methylated spirit should be used to flush the dust into a suitable receptacle. *After the clutch components are wiped clean with rags, dispose of the contaminated rags and cleaner in a sealed, marked container.*

Removal

1 Unless the complete engine/transmission is to be removed from the car and separated for major overhaul (see Chapter 2C Section 4), the clutch can be reached by removing the transmission as described in Chapter 7 Section 5.

2 Before disturbing the clutch, use chalk or a marker pen to mark the relationship of the pressure plate assembly to the flywheel.

3 Working in a diagonal sequence, slacken the pressure plate bolts (Ribe 7) by half a turn at a time, until spring pressure is released and the bolts can be unscrewed by hand **(see illustration)**. Discard the bolts – new ones must be fitted.

4 Prise the pressure plate assembly off its locating dowels, and collect the friction plate, noting which way round the friction plate is fitted.

Inspection

Note: *Due to the amount of work necessary to remove and refit clutch components, it is usually considered good practice to renew the clutch friction plate, pressure plate assembly and release bearing as a matched set, even if only one of these is actually worn enough to require renewal. It is also worth considering the renewal of the clutch components on a preventative basis if the engine and/or transmission have been removed for some other reason.*

5 When cleaning clutch components, read first the warning at the beginning of this Section; remove dust using a clean, dry cloth, and working in a well-ventilated atmosphere.

Note: *Although some friction materials may no longer contain asbestos, it is safest to assume that they DO, and to take precautions accordingly.*

6 Check the friction plate facings for signs of wear, damage or oil contamination. If the friction material is cracked, burnt, scored or damaged, or if it is contaminated with oil or grease (shown by shiny black patches), the friction plate must be renewed.

7 If the friction material is still serviceable, check that the centre boss splines are unworn, that the torsion springs are in good condition and securely fastened, and that all the rivets are tight. If any wear or damage is found, the friction plate must be renewed.

8 If the friction material is fouled with oil, this must be due to an oil leak from the crankshaft left-hand oil seal, from the sump-to-cylinder block joint, or from the transmission input shaft. Renew the seal or repair the joint, as appropriate, before installing the new friction plate.

9 Check the pressure plate assembly for obvious signs of wear or damage; shake it to check for loose rivets or worn or damaged fulcrum rings, and check that the drive straps securing the pressure plate to the cover do not show signs (such as a deep yellow or blue discoloration) of overheating. If the diaphragm spring is worn or damaged, or if its pressure is in any way suspect, the pressure plate assembly should be renewed.

10 Examine the machined bearing surfaces of the pressure plate and of the flywheel; they should be clean, completely flat, and free from scratches or scoring. If either is discoloured from excessive heat, or shows signs of cracks, it should be renewed – although minor damage of this nature can sometimes be polished away using emery paper.

11 Check that the release bearing contact surface rotates smoothly and easily, with no sign of noise or roughness. Also check that the surface itself is smooth and unworn, with no signs of cracks, pitting or scoring. If there is any doubt about its condition, the bearing must be renewed.

Refitting

12 On reassembly, ensure that the bearing surfaces of the flywheel and pressure plate are

5.16 Use a clutch aligning tool to centralise the plate and cover

6.5 Clutch release shaft (1) and upper shaft bush (2)

completely clean, smooth, and free from oil or grease. Use solvent to remove any protective grease from new components.

13 Fit the friction plate so that its spring hub assembly faces away from the flywheel; there may also be a marking showing which way round the plate is to be refitted.

14 Refit the pressure plate assembly, aligning the marks made on dismantling (if the original pressure plate is re-used), and locating the pressure plate on its locating dowels. Fit the new pressure plate bolts, but tighten them only finger-tight, so that the friction plate can still be moved.

15 The friction plate must now be centralised, so that when the transmission is refitted, its input shaft will pass through the splines at the centre of the friction plate.

16 Centralisation can be achieved by passing a screwdriver or other long bar through the friction plate and into the hole in the crankshaft; the friction plate can then

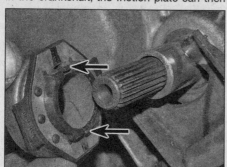

6.14 Engage the release bearing clips with the fork

be moved around until it is centred on the crankshaft hole. Alternatively, a clutch-aligning tool can be used to eliminate the guesswork; these can be obtained from most accessory shops **(see illustration)**. A home-made aligning tool can be fabricated from a length of metal rod or wooden dowel which fits closely inside the crankshaft hole, and has insulating tape wound around it to match the diameter of the friction plate splined hole.

17 When the friction plate is centralised, tighten the pressure plate bolts evenly and in a diagonal sequence to the specified torque setting.

18 Refit the transmission as described in Chapter 7 Section 5.

6 Clutch release mechanism – removal, inspection and refitting

Removal

1 Unless the complete engine/transmission is to be removed from the car and separated for major overhaul (see Chapter 2C Section 4), the clutch release mechanism can be reached by removing the transmission as described in Chapter 7 Section 5.

2 Unhook the release bearing from the fork and slide it off the guide tube.

3 Using circlip pliers extract the circlip from the top of the release fork shaft.

4 Note the position of the arm then slide it off the splines.

5 Using a small drift, tap out the upper release

shaft bush from the transmission casing **(see illustration)**.

6 Lift the release shaft from the lower bush then remove it from inside the transmission casing.

7 Extract the lower bush from the casing.

Inspection

8 Check the release mechanism, renewing any worn or damaged parts. Carefully check all bearing surfaces and points of contact.

9 When checking the release bearing itself, note that it is often considered worthwhile to renew it as a matter of course. Check that the contact surface rotates smoothly and easily, with no sign of roughness, and that the surface itself is smooth and unworn, with no signs of cracks, pitting or scoring. If there is any doubt about its condition, the bearing must be renewed.

Refitting

10 Apply a smear of molybdenum disulphide grease to the shaft pivot bushes and the contact surfaces of the release fork.

11 Tap the lower bush into the casing and refit the release fork and shaft.

12 Slide the upper bush down the shaft and tap it into the casing making sure that the ridge engages with the cut-out, then slide the arm on the splines the correct way round.

13 Refit the circlip in the shaft groove.

14 Slide the release bearing onto the guide tube and engage it with the fork **(see illustration)**.

15 Refit the transmission as described in Chapter 7 Section 5.

Chapter 7
Manual gearbox

Contents

Section number

Gearbox oil – draining and refilling 2
Gearbox overhaul – general information 6
Gearbox – removal and refitting 5
Gearchange lever assembly – removal and refitting 4

Section number

Gearchange selector cables – removal and refitting 3
General information 1
Reversing light switch – testing, removal and refitting 7

Degrees of difficulty

| Easy, suitable for novice with little experience 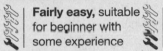 | Fairly easy, suitable for beginner with some experience | Fairly difficult, suitable for competent DIY mechanic | Difficult, suitable for experienced DIY mechanic | Very difficult, suitable for expert DIY or professional |

Specifications

General
TypeT . . . . Transversely-mounted, front wheel drive layout with integral transaxle differential/final drive. 5 or 6 forward speeds, 1 reverse speed
Code . . . . C514.5 (5-speed) or C514.6 (6-speed)

Lubrication
Recommended oil . . . . See 'Lubricants and fluids'
Capacity:
  5-speed transmission . . . . 1.5 litres
  6-speed transmission . . . . 1.7 litres

Torque wrench settings

	Nm	lbf ft
Cylinder block-to-transmission bracket (SOHC 8v only):		
M8	25	18
M10	40	30
M12	55	41
Drain plug	18	13
Filler plug	25	18
Left-hand mounting bracket-to-transmission	70	52
Rear engine mounting:		
Link rod-to-gearbox bracket	100	74
Link rod-to-subframe:		
Stage 1	55	41
Stage 2	Angle-tighten a further 90°	
Bracket-to-gearbox	100	74
Transmission-to-engine	60	44
Transmission-to-sump (DOHC 16v only)	40	30

*Do not re-use

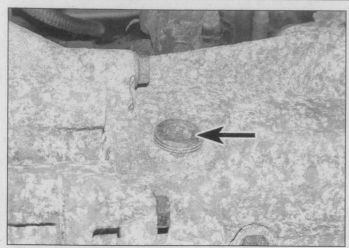
2.2a The filler/level plug is on the front of the transmission...

2.2b... and the drain plug is on the rear/bottom

1 General information

1 The transmission is contained in a cast-aluminium alloy casing bolted to the engine's left-hand end, and consists of the gearbox and final drive differential.

2 Drive is transmitted from the crankshaft via the clutch to the input shaft, which has a splined extension to accept the clutch friction plate and rotates in roller bearings at its right-hand end and ball-bearings at its left-hand end (on 6-speed versions the left-hand extension rotates in a roller bearing). From the input shaft, drive is transmitted to the output shaft which rotates in roller bearings at its right-hand end and ball-bearings at its left-hand end (on 6-speed versions the left-hand extension rotates in ball-bearings). From the output shaft, the drive is transmitted to the differential crownwheel which rotates with the differential case and gears in taper roller bearings, thus driving the sun gears and driveshafts. The rotation of the differential gears on their shaft allows the inner roadwheel to rotate at a slower speed than the outer roadwheel when the car is cornering.

3 The input and output shafts are arranged side-by-side, parallel to the crankshaft and driveshafts, so that their gear pinion teeth are in constant mesh. In the neutral position, the relevant input shaft and output shaft gear pinions rotate freely, so that drive cannot be transmitted to the output shaft and crownwheel.

4 Gear selection is via a floor-mounted lever and twin selector cable mechanism. The selector cables cause the appropriate selector fork to move its respective synchro-sleeve along the shaft, to lock the gear to the synchro-hub. Since the synchro-hubs are splined to the input and output shafts, this locks the gear to the shaft so that drive can be transmitted. To ensure that gearchanging can be made quickly and quietly, a synchromesh system is fitted to all forward gears.

2 Gearbox oil – draining and refilling

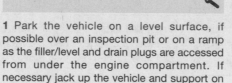

1 Park the vehicle on a level surface, if possible over an inspection pit or on a ramp as the filler/level and drain plugs are accessed from under the engine compartment. If necessary jack up the vehicle and support on axle stands, as described in 'Vehicle jacking and support'.

2 Wipe clean the area around the filler/level and drain plugs, which are on the front and bottom of the transmission (see illustrations).

3 Using an Allen key, unscrew the filler/level plug and clean it.

4 Position a suitable container beneath the transmission, then use the Allen key to unscrew the drain plug. Allow the oil to completely drain.

5 Wipe clean the drain plug then refit and tighten it to the specified torque.

6 Fill the transmission with the correct grade and quantity of oil, referring to Chapter 1 Section 25 when checking the level. Refit and tighten the filler/level plug.

7 Where applicable, lower the vehicle to the ground.

3 Gearchange selector cables – removal and refitting

Removal

1 Remove the battery and battery tray as described in Chapter 5A Section 4.

2 Prise the end of the selector and engagement cables from the levers on the transmission.

3 Pull the locking collars rearwards and slide the outer cables up from the support bracket (see illustration).

4 Raise the front of the vehicle and support it securely on axle stands, as described in 'Vehicle jacking and support'.

5 Unscrew the nuts and disconnect the exhaust front pipe flange from the manifold downpipe. Recover the gasket.

6 Undo the bolts securing the front and rear exhaust system mounting brackets to the underbody. Lower the system and suitably support it.

7 Where an exhaust system front heat shield is fitted, undo the retaining bolts and remove the heat shield.

8 Release the clips and remove the cover from the base of the gear lever housing.

9 Disconnect the gearchange cables end fittings form their attachments at the gear lever linkage.

10 Compress the retaining clips and pull the outer cables from the gear lever housing.

Refitting

11 Refit the gearchange cables to the lever linkage, and engage the outer cables with the lever housing.

12 Refit the lever housing cover.

13 Refit/reconnect the exhaust pipe using a new gasket.

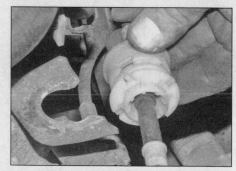
3.3 Pull the collar rearwards and slide the outer cable from the bracket

3.15 Prise up the gaiter and frame

3.16a Lift the reverse inhibitor collar...

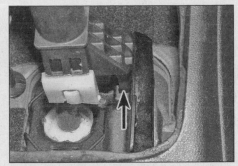

3.16b... rotate it 90°, and engage the lug with the recess in the housing

14 Lower the vehicle to the ground.

15 Prise up the gearchange lever gaiter **(see illustration)**.

16 Raise the reverse inhibitor collar, rotate it clockwise 90° and lower it until it locks in the housing **(see illustrations)**.

17 Refit the outer cables to the support bracket on the transmission.

18 Pull back the locking catch on the selection cable, and depress the spring button – release the catch **(see illustration)**.

19 Press the ends of the cables onto the balljoints on the transmission levers.

20 Pull back the locking catch on the selection cable, and allow the spring button to release, locking the cable adjustment.

21 Release the clip, lift up the inhibitor collar on the gear change lever, and rotate it anti-clockwise 90° **(see illustration)**.

22 The adjustment procedure is now complete.

23 Check the operation of the gear change lever, then refit the battery tray and battery as described in Chapter 5A Section 4.

3.18 Pull back the catch, and depress the spring button

3.21 To release the clip, press it rearwards with a screwdriver

4 Gearchange lever assembly – removal and refitting

Removal

1 Unclip the gear lever gaiter from the centre console **(see illustration 3.15)**, release the Velcro at the top of the gaiter **(see illustration)**. Remove the gaiter.

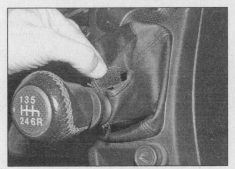

4.1 Release the Velcro at the top of the gaiter

2 Disconnect the gearchange cables from the housing underneath the vehicle as described in Section 3.

3 Undo the bolts and lower the gear lever assembly from place.

Refitting

4 Refitting is a reversal of removal.

5 Gearbox – removal and refitting

Removal

1 Slacken both front roadwheel bolts, then raise the front of the vehicle and support

5.9 Front subframe crossbrace retaining bolts

it securely on axle stands, as described in 'Vehicle jacking and support'. Remove both front roadwheels.

2 Remove the battery and battery tray as described in Chapter 5A Section 4.

3 Drain the transmission oil as described in Section 2.

4 Remove both front driveshafts as described in Chapter 8 Section 2.

5 Remove the air cleaner assembly as described in Chapter 4A Section 2.

6 On DOHC 16v models, release the clamps and remove the air intake hose from the intake manifold.

7 On SOHC 8v models, disconnect the upstream oxygen sensor wiring plug, undo the fasteners and remove the exhaust manifold heat shield.

8 Remove the starter motor as described in Chapter 5A Section 8.

9 Undo the bolts and remove the reinforcing crossbrace from the front subframe **(see illustration)**. Note that the upper part of the crossbrace is marked 'Left' and 'Right' to aid reassembly.

10 Undo the nuts securing the front exhaust pipe to the catalytic converter, and the bolt securing the exhaust pipe support bracket to the transmission bellhousing. Recover the gasket.

11 On SOHC 8v models, undo the bolts and remove the support brace linking the transmission to the cylinder block, then unbolt and remove the cover plate from the lower section of the bellhousing.

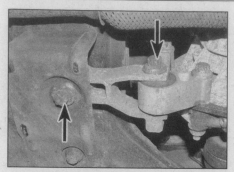

5.12 Remove the rear mounting through-bolts

5.19 Undo the bolts and remove the complete mounting with bracket

7.1 Reversing light switch

12 Undo the through-bolts and remove the rear engine mounting link rod **(see illustration)**.

13 Disconnect the reversing light switch wiring plug **(see illustration 7.1)**.

14 Undo the retaining bolts and move the clutch slave cylinder to one side. There's no need to disconnect the fluid pipe.

15 Undo the nut and disconnect the earth lead from the transmission.

16 With reference to Section 3, detach the gearchange cables from the transmission.

17 Support the weight of the engine using a hoist attached to home-made brackets secured to suitable positions at the left-hand end of the engine.

18 Support the weight of the transmission on a trolley jack then unscrew the engine-to-transmission retaining bolts/nut. Move aside all wiring and support brackets secured by the retaining bolts.

19 Unscrew the bolts securing the left-hand engine/transmission mounting to the body then unscrew the bolts from the transmission and remove the mounting complete with bracket **(see illustration)**.

20 Check that all pipes, hoses and wiring are moved clear then carefully pull the transmission away from the engine. Lower the trolley jack and with the help of an assistant, remove the transmission from under the car.

Caution: Support the transmission to ensure that it remains steady on the jack head. Keep the transmission level until the input shaft is fully withdrawn from the clutch friction plate.

 Warning: Take care, the transmission is heavy!

Refitting

21 Refitting is a reversal of removal, noting the following points:

a) Ensure the gearbox input shaft splines are clean and dry – do not apply any lubricant.

b) Tighten all fasteners to their specified torque, where given.

c) Refill the gearbox with new oil as described in Section 2.

6 Gearbox overhaul – general information

1 Overhauling a manual gearbox unit is a difficult and involved job for the DIY home mechanic. In addition to dismantling and reassembling many small parts, clearances must be precisely measured and, if necessary, changed by selecting shims and spacers. Internal gearbox components are also often difficult to obtain, and in many instances, extremely expensive. Because of this, if the gearbox develops a fault or becomes noisy, the best course of action is to have the unit overhauled by a specialist repairer, or to obtain an exchange reconditioned unit.

2 Nevertheless, it is not impossible for the more experienced mechanic to overhaul the gearbox, provided the special tools are available, and the job is done in a deliberate step-by-step manner, so that nothing is overlooked.

3 The tools necessary for an overhaul include internal and external circlip pliers, bearing pullers, a slide hammer, a set of pin punches, a dial test indicator, and possibly a hydraulic press. In addition, a large, sturdy workbench and a vice will be required.

4 During dismantling of the gearbox, make

careful notes of how each component is fitted, to make reassembly easier and more accurate.

5 Before dismantling the gearbox, it will help if you have some idea what area is malfunctioning. Certain problems can be closely related to specific areas in the gearbox, which can make component examination and replacement easier. Refer to the 'Fault finding 14 Section 9 ' Section of this manual for more information.

7 Reversing light switch – testing, removal and refitting

Testing

1 The reversing light circuit is controlled by a plunger-type switch screwed into the front of the transmission casing **(see illustration)**. If a fault develops, first ensure that the circuit fuse has not blown.

2 To test the switch, disconnect the wiring connector, and use a multimeter (set to the resistance function) or a battery-and-bulb test circuit to check that there is continuity between the switch terminals only when reverse gear is selected. If this is not the case, and there are no obvious breaks or other damage to the wires, the switch is faulty, and must be renewed.

Removal

3 Working in the engine compartment, disconnect the wiring plug, then unscrew the switch from the casing.

Refitting

4 Refit and securely tighten the switch, then reconnect the wiring plug.

Chapter 8
Driveshafts

Contents

	Section number			Section number
Driveshaft overhaul and gaiter renewal	3	General information		1
Driveshaft – removal and refitting	2			

Degrees of difficulty

Easy, suitable for novice with little experience	**Fairly easy,** suitable for beginner with some experience	**Fairly difficult,** suitable for competent DIY mechanic	**Difficult,** suitable for experienced DIY mechanic	**Very difficult,** suitable for expert DIY or professional

Specifications

General

Type	Unequal-length, solid steel shafts, splined to inner and outer constant velocity joints
Lubrication type	Fiat specification 9.55580 grease (Tutela Star 700) or equivalent
Quantity:	
Inner joint	100g
Outer joint:	
1.2L models	70g
1.4L models	85g

Torque wrench settings

	Nm	lbft
Driveshaft nut: *		
Stage 1	70	52
Stage 2	Angle-tighten a further 55°	
Roadwheel bolts	120	89
Shock absorber-to-hub carrier: *		
Stage 1	114	84
Stage 2	Angle-tighten a further 45°	
Trackrod end-to-hub carrier*	40	30

Do not re-use

1 General information

1 Power is transmitted from the differential to the roadwheels by the driveshafts, via inner and outer constant velocity (CV) joints.

2 The outer ball-and-cage type CV joints allow smooth transmission of drive to the wheels at all steering and suspension angles. Drive is transmitted by means of a number of radially static steel balls that run in grooves between the two halves of the joint.

3 The inner CV joints are of the tripod type. Drive is transmitted across the joint by means of three rollers, mounted on the driveshaft in a tripod arrangement, that are radially static but are free to slide in the grooved joint body.

4 The joints are protected by rubber gaiters, and are packed with grease to provide permanent lubrication. If wear is detected in the joint, it can be detached from the driveshaft and renewed. Normally, the CV joints do not require additional lubrication, unless they have been overhauled or the rubber gaiters have been damaged, allowing the grease to become contaminated. Refer to Chapter 1 Section 8 for guidance in checking the condition of the driveshaft gaiters.

5 Both driveshafts are splined at their outer ends, to accept the wheel hubs, and are threaded so that the hubs can be fastened to the driveshafts by means of a staked nut.

2 Driveshaft – removal and refitting

Note: A balljoint separator tool will be required for this operation. A new driveshaft retaining nut and inner CV joint gaiter retaining clip will be required for refitting.

Removal

1 Slacken the front roadwheel bolts, raise the

TOOL TIP

A tool to hold the front hub stationary whilst the driveshaft nut is slackened can be fabricated from two lengths of steel strip (one long, one short) and a nut and bolt; then nut and bolt forming a pivot of a forked tool.

2.4 Tap up the staking of the driveshaft nut

front of the vehicle and support it securely on axle stands, as described in 'Vehicle jacking and support'. Remove the relevant front roadwheel.

2 Drain the gearbox oil as described in Chapter 7 Section 2.

3 If removing the right-hand driveshaft, undo the fasteners and remove the wheelarch lower splashshield.

4 Using a hammer and chisel or similar tool, tap up the staking securing the driveshaft retaining nut in position **(see illustration)**.

5 The front wheel hub must be held stationary in order to loosen the driveshaft nut. Ideally, the hub should be held by a suitable tool bolted into place using two of the roadwheel bolts (see **Tool Tip**). Alternatively, have an assistant firmly apply the foot brake to prevent the hub from rotating. Using a socket and extension bar, slacken and remove the driveshaft retaining nut.

⚠ *Warning: The nut is extremely tight. Discard the nut – a new one must be used on refitting.*

6 Release the brake caliper hydraulic hose (and the ABS wheel speed sensor cable/brake pad wear sensor cable) from the brackets at the base of the suspension strut.

7 Unscrew the nut securing the track rod end to the swivel hub. Release the track rod end tapered shank using a balljoint separator tool.

8 Remove the bolts securing the top of the swivel hub to the base of the suspension strut. Note that new bolts must be fitted.

9 Pull the swivel hub outwards at the top

and withdraw the driveshaft outer constant velocity joint from the hub assembly **(see illustration)**. If necessary, the joint can be tapped out of the hub using a soft-faced mallet. Support the end of the driveshaft – do not allow the end of the driveshaft to hang down as this will strain the joint components and gaiters. Take care not to strain the ABS wheel speed sensor wiring.

10 Insert a lever between the inner joint and the differential casing, and force the driveshaft from the differential **(see illustration)**. Force the right-hand inner driveshaft joint from the transmission using a 70 mm exhaust clamp. With the clamp between the joint and casing, tighten the nuts and the joint will be forced out.

11 Loosely refit one of the strut lower mounting bolts to support the swivel hub while the driveshaft is removed.

Refitting

12 After removing the temporarily-fitted bolt from the strut mounting, pivot the swivel hub away from the car and engage the inner joint with the differential, and the outer CV joint into the hub.

13 Screw on the new driveshaft retaining nut, but do not tighten it at this stage.

14 Refit the suspension strut-to-swivel hub bolts and tighten them to the specified torque.

15 Engage the track rod end with the swivel hub, fit the new retaining nut and tighten it to the specified torque.

16 Refit the brake caliper hydraulic hose (and the ABS wheel speed sensor cable) to the bracket on the base of the suspension strut.

17 Using the method employed on removal to prevent rotation of the hub, tighten the driveshaft retaining nut to the specified torque. Secure the nut by tapping the staking into the two grooves in the end of the CV joint using a hammer and chisel.

18 Where applicable, refit the wheelarch lower splashshield.

19 Refill the gearbox with oil as described in Chapter 7 Section 2.

20 Refit the roadwheel and lower the vehicle to the ground.

2.9 Withdrawn the driveshaft joint from the hub

2.10 Lever between the driveshaft joint and the differetial casing

3.2 Release the rubber gaiter retaining clips by cutting them off with side-cutters

3.10a Slide the small gaiter clip onto the driveshaft...

3.10b... followed by the gaiter...

3 Driveshaft overhaul and gaiter renewal

Outer joint

1 Remove the driveshaft as described in Section 2.

2 Release the rubber gaiter retaining clips by cutting them off with a pair of side-cutters **(see illustration)**. Remove the clips and slide the gaiter down the driveshaft away from the CV joint.

3 The driveshaft is secured in the CV joint by a circlip. Release the circlip and side the joint from the shaft.

4 Slide the old gaiter off the end of the driveshaft.

5 With the constant velocity joint removed from the driveshaft, thoroughly clean the joint using paraffin, or a suitable solvent, and dry it thoroughly. Carry out a visual inspection of the joint.

6 Move the inner splined driving member from side-to-side, to expose each ball in turn at the top of its track. Examine the balls for cracks, flat spots, or signs of surface pitting.

7 Inspect the ball tracks on the inner and outer members. If the tracks have widened, the balls will no longer be a tight fit. At the same time, check the ball cage windows for wear or cracking between the windows.

8 If any of the constant velocity joint components are found to be worn or damaged, it will be necessary to renew the complete joint assembly as the internal parts are not available separately. If the joint is in satisfactory condition, obtain a new gaiter, circlip, retaining clips, and the correct type of grease. These components are all available individually from Fiat dealers, but may be supplied as a complete repair kit from other sources.

9 Commence reassembly by fitting a new joint retaining circlip to the groove in the end of the shaft.

10 Slide the smaller gaiter securing clip onto the driveshaft, followed by the gaiter and the large securing clip **(see illustrations)**.

11 Pack the CV joint with the specified grease, then twist the joint to ensure that all the recesses are filled **(see illustration)**.

12 Fit the CV joint to the driveshaft, and

3.10c... and large clip

engage it with the shaft splines. Use a mallet to tap the joint onto the shaft until the circlip engages correctly.

13 Fill the gaiter with any remaining grease then slide the large end of the gaiter into position over the joint, ensuring that it is seated squarely over the joint body.

14 Locate the large securing clip over the gaiter and secure the clip in place by compressing the raised portion **(see illustration)**.

3.11 Pack the joint with the specified grease, then twist the joint to ensure all recesses are filled

3.14 Secure the clip using driveshaft clip pliers

3.15 Lift the lip of the gaiter to expel air trapped inside

3.16 Slide the small clip into place, and secure it using driveshaft clip pliers

15 Check that the smaller end of the gaiter is located in the driveshaft groove then, using a small screwdriver, lift the lip of the gaiter to expel any air trapped inside (see illustration).
16 Slide the smaller securing clip over the gaiter, and secure it as described previously (see illustration).
17 Refit the driveshaft as described in Section 2.

Inner joint

18 Remove the driveshaft as described in Section 2.
19 Release the rubber gaiter retaining clips by cutting them off with a pair of side-cutters. Remove the clips and slide the gaiter down the driveshaft away from the inner joint.
20 Make alignment marks between the housing and the shaft, then slide the joint housing from the tripod.
21 Remove the circlip securing the tripod to the shaft (see illustration). Discard the circlip – a new one must be fitted.
22 Make alignment marks between the tripod and shaft, then withdraw the tripod and gaiter from the shaft.

23 Thoroughly clean the tripod and rollers, and the end of the driveshaft using paraffin, or a suitable solvent, and dry thoroughly. Carry out a visual inspection of the joint and renew any components as necessary. If the joint is in satisfactory condition, obtain a new gaiter, circlip, retaining clips, and the correct type of grease. These components are all available individually from Fiat dealers, but may be supplied as a complete repair kit from other sources.
24 Commence reassembly by sliding the smaller gaiter securing clip onto the driveshaft, followed by the gaiter.
25 Check that the gaiter is located in the driveshaft groove, then fit the securingclip over the gaiter and secure the clip in place by compressing the raised portion.
26 Refit the tripod and fit a new circlip to secure the tripod to the driveshaft, aligning the previously made marks.
27 Pack the specified grease around the tripod rollers and into the joint body, filling the gaiter with any remaining grease.
28 Align the previously made marks, and slide the housing over the tripod.
29 Slide the gaiter into position over the joint

3.21 Remove the tripod retaining circlip

housing and briefly lift the lip of the gaiter to expel any air trapped inside. Ensure the gaiter is seated squarely over the joint body.
30 Locate a new retaining clip of the rubber gaiter on the inner joint housing. Ensure the clip is seated squarely on the gaiter, then secure the clip in place by compressing the raised portion.
31 Refit the driveshaft as described in Section 2.

Chapter 9
Braking system

Contents

Section number

Anti-lock braking system (ABS) – general information 20
Anti-lock braking system (ABS) components – removal and refitting 21
Front brake caliper – removal, overhaul and refitting 8
Front brake disc – inspection, removal and refitting 6
Front brake pads – renewal 4
General information 1
Handbrake – checking and adjustment 15
Handbrake 'on' warning light switch – removal and refitting 18
Handbrake cables – removal and refitting 16
Handbrake lever – removal and refitting 17
Hydraulic pipes and hoses – renewal 3

Section number

Hydraulic system – bleeding 2
Master cylinder – removal, overhaul and refitting 13
Rear brake caliper – removal, overhaul and refitting 9
Rear brake disc – inspection, removal and refitting 7
Rear brake drum – removal, inspection and refitting 10
Rear brake pads – renewal 5
Rear brake shoes – renewal 11
Rear wheel cylinder – removal, overhaul and refitting 12
Stop-light switch – removal and refitting 14
Vacuum servo unit check valve – removal, testing and refitting 19

Degrees of difficulty

Easy, suitable for novice with little experience	**Fairly easy,** suitable for beginner with some experience	**Fairly difficult,** suitable for competent DIY mechanic	**Difficult,** suitable for experienced DIY mechanic	**Very difficult,** suitable for expert DIY or professional

Specifications

Front brakes

Caliper type	Single piston sliding caliper
All models except 1.2L 10/2006 to 2012 model year:	
Disc type	Ventilated
Diameter	257 mm
Thickness:	
New	22.0 mm
Minimum	20.2 mm
1.2L models 10/2006 to 2012 model year:	
Disc type	Solid
Diameter	257 mm
Thickness:	
New	12.0 mm
Minimum	10.2 mm
Pad friction material minimum thickness	1.5 mm

Rear disc brakes (1.4L Sport models only)

Caliper type .... Single piston sliding caliper
Disc:
  TypeSolid
  Diameter... 264 mm
  Thickness:
    New .... 10.0 mm
    Minimum.. 8.0 mm
Pad friction material minimum thickness .... 1.5 mm

Rear drum brake (except 1.4L Sport models)

Drum inner diameter: ....
  New:
    1.2L models .... 203.25 mm
    1.4L models .... 228.45 mm
  Minimum (wear limit):
    1.2L models .... 204.7 mm
    1.4L models .... 230.0 mm
Minimum brake shoe lining thickness .... 2.0 mm

Torque wrench settings

	Nm	lbf ft
Bleed screw	8	6
Front brake caliper bracket-to-hub carrier......................	105	77
Front caliper guide pin bolts: *...............................	30	22
Disc retaining screw	10	7
Lateral acceleration/yaw rate sensor nuts	10	7
Master cylinder nuts.......................................	20	15
Rear caliper bracket-to-hub carrier bolts......................	57	42
Rear caliper guide pin bolts	30	22
Rear wheel cylinder bolts...................................	10	7
Roadwheel bolts...	120	89
Servo retaining nuts	20	15
Wheel speed sensors:		
Front wheel sensor......................................	8	6
Rear wheel sensor	8	6

*Do not re-use

1 General information

1 The braking system is of the vacuum servo-assisted, dual-circuit hydraulic type. The arrangement of the hydraulic system is such that each circuit operates one front and one rear brake from a tandem master cylinder. Under normal circumstances, both circuits operate in unison. However, in the event of hydraulic failure in one circuit, full braking force will still be available at two diagonally-opposite wheels.

2 All models covered in this manual are fitted with front disc brakes and rear drum brakes, with the exception of 1.4L Sport models, which are fitted with solid rear disc brakes. An Anti-lock Braking System (ABS) is fitted as standard to all models (refer to Section 20 for further information on ABS operation).

3 The front disc brakes are actuated by single-piston sliding type calipers, which ensure that equal pressure is applied to each brake pad.

4 The rear drum brakes incorporate leading and trailing shoes, which are actuated by twin-piston wheel cylinders. A self-adjusting mechanism is incorporated, to automatically compensate for brake shoe wear. As the brake shoe linings wear, the footbrake operation automatically operates the adjuster mechanism to reduce the lining-to-drum clearance. The mechanical handbrake linkage operates the brake shoes via a lever attached to the trailing brake shoe.

5 The rear disc brakes fitted to 1.4L Sport models are actuated by single-piston sliding type calipers, which incorporate a cable-operated handbrake mechanism.

Note: *When servicing any part of the system, work carefully and methodically; also observe scrupulous cleanliness when overhauling any part of the hydraulic system. Always renew components (in axle sets, where applicable) if in doubt about their condition, and use only genuine Fiat replacement parts, or at least those of known good quality. Note the warnings given in 'Safety first!' and at relevant points in this Chapter concerning the dangers of asbestos dust and hydraulic fluid.*

2 Hydraulic system – bleeding

⚠ **Warning: Hydraulic fluid is poisonous; wash off immediately and thoroughly in the case of skin contact, and seek immediate medical advice if any fluid is swallowed or gets into the eyes. Certain types of hydraulic fluid are flammable, and may ignite when allowed into contact with hot components; when servicing any hydraulic system, it is safest to assume that the fluid is flammable, and to take precautions against the risk of fire as though it is petrol that is being handled. Hydraulic fluid is also an effective paint stripper, and will attack plastics; if any is spilt, it should be washed off immediately, using copious quantities of fresh water. Finally, it is hygroscopic (it absorbs moisture from the air) – old fluid may be contaminated and unfit for further use. When topping-up or renewing the fluid, always use the recommended type, and ensure that it comes from a freshly-opened sealed container.**

General

1 The correct operation of any hydraulic system is only possible after removing all air from the components and circuit; and this is achieved by bleeding the system.

2 During the bleeding procedure, add only clean, unused hydraulic fluid of the recommended type; never re-use fluid that has already been bled from the system. Ensure that sufficient fluid is available before starting work.

3 If there is any possibility of incorrect fluid being already in the system, the brake components and circuit must be flushed completely with uncontaminated, correct fluid, and new seals should be fitted throughout the system.

4 If hydraulic fluid has been lost from the system, or air has entered because of a leak, ensure that the fault is cured before proceeding further.

5 Park the car on level ground, switch off the engine and select first or reverse gear, then chock the wheels and release the handbrake.

6 Check that all pipes and hoses are secure, unions tight and bleed screws closed. Remove the dust caps (where applicable), and clean any dirt from around the bleed screws.

7 Unscrew the master cylinder reservoir cap, and top the master cylinder reservoir up to the MAX level line.

Caution: Ensure that the ignition is switched off before starting the bleeding procedure, to avoid any possibility of voltage being applied to the hydraulic modulator before the bleeding procedure is completed. Ideally, the battery should be disconnected. If voltage is applied to the modulator before the bleeding procedure is complete, this will effectively drain the hydraulic fluid in the modulator, rendering the unit unserviceable. Do not, therefore, attempt to 'run' the modulator in order to bleed the brakes.

8 Due to the standard fitment of ABS to all models, a pressure-bleeding kit must be used for bleeding the hydraulic system.

9 These kits are usually operated by the reservoir of pressurised air contained in the spare tyre. However, note that it will probably be necessary to reduce the pressure to a lower level than normal; refer to the instructions supplied with the kit.

Note: *Fiat specify a system pressure of 1.0 bar.*

10 By connecting a pressurised, fluid-filled container to the master cylinder reservoir, bleeding can be carried out simply by opening each screw in turn (in the specified sequence), and allowing the fluid to flow out until no more air bubbles can be seen in the expelled fluid.

11 This method has the advantage that the large reservoir of fluid provides an additional safeguard against air being drawn into the system during bleeding.

12 If the system has been only partially disconnected, and suitable precautions were taken to minimise fluid loss, it should be necessary only to bleed that part of the system.

13 If the complete system is to be bled, then it should be done working in the following sequence:
a) *Right-hand front brake*
b) *Left-hand front brake*
c) *Right-hand rear brake*
d) *Left-hand rear brake*

14 Bleed each brake in turn until clean fluid, free of air bubbles, is seen to emerge. Pause between bleeding each brake to ensure that the fluid level in the reservoir is above the MIN level.

15 When bleeding is complete, and firm pedal feel is restored, wash off any spilt fluid, tighten the bleed screws, and refit their dust caps.

16 Check the hydraulic fluid level in the master cylinder reservoir, and top-up if necessary.

17 Discard any fluid that has been bled from the system; it will not be fit for re-use.

18 Check the feel of the brake pedal. If it feels at all spongy, air must still be present in the system, and further bleeding is required.

⚠️ *Warning: Do not operate the vehicle if you are in doubt about the effectiveness of the braking system. If considerable air was present in the system prior to bleeding, it is possible for some of this air to remain trapped in the hydraulic modulator. If the pedal continues to feel spongy after repeated bleedings, or if any of the brake system warning lights remain on, have the vehicle towed to a Fiat dealer to be bled with the use of Fiat diagnostic equipment.*

3 Hydraulic pipes and hoses – renewal

Note: *Before starting work, refer to the warnings in Section and Section 2.*

1 If any pipe or hose is to be renewed, minimise fluid loss by first removing the master cylinder reservoir cap, then tighten the cap down onto a piece of polythene to obtain an airtight seal. Alternatively, flexible hoses

3.2 Flexible hose spring clip

can be sealed, if required, using a proprietary brake hose clamp; metal brake pipe unions can be plugged (if care is taken not to allow dirt into the system) or capped immediately they are disconnected. Place a wad of rag under any union that is to be disconnected, to catch any spilt fluid.

2 If a flexible hose is to be disconnected, unscrew the brake pipe union nut before removing the spring clip which secures the hose to its mounting bracket **(see illustration)**.

3 To unscrew the union nuts, it is preferable to obtain a brake pipe spanner of the correct size; these are available from most large motor accessory shops. Failing this, a close-fitting open-ended spanner will be required, though if the nuts are tight or corroded, their flats may be rounded-off if the spanner slips. In such a case, a self-locking wrench is often the only way to unscrew a stubborn union, but it follows that the pipe and the damaged nuts must be renewed on reassembly. Always clean a union and surrounding area before disconnecting it. If disconnecting a component with more than one union, make a careful note of the connections before disturbing any of them.

4 If a brake pipe is to be renewed, it can be obtained, cut to length and with the union nuts and end flares in place, from Fiat dealers. All that is then necessary is to bend it to shape, following the line of the original, before fitting it to the vehicle. Alternatively, most motor accessory shops can make up brake pipes from kits, but this requires very careful measurement of the original, to ensure that the replacement is of the correct length. The safest answer is usually to take the original to the shop as a pattern.

5 On refitting, do not overtighten the union nuts. It is not necessary to exercise brute force to obtain a sound joint.

6 Ensure that the pipes and hoses are correctly routed, with no kinks, and that they are secured in the clips or brackets provided. After fitting, remove the polythene from the reservoir, and bleed the hydraulic system as described in Section 2. Wash off any spilt fluid, and check carefully for fluid leaks.

4 Front brake pads – renewal

⚠️ *Warning: Renew both sets of front brake pads at the same time – never renew the pads on only one wheel, as uneven braking may result. Note that the dust created by wear of the pads may contain asbestos, which is a health hazard. Never blow it out with compressed air, and don't inhale any of it. An approved filtering mask should be worn when working on the brakes. DO NOT use petrol or petroleum-based solvents to clean brake parts; use brake cleaner or methylated spirit only.*

1 Apply the handbrake, then slacken the front roadwheel bolts. Jack up the front of the vehicle and support it on axle stands as described in 'Vehicle jacking and support'. Remove both front roadwheels.

2 If new pads are to be fitted, reduce the fluid level in the master cylinder reservoir to the minimum level using a syringe (or similar).

3 Follow the relevant accompanying photos (illustrations 4.3a to 4.3s) for the actual pad replacement procedure. Be sure to stay in order and read the caption under each illustration, and note the following points:

a) New pads may have an adhesive foil on the backplates. Remove this foil prior to installation.

b) Apply a thin smear of anti-seize grease only to the areas shown.

c) When pushing the caliper piston back to accommodate new pads, keep a close eye on the fluid level in the reservoir.

4 Repeat the above procedure on the remaining caliper.

5 Depress the brake pedal repeatedly, until the pads are pressed into firm contact with the brake disc, and normal (non-assisted) pedal pressure is restored.

6 Apply a little anti-seize grease to the hub surface where it contacts the wheel, then refit the roadwheels, lower the vehicle to the ground and tighten the roadwheel bolts to the specified torque.

7 Check the hydraulic fluid level as described in 'Weekly checks'.

Caution: New pads will not give full braking efficiency until they have bedded-in. Be prepared for this, and avoid hard braking as far as possible for the first hundred miles or so after pad renewal.

4.3a Disconnect the pad wear sensor wiring plug, where fitted

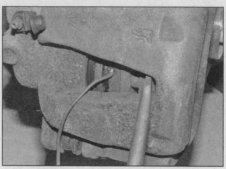
4.3b If there's a wear/rust lip on the outside of the disc, lever the pads away with a screwdriver

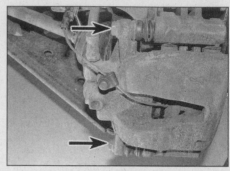
4.3c Unscrew the upper, and lower guide pin bolts

4.3d Slide the caliper from place...

4.3e... and suspend it from the spring using wire, to prevent straining the fluid hose

4.3f Remove the outer brake pad...

4.3g... and the inner brake pad

4.3h Unclip the inner, outer, upper and lower shims

4.3i Clean the mounting bracket with aerosol brake cleaner and a soft brush

4.3j Measure the thickness of the pads friction material – if it's less than 1.5 mm, renew all the front brake pads

4.3k Press the upper, lower, inner and outer shims into place on the mounting bracket

4.3l Apply a thin smear of high-temperature, anti-seize grease to the edge of the pad backplate where It contacts the mounting bracket

4.3m Fit the inner brake pad, with wear sensor wiring (where applicable)...

4.3n... and outer pad. Make sure the friction material is against the disc face!

4.3o If new pads have been fitted, push the piston fully into the caliper body using a piston retraction tool. Keep an eye on the brake fluid reservoir level as the piston is pushed back!

4.3p Slide the caliper into place...

4.3q... insert the new guide pin bolts...

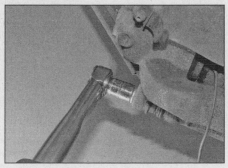

4.3r... and tighten them to the specified torque wrench setting

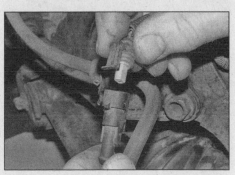

4.3s Reconnect the brake pad wear sensor wiring plug (where fitted)

5 Rear brake pads – renewal

⚠️ **Warning: Renew both sets of rear brake pads at the same time – never renew the pads on only one wheel, as uneven braking may result. Note that the dust created by wear** of the pads may contain asbestos, which is a health hazard. Never blow it out with compressed air, and don't inhale any of it. An approved filtering mask should be worn when working on the brakes. *DO NOT use petrol or petroleum-based solvents to clean brake parts; use brake cleaner or methylated spirit only.*

1 Chock the front wheels, then slacken the rear roadwheel bolts. Jack up the rear of the vehicle and support it on axle stands as described in 'Vehicle jacking and support'. Remove both rear roadwheels.

2 If new pads are to be fitted, reduce the fluid level in the master cylinder reservoir to the minimum level using a syringe (or similar).

3 Follow the relevant accompanying photos (illustrations 5.3a to 5.3p) for the actual pad replacement procedure. Be sure to stay in order and read the caption under each illustration, and note the following points:

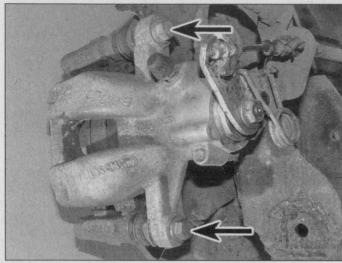

5.3a Unscrew the caliper guide pin bolts

5.3b Slide the caliper from place, and lay it on the top of the hub assembly

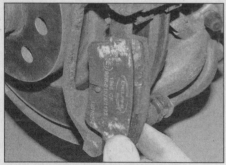

5.3c Remove the outer brake pad...

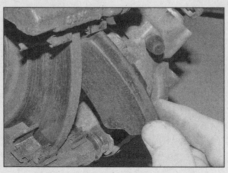

5.3d... and the inner brake pad

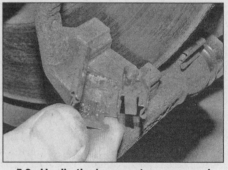

5.3e Unclip the inner, outer, upper and lower shims from the mounting bracket

5.3f Clean the area with aerosol brake cleaner and a soft brush

5.3g Press the inner, outer, upper and lower shims into place

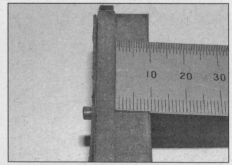

5.3h Measure the thickness of the pads friction material. If it's less than 1.5 mm, renew all 4 pads

a) New pads may have an adhesive foil on the backplates. Remove this foil prior to installation.

b) Apply a thin smear of anti-seize grease only to the areas shown.

c) When pushing the caliper piston back to accommodate new pads, keep a close eye on the fluid level in the reservoir. Note that the right-hand rear caliper piston must be rotated clockwise to retract it, and the left-hand rear caliper must be rotated anti-clockwise to retract it.

d) Upon completion, adjust the handbrake as described in Section 15.

4 Depress the brake pedal repeatedly, until the pads are pressed into firm contact with the brake disc, and normal (non-assisted) pedal pressure is restored.

5 Repeat the above procedure on the remaining rear brake caliper.

6 Apply a little anti-seize grease to the hub surface, then refit the roadwheels, lower the vehicle to the ground and tighten the roadwheel bolts to the specified torque.

7 Check the hydraulic fluid level as described in 'Weekly checks'.

Caution: New pads will not give full braking efficiency until they have bedded-in. Be prepared for this, and avoid hard braking as far as possible for the first hundred miles or so after pad renewal.

5.3i Apply a thin smear of high-temperature, anti-seize grease to the edge of the pad backplate where it contacts the mounting bracket

5.3j Fit the inner brake pad...

5.3k... and outer brake pad. Ensure the friction material is against the disc face!

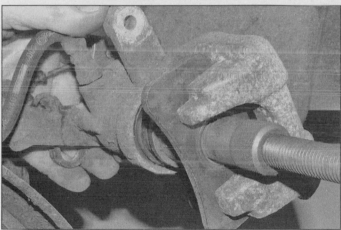

5.3l If new pads are fitted, use a piston retraction tool to press the piston fully back into the caliper body, whist rotating it at the same time – clockwise for the right-hand caliper, and anti-clockwise for the left-hand caliper. Keep an eye on the fluid level in the master cylinder reservoir as the piston is pushed back!

5.3m Rotate the piston so the cut-out in the piston face aligns with the pin on the inner brake pad backplate

5.3n Slide the caliper back into position...

5.3o... refit the caliper guide pin bolts...

5.3p... and tighten them to the specified torque

6.3 Measure the disc thickness using a micrometer

6.9 Caliper mounting bracket retaining bolts

6.10 Undo the Torx screws and remove the disc

6 Front brake disc – Inspection, removal and refitting

Inspection

Note: *If either disc requires renewal, BOTH should be renewed at the same time, to ensure even and consistent braking. New brake pads should also be fitted.*

1 Apply the handbrake, then jack up the front of the car and support it on axle stands as described in *'Vehicle jacking and support'*. Remove the appropriate front roadwheel.

2 Slowly rotate the brake disc so that the full area of both sides can be checked; remove the brake pads if better access is required to the inboard surface. Light scoring is normal in the area swept by the brake pads, but if heavy scoring or cracks are found, the disc must be renewed.

3 It is normal to find a lip of rust and brake dust around the disc's perimeter; this can be scraped off if required. If, however, a lip has formed due to excessive wear of the brake pad swept area, then the disc's thickness must be measured using a micrometer **(see illustration)**. Take measurements at several places around the disc, at the inside and outside of the pad swept area; if the disc has worn at any point to the specified minimum thickness or less, the disc must be renewed.

4 If the disc is thought to be warped, it can be checked for run-out. Either use a dial gauge mounted on any convenient fixed point, while the disc is slowly rotated, or use feeler blades to measure (at several points all around the disc) the clearance between the disc and a fixed point, such as the caliper mounting bracket. If the measurements obtained are at the specified maximum or beyond, the disc is excessively warped, and must be renewed; however, it is worth checking first that the hub bearing is in good condition (Chapters 1 and/ or 10). If the run-out is excessive, the disc must be renewed.

5 Check the disc for cracks, especially around the wheel stud holes, and any other wear or damage, and renew if necessary.

Removal

6 Mark the relationship between the disc and the hub with chalk or a marker pen, to allow correct refitting.

7 Remove the brake pads as described in Section 4.

8 Suspend the caliper from a rigid point on the suspension, using wire or a cable tie. Do not allow it to hang unsupported as this will strain the brake hose.

9 Undo the 2 retaining bolts and remove the caliper mounting bracket **(see illustration)**.

10 Undo the retaining screw(s) and remove the disc from the hub **(see illustration)**. If necessary, liberally apply releasing fluid to the area between the disc and hub, and use a large hammer to force the disc from the hub.

Refitting

11 If a new disc is being fitted, remove the protective coating from the surface using an appropriate cleaner.

12 Locate the disc on the hub so that the roadwheel bolt and retaining screw holes are all correctly lined up; use the alignment marks made during removal.

13 Refit the disc retaining screw(s) and tighten them to the specified torque.

14 Refit the caliper mounting bracket, then apply a little thread-locking compound and tighten the bolts to the specified torque.

15 Refit the brake pads as described in Section 4.

7 Rear brake disc – inspection, removal and refitting

Inspection

Note: *If either disc requires renewal, BOTH should be renewed at the same time, to ensure even and consistent braking. New brake pads should also be fitted.*

1 Firmly chock the front wheels, then jack up the rear of the car and support it on axle stands as described in *'Vehicle jacking and support'*. Remove the appropriate rear roadwheel. Release the handbrake.

2 Inspect the disc as described in Section 6.

Removal

3 Remove the brake pads as described in Section 5.

4 Undo the 2 caliper mounting bracket bolts, and slide the bracket from place.

5 Slacken and remove the brake disc retaining Torx screws.

6 If the disc is to be refitted, make alignment marks between the disc and hub.

7 It should now be possible to withdraw the brake disc from the rear hub by hand. If it is tight, lightly tap its rear face with a hide or plastic mallet.

Refitting

8 If a new disc is been fitted, use a suitable solvent to wipe any preservative coating from the disc. Ensure the disc mounting surface on the hub is free from dirt and corrosion.

9 Align (if applicable) the marks made on removal, then fit the disc and tighten the retaining screws to the specified torque.

10 Refit the caliper mounting bracket, and tighten the bolts to the specified torque.

11 Fit the brake pads as described in Section 5.

8 Front brake caliper – removal, overhaul and refitting

Caution: Before starting work, refer to the warnings at the beginning of Section 2 and Section 4 concerning the dangers of hydraulic fluid and asbestos dust.

Removal

1 Remove the front brake pads as described in Section 4.

2 To minimise fluid loss during the following operations, remove the master cylinder reservoir filler cap, then tighten it down onto a piece of polythene, to obtain an airtight seal. Alternatively, use a brake hose clamp to seal off the flexible hydraulic hose running to the caliper.

Caution: Do not use an ordinary G-clamp or mole grips for this purpose, as these can easily damage the hydraulic hose internally, possibly leading to failure.

3 Clean the area surrounding the brake hose union, then slacken the union half a turn.
4 Hold the brake hose and rotate the caliper to unscrew the hose union from the caliper body. Cover the open ends of the union and the caliper fluid inlet, to prevent dirt ingress. Alternatively, the flexible brake hose may be separated from the rigid brake pipe at the bracket mounted on the inner wheel arch.

Overhaul

5 At the time of writing, no replacement parts appear to be available for the front calipers. If they are defective, replacement calipers must be fitted.

Refitting

6 Hold the brake hose and rotate the caliper to screw the hose union back into the caliper body.
7 Refit the brake pads as described in Section 4, then tighten the brake hose securely.
8 Bleed the brake hydraulic system as described in Section 2.

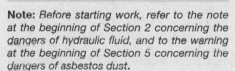

9 Rear brake caliper – removal, overhaul and refitting

Note: *Before starting work, refer to the note at the beginning of Section 2 concerning the dangers of hydraulic fluid, and to the warning at the beginning of Section 5 concerning the dangers of asbestos dust.*

Removal

1 To minimise fluid loss during the following operations, remove the master cylinder reservoir filler cap, then tighten it down onto a piece of polythene, to obtain an airtight seal. Alternatively, use a brake hose clamp to seal off the flexible hydraulic hose running to the caliper.
Caution: Do not use an ordinary G-clamp or mole grips for this purpose, as these can easily damage the hydraulic hose internally, possibly leading to failure.
2 Clean the area surrounding the brake hose union, then slacken the union half a turn.
3 Remove the rear brake pads as described in Section 5.
4 Hold the brake hose and rotate the caliper to unscrew the hose union from the caliper body. Cover the open ends of the union and the caliper fluid inlet, to prevent dirt ingress. Alternatively, the flexible brake hose may be separated from the rigid brake pipe at the bracket mounted on the inner wheel arch.

Overhaul

5 At the time of writing, it would appear that no replacement parts are available for the rear caliper. If defective, the complete caliper must be replaced.

Refitting

6 Screw the caliper onto the end of the brake hose.

7 Refit the brake pads as described in Section 5.
8 tighten the brake hose union securely.
9 Bleed the brake hydraulic system as described in Section 2.

10 Rear brake drum – removal, inspection and refitting

 Warning: Before starting work, refer to the warning at the beginning of Section 4 concerning the dangers of asbestos dust.

Removal

1 Chock the front wheels, slacken the rear wheel bolts, raise the rear of the vehicle and support it securely on axle stands, as described in 'Vehicle jacking and support'. Fully release the handbrake, and remove the rear roadwheels.
2 If the original drum is to be refitted, mark the relationship between the drum and the hub. Slacken and remove the two retaining bolts and pull the drum from the hub.
3 If the drum is binding on the brake shoes, screw two M10 bolts into the threaded holes in the drum and progressively tighten them against the hub flange to push the drum from the hub **(see illustration)**.

Inspection

Note: *If either drum requires renewal, BOTH should be renewed at the same time, to ensure even and consistent braking. New brake shoes should also be fitted.*
4 Working carefully, remove all traces of brake dust from the drum, but avoid inhaling the dust, as it is a health hazard.
5 Clean the outside of the drum, and check it for obvious signs of wear or damage, such as cracks around the roadwheel stud holes; renew the drum if necessary.
6 Carefully examine the inside of the drum. Light scoring of the friction surface is normal, but if heavy scoring is found, the drum must be renewed.
7 It is usual to find a lip on the drum's inboard edge which consists of a mixture of rust and brake dust; this should be carefully scraped away, to leave a smooth surface which can be polished with fine (120- to 150-grade) emery paper. If, however, the lip is due to the friction surface being recessed by excessive wear, then the drum must be renewed.
8 If the drum is thought to be excessively worn, or oval, its internal diameter must be measured at several points using an internal micrometer. Take measurements in pairs, the second at right-angles to the first, and compare the two, to check for signs of ovality. Provided that it does not enlarge the drum to beyond the specified maximum diameter, it may be possible to have the drum refinished by skimming or grinding; if this is not possible, the drums on both sides must be renewed.

10.3 Use two M10 bolts to force the drum from the hub

Note that if the drum is to be skimmed, BOTH drums must be refinished, to maintain a consistent internal diameter on both sides.

Refitting

9 If a new brake drum is to be installed, use a suitable solvent to remove any preservative coating that may have been applied to its internal friction surfaces. Note that it may also be necessary to shorten the adjuster strut length, by rotating the serrated strut wheel, to allow the drum to pass over the brake shoes – see Section 11 for details.
10 If the original drum is being refitted, align the marks made on the drum and hub before removal, then fit the drum over the hub. Refit the locating studs and tighten them to the specified torque.
11 Depress the footbrake repeatedly to expand the brake shoes against the drum, and ensure that normal pedal pressure is restored.
12 Chock and if necessary adjust the handbrake as described in Section 15.
13 Refit the roadwheels, and lower the vehicle to the ground.

11 Rear brake shoes – renewal

 Warning: Renew BOTH sets of rear brake shoes at the same time – NEVER renew the shoes on only one wheel, as uneven braking may result.

 Warning: Before starting work, refer to the warning given at the beginning of Section 4, concerning the dangers of asbestos dust.

1 Remove the rear brake drums as described in Section 10.
2 Working carefully, and taking the necessary precautions, remove all traces of brake dust from the brake drum, backplate and shoes.
3 Measure the thickness of the friction material of each brake shoe at several points; if either shoe is worn at any point to the specified minimum thickness or less, all four shoes must be renewed as a set. The shoes

11.5 Note the positions of the brake components – drivers side brake assembly shown

11.6 Depress the hold-down clip and slide it from place

should also be renewed if any are fouled with hydraulic fluid, oil or grease; there is no satisfactory way of degreasing friction material, once contaminated.

4 If any of the brake shoes are worn unevenly, or contaminated, trace and rectify the cause before reassembly.

5 Note the position of each shoe, and the location of the return springs and self-adjuster mechanism to aid refitting later **(see illustration)**.

6 Depress the leading brake shoe hold-down spring clip and slide the clip out from under the pin head, while holding the pin from the rear **(see illustration)**. Remove the pin from the rear of the backplate.

7 Pull out the leading shoe a little, detach the lower return spring, pull the top of the leading shoe from the cylinder piston, then pivot the shoe upwards, remove the self-adjusting mechanism, and detach the upper return spring **(see illustrations)**.

8 Remove the hold-down spring clip and pin from the trailing brake shoe, then withdraw the shoe from the backplate.

9 Slide the handbrake cable end out of the lever on the trailing shoe **(see illustration)**. Remove the trailing brake shoe.

10 Retain the wheel cylinder pistons in the wheel cylinder using a cable tie or a strong elastic band. Do not depress the brake pedal until the brakes are reassembled.

11 Carefully examine the self-adjuster mechanism for signs of wear or damage. Pay particular attention to the threads and the toothed adjuster wheel, and renew if necessary.

12 Check the condition of all return springs and renew any that show signs of distortion or other damage.

13 Peel back the rubber protective caps, and check the wheel cylinder for fluid leaks or other damage; check that both cylinder pistons are free to move easily. Refer to Section 12, if necessary, for information on wheel cylinder renewal.

14 Prior to installation, clean the backplate, and apply a thin smear of high-temperature brake grease or anti-seize compound to all those surfaces of the backplate which bear on the shoes, particularly the wheel cylinder pistons and lower pivot point. Do not allow the lubricant to foul the friction material.

15 Connect the handbrake cable to the lever on the trailing brake shoe, locate the trailing shoe on the backplate and secure in position with the pin and hold-down spring clip.

16 Fit upper brake shoe return spring, and the self-adjuster mechanism into the recess in the trailing brake shoe, then engage the leading shoe with the other end of the adjuster mechanism **(see illustrations)**.

17 Fit the lower brake shoe return spring, engaging it with the slots in the shoes **(see**

11.7a Detach the lower return spring

11.7b Remove the self-adjusting mechanism...

11.7c... and upper return spring

11.9 Detach the handbrake cable from the lever

11.16a Engage the self-adjusting mechanism with the trailing shoe...

11.16b... and leading shoe

illustration). Remove the elastic band or cable tie from the wheel cylinder.

18 Manoeuvre the leading shoe into position and secure it with the hold-down pin and spring clip.

19 Turn the serrated wheel at the end of the self-adjuster mechanism, to retract the brake shoes – this will give additional clearance to allow the drum to pass over the shoes during refitting.

20 Refit the brake drum as described in Section 10.

21 Repeat the above procedure on the remaining rear brake.

22 Apply the brake pedal and handbrake lever several times to settle the self-adjusting mechanism. With both rear roadwheels refitted and the rear of the car still raised, turn the wheels by hand to check that the brake shoes are not binding. Check and if necessary adjust the operation of the handbrake, as described in Section 15.

23 On completion, check the brake hydraulic fluid level in the master cylinder reservoir as described in 'Weekly checks'.

24 Note that new shoes will not give full braking efficiency until they have bedded-in. Be prepared for this, and avoid hard braking as far as possible for the first hundred miles or so after shoe renewal.

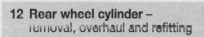

12 Rear wheel cylinder – removal, overhaul and refitting

Warning: Before starting work, refer to the warnings at the beginning of Section 2 and Section 4 concerning the dangers of hydraulic fluid and asbestos dust.

Removal

1 Remove the rear brake shoes as described in Section 11.

2 To minimise fluid loss during the following operations, remove the master cylinder reservoir filler cap, then tighten it down onto a piece of polythene, to obtain an airtight seal.

3 Clean the brake backplate around the wheel cylinder mounting bolts and the hydraulic pipe union, then unscrew the union nut and disconnect the hydraulic pipe **(see illustration)**. Cover the open ends of the pipe and the wheel cylinder to prevent dirt ingress.

4 Remove the two securing bolts, then withdraw the wheel cylinder from the backplate.

Overhaul

5 At the time of writing, it would appear that no replacement parts are available for the rear wheel cylinders. If defective, the complete cylinders must be replaced.

Refitting

6 Refitting is a reversal of removal, noting the following points:

11.17 Refit the lower return spring

a) Tighten the mounting bolts to the specified torque.

b) Refit the brake shoes as described in Section 11.

c) Before refitting the roadwheel and lowering the car to the ground, remove the polythene from the fluid reservoir, and bleed the hydraulic system as described in Section 2. Note that if no other part of the system has been disturbed, it should only be necessary to bleed the relevant rear circuit.

13 Master cylinder – removal, overhaul and refitting

Note. Before starting work, refer to the warning at the beginning of Section 2 concerning the dangers of hydraulic fluid.

Removal

1 Remove the master cylinder fluid reservoir filler cap, and syphon the hydraulic fluid from the reservoir. Do not syphon the fluid by mouth, as it is poisonous; use a syringe or an old poultry baster. Alternatively, open any convenient bleed screw in the system, and gently pump the brake pedal to expel the fluid through a tube connected to the screw (see Section 2).

2 Mark their positions, then undo the union nuts and disconnect the rigid brake pipes from the master cylinder **(see illustration)**.

13.2 Disconnect the rigid brake pipes from the master cylinder

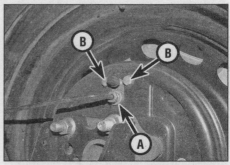

12.3 Wheel cylinder hydraulic pipe union (A) and retaining bolts (B)

3 Depress the release tabs and disconnect the fluid supply hose(s) from the master cylinder **(see illustration)**.

4 Undo the retaining nuts and detach the master cylinder from the servo unit. Recover the O-ring seal.

Refitting

5 Remove all traces of dirt from the master cylinder and servo unit mating surfaces and, where applicable, fit a new seal between the master cylinder body and the servo.

6 Fit the master cylinder to the servo unit, ensuring that the servo unit pushrod enters the master cylinder bore centrally. Refit the master cylinder mounting nuts, and tighten them to the specified torque.

7 Wipe clean the brake pipe unions, then refit them to the correct master cylinder ports, as noted before removal, and tighten the union nuts securely.

8 Reconnect the brake fluid supply hose(s) to the master cylinder.

9 Refill the master cylinder reservoir with fresh hydraulic fluid of the specified type (see Lubricants and fluids 0 Section 5), and bleed the complete hydraulic system as described in Section 2. Note that it may also be necessary to bleed the clutch hydraulic system as described in Chapter 6 Section 2.

10 On completion, thoroughly check the operation of the brake and clutch systems.

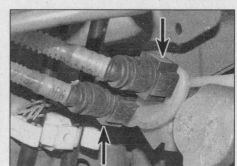

13.3 Fluid supply hoses release tabs

14 Stop-light switch – removal and refitting

Removal

1 Working under the drivers side of the facia, undo the retaining bolt and unclip the footwell air duct.

Models upto 10/2008

2 Depress the brake pedal, then secure it in this position by inserting a screwdriver between the pedal pivot lugs.
3 Pull the switch plunger outwards to the full extent of it's travel.
4 Pull the plunger red collar out to its full extent **(see illustration)**.
5 Depress the clip each side and manoeuvre the switch from the pedal bracket **(see illustration)**.
6 Disconnect the switch wiring plug.

Models from 10/2008

7 Reach up under the facia, and rotate the brake switch 45° anti-clockwise, and withdraw it from the pedal bracket. Disconnect the wiring plug as the switch is withdrawn.

Refitting

Models upto 10/2008

8 Ensure the brake pedal is still in its depressed position, as described earlier in this Section.
9 Pull the switch plunger out to its full extent, then pull the red collar out to its full extent.
10 Reconnect the switch wiring plug, then press the switch into position on the pedal bracket. The switch will only fit in one position.
11 Hold the pedal, remove the screwdriver, and allow the pedal to return to its 'at-rest' position.
12 Check the operation of the brake lights, then refit the footwell air duct.

Models from 10/2008

13 Depress the brake pedal, insert the switch into position on the pedal bracket, and rotate it 45° clockwise.
14 Reconnect the switch wiring plug.
15 Slowly release the pedal, check the operation of the brake lights, and refit the footwell air duct.

15.8 Prise up the panel around the handbrake lever

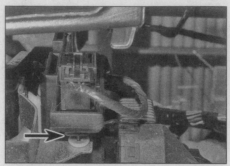
14.4 Pull the red collar out to its full extent

15 Handbrake – checking and adjustment

Checking

1 The handbrake should be capable of holding the parked vehicle stationary, even on steep slopes, when applied with moderate force. The mechanism should be firm and positive in feel, with no trace of stiffness or sponginess from the cables, and the mechanism should release immediately the handbrake lever is released. If the mechanism does not operate satisfactorily, it should be checked immediately.
2 To check the operation of the handbrake, chock the front wheels, raise the rear of the vehicle and support it securely on axle stands, as described in 'Vehicle jacking and support'. Release the handbrake lever.
3 Depress the brake pedal several times to establish the correct shoe-to-drum/pad-to-disc clearance.
4 With the pedal released, check that the rear roadwheels can be rotated – slight dragging is acceptable, but it should be possible to turn each wheel easily.
5 Apply the handbrake lever and check that the rear roadwheels start to drag after one click of the ratchet mechanism, and are fully locked within 5 clicks of the ratchet.
6 Fully release the handbrake, and check that the rear roadwheels can again be rotated by hand.
7 If the handbrake does not operate as

15.9 Handbrake adjuster nut

14.5 Depress the clip each side of the switch

described, carry out the adjustment procedure as follows.

Adjustment

8 Carefully prise up the trim panel adjacent to the handbrake lever **(see illustration)**.
9 Using a spanner or suitable socket, turn the adjuster nut clockwise to apply tension to the cables, or anti-clockwise to release the tension on the cables, as necessary **(see illustration)**. Check the operation of the handbrake as described previously and repeat the adjustment procedure as required.
10 On completion, refit the trim panel, and lower the vehicle to the ground.

16 Handbrake cables – removal and refitting

Removal

1 There are two rear handbrake cables, one on each side of the car. To renew either rear cable, proceed as follows.
2 Carefully prise up the trim panel adjacent to the handbrake lever **(see illustration 18.1)**.
3 At the base of the handbrake lever, fully slacken the handbrake adjuster nut, to remove all tension from the cable draw bar, then disconnect the relevant handbrake inner cable from the draw bar.
4 Depress the retaining tabs and release the outer cables from the floorpan **(see illustration)**.
5 Chock the front wheels then jack up the

16.4 Depress the tabs and pull the outer cables from the floorpan

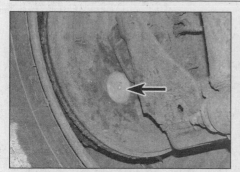

16.7 Prise the access flap from the brake backplate

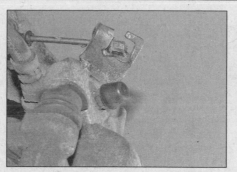

16.8 Detach the handbrake cable from the caliper lever

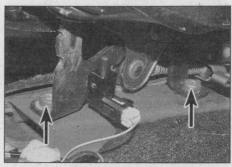

17.3 Handbrake lever retaining bolts

rear of the car and securely support it on axle stands, as described in 'Vehicle jacking and support'.

6 Working along the length of the relevant cable, release the retaining clips/bracket.

7 On models with rear drum brakes, prise out the access cap from the brake backplate, and use a thin-nosed pair of pliers to detach the cable end fitting from the lever on the brake shoe, and pull the outer cable from the backplate (see illustration).

8 On models with rear disc brakes detach the cable end fitting from the caliper lever, and pull the outer cable from support bracket (see illustration).

9 Manoeuvre the cable(s) from under the vehicle.

Refitting

10 Refitting is a reversal of removal. On completion, adjust the handbrake as described in Section 15.

17 Handbrake lever – removal and refitting

Removal

1 Detach both handbrake cables from the lever draw bar, as described in Section 16.

2 Pull up the handbrake lever gaiter a little, and disconnect the warning switch wiring plug.

3 Undo the retaining bolts, and manoeuvre

the handbrake lever assembly from place (see illustration).

Refitting

4 Refitting is a reversal of removal. On completion, adjust the handbrake as described in Section 15.

18 Handbrake 'on' warning light switch – removal and refitting

Removal

1 Carefully prise up the trim panel adjacent to the handbrake lever (see illustration).

2 Disconnect the switch wiring plug.

3 Release the retaining clip and remove the switch from its location (see illustration).

Refitting

4 Refitting is a reversal of removal.

19 Vacuum servo unit check valve – removal, testing and refitting

Removal

1 Disconnect the vacuum pipe at the quick-release connector between the check valve and the servo.

2 Disconnect the vacuum hose from the throttle body or manifold as applicable (see illustration).

3 The valve is integral with the hose. If the valve is faulty, the complete hose assembly must be renewed.

Testing

4 Examine the vacuum hose, check the valve for signs of damage, and renew if necessary.

5 The valve may be tested by blowing through the hose in both directions; air should glow through the valve in one direction only – when blown through the from the servo unit end of the hose. Renew the hose assembly is this not the case.

Refitting

6 Refitting is a reversal of removal.

7 On completion, start the engine and check the valve to servo unit connection for signs of air leaks. Test the operation of the braking system before venturing out onto the road.

20 Anti-lock braking system (ABS) – general information

General information

1 ABS is fitted as standard equipment on all models covered by this manual. The purpose of the system is to prevent the wheels locking during heavy braking. This is achieved by automatic release of the brake on the relevant wheel, followed by modulated re-application of the brake. The system comprises an electronic control unit, a hydraulic modulator,

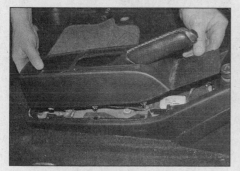

18.1 Pull up the panel around the handbrake lever

18.3 Handbrake 'on' warning light switch

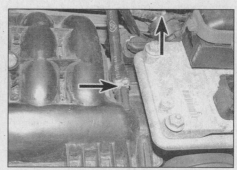

19.2 Vacuum hose quick-release connector and manifold connection

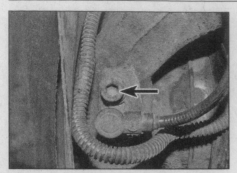

21.14 Front wheel speed sensor retaining bolt

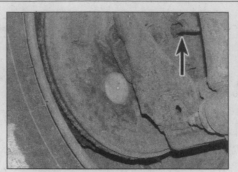

21.19 Rear wheel speed sensor retaining bolt – drum brake model shown

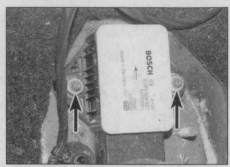

21.23 Lateral acceleration/yaw rate sensor retaining nuts

hydraulic solenoid valves (located in the modulator unit), an electrically-driven fluid return pump, and four wheel speed sensors.

2 The solenoids (which control the fluid pressure to the calipers/wheel cylinders) are controlled by the electronic control unit, which itself receives signals from the wheel speed sensors. The wheel speed sensors monitor the speed of rotation of each wheel. By comparing the speed signals from the four wheels, the control unit can determine when a wheel is decelerating at an abnormal rate, compared to the speed of the of the other wheels. Using this information, the control unit can predict when a wheel is about to lock, and is able to reduce the fluid pressure to the brake on the relevant wheel to prevent it locking. Once the rotational speed of the monitored wheel returns to approximately that of the other wheels, the hydraulic fluid pressure is increased in stages, to enable braking to continue.

3 During normal operation, the system functions in the same way as a conventional non-ABS braking system.

21 Anti-lock braking system (ABS) components – removal and refitting

ABS hydraulic and electronic control unit

Removal

1 Remove the battery and battery tray as described in Chapter 5A Section 4.

2 Release the locking clip and disconnect the ECU wiring harness connector.

3 Wipe clean the area around the brake pipe unions on the side of the unit, and place absorbent rags beneath the pipe unions to catch any surplus fluid. Make a note of the correct fitted positions of the unions, then unscrew the union nuts and carefully withdraw the pipes. Plug or tape over the pipe ends and unit orifices to minimise the loss of fluid, and to prevent the entry of dirt into the system.

4 Undo the retaining nuts/bolts, and remove

the unit from the engine compartment.

Refitting

5 If a new control unit assembly is being fitted, it will be supplied prefilled with hydraulic fluid, and sealed with blanking plugs. Leave the plugs in position until just before connecting the brake pipes.

6 Locate the control unit in position and refit the retaining nuts/bolts.

7 Reconnect the brake pipes to their correct locations as noted during removal and tighten the union nuts securely.

8 Reconnect the ECU wiring connector.

9 Refit the battery tray and battery as described in Chapter 5A Section 4.

10 Bleed the complete brake hydraulic system as described in Section 2. Note that it may also be necessary to bleed the clutch hydraulic system as described in Chapter 6 Section 2.

Front wheel speed sensor

Removal

11 Slacken the front roadwheel bolts, raise the front of the vehicle and support it securely on axle stands, as described in 'Vehicle jacking and support'. Remove the relevant front wheel.

12 Disconnect the battery negative lead as described in Chapter 5A Section 4.

13 Trace the wiring back from the sensor, and separate the two halves of the wiring connector. Note the routing of the wiring to aid correct refitting.

14 Unscrew the retaining bolt and withdraw the sensor from the hub carrier (see illustration).

Refitting

15 Refitting is a reversal of removal, noting the following points:

a) Ensure that the mating faces of the sensor and the hub carrier are clean, and apply a smear of high melting-point brake grease to the sensor location in the swivel hub before refitting.

b) Ensure that the end face of the sensor is clean.

c) Route the wiring as noted before removal.

Rear wheel sensor

Removal

16 Chock the front roadwheels, slacken the rear roadwheel bolts, raise the rear of the vehicle and support it securely on axle stands, as described in 'Vehicle jacking and support'. Remove the relevant rear roadwheel.

17 Disconnect the battery negative lead as described in Chapter 5A Section 4.

18 Trace the wiring back from the sensor, disconnect the wiring plug, and release the harness from the retaining clips.

19 Undo the retaining bolt, and withdraw the sensor from the hub carrier (see illustration).

Refitting

20 Refitting is a reversal of removal, noting the following points:

a) Ensure that the mating faces of the sensor and the hub carrier are clean, and apply a smear of high melting-point brake grease to the sensor location in the swivel hub before refitting.

b) Ensure the end face of the sensor is clean.

c) Tighten the sensor retaining bolt to the specified torque.

Lateral acceleration/yaw rate sensor

Removal

21 Disconnect the battery negative lead as described in Chapter 5A Section 4.

22 Prise up the trim panel adjacent to the handbrake lever (see illustration 18.1).

23 Disconnect the wiring plug, undo the retaining nuts and manoeuvre the sensor from place (see illustration).

Refitting

24 Refitting is a reversal of removal, noting the following points:

a) Tighten the sensor retaining nuts to the specified torque.

b) Ensure the arrow on the sensor points forwards.

c) If a new sensor has been fitted, it must be calibrated using Fiat diagnostic equipment (Witech/Examiner or equivalent). Entrust this task to a Fiat dealer or suitably equipped repairer.

Chapter 10
Suspension and steering

Contents

Section number

Front anti-roll bar – removal and refitting 8
Front hub bearings – renewal. 3
Front hub carrier assembly – removal and refitting 2
Front subframe – removal and refitting 9
Front suspension lower arm – removal and refitting 6
Front suspension lower arm balljoint – renewal 7
Front suspension strut – overhaul 5
Front suspension strut – removal and refitting. 4
General information 1

Section number

Power steering electric motor – removal and refitting 14
Rear hub assembly – removal and refitting 10
Rear suspension components – removal and refitting. 11
Steering column – removal, inspection and refitting 13
Steering rack – removal, overhaul and refitting 15
Steering rack rubber gaiters – renewal. 16
Steering wheel – removal and refitting 12
Track rod end – removal and refitting. 17
Wheel alignment and steering angles – general information 18

Degrees of difficulty

Easy, suitable for novice with little experience	Fairly easy, suitable for beginner with some experience	Fairly difficult, suitable for competent DIY mechanic	Difficult, suitable for experienced DIY mechanic	Very difficult, suitable for expert DIY or professional

Specifications

Front suspension

Type . . . . Independent, with MacPherson struts and transverse lower suspension arms. Anti-roll bar fitted to all models.

Rear suspension

Type . . . . Semi-independent torsion beam axle, with coil springs and telescopic shock absorbers

Steering system

Type . . . . Rack-and-pinion with electrically-operated power assistance

Front wheel alignment and steering angles

Toe-in . . . . 0°4' ± 4' (1.0 mm ± 1.0 mm)

Rear wheel alignment angles

Toe-in . . . . 0°8' ± 10' (1.9 mm ± 2.0 mm)

Tyre pressures . . . . See end of 'Weekly checks'

Torque wrench settings

	Nm	lbf ft
Front suspension:		
Anti-roll bar clamp bolts	25	18
Anti-roll bar link rod nut	50	37
Lower arm-to-hub carrier*	60	44
Lower arm-to-subframe:*		
Stage 1	55	41
Stage 2	Angle-tighten a further 90°	
Driveshaft nut:*		
Stage 1	70	52
Stage 2	Angle-tighten a further 55°	
Hub carrier-to-strut:*		
Stage 1	115	85
Stage 2	Angle-tighten a further 45°	
Subframe bolts (M12)	130	96
Suspension strut piston rod top nut	40	30
Suspension strut upper mounting cup-to-piston nut	50	37
Roadwheel bolts	120	89
Rear suspension		
Drum brake backplate bolts (M8)	25	18
Hub nut*	280	207
Shock absorber lower mounting bolts	130	96
Shock absorber upper mounting bolts	80	59
Stub axle bolts	125	92
Rear axle-to-front mounting bracket bolt	130	96
Rear axle front mounting bracket-to-body bolts	80	59
Steering		
Column mounting bolts/nuts	20	15
Column universal joint pinch bolt*	55	41
Steering rack mounting bolts	100	74
Steering wheel bolt	30	22
Track rod end-to-hub carrier*	40	30

Do not re-use

1 General information

Front suspension

1 The front suspension is independent, comprising transverse lower wishbones, coil spring-over-damper MacPherson strut units and an anti-roll bar. The swivel hubs are bolted to the base of the strut units and are linked to the lower arms by means of balljoints. The entire front suspension assembly is mounted on a subframe, which is in turn bolted to the vehicle body.

Rear suspension

2 The rear suspension incorporates a torsion beam axle with trailing arms, coil springs and separate double-acting telescopic shock absorbers. The components form a discrete sub-assembly which can be unbolted from the underside of the vehicle separately or as a complete unit. No anti-roll bar is fitted.

Steering

3 The two-piece steering shaft runs in a tubular column assembly, which is bolted to a bracket mounted on the vehicle bulkhead. The upper shaft is attached to the intermediate shaft by means of a universal joint and the intermediate shaft is similarly connected to the steering gear pinion by a second universal joint.

4 The rack-and-pinion steering gear is mounted on the front subframe, and is connected by means of track rods to the steering arms projecting rearwards from the swivel hubs. The track rods are fitted with balljoints at their inner and outer ends, to allow for suspension movement, and are threaded to facilitate adjustment.

5 Dualdrive electrically-operated power steering is fitted to all models. The power assistance is provided by an electric motor and gearbox assembly which is integral with the steering column. The system is controlled by an electronic control unit and provides the driver with two operating strategies – one for normal driving and one for 'city' driving. A control button on the facia is used to switch between the two functions. When the 'city' function is activated, a greater degree of power assistance is provided for ease of town driving and parkingmanoeuvres.

2 Front hub carrier assembly – removal and refitting

Note: *A balljoint separator tool will be required for this operation and a new driveshaft retaining nut will be required for refitting.*

Removal

1 Slacken the front roadwheel bolts, raise the front of the vehicle and support it securely on axle stands, as described in *'Vehicle jacking and support'*. Remove the relevant roadwheel.

2 Using a hammer and chisel or similar tool, tap up the staking securing the driveshaft retaining nut in position.

3 The front wheel hub must be held stationary in order to loosen the driveshaft nut. Ideally, the hub should be held by a suitable tool bolted into place using two of the roadwheel bolts (see **Tool Tip**). Alternatively, have an assistant firmly apply the foot brake to prevent the hub from rotating. Using a socket and extension bar, slacken and remove the driveshaft retaining nut.

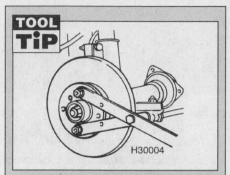

H30004

A tool to hold the front hub stationary whilst the driveshaft nut is slackened can be fabricated from two lengths of steel strip (one long, one short) and a nut and bolt; the nut and bolt forming the pivot of a forked tool.

2.9 Undo the nuts, and withdraw the hub carrier-to-strut bolts

2.11 Undo the nut and withdraw the clamp bolt

Caution: The nut is extremely tight. Discard the nut – a new one must be fitted.

4 Release the brake caliper hydraulic hose from the bracket at the base of the suspension strut.

5 Remove the front brake disc as described in Chapter 9 Section 6.

6 Release the wheel speed sensor cable from the brackets at the base of the suspension strut. Undo the sensor retaining bolt, withdraw the sensor from the hub carrier and suspend it away from the working area, to avoid the possibility of damage.

7 Undo the retaining bolts and remove the brake disc shield.

8 Unscrew the nut securing the track rod end to the hub carrier. Release the track rod end tapered shank using a balljoint separator tool.

9 Unscrew the two nuts and remove the bolts securing the top of the hub carrier to the base of the suspension strut **(see illustration)**. When refitting, insert the bolts from the front.

10 Pull the hub carrier outwards at the top to release the driveshaft outer constant velocity joint from the wheel hub. If necessary, the joint can be tapped free using a soft-faced mallet.

11 Slacken and remove the nut, then withdraw the suspension lower arm balljoint clamp bolt from the hub carrier **(see illustration)**.

12 Tap a small chisel into the split on the hub carrier to spread the hub carrier slightly, then lift the swivel hub assembly up and off the balljoint shank.

Refitting

13 Locate the hub carrier over the suspension lower arm balljoint, pushing it fully into engagement with the balljoint shank. Refit the clamp bolt and secure with the nut tightened to the specified torque.

14 Engage the outer CV joint into the wheel hub, then pivot the top of the hub carrier back towards the car. Screw on the new driveshaft retaining nut, but do not tighten it at this stage.

15 Refit the suspension strut-to-hub carrier bolts, screw on the two nuts and tighten them to the specified torque.

16 Engage the track rod end with the hub carrier, refit the retaining nut and tighten the nut to the specified torque.

17 Ensure that the mating faces of the wheel speed sensor and the hub carrier are clean, and apply a smear of high melting point brake grease to the sensor location in the hub carrier. Ensure that the end face of the sensor is clean, then locate it in position and secure with the retaining bolt. Refit the sensor cable to the brackets on the suspension strut.

18 Refit the brake disc shield and tighten the retaining bolts securely.

19 Refit the brake disc as described in Chapter 9 Section 6.

20 Using the method employed on removal to prevent rotation of the hub, tighten the driveshaft retaining nut to the specified torque. Secure the nut by tapping the staking into the two grooves in the end of the CV joint using a hammer and chisel.

21 Refit the roadwheel, and lower the car to the ground. Depress the brake pedal several times to bring the brake pads into contact with the disc.

22 It is advisable to have the front wheel toe setting checked at the earliest opportunity.

3 Front hub bearings – renewal

Note: *Various special tools, including a hydraulic press will be required for this operation (see text). If the necessary tools are not available, the hub carrier assembly should be removed as described in Section 2 and taken to a suitably-equipped engineering works for renewal of the bearing.*

1 Remove the hub carrier assembly as described in Section 2.

2 Press the wheel hub flange from the bearing and extract the hub, together with the bearing inner race.

3 The bearing inner race must now be removed from the wheel hub using a suitable puller. To provide sufficient clearance for the puller legs, force the inner race away from the hub flange using a hammer and small chisel inserted between the inner race and the hub flange. When sufficient clearance exists, engage the puller legs behind the inner race and draw the race off the wheel hub.

4 Using a pair of screwdrivers, extract the circlip from the hub carrier **(see illustration)**.

5 Press the bearing out of the hub. Note that a flange on the outboard side of the hub carrier means that the bearing can only be removed in one direction.

6 Before installing the new bearing, thoroughly clean the bearing location in the hub carrier.

7 Fit the new bearing from the inboard side the hub carrier and press it fully into position, applying pressure only to the bearing outer race.

8 Fit the bearing retaining circlip to its groove in the hub carrier so that the circlip's gap is aligned with the aperture for the ABS wheel speed sensor (otherwise the sensor will not function correctly and the ABS failure warning lamp will illuminate).

9 Suitably support the bearing inner race on the press bed and press the wheel hub into the bearing.

10 On completion, check that the wheel hub rotates freely in the bearing without resistance or roughness.

11 Refit the hub carrier assembly as described in Section 2.

3.4 Remove the bearing retaining circlip

4 Front suspension strut – removal and refitting

Removal

1 Slacken the front wheel bolts, raise the front of the vehicle and support it securely on axle stands, as described in *'Vehicle jacking and support'*.
2 Release the brake caliper hydraulic hose (and the ABS wheel speed sensor cable) from the brackets at the base of the suspension strut.
3 Unscrew the two nuts and remove the bolts securing the base of the suspension strut to the top of the hub carrier **(see illustration 2.9)**. New bolts/nuts will be required.
4 Pull the hub carrier outwards at the top to release it from the suspension strut.
5 Undo the nut securing the front anti-roll bar link rod to the strut **(see illustration)**. Counter

hold the nut with an open ended spanner on the rod balljoint shank.
6 Remove both front wiper arms as described in Chapter 12 Section 13.
7 Undo the 3 screws and remove the windscreen base trim along with the rubber sealing strip **(see illustrations)**.
8 Have an assistant support the strut from underneath the wheel arch. Working in the engine compartment, unscrew the nut securing the upper mounting cup to the strut piston rod while counterholding the piston rod with a suitable Allen key. Lift off the upper mounting cup and withdraw the assembly from under the wheel arch **(see illustrations)**.

Refitting

9 Manoeuvre the strut assembly into position under the wheel arch and locate the upper mounting cup over the strut piston. Refit the retaining nut and moderately tighten it at this stage. Final tightening of this nut is carried out with the car resting on its roadwheels.

4.5 Counterhold with an open-ended spanner on the balljoint shank

10 Engage the lower end of the strut with the hub carrier, then fit the new securing bolts and nuts. Tighten the nuts to the specified torque.
11 The remainder of refitting is a reversal of removal. With the car resting on its' roadwheels, tighten the suspension strut upper mounting cup retaining nut to the specified torque.

4.7a Undo the 3 screws at the front edge of the windscreen base trim...

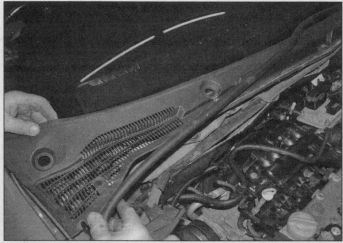

4.7b... then pull up the trim panel along with the rubber sealing strip

4.8a Counterhold the piston rod with an Allen bet/key, then undo the strut retaining nut

4.8b Recover the upper mounting cup

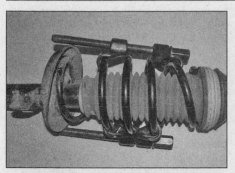

5.2 Fit compressors to the coil spring

5.3 Hold the piston rod nut with an Allen bit/key, then undo the retaining nut

5.4a Withdraw the upper mounting/spring seat...

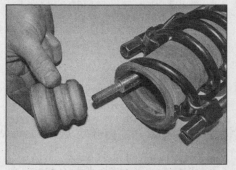

5.4b... bump stop...

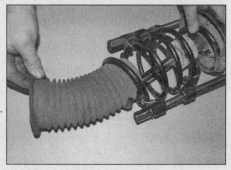

5.4c... and gaiter

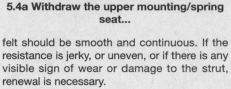

5 Front suspension strut – overhaul

Note: *Suitable compressor tools will be required for this operation.*

1 Remove the front suspension strut as described in Section 4.

2 Fit suitable spring compressors to the coil spring, and compress the spring sufficiently to enable the upper mounting to be turned by hand **(see illustration)**.

⚠️ *Warning: Ensure that the coil spring is compressed sufficiently to remove all the tension from the upper mounting, before attempting to remove the piston rod nut.*

3 Unscrew the nut securing the strut piston rod to the upper mounting, while counterholding the piston with a suitable Allen key **(see illustration)**.

4 Withdraw the upper mounting/spring seat, then withdraw the bump stop and gaiter **(see illustrations)**.

5 Carefully remove the spring, complete with compressors **(see illustration)**.

6 With the strut assembly now dismantled, examine all the components for wear, damage or deformation. Renew any components as necessary.

7 Examine the strut body for signs of fluid leakage or damage and the piston rod for signs of pitting or scoring. While holding it in an upright position, test the operation of the strut by moving the piston rod through a full stroke, and then through short strokes of 50 to 100 mm. In both cases, the resistance felt should be smooth and continuous. If the resistance is jerky, or uneven, or if there is any visible sign of wear or damage to the strut, renewal is necessary.

8 If any doubt exists about the condition of the coil spring, carefully remove the spring compressors, and check the spring for distortion and signs of cracking. Renew the spring if it is damaged or distorted, or if there is any doubt about its condition.

Caution: Coil springs are classified by their height when under load – this is indicated by a coloured paint marking on the side of the coil windings. All coil springs fitted to the vehicle must be of the same classification to ensure the correct ride height.

9 Begin reassembly by refitting the dust cover and bump rubber.

10 Ensure that the coil spring is compressed sufficiently to enable the upper mounting components to be fitted, then fit the spring over the piston rod, ensuring that the lower end of the spring is correctly located in the recess on the lower spring seat **(see illustration)**.

11 Locate the upper spring seat/mounting over the piston rod.

12 Fit the piston rod top nut, then tighten the nut to the specified torque, counterholding the piston rod in a manner similar to that used during dismantling.

13 Remove the spring compressors and refit the strut to the car as described in Section 4.

6 Front suspension lower arm – removal and refitting

Removal

1 Slacken the front wheel bolts, raise the front of the vehicle and support it securely on axle stands, as described in *'Vehicle jacking and support'*. Remove the front roadwheels.

2 Undo the fasteners and remove the engine undershield (where fitted).

3 Detach the track rod end from the hub carrier, as described in Section 17.

4 Slacken and remove the nut, then withdraw the suspension lower arm balljoint clamp bolt

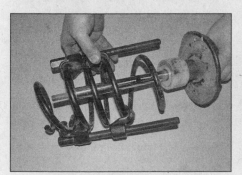

5.5 Remove the spring with the compressors

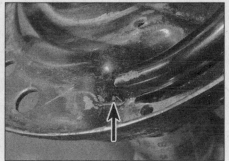

5.10 Ensure the end of the spring locates in the recess

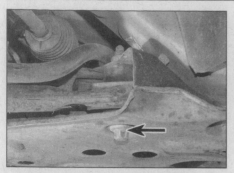

6.6 Remove the arm rear mounting bolt

6.7 Lower arm front mounting bolt/nut

from the hub carrier **(see illustration 2.11)**.

5 Tap a small chisel into the split on the hub carrier to spread the hub slightly, then lever the end of the suspension lower arm down to release it from the base of the hub carrier.

6 Unscrew the bolt securing the suspension lower arm rear mounting to the subframe **(see illustration)**. Discard the bolt – a new one must be fitted.

7 Slacken and remove the nut from the through-bolt at the lower arm front mounting **(see illustration)**. Withdraw the bolt and discard it – a new one must be fitted.

8 Manoeuvre the suspension lower arm from its mounting locations and remove it from under the vehicle.

9 With the lower arm removed, examine the arm itself, and the mounting bushes, for wear, cracks or damage.

10 Check the balljoint for wear, excessive play, or stiffness. Also check the balljoint dust boot for cracks or damage.

11 The mounting bushes and balljoint assembly are integral with the suspension lower arm, and cannot be renewed independently. If either the bushes or the balljoint are worn or damaged, the complete suspension lower arm assembly must be renewed.

Refitting

Caution: Final tightening of the suspension lower arm and anti-roll bar attachments must be carried out with the car resting on its roadwheels, or damage to the rubber bushes will result.

12 Locate the suspension lower arm in its mountings. Fit the through-bolt to the front mounting bracket and engage it with the lower arm bush. Fit the securing nut, but do not fully tighten it at this stage.

13 Fit the rear mounting bolt, but do not fully tighten the bolt at this stage.

14 Engage the lower arm balljoint with the hub carrier, then refit the balljoint clamp bolt and nut. Tighten the clamp bolt nut to the specified torque.

15 The remainder of refitting is a reversal of removal, noting the following points:

a) *Refit the roadwheel, and lower the car to the ground.*

b) *Make sure that the car is parked on level ground, then release the handbrake. Roll the vehicle backwards and forwards, and bounce the front of the vehicle to settle the suspension components.*

c) *Chock the wheels, then tighten all the suspension arm mounting nuts and bolts to the specified torque.*

d) *On completion, have the front wheel toe setting checked at the earliest opportunity.*

7 Front suspension lower arm balljoint – renewal

1 The balljoint is integral with the suspension lower arm. If the balljoint is worn or damaged, the complete lower arm must be renewed, as described in Section 6.

8.2 Detach the lower end of the link rods from the anti-roll bar

8.5 Rear engine mounting-to-subframe bolt

8 Front anti-roll bar – removal and refitting

Removal

1 Slacken the front wheel bolts, raise the front of the vehicle and support it securely on axle stands, as described in *'Vehicle jacking and support'*. Remove the front roadwheels.

2 Undo the nut each side, securing the link rods to the ends of the anti-roll bar. Use an Allen key in the balljoint shank to counterhold the nut **(see illustration)**.

3 Undo the bolts securing the anti-roll bar clamps to the front subframe.

4 Undo the bolts securing the steering rack to the subframe **(see illustration 15.7)**.

5 Undo the bolt securing the rear engine mounting to the subframe **(see illustration)**.

6 Paint alignment marks between the subframe and vehicle body to aid refitting.

7 Place a workshop/trolley jack under the front subframe, then slacken the retaining bolts and lower the front subframe slightly **(see illustration 8.8a and 8.8b)**.

8 Manoeuvre the anti-roll bar assembly through the wheelarch aperture.

9 Inspect the rubber bushes for cracks or deterioration. If renewal is necessary, at the time of writing, it would appear that the complete anti-roll bar must be replaced – the bushes are not available separately. Check with a Fiat dealer or parts specialist.

10 Check the anti-roll bar for signs of damage, wear or serious corrosion.

Refitting

11 Refitting is a reversal of removal, bearing in mind the following points:

a) *Moderately tighten the anti-roll bar mountings initially, then tighten them all to the specified torque after the car has been lowered to the ground and is resting on its roadwheels.*

b) *Tighten all fasteners to their specified torque where given.*

c) *Align the previously made marks prior to tightening the subframe mounting bolts.*

9 Front subframe – removal and refitting

Removal

1 Remove both front suspension lower arms as described in Section 6.

2 Undo the bolts and remove the rear, lower engine mounting link rod **(see illustration 8.5)**.

3 On 1.4L 16v models, undo the bolts and remove the front subframe cross brace **(see**

9.3 Undo the bolts and remove the subframe cross brace

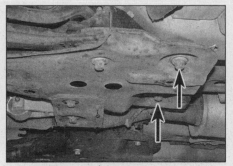

9.8a Subframe left-hand side rear mounting bolts...

9.8b... and front mounting bolt

illustration). Note that the cross brace is marked Left and Right on the upper surface to aid refitting.

4 Remove the rear silencer and centre exhaust pipe as described in Chapter 4A Section 13.

5 Undo the bolts securing the anti-roll bar clamps to the subframe.

6 Working underneath the facia, undo the steering column universal joint pinch bolt, and slide the steering column upwards from the rack pinion (see illustration 13.8). Discard the bolt – a new one must be fitted.

7 Paint alignment marks between the subframe and the vehicle body to aid refitting.

8 Position a workshop/trolley jack under the subframe, then undo the retaining bolts and lower the subframe from place (see illustrations).

Refitting

9 Raise the subframe into position, align the previously made marks, then tighten the retaining bolts to the specified torque.

10 The remainder of refitting is a reversal of removal, noting the following points:
a) Tighten all fasteners to their specified torque where given.
b) Moderately tighten the anti-roll bar mountings initially, then tighten them all to the specified torque after the car has been lowered to the ground and is resting on its roadwheels.
c) Have the front wheel alignment checked at the earliest opportunity.

11.4 Shock absorber lower retaining bolt/ nut

10 Rear hub assembly – removal and refitting

Note: *A new rear hub retaining nut must be used on refitting.*

Removal

1 The rear hub bearings are integral with the hubs themselves, and cannot be renewed separately. If the bearings require renewal, the complete hub assembly must be renewed.

2 Remove the brake drum as described in Chapter 9 Section 10, or the rear brake disc as described in Chapter 9 Section 7.

3 Prise the dust cap from the hub, using a mallet and chisel.

4 Slacken and remove the hub nut and recover the spacers.

Caution: The nut is tightened to a very high torque. Use a long extension bar to remove the nut and ensure that you have access to torque wrench capable of tightening the new nut to the specified torque before removing the existing nut.

5 Withdraw the hub and bearing assembly from the stub axle, and recover the inner spacer. Discard the hub nut – a new one must be used on refitting.

Refitting

6 Thoroughly clean the stub axle, then slide the inner spacer and the hub assembly into position.

7 Fit the outer spacer, then thread a new hub nut onto the end of the stub axle.

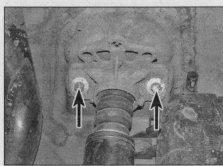

11.6 Rear shock absorber upper mounting bolts

8 Tighten the hub nut to the specified torque, then check that the hub spins smoothly and freely. Carefully tap the dust cap into position over the nut.

9 Refit the brake drum as described in Chapter 9 Section 10, or the brake disc as described in Chapter 9 Section 7.

10 Refit the roadwheel and lower the vehicle to the ground.

11 Rear suspension components – removal and refitting

1 Chock the front wheels, slacken the rear roadwheel bolts, raise the rear of the vehicle and support it securely on axle stands, as described in 'Vehicle jacking and support'. Remove the rear roadwheels.

Shock absorber

Removal

2 Remove the rear wheelarch liner

3 Using a trolley jack positioned under the rear axle trailing arm, raise the trailing arm to take the strain from the shock absorber.

4 Slacken and withdraw the shock absorber lower retaining bolt (see illustration).

5 Lower the jack and allow the shock absorber to separate from the trailing arm. Take care to avoid displacing the coil spring.

6 Undo the 2 bolts securing the shock absorber upper mounting to the vehicle body (see illustration).

7 Manoeuvre the shock absorber from the wheelarch. Note that to avoid confusion when refitting, the right-hand mounting only has an identification hole.

8 Examine the shock absorber for signs of fluid leakage or damage. While holding it in an upright position, test the operation of the shock absorber by moving the piston through a full stroke, and then through short strokes of 50 to 100 mm. In both cases, the resistance felt should be smooth and continuous. If the resistance is jerky, or uneven, or if there is any visible sign of wear or damage, renewal is necessary.

9 If required, undo the nut and detach the upper mounting assembly from the shock absorber.

Refitting

10 Refitting is a reversal of removal. Tighten the shock absorber upper and lower retaining bolts to the specified torque, but delay this operation until the full weight of the car is resting on its roadwheels.

Coil spring

Removal

11 Using a trolley jack positioned under the rear axle trailing arm, raise the trailing arm to take the strain from the shock absorbers.
12 Slacken and withdraw the shock absorber lower retaining bolts on both sides.
13 Lower the trailing arm gradually using a trolley jack, until the coil spring is released from its lower seat on the trailing arm and its upper seat on the underbody. Make a note of the orientation of the coil spring, to aid correct refitting later.

Refitting

14 Refitting is a reversal of removal. Tighten the shock absorber retaining bolts to the specified torque, but delay this operation until the full weight of the car is resting on its roadwheels.

Stub axle

Removal

15 Remove the rear hub assembly as described in Section 10.

Drum brake models

16 Using a brake hose clamp, clamp the brake flexible hydraulic hose located adjacent to the rear axle mounting.
17 Clean the brake backplate around the wheel cylinder hydraulic pipe union, then unscrew the union nut and disconnect the hydraulic pipe. Cover the open ends of the pipe and the wheel cylinder to prevent dirt ingress.
18 Slacken and remove the bolt securing the rear wheel speed sensor to the rear of the stub axle and withdraw the sensor from its location. Suspend the sensor away from the working area, to avoid the possibility of damage.
19 Prise out the cap, and use a pair of thin-nosed pliers to disconnect the handbrake cable from the lever on the brake shoe as described in Chapter 9 Section 16.
20 Release the handbrake outer cable from the brake backplate.
21 Undo the two bolts and remove the brake backplate/shoe assembly from the stub axle.
22 Undo the four bolts and remove the stub axle from the rear axle bracket.

Disc brake models

23 Undo the bolts and remove the brake disc shield.
24 Undo the 4 retaining bolts and remove the stub axle.

Refitting

25 Refitting is a reversal of removal, noting the following points:
a) *Tighten all fasteners to their specified torque where given.*
b) *Bleed the brake hydraulic system as described in Chapter 9 Section 2. Drum brake models only.*
c) *Adjust the handbrake as described in Chapter 9 Section 15. Drum brake models only.*

Rear axle assembly

Removal

26 On models with rear drum brakes, remove the rear brake shoes on both sides as described in Chapter 9 Section 11.
27 Using brake hose clamps, clamp the brake flexible hydraulic hoses located adjacent to each rear axle mounting.
28 Clean the area around the brake pipe-to-flexible hose union nuts, and unscrew the pipe unions on each side. Extract the retaining clips and detach the flexible hoses from the brackets on the rear axle. Cover the open ends of the pipes and hoses to prevent dirt ingress.
29 Slacken and remove the bolts securing the rear wheel speed sensors to the rear of the stub axles and withdraw the sensors from their location. Suspend the sensors away from the working area, to avoid the possibility of damage.
30 On models with rear disc brakes, detach the cable each side from the brake caliper and support bracket, as described in Chapter 9 Section 16.
31 Release the handbrake cables, and the rear wheel speed sensor cables from their clips on the rear axle.
32 Remove both rear coil springs as described previously in this Section.
33 Suitably support the rear axle assembly on a trolley jack and engage the help of an assistant.
34 Undo the bolts securing the rear axle mounting brackets to the underbody on both sides. Slowly lower the jack and guide the axle assembly down and out from under the car.
35 If the mounting bushes require renewal, undo the nuts/bolts and remove the mounting bracket from the front end of the axle.
36 Note the fitted position of the bushes, then using a combination of washers, spacers, a length of threaded rod and nuts, draw the bush from place each side. Note that Fiat special tool No. 2.000.025.800 may be available for this task.
37 Using soapy water as a lubricant, position the new bushes on the axle, and draw them into place using the same method as removal.
38 Refit the mounting brackets and tighten the nuts/bolts to the specified torque.

Refitting

39 Guide the axle assembly into position,

refit the mounting bracket retaining bolts and tighten them to the specified torque.
40 Refit the rear coil springs as described previously in this Section.
41 Ensure that the mating faces of the wheel speed sensors and the stub axles are clean, and apply a smear of high melting-point brake grease to the sensor locations in the stub axles. Clean the end face of the sensors, locate them place and secure with the retaining bolts.
42 Refit the flexible brake hydraulic hoses to their mounting brackets and secure with the retaining clips. Reconnect the brake pipe union to each hose and tighten the union nut securely. Remove the brake hose clamps from the hoses.
43 Secure the handbrake cables, and the rear wheel speed sensor cables in their clips on the rear axle.
44 Refer to Chapter 9 and refit the rear brake shoes (where applicable) then bleed the brake hydraulic system. Note that if no other part of the system has been disturbed, it should only be necessary to bleed the rear circuits.
45 On disc brake models, reconnect the handbrake cable, and if necessary adjust the cable as described in Chapter 9.
46 Have the wheel alignment checked at the earliest opportunity.

12 Steering wheel – removal and refitting

Removal

1 Remove the airbag unit from the steering wheel as described in Chapter 12 Section 20.
2 Ensure the steering wheel is in its centre position, and the roadwheels are pointing straight-ahead.
3 Slacken and remove the steering wheel retaining bolt **(see illustration)**. Counterhold the steering wheel to prevent rotation as the bolt is released.
4 If no marks are visible, make alignment marks between the steering wheel and the

12.3 Steering wheel retaining bolt

12.4 Make alignment marks between the column shaft and wheel

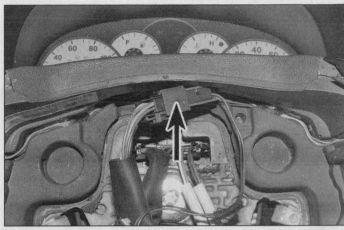

12.5 Disconnect the wiring plug and remove the steering wheel

end of the steering column shaft, to aid correct refitting later **(see illustration)**.

5 Disconnect the steering wheel switches wiring plug, and lift the steering wheel off the column splines. If it is tight, twist it from side-to-side, whilst pulling upwards to release it from the shaft splines **(see illustration)**. Once the wheel is free, feed the airbag and horn switch wiring through the aperture in the steering wheel and remove the wheel from the car.

6 With the steering wheel removed, the clock spring assembly should be locked in place. It is advisable to secure the moving and fixed portions of the clock spring together using tape to prevent rotation with the steering wheel removed.

Refitting

7 Check that the airbag clock spring is still centred correctly as previously described. Remove the tape used to secure the clock spring moving and fixed portions together.

8 Feed the airbag and horn switch wiring through the steering wheel and locate the wheel on the column splines. Ensure that the marks made on the steering wheel and column shaft are aligned.

9 Fit the steering wheel retaining bolt, and tighten it to the specified torque.

10 Reconnect the horn wiring plug.

11 Refit the airbag unit as described in Chapter 12 Section 20.

---

13 Steering column – removal, inspection and refitting

Removal

1 Remove the steering wheel as described in Section 12.

2 Remove the steering column combination switch assembly as described in Chapter 12 Section 5.

3 Pull the drivers side storage compartment/cover rearwards to release the clips **(see illustration)**.

13.3 Pull the storage compartment/cover rearwards

13.5 Unclip the transponder aerial from around the ignition switch

4 Undo the retaining bolt, and unclip the footwell airduct **(see illustration)**.

5 Release the clips and slide the transponder aerial from the ignition switch **(see illustration)**. Disconnect the wiring plug as the aerial is withdrawn.

6 Note their fitted positions, then disconnect the wiring plugs from the steering column, and release the wiring harness from any retaining clips.

7 If required, drill-out the shear bolts and remove the steering lock assembly **(see illustration)**.

8 Working under the facia, slacken and remove the steering column lower universal joint pinch bolt **(see illustration)**. The joint

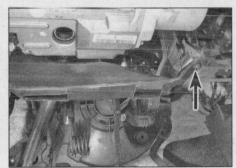

13.4 Footwell airduct retaining bolt

13.7 Steering column lock shear bolts

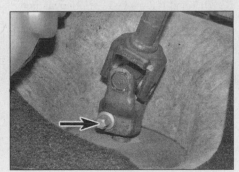

13.8 Remove the steering column pinch bolt

13.9a The column is secured by 2 nuts at the underneath at the rear...

13.9b... and a bolt each side

and rack pinion are equipped with a master spline, so they will only align in one position. Discard the bolt – a new one must be fitted.

9 Undo the steering column retaining nuts/bolts and manoeuvre the assembly away from the bulkhead bracket **(see illustrations)**.

10 Disconnect the universal joint from the steering gear pinion, and remove the steering column from the car.

Caution: If the column is to be refitted to the vehicle, do not release the column adjustment lever, otherwise the column may be irreparably damaged.

Inspection

11 The steering column incorporates a telescopic safety feature. In the event of a front-end crash, the lower section of the shaft collapses and prevents the steering wheel injuring the driver. Before refitting the steering column, examine the column and mountings for signs of damage and deformation, and renew as necessary.

12 Check the steering shaft for signs of free play in the column bushes. If any damage or wear is found on the steering column bushes, it may be possible to have the column overhauled. Consult a Fiat dealer or specialist.

Refitting

13 Refitting is a reversal of removal, noting the following points:

a) Ensure that the roadwheels are in the straight-ahead position then engage the universal joint with the steering gear pinion, aligning the marks made on removal.

b) Tighten all retaining nuts and bolts to the specified torque.

c) Refit the steering column combination switch assembly as described in Chapter 12 Section 5.

d) Refit the steering wheel as described in Section 12.

e) If a new column has been fitted, it may need to be calibrated using Fiat diagnostic

equipment (Examiner – or equivalent). Entrust this task to a Fiat dealer or suitably equipped repairer.

14 Power steering electric motor – removal and refitting

1 It would appear at the time of writing, that no separate parts are available for the steering column (except for the steering lock/ignition switch assembly – see Chapter 5A Section 10). Consequently, if faulty, the complete steering column assembly must be renewed. Consult a Fiat parts specialist.

15 Steering rack – removal, overhaul and refitting

Removal

1 Turn the steering wheel to its centre position, so that the roadwheels are pointing straight-ahead.

2 Slacken the front roadwheel bolts, raise the front of the vehicle and support it securely on axle stands, as described in 'Vehicle jacking and support'.

3 On DOHC 16v models, undo the bolts and remove the front subframe crossbrace **(see illustration 9.3)**. Note the upper part of the crossbrace is marked 'Left' and 'Right' to aid refitment.

4 Undo the bolt securing the rear engine/transmission mounting to the subframe.

5 Working in the driver's footwell, unscrew the clamp bolt securing the intermediate shaft lower universal joint. Make suitable alignment marks on the steering gear pinion and universal joint to ensure correct orientation when refitting. Discard the bolt – a new one must be fitted.

6 Unscrew the nut securing the track rod end

to the hub carrier. Release the track rod end tapered shank using a balljoint separator tool.

7 Undo the bolts securing the steering rack to the subframe **(see illustration)**.

8 Undo the nuts securing the front exhaust pipe to the catalytic converter, remove the bolt securing the pipe support bracket to the transmission bell housing, then release the rubber mounting and move the exhaust pipe to one side. Recover the gasket.

9 Position a workshop jack under the engine/transmission assembly, then move the assembly forwards a little, and with the help of an assistant, manoeuvre the steering rack forwards from place.

Overhaul

10 Examine the steering rack assembly for signs of wear, leakage or damage. If overhaul of the steering rack assembly is necessary, the task must be entrusted to a Fiat dealer or specialist.

Refitting

11 Refitting is a reversal of removal, bearing in mind the following points:

a) Centralise the steering rack by turning the pinion so that the rack moves to full left lock. Now move the rack to full right lock, counting the number of turns of the pinion.

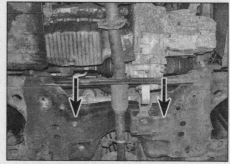

15.7 Steering rack mounting bolts

16.3 Gaiter securing clips

Turn the pinion back by half the number of turns counted.
b) *Ensure that the roadwheels are in the straight-ahead position then engage steering gear pinion with the universal joint, aligning the marks made on removal.*
c) *Tighten all retaining nuts and bolts to the specified torque.*
d) *Have the front wheel toe setting checked at the earliest opportunity.*

16 Steering rack rubber gaiters – renewal

1 Remove the relevant track rod end as described in Section 17.
2 Make an alignment mark between the track rod end locknut and the track rod, to allow the locknut to be accurately positioned when refitting. Unscrew the locknut from the end of the track rod.
3 Mark the correct fitted position of the gaiter on the track rod, then release the gaiter securing clips (see illustration). Slide the gaiter from the steering gear, and off the end of the track rod.
4 Thoroughly clean the track rod and the steering gear housing, using fine abrasive paper to polish off any corrosion, burrs or sharp edges which might damage the new gaiter sealing lips on installation. Scrape off all the grease from the old gaiter, and apply it to the track rod inner balljoint. (This assumes that grease has not been lost or contaminated

as a result of damage to the old gaiter. Use fresh grease if in doubt.)
5 Carefully slide the new gaiter onto the track rod, and locate it on the steering gear housing. Align the outer edge of the gaiter with the mark made on the track rod prior to removal, then secure it in position with new retaining clips.
6 Screw the track rod end locknut onto the end of the track rod and position it accurately in accordance with the mark made on removal.
7 Refit the track rod end as described in Section 17.

17 Track rod end – removal and refitting

Removal

1 Slacken the front roadwheel bolts, raise the front of the vehicle and support it securely on axle stands, as described in *'Vehicle jacking and support'*.
2 Hold the track rod, and unscrew the track rod end locknut by a quarter of a turn (see illustration). Do not move the locknut from this position, as it will serve as a handy reference mark on refitting.
3 Partially unscrew the nut securing the track rod end to the hub carrier.
4 Using a balljoint separator tool, separate the track rod end from the hub carrier (see illustration). Remove the nut and lift the track rod end from the hub carrier.
5 Counting the exact number of turns necessary to do so, unscrew the track rod end from the track rod.

Refitting

6 Carefully clean the track rod end and the track rod threads.
7 Renew the track rod end if the rubber dust cover is cracked, split or perished, or if the movement of the balljoint is either sloppy or too stiff. Also check for other signs of damage such as worn threads.
8 Screw the track rod end onto the track rod by the number of turns noted during removal. This should bring it to within a quarter of a

turn from the locknut. Hold the track rod and securely tighten the locknut.
9 Ensure that the balljoint taper is clean, then engage the taper with the hub carrier.
10 Refit the track rod end retaining nut, and tighten the nut to the specified torque.
11 Refit the roadwheel, and lower the car to the ground.
12 Have the front wheel toe setting checked at the earliest opportunity.

18 Wheel alignment and steering angles – general information

Definitions

1 A car's steering and suspension geometry is defined in four basic settings (see illustration) – all angles are usually expressed

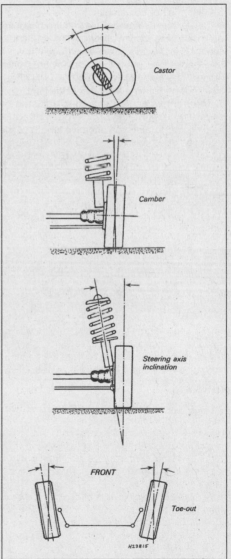

18.1 Steering/suspension geometry details

17.2 Slacken the trackrod end locknut a quarter of a turn

17.4 Use a balljoint separator tool to separate the track rod end from the hub carrier

in degrees (toe settings are also expressed as a measurement); the steering axis is defined as an imaginary line drawn through the axis of the suspension strut, extended where necessary to contact the ground.

2 Camber is the angle between each roadwheel and a vertical line drawn through its centre and tyre contact patch, when viewed from the front or rear of the car. Positive camber is when the roadwheels are tilted outwards from the vertical at the top; negative camber is when they are tilted inwards.

3 The front camber angle is not adjustable.

4 Castor is the angle between the steering axis and a vertical line drawn through each roadwheel's centre and tyre contact patch, when viewed from the side of the car. Positive castor is when the steering axis is tilted so that it contacts the ground ahead of the vertical; negative castor is when it contacts the ground behind the vertical.

5 Castor is not adjustable.

6 Toe is the difference, viewed from above, between lines drawn through the roadwheel centres and the car's centre-line. "Toe-in" is when the roadwheels point inwards, towards each other at the front, while "toe-out" is when they splay outwards from each other at the front.

7 The front wheel toe setting is adjusted by screwing the right-hand track rod in or out of its balljoint, to alter the effective length of the track rod assembly.

8 Rear wheel toe setting is also adjustable. The toe setting is adjusted by slackening the trailing arm mounting bracket bolts and repositioning the bracket.

Checking and adjustment

Front wheel toe setting

9 Due to the special measuring equipment necessary to check the wheel alignment, and the skill required to use it properly, the checking and adjustment of these settings is best left to a Fiat dealer or similar expert. Note that most tyre-fitting shops now possess sophisticated checking equipment.

10 To check the toe setting, a tracking gauge must first be obtained. Two types of gauge are available, and can be obtained from motor accessory shops. The first type measures the distance between the front and rear inside edges of the roadwheels, as previously described, with the car stationary. The second type, known as a "scuff plate", measures the actual position of the contact surface of the tyre, in relation to the road surface, with the car in motion. This is achieved by pushing or driving the front tyre over a plate, which then moves slightly according to the scuff of the tyre, and shows this movement on a scale. Both types have their advantages and disadvantages, but either can give satisfactory results if used correctly and carefully.

11 Make sure that the steering is in the straight-ahead position when making measurements.

12 If adjustment is necessary, apply the handbrake then jack up the front of the car and support it securely on axle stands.

13 First clean the track rod threads; if they are corroded, apply penetrating fluid before starting adjustment. Release the rubber gaiter outer clips, peel back the gaiters and apply a smear of grease so that both are free and will not be twisted or strained as their respective track rods are rotated.

14 Retain the track rod with a suitable spanner and slacken the locknut. Alter the length of the track rod, by screwing them into or out of the balljoints by rotating the track rod using an open-ended spanner fitted to the track rod flats provided; shortening the track rods (screwing them onto their balljoints) will reduce toe-in/increase toe-out.

15 When the setting is correct, hold the track rod and tighten the locknut to the specified torque setting.

16 Check that the toe setting has been correctly adjusted by lowering the car to the ground and re-checking the toe setting; re-adjust if necessary. Ensure that the rubber gaiters are seated correctly and are not twisted or strained, and secure them in position with the retaining clips; where necessary fit a new retaining clip.

Chapter 11
Bodywork and fittings

Contents

Section number

Body exterior fittings – removal and refitting 20
Bonnet – removal and refitting 10
Bonnet lock assembly – removal and refitting 11
Bonnet release cable – removal and refitting 12
Bumpers – removal and refitting 6
Centre console – removal and refitting. 24
Door – removal and refitting 14
Door handle and lock components – removal and refitting 15
Door inner trim panel – removal and refitting 13
Door window glass and regulator – removal and refitting 17
Exterior mirror components – removal and refitting 16
Facia panels – removal and refitting. 25
General information 1

Section number

Interior trim – removal and refitting 23
Maintenance – bodywork and underframe. 2
Maintenance – upholstery and carpets 3
Major body damage – repair 5
Minor body damage – repair 4
Seat belts – removal and refitting. 22
Seats – removal and refitting 21
Sunroof – general information 19
Tailgate – removal, refitting and adjustment. 7
Tailgate lock components – removal and refitting 9
Tailgate strut – removal and refitting 8
Windscreen and fixed window glass – general information 18

Degrees of difficulty

Easy, suitable for novice with little experience | **Fairly easy,** suitable for beginner with some experience | **Fairly difficult,** suitable for competent DIY mechanic | **Difficult,** suitable for experienced DIY mechanic | **Very difficult,** suitable for expert DIY or professional

Specifications

Torque wrench settings	Nm	lbf ft
Seat belt anchorage	35	26
Seat belt inertia reel	35	26
Seat belt stalks	35	26

1 General information

1 The bodyshell is composed of pressed-steel sections which are welded together, although some use of structural adhesives is made. In addition, the front wings are bolted on.
2 The bonnet, door and some other panels vulnerable to corrosion are fabricated from zinc-coated metal. Almost 90% (by weight) of the vehicle body is galvanised to resist corrosion. A coating of anti-chip primer, applied prior to paint spraying provides further protection.
3 Extensive use is made of plastic materials, mainly in the interior, but also in exterior components. The outer sections of the front and rear bumpers are injection-moulded from a synthetic material which is very strong, and yet light. Plastic components such as wheel arch liners are fitted to the underside of the vehicle, to improve the body's resistance to corrosion.

2 Maintenance – bodywork and underframe

1 The general condition of a vehicle's bodywork is the one thing that significantly affects its value. Maintenance is easy but needs to be regular. Neglect, particularly after minor damage, can lead quickly to further deterioration and costly repair bills. It is important also to keep watch on those parts of the vehicle not immediately visible, for instance the underside, inside all the wheel arches and the lower pan of the engine compartment.
2 The basic maintenance routine for the bodywork is washing – preferably with a lot of water, from a hose. This will remove all the loose solids, which may have stuck to the vehicle. It is important to flush these off in such a way as to prevent grit from scratching the finish. The wheel arches and underframe need washing in the same way to remove any accumulated mud, which will retain moisture and tend to encourage rust. Paradoxically, the best time to clean the underframe and wheel arches is in wet weather when the mud is thoroughly wet and soft. In very wet weather the underframe is usually cleaned of large accumulations automatically and this is a good time for inspection.
3 Periodically, except on vehicles with a wax-based underbody protective coating, it is a good idea to have the whole of the underframe of the vehicle steam cleaned, engine compartment included, so that a thorough inspection can be carried out to see what minor repairs and renovations are necessary. Steam cleaning is available at many garages and is necessary for removal of the accumulation of oily grime, which sometimes is allowed to become thick in certain areas. If steam-cleaning facilities are not available, there are some excellent grease solvents available which can be brush applied. The

dirt can then be simply hosed off. Note that these methods should not be used on vehicles with wax-based underbody protective coating or the coating will be removed. Such vehicles should be inspected annually, preferably just prior to winter, when the underbody should be washed down and any damage to the wax coating repaired. Ideally, a completely fresh coat should be applied. It would also be worth considering the use of such wax-based protection for injection into door panels, sills, box sections, etc, as an additional safeguard against rust damage where such protection is not provided by the vehicle manufacturer.

4 After washing paintwork, wipe off with a chamois leather to give an unspotted clear finish. A coat of clear protective wax polish will give added protection against chemical pollutants in the air. If the paintwork sheen has dulled or oxidised, use a cleaner/polisher combination to restore the brilliance of the shine. This requires a little effort, but such dulling is usually caused because regular washing has been neglected. Care needs to be taken with metallic paintwork, as special non-abrasive cleaner/polisher is required to avoid damage to the finish. Always check that the door and ventilator opening drain holes and pipes are completely clear so that water can be drained out. Bright work should be treated in the same way as paintwork. Windscreens and windows can be kept clear of the smeary film that often appears by the use of a proprietary glass cleaner. Never use any form of wax or other body or chromium polish on glass.

3 Maintenance – upholstery and carpets

1 Mats and carpets should be brushed or vacuum cleaned regularly to keep them free of grit. If they are badly stained remove them from the vehicle for scrubbing or sponging and make quite sure they are dry before refitting. Seats and interior trim panels can be kept clean by wiping with a damp cloth. If they do become stained (which can be more apparent on light coloured upholstery) use a little liquid detergent and a soft nail brush to scour the grime out of the grain of the material. Do not forget to keep the headlining clean in the same way as the upholstery. When using liquid cleaners inside the vehicle do not over-wet the surfaces being cleaned. Excessive damp could get into the seams and padded interior causing stains, offensive odours or even rot. If the inside of the vehicle gets wet accidentally it is worthwhile taking some trouble to dry it out properly, particularly where carpets are involved. Do not leave oil or electric heaters inside the vehicle for this purpose.

4 Minor body damage – repair

Minor scratches

1 If the scratch is very superficial, and does not penetrate to the metal of the bodywork, repair is very simple. Lightly rub the area of the scratch with a paintwork renovator, or a very fine cutting paste, to remove loose paint from the scratch and to clear the surrounding bodywork of wax polish. Rinse the area with clean water.

2 In the case of metallic paint, the most commonly found scratches are not in the paint, but in the lacquer top coat, and appear white. If care is taken, these can sometimes be rendered less obvious by very careful use of paintwork renovator (which would otherwise not be used on metallic paintwork); otherwise, repair of these scratches can be achieved by applying lacquer with a fine brush.

3 Apply touch-up paint to the scratch using a fine paintbrush; continue to apply fine layers of paint until the surface of the paint in the scratch is level with the surrounding paintwork. Allow the new paint at least two weeks to harden, and then blend it into the surrounding paintwork by rubbing the scratch area with a paintwork renovator or a very fine cutting paste. Finally, apply wax polish.

4 Where the scratch has penetrated right through to the metal of the bodywork, causing the metal to rust, a different repair technique is required. Remove any loose rust from the bottom of the scratch with a penknife, and then apply rust-inhibiting paint to prevent the formation of rust in the future. Using a rubber or nylon applicator, fill the scratch with bodystopper paste. If required, this paste can be mixed with cellulose thinners to provide a very thin paste, which is ideal for filling narrow scratches. Before the stopper-paste in the scratch hardens, wrap a piece of smooth cotton rag around the top of a finger. Dip the finger in cellulose thinners, and then quickly sweep it across the surface of the stopper-paste in the scratch; this will ensure that the surface of the stopper-paste is slightly hollowed. The scratch can now be painted over as described earlier in this Section.

Dents

5 When deep denting of the vehicle's bodywork has taken place, the first task is to pull the dent out, until the affected bodywork almost attains its original shape. There is little point in trying to restore the original shape completely, as the metal in the damaged area will have stretched on impact and cannot be reshaped fully to its original contour. It is better to bring the level of the dent up to a point which is about 3 mm below the level of the surrounding bodywork. In cases where the dent is very shallow anyway, it is not worth trying to pull it out at all. If the underside of the dent is

accessible, it can be hammered out gently from behind, using a mallet with a wooden or plastic head. Whilst doing this, hold a suitable block of wood firmly against the outside of the panel to absorb the impact from the hammer blows and thus prevent a large area of the bodywork from being 'belled-out'.

6 Should the dent be in a section of the bodywork, which has a double skin or some other factor making it inaccessible from behind, a different technique is called for. Drill several small holes through the metal inside the area – particularly in the deeper section. Then screw long self-tapping screws into the holes just sufficiently for them to gain a good purchase in the metal. Now the dent can be pulled out by pulling on the protruding heads of the screws with a pair of pliers.

7 The next stage of the repair is the removal of the paint from the damaged area, and from an inch or so of the surrounding 'sound' bodywork. This is accomplished most easily by using a wire brush or abrasive pad on a power drill, although it can be done just as effectively by hand using sheets of abrasive paper. To complete the preparation for filling, score the surface of the bare metal with a screwdriver or the tang of a file, or alternatively, drill small holes in the affected area. This will provide a really good 'key' for the filler paste.

8 To complete the repair see the Section on filling and re-spraying.

Rust holes or gashes

9 Remove all paint from the affected area and from an inch or so of the surrounding 'sound' bodywork, using an abrasive pad or a wire brush on a power drill. If these are not available a few sheets of abrasive paper will do the job just as effectively. With the paint removed you will be able to gauge the severity of the corrosion and therefore decide whether to renew the whole panel (if this is possible) or to repair the affected area. New body panels are not as expensive as most people think and it is often quicker and more satisfactory to fit a new panel than to attempt to repair large areas of corrosion.

10 Remove all fittings from the affected area except those, which will act as a guide to the original shape of the damaged bodywork. Then, using tin snips or a hacksaw blade, remove all loose metal and any other metal badly affected by corrosion. Hammer the edges of the hole inwards in order to create a slight depression for the filler paste.

11 Wire-brush the affected area to remove the powdery rust from the surface of the remaining metal. Paint the affected area with rust -inhibiting paint – if the back of the rusted area is accessible, treat this also.

12 Before filling can take place it will be necessary to block the hole in some way. This can be achieved by the use of aluminium or plastic mesh, or aluminium tape.

13 Aluminium or plastic mesh is probably the best material to use for a large hole. Cut

a piece to the approximate size and shape of the hole to be filled, then position it in the hole so that its edges are below the level of the surrounding bodywork. It can be retained in position by several blobs of filler paste around its periphery.

14 Aluminium tape should be used for small or very narrow holes. Pull a piece off the roll and trim it to the approximate size and shape required, then pull off the backing paper (if used) and stick the tape over the hole; it can be overlapped if the thickness of one piece is insufficient. Burnish down the edges of the tape with the handle of a screwdriver or similar, to ensure that the tape is securely attached to the metal underneath.

Filling and re-spraying

15 Before using this Section, see the Sections on dent, deep scratch, rust holes and gash repairs.

16 Many types of bodyfiller are available, but generally speaking those proprietary kits which contain a tin of filler paste and a tube of resin hardener are best for this type of repair. A wide, flexible plastic or nylon applicator will be found invaluable for imparting a smooth and well-contoured finish to the surface of the filler.

17 Mix up a little filler on a clean piece of card or board – measure the hardener carefully (follow the maker's instructions on the pack) otherwise the filler will set too rapidly or too slowly. Using the applicator, apply the filler paste to the prepared area; draw the applicator across the surface of the filler to achieve the correct contour and to level the filler surface. As soon as a contour that approximates to the correct one is achieved, stop working the paste – if you carry on too long, the paste will become sticky and begin to 'pick up' on the applicator. Continue to add thin layers of filler paste at twenty-minute intervals until the level of the filler is just proud of the surrounding bodywork.

18 Once the filler has hardened, excess can be removed using a metal plane or file. From then on, progressively finer grades of abrasive paper should be used, starting with a 40-grade production paper and finishing with 400-grade (or higher) wet-and-dry paper. Always wrap the abrasive paper around a flat rubber, cork, or wooden block – otherwise the surface of the filler will not be completely flat. During the smoothing of the filler surface, the wet-and-dry paper should be periodically rinsed in water. This will ensure that a very smooth finish is imparted to the filler at the final stage.

19 At this stage the 'dent' should be surrounded by a ring of bare metal, which in turn should be encircled by the finely 'feathered' edge of the good paintwork. Rinse the repair area with clean water, until all of the dust produced by the rubbing-down operation has gone.

20 Spray the whole repair area with a light coat of primer – this will show up any imperfections in the surface of the filler. Repair these imperfections with fresh filler paste or bodystopper, and once more smooth the surface with abrasive paper. If bodystopper is used, it can be mixed with cellulose thinners to form a really thin paste, which is ideal for filling small holes. Repeat this spray-and-repair procedure until you are satisfied that the surface of the filler, and the feathered edge of the paintwork are perfect. Clean the repair area with clean water, and allow to dry fully.

21 The repair area is now ready for final spraying. Paint spraying must be carried out in a warm, dry, windless and dust-free atmosphere. This condition can be created artificially if you have access to a large indoor working area, but if you are forced to work in the open, you will have to pick your day very carefully. If you are working indoors, dousing the floor in the work area with water will help to settle the dust that would otherwise be in the atmosphere. If the repair area is confined to one body panel, mask off the surrounding panels; this will help to minimise the effects of a slight mis-match in paint colours. Bodywork fittings (e.g. rubbing strips, door handles, etc) will also need to be masked off. Use genuine masking tape and several thicknesses of newspaper for the masking operations.

22 Before commencing to spray, agitate the aerosol can thoroughly, and then spray a test area (an old tin, or similar) until the technique is mastered. Cover the repair area with a thick coat of primer; the thickness should be built up using several thin layers of paint rather than one thick one. Using 400-grade (or higher) wet-and-dry paper, rub down the surface of the primer until it is really smooth. While doing this, the work area should be thoroughly doused with water, and the wet-and-dry paper periodically rinsed in water. Allow to dry before spraying on more paint.

23 Spray on the top coat, again building up the thickness by using several thin layers of paint. Start spraying at the top of the repair area and then, using a side-to-side motion, work downwards until the whole repair area and about 2 inches of the surrounding original paintwork is covered. Remove all masking material 10 to 15 minutes after spraying on the final coat of paint.

24 Allow the new paint at least two weeks to harden, then, using a paintwork renovator or a very fine cutting paste, blend the edges of the paint into the existing paintwork. Finally, apply wax polish.

Plastic components

25 With the use of more and more plastic body components by the vehicle manufacturers (e.g. bumpers, spoilers, and in some cases major body panels), rectification of more serious damage to such items has become a matter of either entrusting repair work to a specialist in this field, or renewing complete components. Repair of such damage by the DIY owner is not really feasible, owing to the cost of the equipment and materials required for effecting such repairs. The basic technique involves making a groove along the line of the crack in the plastic using a rotary burr in a power drill. The damaged part is then welded back together by using a hot-air gun to heat up and fuse a plastic filler rod into the groove. Any excess plastic is then removed and the area rubbed down to a smooth finish. It is important that a filler rod of the correct plastic is used, as body components can be made of a variety of different types (e.g. polycarbonate, ABS, polypropylene).

26 Damage of a less serious nature (abrasions, minor cracks etc) can be repaired by the DIY owner using a two-part epoxy filler repair material. Once mixed in equal proportions, this is used in similar fashion to the bodywork filler used on metal panels. The filler is usually cured in twenty to thirty minutes, ready for sanding and painting.

27 If the owner is renewing a complete component himself, or if he has repaired it with epoxy filler, he will be left with the problem of finding a suitable paint for finishing which is compatible with the type of plastic used. At one time the use of a universal paint was not possible, owing to the complex range of plastics encountered in body component applications. Standard paints, generally speaking, will not bond to plastic or rubber satisfactorily. However, it is now possible to obtain a plastic body parts finishing kit, which consists of a pre-primer treatment, a primer and coloured top coat. Full instructions are normally supplied with a kit, but basically the method of use is to first apply the pre-primer to the component concerned and allow it to dry for up to 30 minutes. Then the primer is applied and left to dry for about an hour before finally applying the special coloured top coat. The result is a correctly coloured component where the paint will flex with the plastic or rubber, a property that standard paint does not normally possess.

5 Major body damage – repair

1 Where serious damage has occurred, or large areas need renewal due to neglect, it means that complete new panels will need welding in, and this is best left to professionals. If the damage is due to impact, it will also be necessary to completely check the alignment of the bodyshell, and this can only be carried out accurately by a Mercedes-Benz dealer using special jigs. If the body is left misaligned, it is primarily dangerous as the car will not handle properly, and secondly, uneven stresses will be imposed on the steering, suspension and possibly transmission, causing abnormal wear, or complete failure, particularly to such items as the tyres.

6 Bumpers – removal and refitting

Front bumper

Removal

1 For improved access, firmly apply the handbrake, then jack up the front of the car and support it securely on axle stands, as described in 'Vehicle jacking and support'.

Grande Punto models

2 Undo the nut/bolts securing the front section of the wheel arch liner each side.

3 Pull the front section of the wheel arch liners rearwards a little, and undo the bolts securing the bumper to the wing (see illustration).

4 Disconnect the fog light wiring plugs.

5 Undo the 4 bolts securing the lower edge of the bumper.

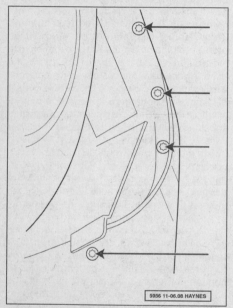

6.8 Bumper-to-wheel arch liner and wing screws

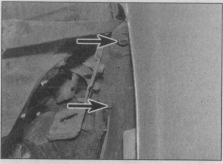

6.3 Undo the bolts each side securing the bumper to the wing

6 Undo the 4 bolts at the upper edge of the bumper (see illustration).

7 With the help of an assistant, manoeuvre the bumper forwards from position.

Punto Evo/Punto models

8 Undo the screws securing the wheel arch liner to the bumper, and the wing to the bumper (see illustration).

9 Turn the steering wheel as necessary to gain access, then undo the bolts and remove the wheel arch liner access cover (see illustration).

10 Reach through the aperture in the wheel

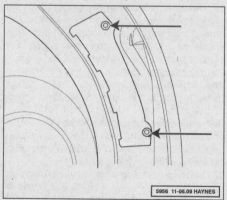

6.9 Undo the bolts and remove the access cover

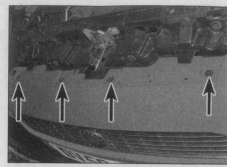

6.6 Undo the bolts at the upper edge of the bumper

arch liner, and disconnect the wiring plugs from the directional indicators and the fog lights.

11 Undo the 4 retaining bolts at the lower edge of the bumper.

12 Undo the 4 retaining bolts at the upper edge of the bumper (see illustration 6.6).

13 With the help of an assistant, pull the rear edges of the bumper outwards a little to release the guide clips, and carefully manoeuvre the bumper forwards.

Refitting

14 Refitting is a reversal of removal. If necessary, adjust the fog light aim as described in Chapter 12 Section 8.

Rear bumper

Removal

15 Chock the front wheels, slacken the rear roadwheel bolts, raise the rear of the vehicle and support it securely on axle stands, as described in 'Vehicle jacking and support'.

16 Undo the 3 bolts, 1 nut, and remove the rear section of the wheel arch liner each side (see illustration).

17 Remove the number plate light assembly as described in Chapter 12 Section 8.

18 Pull forward the rear section of the wheelarch liner, then undo the Torx bolt securing the bumper to the wing each side (see illustration).

6.16 The rear section of the liner is secured by 3 bolts, and 1 nut

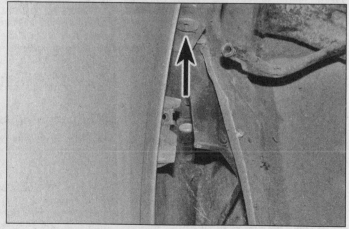

6.18 Undo the Torx bolt securing the bumper to the wing

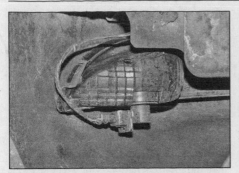
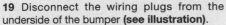

6.19 Disconnect the wiring plug each side of the bumper

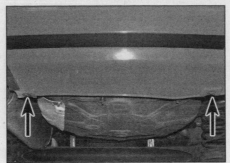

6.20a Bumper lower edge bolts – Grande Punto

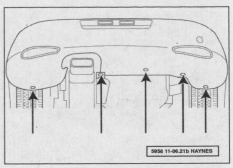

6.20b Bumper lower edge bolts – Punto Evo/2012

19 Disconnect the wiring plugs from the underside of the bumper **(see illustration)**.
20 Undo the bolts at the lower edge of the bumper **(see illustrations)**.
21 Open the tailgate and remove the 2 bolts at the upper edge of the bumper **(see illustration)**.
22 With the help of an assistant, manoeuvre the bumper rearwards from place.

Refitting

23 Refitting is a reversal of removal, ensuring the upper edge of the bumper engages correctly with the guide clips at the base of the tailgate aperture.

7 Tailgate – removal, refitting and adjustment

Removal

1 Open the tailgate, and remove the parcel shelf.
2 Remove the tailgate inner trim panel as described in Section 23.
3 Remove the high-level brake light as described in Chapter 12 Section 8.
4 Disconnect the wiring connectors for the tailgate lock and tailgate wiper motor and unbolt the earth leads. Check for any other wiring connectors which must be disconnected to facilitate tailgate removal. Carefully label each wiring harness connector to aid correct refitting.
5 Tie a length of cord to the wiring harness,

then bind the loose ends of the cabling together using PVC tape. Prise the wiring harness grommet from the upper edge of the tailgate, then feed the wiring through the aperture in the tailgate. Untie the cord from the harness, but leave it in place in the tailgate, to aid refitting later.
6 Disconnect the fluid hose from the tailgate washer nozzle, then tie a length of cord to the hose and draw it out of the tailgate, using the same procedure carried out on the wiring harness.
7 Have an assistant support the tailgate in the open position.
8 Detach the upper ends of the support struts from the tailgate as described in Section 8.
9 Make alignment marks between the tailgate hinges and the vehicle body, then slacken and unscrew the bolts securing the hinges to the tailgate, and lift the tailgate from the vehicle **(see illustration)**.

Refitting

10 Refitting is a reversal of removal, bearing in mind the following points:
a) Tie the cord to the wiring harness and use it to pull the harness through the aperture and into the tailgate. Repeat the procedure on the washer fluid hose.
b) Do not fully tighten the hinge bolts until the tailgate adjustment has been checked, as described in the following paragraphs.

Adjustment

11 Close the tailgate carefully, in case the alignment is incorrect, which may cause

scratching on the tailgate or the body as the tailgate is closed, and check for alignment with the adjacent panels. If necessary, slacken the bolts that secure the hinges to the bodywork and re-align the tailgate to suit. Once the tailgate is correctly aligned, tighten the hinge bolts securely.
12 Check that the tailgate fastens and releases in a satisfactory manner. If adjustment is necessary, slacken the striker plate retaining bolts, and adjust the position of the striker to suit. Once the lock is operating correctly, securely tighten the striker plate retaining bolts.
13 If necessary, adjust the protrusion of the rubber buffers at the lower edge of the tailgate by screwing them in or out, as appropriate.

8 Tailgate strut – removal and refitting

Removal

1 Open the tailgate and support it using suitable wooden props.
2 At the upper end of each strut, lever out the balljoint spring clip a little, then compress the strut slightly by hand and then prise the strut balljoint from the stud on the tailgate **(see illustration)**.

⚠ **Warning: The strut may still be under tension and could extend suddenly once detached from its mountings.**

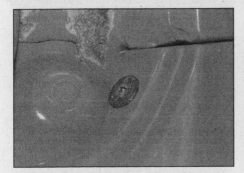

6.21 Undo the bolt each side at the upper edge of the bumper

7.9 Tailgate hinge bolts

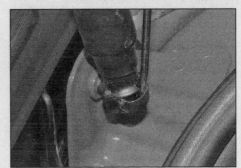

8.2 Prise the clip out a little, and pull the strut from the stud

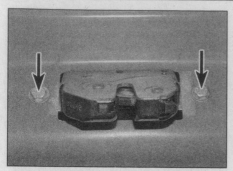

9.2 Tailgate lock retaining bolts

3 Release the lower end of each strut in the same way.

Refitting

4 Refitting is a reversal of removal.

9 Tailgate lock components – removal and refitting

Tailgate lock

Removal

1 Remove the tailgate inner trim panel as described in Section 23.
2 Undo the lock retaining bolts, manoeuvre the lock from place and disconnect the wiring plug **(see illustration)**.

Refitting

3 Refitting is a reversal of removal. Ensure the lock operates correctly prior to closing the tailgate.

Tailgate release control

Removal

4 Remove the tailgate inner trim panel as described in Section 23.
5 Disconnect the wiring plug, undo the 2 retaining nuts and remove the release control assembly. Recover the seal.

Refitting

6 Refitting is a reversal of removal.

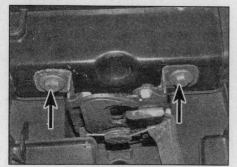

11.2 Bonnet lock is secured by 2 bolts at the front, and 1 behind (hidden)

10.3 Bonnet-to-hinge bolts

Striker plate

Removal

7 Mark the position of the striker plate in relation to the bodywork using a pencil or marker pen, to aid accurate refitting.
8 Slacken and unscrew the bolts securing the striker plate to the body.

Refitting

9 Refitting is a reversal of removal. Use the markings made during removal to give the correct alignment.
10 Check that the tailgate fastens and releases in a satisfactory manner. If adjustment is necessary, slacken the striker plate retaining bolts, and adjust the position of the plate to suit. Once the lock is operating correctly, securely tighten the striker plate retaining bolts.

10 Bonnet – removal and refitting

Removal

1 Open the bonnet and prop it up with a stout pole.
2 Disconnect the washer jet hose at the bonnet connector.
3 Mark the relationship between the hinges and the edge of the bonnet using a soft pencil or marker pen. Slacken and unscrew the bolts; have an assistant support the bonnet as the last bolts are removed **(see illustration)**.

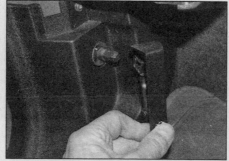

12.3 Pull the release handle from the spindle

4 With the help of an assistant, lift off the bonnet and set it down on its edge, using a dust sheet to protect the paintwork.

Refitting

5 Refit the bonnet and retaining bolts, using the markings made during removal to achieve the correct alignment. Note that the bolt mounting holes are slotted to allow adjustment if required. On completion, tighten the bolts to the specified torque.
6 Reconnect the washer hose, then check that the bonnet fastens and releases in a satisfactory manner. If necessary, adjust the bonnet lock assembly, as described in Section 11.

11 Bonnet lock assembly – removal and refitting

Removal

1 Open the bonnet and mark the relationship between the lock assembly and the front body panel using a soft pencil or marker pen.
2 Slacken and unscrew the 3 nuts/bolts and withdraw the lock assembly from its location **(see illustration)**.
3 Disconnect the release cable and remove the lock assembly.

Refitting

4 Refitting is a reversal of removal. Use the alignment markings made during removal to aid accurate refitting. Check that the bonnet fastens and releases in a satisfactory manner, noting that the mounting holes are slotted to allow adjustment of the lock, if required. On completion, tighten the bolts securely.
5 If necessary, adjust the protrusion of the rubber buffers on the front body panel (located above each headlamp unit) by screwing them in or out, as appropriate. When the rubber buffers are correctly adjusted, there should be just enough free movement to allow the bonnet to be closed and locked easily, without using excessive force, but not enough to allow the bonnet to rattle when secured in the locked position.

12 Bonnet release cable – removal and refitting

Removal

1 Disconnect the release cable from the bonnet lock assembly as described in Section 11.
2 Open the door, undo the screws, then using a blunt, flat-bladed tool carefully prise up the door sill trim to release the retaining clips.
3 Pull the bonnet release handle from the spindle **(see illustration)**.

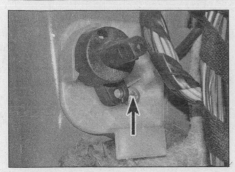

12.5 Release lever retaining bolt

13.1a Use a shop rag...

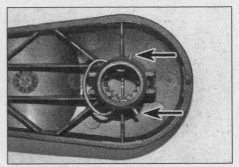

13.1b...to dislodge the clip, and remove the winder handle

4 Undo the retaining bolts and remove the lower A-pillar trim panel.

5 Undo the release lever retaining bolt, rotate the lever assembly slightly to disengage it from the pillar, then disconnect the release cable (see illustration).

6 Working around the engine bay, extract the release cable from its securing clips.

7 Tie a length of string to the end of the cable in the engine compartment, then carefully pull the cable through the bulkhead grommet into the passenger's compartment. Untie the string from the cable, but leave it in place in the bulkhead, to aid refitting.

Refitting

8 Refitting is a reversal of removal, using the string to draw the cable through the bulkhead into the engine compartment. Reconnect the cable to the bonnet lock and adjust the lock position as described in Section 11.

13 Door inner trim panel – removal and refitting

Removal

Grande Punto models

1 On models with manual rear window winders, use a shop rag to release the clip and pull the handle from place (see illustrations).

2 On models with electric windows, using a blunt, flat bladed tool, carefully prise up the switch panel from the armrest (see illustration). Disconnect the wiring plugs as the panel is withdrawn.

3 Prise out the courtesy light (where fitted) from the lower edge of the trim panel. Disconnect the wiring plug as the light is withdrawn.

4 Prise out the plastic covers (where fitted), and undo the 2 screws in the grab handle aperture (see illustration).

5 Prise out the plastic cap and undo the screw in the interior release handle panel (see illustration).

6 Undo the screws at the lower edge of the inner trim panel. Front door panels are retained by 5 screws, whilst rear door panels are retained by 2 screws (see illustrations).

7 Using a blunt, flat-bladed tool, carefully prise the front and rear edges of the inner trim panel away from the door to release the retaining clips (see illustration).

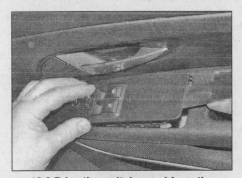

13.2 Prise the switch panel from the armrest

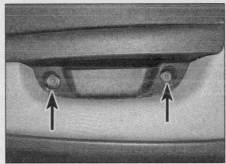

13.4 Prise out the covers, and undo the screws

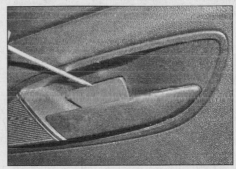

13.5 Prise out the cap in the interior handle panel

13.6a Front door panels are retained by 5 screws

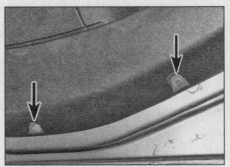

13.6b Rear door panels are retained by 2 screws at the lower edge

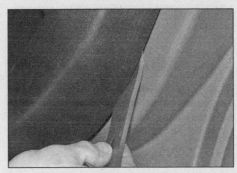

13.7 Carefully prise the panel from the door

13.9 Disconnect the interior release handle cable

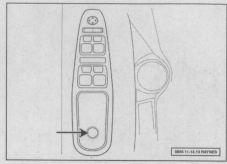

13.10 Prise out the cap and undo the screw

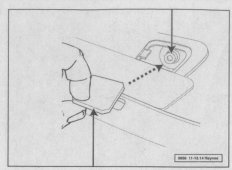

13.14 Prise out the cap and undo the screw

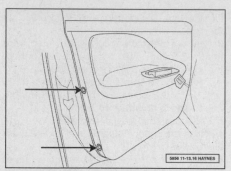

13.16 Undo the screws at the rear edge of the panel

13.19 Use a sharp blade to cut through the sealing sheet sealant

8 With all the retaining clips released, lift the panel slightly and move it away from the door.
9 Disconnect the panel wiring plugs as they become accessible, then disconnect the interior release cable from the handle (see illustration).

Punto Evo/Punto 2012 models

10 Use a small screwdriver to prise out the plastic cap in the arm rest storage tray, and undo the screw exposed (see illustration).
11 On models with electrically operated windows, carefully prise the switch panel from the armrest, and disconnect the wiring plugs.
12 Prise out the courtesy light (where fitted) from the lower edge of the trim panel. Disconnect the wiring plug as the light is withdrawn.
13 On models with manually operated windows, remove the handle as described in the first paragraph of this Section (see illustrations 13.1a and 13.1b).

14 Carefully prise out the plastic cover in the the interior release handle panel, and undo the screw exposed (see illustration).
15 Undo the 2 screws in the switch panel aperture.
16 Undo the 2 screws at the rear edge of the door inner trim panel (see illustration).
17 Using a blunt, flat-bladed tool, working around the front, rear and lower edges, prise the inner trim panel away from the door to release the push-in clips (see illustration 3.7).
18 Lift the panel slightly to release the upper edge, then disconnect the panel wiring plugs, and interior release handle cable (see illustration 3.9).

All models

19 If work is to be carried out on the door internal components, it will be necessary to remove the plastic sealing sheet from the inside of the door. Remove the door speaker

(Chapter 12 Section 17), then start at one corner of the sheet and carefully peel it away, using a sharp blade to split the sealant bead, if necessary (see illustration).
20 Store the detached sealing sheet such that it cannot become contaminated with dust; this will allow it to be re-used later.

Refitting

21 Refitting is a reversal of removal, bearing in mind the following points:
a) Ensure that the sealing sheet is correctly refitted, press it on firmly to ensure that it is adequately sealed around its edges. It should be possible to use the original sealant, but if necessary, new sealant can be obtained from a Fiat dealer.
b) Make sure that the weatherstrip engages securely with the edge of the door as the panel is refitted.

14 Door – removal and refitting

Removal

1 Fully lower the window glass, then open the door, and disconnect the battery negative lead as described in Chapter 5A Section 4.
2 Unplug the multi-way electrical connector from the door pillar (front door) or door frame (rear door) (see illustration).
3 Undo the bolt securing the check strap to the pillar.
4 Undo the hinge bolts, and lift the door from place (see illustration).

Refitting

5 Refitting is a reversal of removal.

15 Door handle and lock components – removal and refitting

Front door exterior handle

Removal

1 Fully raise the window glass.
2 Remove the door inner trim panel and

14.2 Lever over the catch and disconnect the wiring plug

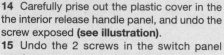

14.4 Undo the door hinge bolts

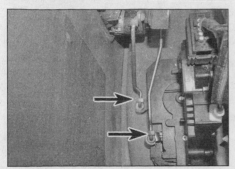

15.3 Rotate the clips anti-clockwise, then disconnect the handle and lock cylinder link rods

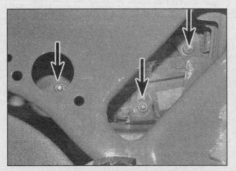

15.5a Undo the retaining nuts...

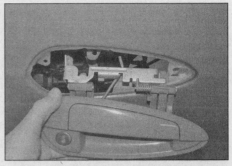

15.5b... and manoeuvre the exterior handle from the door

plastic sealing sheet, as described in Section 13.

3 Release the clip and disconnect the the exterior handle-to-lock link rod from the lock **(see illustration)**.

4 Where applicable, release the clip and disconnect the key lock link rod from the cylinder **(see illustration 15.3)**.

5 Undo the 3 retaining nuts, and manoeuvre the handle assembly from the outside of the door **(see illustrations)**.

Refitting

6 Locate the handle in position and connect the link rod to the door lock mechanism, and where applicable, the link rod to the key lock cylinder.

7 Refit the handle retaining nuts and tighten them securely.

8 Where applicable, refit the security shield and secure it with new rivets, then clip the release cable back into place.

9 Refit the sealing sheet and door inner trim panel as described in Section 13.

Front door lock cylinder

Removal

10 Remove the exterior handle as described previously in this Section.

11 Undo the retaining screw, rotate the cylinder and remove it from the handle **(see illustrations)**.

12 Insert the key, hold the cylinder vertical, extract the clip, press-in the lever and slide the barrel from the cylinder **(see illustrations)**.

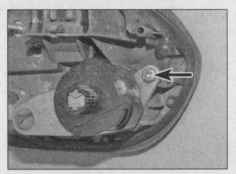

15.11a Undo the screw...

Once the barrel has been extracted, slowly release the lever.

Refitting

13 Press-in the lever, and with the key inserted, slide the barrel into the cylinder. Once inserted, refit the clip, release the lever and remove the key.

14 Refit the cylinder to the exterior handle, engage the clip and tighten the retaining screw securely.

15 Refit the exterior handle.

Front door interior handle

Removal

16 Remove the door inner trim panel as described in Section 13.

17 Holding the return spring in place, carefully extract the retaining pin, and remove the door handle from the panel **(see**

15.11b... rotate the cylinder anti-clockwise and remove it

illustration). Release the spring as the handle is withdrawn.

Refitting

18 Position the handle on the door trim, hold the spring in place and insert the retaining pin.

19 Refit the door inner trim panel as described in Section 13.

Front door lock mechanism

Removal

20 Fully raise the window glass

21 Remove the front door inner trim panel and sealing sheet as described in Section 13. Note that it's only necessary to remove the sealing sheet in the area of the door lock.

22 Disconnect the wiring plug from the door lock.

23 Unclip the operating link rods from the door lock **(see illustration 15.3)**.

15.12a Prise out the barrel retaining clip

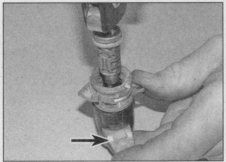

15.12b Press-in the lever, and slide the barrel from the cylinder

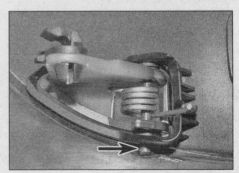

15.17 Interior release handle retaining pin

15.24a Front door lock retaining bolts

15.24b Slide out the red locking catch to disconnect the wiring plug

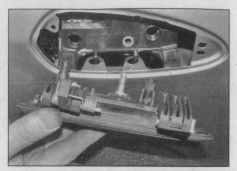

15.27 Remove the handle from the door

24 Unclip the interior release cable, then undo the 3 retaining bolts and manoeuvre the lock assembly, complete with the cable from the door frame **(see illustrations)**. Disconnect the wiring plug as the lock assembly is withdrawn.

Refitting

25 Refitting is a reversal of removal. Secure the security shield using new rivets.

Rear door exterior handle

Removal

26 Undo the 3 bolts securing the lock mechanism to the door, and the 2 nuts securing the exterior handle/frame, as described later in this Section.

27 Manoeuvre the exterior handle assembly from the outside of the door **(see illustration)**.

Refitting

28 Refitting is a reversal of removal.

Rear door interior handle

29 The rear door interior handle removal and refitting procedure is identical to that for the front door, as described previously in this Section.

Rear door lock mechanism

Removal

30 Fully raise the window, then remove the door inner trim panel and sealing sheet as described in Section 13. Note that it's only

necessary to remove the sealing sheet in the area of the door lock.

31 Undo the 2 retaining nuts, unclip the interior handle release cable, and manoeuvre the security shield from the door frame **(see illustration)**.

32 Undo the 3 retaining bolts securing the lock mechanism to the door frame **(see illustration)**.

33 Undo the 2 nuts securing the exterior handle/frame to the door **(see illustration)**.

34 Disconnect the wiring plug and manoeuvre the lock mechanism from the door frame **(see illustrations)**.

Refitting

35 Refitting is a reversal of removal

15.31 Security shield retaining nuts

15.32 Door lock retaining bolts

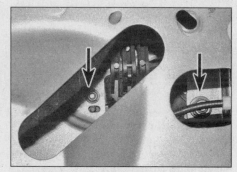

15.33 Exterior handle/frame retaining nuts

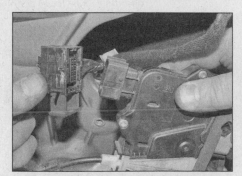

15.34a Prise out the red locking catch and disconnect the wiring plug

15.34b Manoeuvre the lock/frame assembly from the door

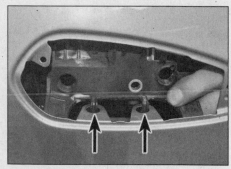

15.34c Note how the handle frame locates in the door skin (handle removed for clarity)

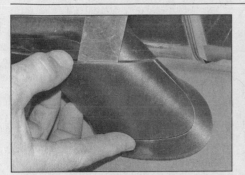

16.1 Starting at the top, prise the mirror base trim from place

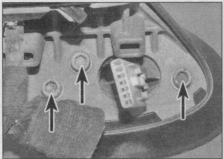

16.3 Exterior mirror retaining bolts

16.6 Carefully release the mirror glass clips

16 Exterior mirror components – removal and refitting

Mirror assembly

Removal

1 Starting at the upper edge, carefully prise the trim panel from door adjacent to the mirror **(see illustration)**.
2 Disconnect the mirror wiring plug.
3 Undo the 3 retaining bolts and remove the mirror assembly **(see illustration)**.

Refitting

4 Refitting is a reversal of removal.

Mirror glass

Removal

5 Push the lower edge of the glass inwards to create an opening between the upper edge of the glass and the mirror body.
6 Insert a small screwdriver between the mirror glass and the mirror body, and carefully release the mirror glass securing clips **(see illustration)**.

 Warning: Protect your hands and eyes from glass splinters.

7 Where applicable, disconnect the heater element wiring from the rear of the glass, and withdraw the glass from the mirror assembly.

Refitting

8 Where applicable, reconnect the wires to the rear of the mirror glass, then push the glass into position to engage the securing clips.

17 Door window glass and regulator – removal and refitting

Front window glass

Removal

1 Fully lower the window, then remove the door inner trim panel and sealing sheet as described in Section 13.
2 Using a blunt, flat-bladed tool, carefully prise the window outer weatherstrip from the door frame **(see illustrations)**.

3 Carefully pull the window guide channel from the door/window frame **(see illustration)**.
4 Reconnect the window switch, and raise the window until the glass retaining clip is accessible through the door aperture.
5 Support the glass, then unclip the plastic fastener that secures the window glass to the regulator mechanism. To do this, engage a screwdriver over the strap at the base of the fastener and push downwards. This will release the fastener from its retaining peg **(see illustrations 17.24a and 17.24b)**.
6 With the plastic fastener released, disengage the regulator mechanism from the hole at the base of the window glass.
7 Lift the glass upwards at the rear and remove it from the inside of the door frame.

Refitting

8 Locate the glass in the door, engage the regulator mechanism with the hole at the

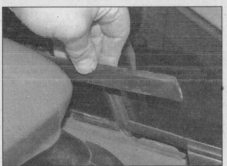

17.2a Carefully prise up the front edge of the outer weatherstrip...

17.3 Pull the rubber guide channel from the frame

base of the glass, then reach up behind and reconnect the plastic fastener.
9 Refit the window guide channel and outer weatherstrip to the door.
10 Refit the door sealing sheet and inner trim panel as described in Section 13.

Front window regulator

Removal

11 Detach the window glass from the regulator as described previously in this Section, then fully raise the window glass, and secure it in position using suitable tape, or by wedging the glass in position using rags between the glass and the edge of the door – ensure that the glass cannot drop into the door.
12 Disconnect the wiring plug, undo the 3 retaining nuts, and manoeuvre the regulator assembly from the door frame **(see illustration)**.

17.2b... then slide it forwards to release the rear lug

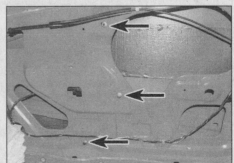

17.12 Front window regulator retaining nuts

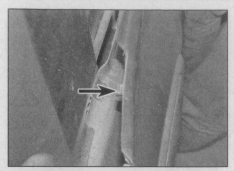

17.15a Pull out the rear edge of the weatherstrip to disengage the pin, then pull the strip upwards...

17.15b... and slide it rearwards to unhook the front edge

17.16 Remove the rubber window guide channel from the door/window frame

Refitting

13 Refitting is a reversal of removal, noting the following points:

a) *Attach the window glass to the regulator as described previously, before tightening the regulator retaining nuts.*

b) *Check the operation of the window mechanism before refitting the door inner trim panel.*

c) *Refit the door sealing sheet and inner trim panel as described in Section 13.*

Rear window glass

Removal

14 Remove the window regulator assembly as described later in this Section.

15 Using a blunt, flat-bladed tool, carefully prise the rear edge of the window outer weatherstrip outwards, then pull it upwards from the door frame, and unhook the front edge **(see illustrations)**.

16 Lower the window into the door, then carefully pull the window guide channel from the door/window frame **(see illustration)**. Take care not to damage the sliding pad.

17 Raise the rear of the window, and manoeuvre it from the door frame.

Refitting

18 Insert the window glass into the door, and refit the window guide channel.

19 Engage the regulator mechanism with the

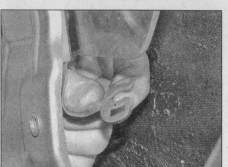

17.24a Reach into the door and pull the glass retaining fastener downwards

17.24b The fastener locates over the window glass support pin

hole at the base of the glass, then reach up behind and reconnect the plastic fastener.

20 Refit the window aperture outer weatherstrip.

21 Refit the window regulator assembly as described later in this Section.

Rear window regulator

Removal

22 Remove the door inner trim panel and sealing sheet as described in Section 13.

23 Reconnect the window switch/refit the winder handle (as applicable) and move the window until the glass retaining clip is accessible.

24 Support the glass, then unclip the plastic fastener that secures the window glass to the regulator mechanism. To do this, engage a screwdriver over the strap at the base of the fastener and push downwards. This will

release the fastener from its retaining peg **(see illustrations)**.

25 Fully raise the window glass, and secure it in position using suitable tape, or by wedging the glass in position using rags between the glass and the edge of the door – ensure that the glass cannot drop into the door.

26 Disconnect the wiring plug, undo the 4 retaining nuts, and manoeuvre the regulator assembly from the door aperture **(see illustrations)**.

Refitting

27 Refitting is a reversal of removal, noting the following points:

a) *Attach the window to the regulator before tightening the retaining nuts.*

b) *Check the operation of the regulator before refitting the sealing sheet and door inner trim panel.*

17.26a Undo the retaining nuts...

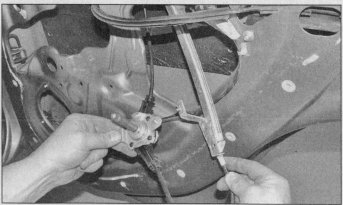

17.26b... and manoeuvre the regulator from the door

20.2 Undo the 3 screws along the front edge of the scuttle panel

20.3 Pull up the scuttle panel along with the rubber sealing strip

18 Windscreen and fixed window glass – general information

1 Due to the methods of attachment, and the special equipment required to complete the task successfully, removal and refitting of the windscreen, tailgate window (and rear side windows on 3-door models) should be entrusted to a dealer or an automotive glass specialist.

19 Sunroof – general information

1 Due to the complexity of the sunroof mechanism, considerable expertise is needed to repair, renew or adjust the sunroof components successfully. Removal of the roof first requires the headlining to be removed, which is a complex and tedious operation, and not a task to be undertaken lightly. Therefore, any problems with the sunroof should be referred to a Fiat dealer.
2 If the sunroof motor fails to operate, first check the relevant fuse. If the fault cannot be traced and rectified, the sunroof can be opened and closed manually, using the special crank handle supplied in the vehicle toolkit to turn the motor spindle.
3 To gain access to the motor spindle, ensure that the ignition key is in the 'off' position, then carefully prise the overhead console from

its location. Engage the crank handle with the spindle, and turn the handle to open or close the sunroof (see illustrations).
4 Once the roof is closed, remove the crank handle, and clip the overhead console back into place.

20 Body exterior fittings – removal and refitting

Windscreen scuttle panel

1 Remove the wiper arms as described in Chapter 12 Section 13.
2 Undo the 3 screws at the front edge of the scuttle panel (see illustration).
3 Carefully pull the windscreen scuttle panel upwards to release the clips at the base of the windscreen, and remove it along with the rubber sealing strip (see illustration).
4 Refitting is a reversal of removal.

Wheel arch liners

5 The wheel arch liners are secured by a combination of plastic nuts, push-in clips and screws – removal is self-evident and straightforward. Multiple liner panels are used which overlap each other at their edges. In some instances it may be necessary to move aside adjoining panels for access to a specific panel.

Body trim strips and badges

6 The various body trim strips and badges are held in position with a special adhesive tape.

Removal requires the trim/badge to be heated, to soften the adhesive, and then cut away from the surface. Due to the high risk of damage to the vehicle paintwork during this operation, it is recommended that this task should be entrusted to a Fiat dealer or specialist.

21 Seats – removal and refitting

Front seats

⚠ **Warning: Certain models are equipped with side airbags built into the outer sides of the front seats. Refer to Chapter 12 Section 19 for the precautions which should be observed when dealing with an airbag system. Do not tamper with the airbag unit in any way, and do not attempt to test any airbag system components. Note that the airbag is triggered if the mechanism is supplied with an electrical current (including via an ohmmeter), or if the assembly is subjected to a temperature of greater than 100°C.**

Removal

1 Disconnect the battery negative lead as described in Chapter 5A Section 4, then wait at least 10 minutes for any residual electrical energy in the SRS system to dissipate.
2 Slide the seat towards the front of the car to gain access to the two bolts at the rear, then slacken and remove them (see illustration).

3-door models

3 Slide the seat rearwards, prise the plastic clips forwards, and remove the cover forwards to expose the seat wiring plugs, then disconnect the plugs (see illustration 21.6).
4 Undo the bolts at the front of the seat rails, and manoeuvre the seat from the vehicle.

5-door models

5 Unclip the seat belt trim panel from the seat base, undo the bolt and detach the belt from the seat (see illustration).
6 Slide the seat fully rearwards, prise forward the clips and remove the plastic cover forwards to expose the seat wiring plugs, then disconnect the plugs (see illustration).

21.2 Undo the bolts at the rear of the seat rails

21.5 Carefully pull the trim panel outwards to release the clips

21.6 Prise forwards the plastic clips and remove the wiring plug(s) cover

21.9 Undo the bolt each side of the front lower edge of the cushion

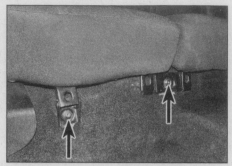

21.11 Two piece rear seat cushion retaining bolts (centre and right-hand bolts arrowed)

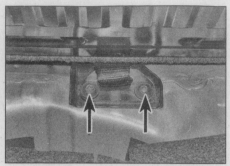

21.15 Rear seat backrest strap bolts

7 Undo the bolts at the front of the seat rails, and manoeuvre the seat from the vehicle.

Refitting

8 Refitting is a reversal of removal. On 5-door models, tighten the seat belt lower anchorage bolt to the specified torque.

Rear seat

Rear seat cushion – one piece

9 Undo the retaining bolt each side, move the cushion forwards, and manoeuvre it from place (see illustration).
10 Refitting is a reversal of removal.

21.17 Slide the retainers inwards and release the backrest

Rear seat cushion – two piece

11 Undo the outer and inner bolts at the front edge of the cushion, then manoeuvre the cushion from place (see illustration).
12 Refitting is a reversal of removal.

Rear seat backrest – one piece

13 Fold forwards the seat cushion, release the side catches and fold the backrest forwards a little.
14 Remove the luggage compartment floor covering.
15 Undo the backrest strap fixing bolts (see illustration).
16 Undo the centre seat belt lower anchorage bolt.
17 Release the side retainers and remove the backrest (see illustration).
18 Refitting is a reversal of removal.

Rear seat backrest – two piece

19 Fold the rear seat cushions forwards, release the side catches and fold the seat backrests forwards a little.
20 Release the side retainer, lift the outer edge of the right-hand backrest, and slide it from the centre hinge pin (see illustration).
21 Remove the luggage compartment floor covering.
22 Undo the bolts securing the centre hinge assembly (see illustration).

23 Undo the seat belt lower anchorage bolt.
24 Release the side catch and fold the backrest forwards a little.
25 Release the side retainer and manoeuvre the backrest from place.
26 Refitting is a reversal of removal. Tighten the seat belt anchorage bolt to the specified torque.

22 Seat belts – removal and refitting

Note: *Record the positions of the washers and spacers on the seat belt anchors, and ensure they are refitted in their original positions.*

Front seat belt

Removal

⚠ *Warning: On certain models, the front seat belt inertia reels are equipped with a pyrotechnic pretensioner mechanism. Refer to the airbag system precautions contained in Chapter 12 Section 19 which apply equally to the seat belt pretensioners. Do not tamper with the inertia reel pretensioner unit in any way, and do not attempt to test the unit.*

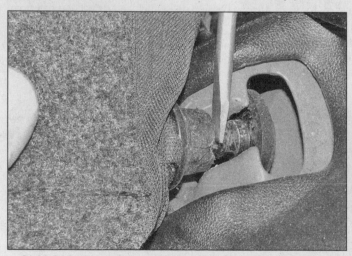

21.20 Slide the retainer inwards, and lift the outer edge of the backrest

21.22 Centre hinge retaining bolts

22.7 Lower anchorage bar retaining bolt

22.10 Upper seat belt anchorage bolt

22.11a Front seat belt inertia reel retaining bolt

1 De-activate the airbag system (which will also de-activate the pyrotechnic pretensioner mechanism, where fitted), as described in Chapter 12 Section 19, before attempting to remove the seatbelt.

3-door models

2 Remove the left-, or right-hand rear side panel (as appropriate) as described in Section 23.

3 Remove the left-,or right-hand side B-pillar trim panel (as appropriate) as described in Section 23.

4 Unclip and remove the seat belt guide from the B-pillar.

5 Undo the bolt and detach the upper seat belt anchorage **(see illustration 22.10)**.

6 Disconnect the wiring plug, undo the retaining bolt and manoeuvre the seat belt inertia reel from position.

7 Undo the retaining bolt, and slip the seat belt from the lower anchorage bar **(see illustration)**.

5-door models

8 Remove the upper and lower B-pillar trim panel, as described in Section 23.

9 Unclip the seat belt guide from the B-pillar.

10 Undo the bolt and detach the upper seat belt anchorage **(see illustration)**.

11 Squeeze together the clips (one above, one below) and pull the wiring plug from the reel, then undo the retaining bolt and manoeuvre the seat belt inertia reel from position **(see illustrations)**.

Refitting

12 Refitting is a reversal of removal. Tighten the seat belt bolts to their specified torque.

Rear seat belts

Removal

Outer seat belts

13 Remove the C-pillar trim panel as described in Section 23.

14 Unclip the inertia reel cover downwards (where fitted).

15 Undo the retaining bolt and manoeuvre the seat belt inertia reel from position **(see illustration)**.

Centre seat belt

16 Removal of the centre inertia reel involves

22.11b Squeeze together the clips and pull the wiring plug from the reel

removal of the seat backrest cover. This is an involved procedure, which we recommend is best entrusted to a Fiat dealer, repairer or upholstery specialist.

Refitting

17 Refitting is a reversal of removal. Tighten the seat belt fasteners to their specified torque.

Seat belt stalks

Front seat belt stalks

Models with inertia reel pretensioners

18 Remove the relevant front seat as described in Section 21.

19 Unclip the wiring harness, undo the retaining bolt and detach the stalk from the seat frame **(see illustration)**.

20 Refitting is a reversal of removal,

22.19 Seat belt stalk retaining bolt

22.15 Rear outer seat belt inertia reel retaining bolt

tightening the stalk retaining bolt to the specified torque.

Models with stalk pretensioners (3-door models)

21 Remove the rear side panel as described in Section 23.

Models with stalk pretensioners (5-door models)

22 Slide the front seat fully forwards, depress the central retaining clip and disconnect the seat belt from the stalk **(see illustration)**.

23 Undo the screw at each end, and prise up the door sill trim panel to release the retaining clips.

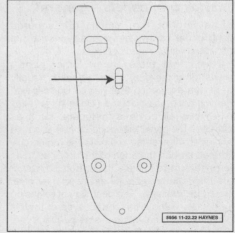

22.22 Depress the clip and detach the seat belt

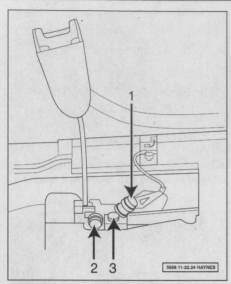

22.24 Stalk pretensioner wiring plug (1), retaining bolt (2) and retainer (3)

24 Disconnect the wiring plug, undo the retaining bolt, and manoeuvre the stalk and pretension assembly from place **(see illustration)**.

All models

25 Refitting is a reversal of removal, tightening the stalk retaining bolts to the specified torque.

Rear seat stalks

26 Fold the rear seat cushion forwards, undo the retaining bolts and remove the relevant seat belt stalk.
27 Refitting is a reversal of removal, tightening the seat belt stalk retaining bolts to their specified torque.

23 Interior trim – removal and refitting

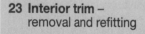

Interior trim panels – general

1 The interior trim panels are secured using either screws or various types of trim fasteners, usually studs or clips.
2 Check that there are no other panels overlapping the one to be removed; usually there is a sequence that has to be followed that will become obvious on close inspection.
3 Remove all obvious fasteners, such as screws. If the panel will not come free, it is held by hidden clips or fasteners. These are usually situated around the edge of the panel and can be prised up to release them; note, however, that they can break quite easily so new ones should be available. The best way of releasing such clips, without the correct type of tool, is to use a large flat-bladed screwdriver. Note that some panels are secured by plastic expanding rivets, where the centre pin must be prised up before the rivet can be removed.

23.7 Undo the bolt in the handle recess

Note in many cases that the adjacent sealing strip must be prised back to release a panel.
4 When removing a panel, never use excessive force or the panel may be damaged; always check carefully that all fasteners have been removed or released before attempting to withdraw a panel.
5 Refitting is the reverse of the removal procedure; secure the fasteners by pressing them firmly into place and ensure that all disturbed components are correctly secured to prevent rattles.

Door inner trim panels

6 Refer to Section 13.

Tailgate inner trim panel

7 Undo the bolt in the trim panel handle recess **(see illustration)**.
8 Starting at the lower rear corner, pull the panel downwards to release the securing clips, then remove the panel from the tailgate.
9 To refit the panel, locate it in position, ensuring that the retaining clips engage, and secure with the bolt in the handle recess.

A-pillar trim panel

10 Due to the proximity of the headlining airbag, disconnect the battery negative lead as described in Chapter 5A Section 4, then wait at least 10 minutes for any residual electrical energy to dissipate.
11 Pull the rubber weatherstrip away adjacent to the A-pillar.
12 Using a blunt-, flat-bladed tool, carefully prise the top of the A-pillar trim panel from place, then pull it upwards. Undo the safety

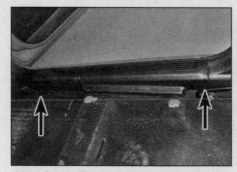

23.14 Door sill trim panel retaining screws

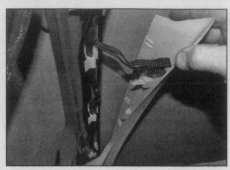

23.12 Prise the top of the trim panel away from the pillar

strap screw as the panel is withdrawn **(see illustration)**.
13 Refitting is a reversal of removal; secure the fasteners by pressing them firmly into place and ensure that all disturbed components are correctly secured to prevent rattles.

B-pillar trim panel

3-door models

14 Undo the screw at the front and rear, then prise up the door sill trim panel to release the retaining clips **(see illustration)**.
15 Remove the rear seat cushion as described in Section 21.
16 Pull away the rubber weatherstrip adjacent to the B-pillar.
17 Undo the retaining bolt at the lower, front edge, and carefully prise the front/upper part of the rear side panel from place **(see illustration)**.
18 Undo the bolt and detach the seat belt lower anchorage rail from the vehicle body, or depress the clip and detach the belt from the stalk (as applicable).
19 Release the lower retaining clips, and pull the B-pillar trim panel downwards. Note the lugs at the top of the panel **(see illustration 23.28a and 23.28b)**.
20 If required, feed the seat belt through the panel as it's withdrawn.
21 Refitting is a reversal of removal.

5-door models

22 Undo the screws along the inner edge, then carefully prise up the front door sill

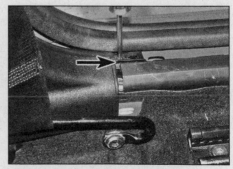

23.17 Undo the screw at the lower, front edge of the side panel

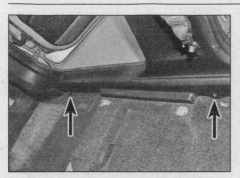

23.22 Door sill trim retaining screws

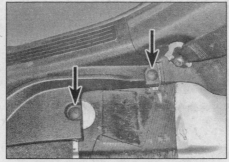

23.24 Unscrew the plastic fasteners at the rear of the sill trim panel

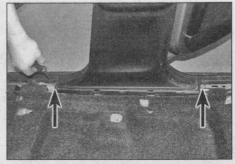

23.26a Undo the screws at the lower edge...

trim panel to release the retaining clips **(see illustration)**.

23 Move the front seat fully forwards, and fold forward the rear seat cushion.

24 Release the plastic fasteners and prise up the rear door sill trim panel **(see illustration)**.

25 Pull away the rubber weatherstrips each side of the B-pillar.

26 Undo the screw at the front, and rear of the lower B-pillar base, and pull the lower trim panel away from the pillar **(see illustrations)**.

27 Unclip the panel from the seat base, undo the retaining bolt and detach the seat belt from the seat frame.

28 Undo the lower retaining screw, and pull the B-pillar trim panel inwards to release the clips. Note the lugs at the top of the panel **(see illustrations)**.

29 If required, feed the seat belt through the panel as it's withdrawn.

30 Refitting is a reversal of removal.

C-pillar trim panel

31 Remove the rear parcel shelf.

32 Prise out the luggage compartment light, and disconnect the wiring plug **(see illustration)**.

33 Fold forwards the rear seat cushion, undo undo the seat belt lower anchorage **(see illustration)**.

34 Pull away the rubber weatherstrip adjacent to the C-pillar trim panel.

35 Undo the 2 bolts at the lower edge of the C-pillar trim panel, then carefully prise the panel inwards to release the retaining clips **(see illustrations)**.

23.26b... and pull the trim panel from the B-pillar

23.28a Undo the lower retaining screw...

23.28b... and pull the pillar trim panel inwards to release the clips

23.32 Carefully prise out the luggage compartment light

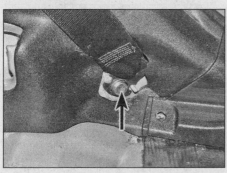

23.33 Rear seat belt lower anchorage bolt

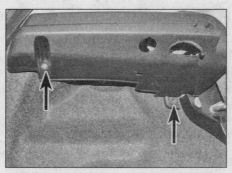

23.35a Undo the bolts at the lower edge...

23.35b... then pull the C-pillar trim panel inwards to release the clips

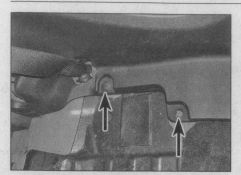

23.42 Unscrew the plastic fasteners at the lower edge (where fitted)

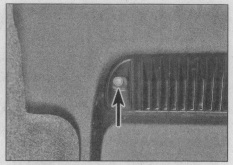

23.47a The tailgate sill trim panel is secured by a bolt each side at the front...

23.47b... and a bolt along the rear edge

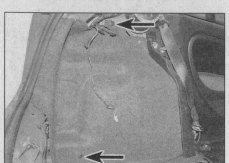

23.49 Prise out the plastic fasteners

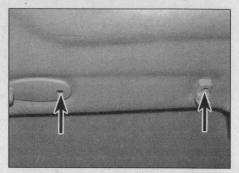

23.51 Undo the screws and remove the sunvisor mountings

47 Undo the 3 retaining bolts, and prise the tailgate sill trim panel upwards to release the retaining clips (see illustrations).
48 Remove the C-pillar trim panel as described previously in this Section.
49 Prise out the plastic fasteners, and carefully pull the side trim panel inwards to release the clips (see illustration). Disconnect any wiring plugs as they become accessible.
50 Refitting is a reversal of removal.

Sunvisors

51 The sunvisors are secured by 1 screw at the inner end, and 1 screw at the outer (see illustration). Undo the screws and remove the sunvisor.
52 Refitting is a reversal of removal.

Grab handles

53 Fold open the covers, undo the bolts and remove the grab handle.
54 Refitting is a reversal of removal.

Carpet

55 The passenger compartment floor carpet is in one piece (with a separate piece used in the luggage area), and is secured at its edges by screws or clips, usually the same fasteners used to secure the various adjoining trim panels.
56 Carpet removal and refitting is reasonably straightforward, but very time-consuming, due to the fact that all adjoining trim panels must be removed first, as must components such as the seats, the centre console and seat belt lower anchorages.

36 If required, feed the seat belt through the panel as it's withdrawn.
37 Refitting is a reversal of removal, tightening the seat belt lower anchorage bolt to the specified torque.

Rear side trim panel – 3-door models

38 Remove the C-pillar trim panel as described previously in this Section.
39 Undo the 2 screws, and prise up the door sill trim panel to release the retaining clips (see illustration 23.14).
40 Remove the rear seat cushion and backrest as described in Section 21.
41 Pull away the rubber weatherstrip from the door aperture adjacent to the side panel.
42 Undo the bolt at the front, lower edge (see illustration 23.17), remove the plastic fasteners at the lower edge, and carefully

prise the side panel inwards to release the clips (see illustration).
43 Refitting is a reversal of removal.

Headlining

44 The rigid headlining is clipped to the roof, and can only be withdrawn once all fittings such as the grab handles, sunvisors, interior light, and related trim panels have been removed, and the door, tailgate and sunroof aperture sealing strips have been prised clear.
45 As with carpet removal, taking out the headlining is not especially difficult, just time-consuming.

Luggage compartment side trim panel

46 Remove the parcel shelf, and lift out the luggage compartment floor covering.

24.1a Undo the screw on the drivers side

24.1b Pull out the rear edge, and slide the panel each side rearwards

24 Centre console – removal and refitting

Removal

1 Undo the screw securing the drivers side panel, then carefully prise the rear edge of the centre console front side panels away to release the clips, then side them rearwards to release the front lugs (see illustrations).

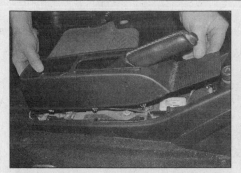

24.2 Prise up the panel around the hand brake lever

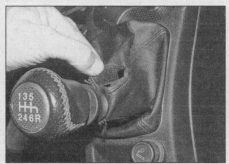

24.3a Release the Velco...

24.3b... and prise up the gaiter/frame

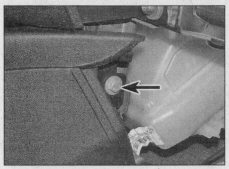

24.4 Remove the screw each side at the front of the console

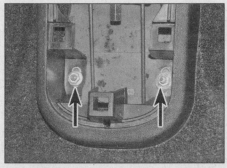

24.6a Undo the nuts at the rear...

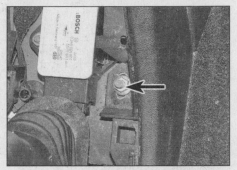

24.6b... and one in the centre...

2 Prise up the centre console panel adjacent to the handbrake lever **(see illustration).**

3 Release the Velco strap at the top, and unclip the gear lever gaiter from the centre console **(see illustrations).**

4 Undo the screw each side at the front of the centre console **(see illustration).**

5 Disconnect the wiring plug at the rear of the gear lever aperture.

6 Undo the 2 nuts at the rear, 1 in the centre, and manoeuvre the centre console from place **(see illustrations).** Disconnect any wiring plugs as they become accessible.

7 ... then remove the centre console

Refitting

8 Refitting is a reversal of removal.

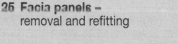 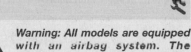
25 Facia panels – removal and refitting

⚠ *Warning: All models are equipped with an airbag system. The driver's airbag is mounted in the steering wheel centre pad and, where fitted, the passenger's airbag is mounted in the passenger's side of the facia. Make sure that the safety precautions given in Chapter 12 Section 19 are followed, to prevent personal injury.*

Grande Punto models
Glovebox
Removal

1 Open the glovebox and use a small

screwdriver to extract the outboard plastic hinge pin **(see illustration).**

2 With the hinge pin removed, manoeuvre the glovebox from the facia.

Refitting

3 Refitting is a reversal of removal.

Drivers side lower facia panel
Removal

4 Starting at the upper edge, pull the storage compartment/cover from the facia **(see illustration).**

5 Remove the steering column lower shroud as described in this Section.

6 Prise the lower facia panel rearwards to release the clips **(see illustration).**

Refitting

7 Refitting is a reversal of removal.

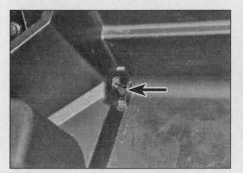

25.1 Prise out the hinge pin

25.4 Pull the storage compartment/cover rearwards

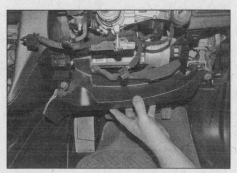

25.6 Pull the lower facia panel rearwards

Steering column shrouds

Removal

8 Fully lower and extend the steering column.
9 The lower shroud is retained by 7 screws. Undo the screws and remove the lower shroud (see illustration).
10 Unclip the column switch stalk panel (see illustration).
11 Undo the 2 retaining screws and remove the upper shroud (see illustrations).

Refitting

12 Refitting is a reversal of removal.

Instrument panel surround

Removal

13 Fully lower and extend the steering column.
14 Release the retaining clips for the gaiter at the lower edge of the instrument panel surround (see illustration 25.11b).
15 Undo the 4 retaining screws, and remove the instrument panel surround (see illustrations).

Refitting

16 Refitting is a reversal of removal.

Audio unit support frame

Removal

17 Remove the facia mounted audio unit as described in Chapter 12 Section 16.
18 Slacken the 4 retaining screws, and pull the support frame rearwards from the facia (see illustration).

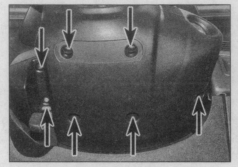

25.9 Steering column lower shroud retaining bolts

Refitting

19 Refitting is a reversal of removal.

Central switch/air vent panel

Removal

20 Remove the audio unit surround panel as described previously in this Section.
21 Undo the 3 retaining screws on the underside of the switch/vent panel (see illustration). Disconnect the wiring plug as the panel is withdrawn.

Refitting

22 Refitting is a reversal of removal.

Complete facia assembly

Removal

23 Disconnect the battery negative lead as described in Chapter 5A Section 4.

25.10 Unclip the panel around the switch stalk

24 Remove the audio unit support frame as described previously in this Section.
25 Remove the heater/air conditioning control panel as described in Chapter 3 Section 8.
26 Remove the central switch/air vent panel as described previously in this Section.
27 Remove the steering column combination switch assembly as described in Chapter 12 Section 5.
28 Remove the instrument cluster as described in Chapter 12 Section 10.
29 Remove the drivers side lower facia panel as described previously in this Section.
30 Remove the drivers side switch panel from the facia, as described in Chapter 12 Section 5.
31 Remove the glovebox as described previously in this Section.

25.11a Undo the upper shroud screws...

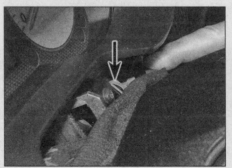

25.11b... and pull the gaiter rearwards to unclip it

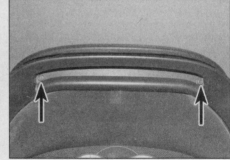

25.15a Undo the screws at the top...

25.15b... and base of the instrument panel surround

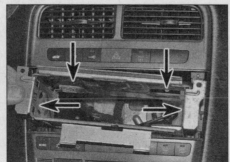

25.18 Undo the screws and remove the support frame

25.21 Central switch/air vent panel retaining screws

25.32 Remove the document holder or control unit

25.33 Carefully prise the solar sensor upwards from the facia

25.34 Prise the central demister grille upwards to release the clips

32 Slacken the screws, and remove the document holder/control unit from the glovebox aperture **(see illustration)**.

33 Where applicable, prise up the solar sensor from the centre of the facia, releasing the clips, and disconnect the wiring plug **(see illustration)**.

34 Release the retaining clips and remove the central demister grille from the facia **(see illustration)**.

35 Remove both A-pillar trim panels as described in Section 23.

36 Remove the centre console as described in Section 24.

37 Where applicable, remove the 2 shear bolts securing the facia at the passengers, lower section **(see illustration)**.

38 The facia is now secured by a total of 15 screws. Undo the screws, check that nothing remains connected between the facia and the bulkhead, and with the help of an assistant, manoeuvre the facia rearwards, and out from the cabin **(see illustrations)**.

Refitting

39 Refitting is a reversal of removal, noting the following points:

a) Reinstate all electrical connections according to the labels made during removal and ensure that cables are secured in their clips, using the original routing.

b) Refer to the Chapters/Sections indicated and refit all components disturbed during the removal process.

c) On completion, reconnect the battery negative terminal and check the operation of all controls, gauges and instruments

disturbed during the removal process, including the heating/air conditioning system.

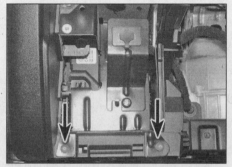

25.37 Remove the shear bolts at the passengers end of the facia

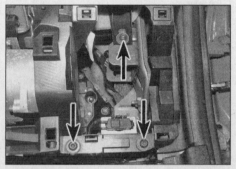

25.38a The facia is secured by 3 bolts on the drivers side...

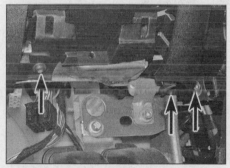

25.38b... 3 bolts in the lower, centre section of the facia...

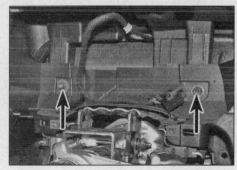

25.38c... 2 bolts in the instrument panel aperture...

25.38d... 3 bolts at the front edge of the facia (centre bolt arrowed)...

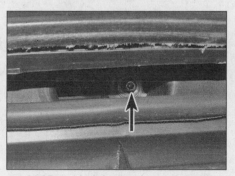

25.38e... 1 bolt in the centre air vent aperture...

25.38f... and 3 bolts on the passengers side

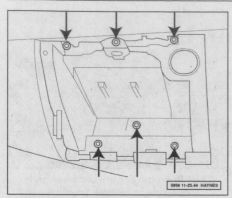

25.44 Glovebox retaining screws – LHD shown

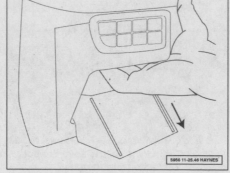

25.46 Pull the upper edge of the panel rearwards – LHD shown

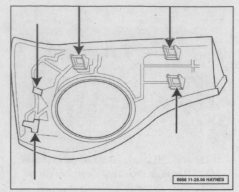

25.56 Pull the vent surround panel rearwards to release the clips – LHD shown

Punto Evo/Punto (2012 model year-on)

Glovebox

Removal

40 Carefully prise the glovebox light from place, and disconnect the wiring plug.

41 Squeeze together the lugs and remove the retaining pin securing the glovebox lid support strap.

42 Lower the glovebox lid, depress the clip on the plastic bracket and manoeuvre the lid from the facia.

43 Release the clips and pull the glovebox tray rearwards from place.

44 Undo the 6 retaining screws, and manoeuvre the glovebox rearwards, disconnecting the wiring plug(s) as they become accessible **(see illustration)**.

Refitting

45 Refitting is a reversal of removal.

Drivers side lower facia panel

Removal

46 Open the drivers side storage compartment, reach into the aperture and pull the switch panel rearwards at the upper edge (see illustration). Disconnect the wiring plugs and lift the panel from place.

47 Undo the 2 retaining screws, then pull the drivers side lower facia panel rearwards to release the clips.

Refitting

48 Refitting is a reversal of removal.

Steering column shrouds

Removal

49 Fully lower and extend the steering column.

50 The lower shroud is retained by 7 screws, and one clip. Undo the screws, release the clip and remove the lower shroud **(see illustration 25.9)**.

51 Unclip the column switch stalk panel **(see illustration 25.10)**.

52 Undo the 2 retaining screws and remove the upper shroud **(see illustration 25.11)**.

Refitting

53 Refitting is a reversal of removal.

Drivers side vent surround trim

Removal

54 Set the vent to the open position, with the fins set in the horizontal position.

55 Fashion a hook on 2 lengths of welding wire, inset the wire into the lowest opening, and pull the vent from place.

56 Carefully pull the vent surround trim from the facia **(see illustration)**.

Refitting

57 Refitting is a reversal of removal.

Passengers side facia trim panel

Removal

58 Remove the facia audio unit as described in Chapter 12 Section 16.

59 Remove the facia panel centre frame as described in this Section.

60 Open the facia central storage compartment, lift out the rubber mat, undo the single retaining bolt and pull the storage compartment/vent assembly rearwards from the facia. Disconnect any wiring plugs as the assembly is withdrawn.

61 Open the glovebox, and remove the 2 retaining screws at the lower edge of the facia trim panel in the glovebox aperture **(see illustration)**. Recover the washers.

62 Carefully prise the passengers side facia trim panel rearwards to release the retaining clips **(see illustration)**. Take care not to mark the facia or trim panel.

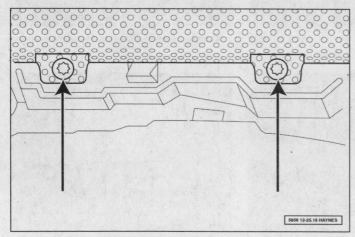

25.61 Undo the screws at the lower edge of the facia trim panel

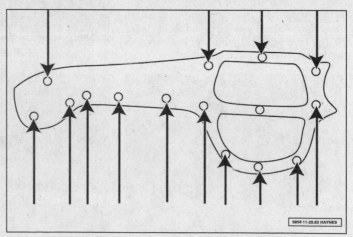

25.62 Passengers side facia panel retaining clips

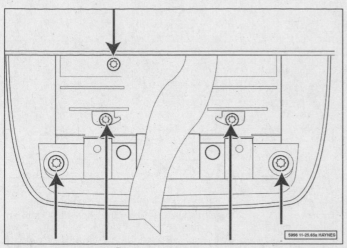

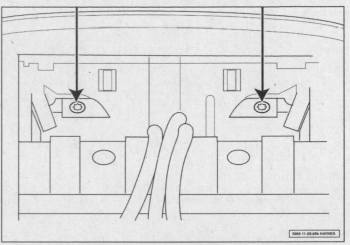

25.65a The central frame is secured by 5 screws in the aperture... **25.65b... and 2 screws at the top**

Refitting

63 Refitting is a reversal of removal.

Facia panel central frame

Removal

64 Remove the facia audio unit as described in Chapter 12 Section 16.

65 Undo the 7 retaining screws in the audio unit aperture, and pull the central frame rearwards **(see illustrations)**. Disconnect the wiring plugs, and unclip the wiring harness as they become accessible.

Refitting

66 Refitting is a reversal of removal.

Complete facia assembly

Removal

67 Disconnect the battery negative lead as described in Chapter 5A Section 4.

68 Remove the drivers side lower facia panel as described previously in this Section, or remove the drivers knee airbag (Chapter 12 Section 20) as applicable.

69 Remove the passengers side facia trim panel as described previously in this Section.

70 Remove the facia panel central frame as described previously in this Section.

71 Remove the heat/air conditioning control panel as described in Chapter 3 Section 8.

72 Prise out the glovebox light and disconnect the wiring plug.

73 Remove the glovebox as described previously in this Section.

74 Remove the passengers air bag as described in Chapter 12 Section 20.

75 Remove the instrument cluster as described in Chapter 12 Section 10.

76 Remove the steering column combination switch assembly as described in Chapter 12 Section 5.

77 Remove the drivers side vent surround trim as described previously in this Section.

78 Unclip the transponder aerial from the ignition switch, and disconnect the wiring plug.

79 Carefully prise the solar sensor (where fitted) from the centre of the facia, and disconnect the wiring plug **(see illustration 25.33)**.

80 Prise the central demister vent grille up from the facia **(see illustration 25.34)**.

81 Remove the centre console as described in Section 24.

82 Remove both A-pillar trim panels as described in Section 23.

83 Working in the central vent area,

disconnect the wiring plug for the facia light guide.

84 The facia is now secured by 10 screws on the drivers side, and 5 screws on the passengers side. Undo the screws, check that nothing remains connected between the facia and the bulkhead, and with the help of an assistant, manoeuvre the facia rearwards, and out from the cabin **(see illustrations 25.38a to 25.38b)**.

Refitting

85 Refitting in a reversal of removal, noting the following points:

a) *Reinstate all electrical connections according to the labels made during removal and ensure that cables are secured in their clips, using the original routing.*

b) *Refer to the Chapters/Sections indicated and refit all components disturbed during the removal process.*

c) *On completion, reconnect the battery negative terminal and check the operation of all controls, gauges and instruments disturbed during the removal process, including the heating/air conditioning system.*

Chapter 12
Body electrical systems

Contents

Section number

Airbag system – general information, precautions and system de-activation................................. 19
Airbag system components – removal and refitting............. 20
Anti-theft system and engine immobiliser – general information.... 18
Body computer – removal and refitting....................... 22
Bulbs (exterior lights) – renewal........................... 6
Bulbs (interior lights) – removal and refitting................. 7
Electrical connectors – general information................... 4
Electrical fault finding – general information.................. 2
Exterior light units – removal and refitting................... 8
Fuses and relays – general information...................... 3
General information and precautions........................ 1
Headlight beam adjustment – general information............. 9

Section number

Horns – removal and refitting.............................. 12
Infotainment units – removal and refitting.................... 16
Instrument panel – removal and refitting.................... 10
Parking obstacle detection system – general information and component renewal.................................... 21
Rain sensor – removal and refitting......................... 11
Speakers – removal and refitting........................... 17
Switches – removal and refitting........................... 5
Windscreen wiper motor and linkage – removal and refitting..... 14
Windscreen/tailgate washer system components – removal and refitting.. 15
Wiper arm – removal and refitting.......................... 13

Degrees of difficulty

Easy, suitable for novice with little experience 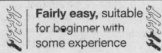	Fairly easy, suitable for beginner with some experience	Fairly difficult, suitable for competent DIY mechanic	Difficult, suitable for experienced DIY mechanic	Very difficult, suitable for expert DIY or professional

Specifications

Bulbs — Wattage

Exterior lights:
Direction indicators	21 PY
Direction indicator side repeater	5 capless
Front foglight (Grande Punto)	55 H1
Front foglight (Punto Evo/Punto 2012 MY-on)	55 H11
Front sidelight	5 capless
Headlight	55/60 H4
High level stop light	2.3 capless
Number plate light	5 capless
Rear fog light (Grande Punto)	21
Rear fog light (Punto Evo/Punto 2012 MY-on)	16 capless
Rear side light	5 capless
Reverse (Grande Punto)	21
Reverse (Punto Evo/Punto 2012 MY-on)	16 capless
Stop/tail light (Grande Punto)	21/5
Stop light (Punto Evo/Punto 2012 MY-on)	21
Tail light (Punto Evo/Punto 2012 MY-on)	LED

Interior lights:
Front courtesy lights	10 festoon
Luggage compartment lights	5 capless

Torque wrench settings	Nm	lbf ft
Airbag control unit bolts	8	6
Impact sensor bolts	8	6
Passengers air bag bolt	8	6

1 General information and precautions

1 The electrical system is of 12 volt negative earth type. Power for the lights and all electrical accessories is supplied by a lead-acid type battery, which is charged by the alternator.

2 This Chapter covers repair and service procedures for the various electrical components not associated with the engine. Information on the battery, alternator and starter motor can be found in Chapter 5A.

3 It should be noted that, prior to working on any component in the electrical system, the battery negative terminal should first be disconnected, to prevent the possibility of electrical short-circuits and/or fires (refer to Chapter 5A Section 4).

⚠ *Warning: Before carrying out any work on the electrical system, read through the precautions given in 'Safety first!' at the beginning of this manual, and in Chapter 5A.*

⚠ *Warning: All models are equipped with an airbag system and may also have pyrotechnic seat belt pretensioners. When working on the electrical system, refer to the precautions given in Section 19, to avoid the possibility of personal injury.*

2 Electrical fault finding – general information

General

1 A typical electrical circuit consists of an electrical component; any switches, relays, motors, fuses, fusible links or circuit breakers related to that component, and the wiring and connectors which link the component to both the battery and the chassis. To help to pin-point a problem in an electrical circuit, wiring diagrams are included at the end of this Chapter.

2 Before attempting to diagnose an electrical fault, first study the appropriate wiring diagram to obtain a complete understanding of the components included in the particular circuit concerned. The possible sources of a fault can be narrowed down by noting if other components related to the circuit are operating properly. If several components or circuits fail at one time, the problem is likely to be related to a shared fuse or earth connection.

3 Electrical problems usually stem from simple causes, such as loose or corroded connections, a faulty earth connection, a blown fuse, a melted fusible link, or a faulty relay (refer to Section 3 for details of testing relays). Visually inspect the condition of all fuses, wires and connections in a problem circuit before testing the components. Use the wiring diagrams to determine which terminal connections will need to be checked in order to pin-point the trouble spot.

4 The basic tools required for electrical fault finding include a circuit tester or voltmeter (a 12 volt bulb with a set of test leads can also be used for certain tests); a self-powered test light (sometimes known as a continuity tester); an ohmmeter (to measure resistance); a battery and set of test leads; and a jumper wire, preferably with a circuit breaker or fuse incorporated, which can be used to bypass suspect wires or electrical components. Before attempting to locate a problem with test instruments, use the wiring diagram to determine where to make the connections.

⚠ *Warning: Under no circumstances may live measuring instruments such as ohmmeters, voltmeters or a bulb and test leads be used to test any of the airbag circuitry. Any testing of these components must be left to a Fiat dealer or specialist, as there is a danger of activating the system if the correct procedures are not followed.*

5 To find the source of an intermittent wiring fault (usually due to a poor or dirty connection, or damaged wiring insulation), a 'wiggle' test can be performed on the wiring. This involves wiggling the wiring by hand to see if the fault occurs as the wiring is moved. It should be possible to narrow down the source of the fault to a particular section of wiring. This method of testing can be used in conjunction with any of the tests described in the following sub-Sections.

6 Apart from problems due to poor connections, two basic types of fault can occur in an electrical circuit – open-circuit, or short-circuit.

7 Open-circuit faults are caused by a break somewhere in the circuit, which prevents current from flowing. An open-circuit fault will prevent a component from working, but will not cause the relevant circuit fuse to blow.

8 Short-circuit faults are caused by a 'short' somewhere in the circuit, which allows the current flowing in the circuit to 'escape' along an alternative route, usually to earth. Short-circuit faults are normally caused by a breakdown in wiring insulation, which allows a feed wire to touch either another wire, or an earthed component such as the bodyshell. A short-circuit fault will normally cause the relevant circuit fuse to blow.

Finding an open-circuit

9 To check for an open-circuit, connect one lead of a circuit tester or voltmeter to either the negative battery terminal or a known good earth.

10 Connect the other lead to a connector in the circuit being tested, preferably nearest to the battery or fuse.

11 Switch on the circuit, bearing in mind that some circuits are live only when the ignition switch is moved to a particular position.

12 If voltage is present (indicated either by the tester bulb lighting or a voltmeter reading, as applicable), this means that the section of the circuit between the relevant connector and the battery is problem-free.

13 Continue to check the remainder of the circuit in the same fashion.

14 When a point is reached at which no voltage is present, the problem must lie between that point and the previous test point with voltage. Most problems can be traced to a broken, corroded or loose connection.

Finding a short-circuit

15 To check for a short-circuit, first disconnect the load(s) from the circuit (loads are the components which draw current from a circuit, such as bulbs, motors, heating elements, etc).

16 Remove the relevant fuse from the circuit, and connect a circuit tester or voltmeter to the fuse connections.

17 Switch on the circuit, bearing in mind that some circuits are live only when the ignition switch is moved to a particular position.

18 If voltage is present (indicated either by the tester bulb lighting or a voltmeter reading, as applicable), this means that there is a short-circuit.

19 If no voltage is present, but the fuse still blows with the load(s) connected, this indicates an internal fault in the load(s).

Finding an earth fault

20 The battery negative terminal is connected to 'earth' – the metal of the engine/transmission and the car body – and most systems are wired so that they only receive a positive feed, the current returning through the metal of the car body **(see illustrations)**.

2.20a Main earth connection between the engine/transmission and the vehicle body

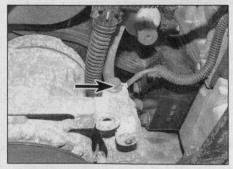

2.20b Other earth connections may be on the compressor/alternator bracket...

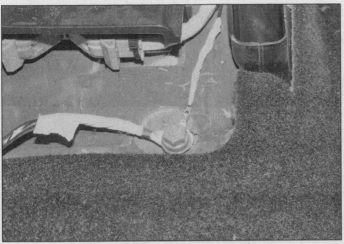

2.20c... beneath the centre console...

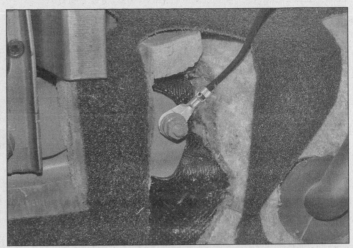

2.20d... right-hand side of the centre tunnel...

2.20e... the passengers side lower A-pillar...

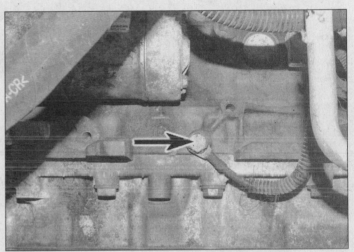

2.20f... and the rear of the engine block

This means that the component mounting and the body form part of that circuit. Loose or corroded mountings can therefore cause a range of electrical faults, ranging from total failure of a circuit, to a puzzling partial fault. In particular, lights may shine dimly (especially when another circuit sharing the same earth point is in operation), motors (eg, wiper motors or the heater fan motor) may run slowly, and the operation of one circuit may have an apparently unrelated effect on another.

21 Note that on many vehicles, earth straps are used between certain components, such as the engine/transmission and the body, usually where there is no metal-to-metal contact between components due to flexible rubber mountings, etc.

22 To check whether a component is properly earthed, disconnect the battery and connect one lead of an ohmmeter to a known

good earth point. Connect the other lead to the wire or earth connection being tested. The resistance reading should be zero; if not, check the connection as follows.

23 If an earth connection is thought to be faulty, dismantle the connection and clean back to bare metal both the bodyshell and the wire terminal or the component earth connection mating surface. Be careful to remove all traces of dirt and corrosion, and then use a knife to trim away any paint, so that a clean metal-to-metal joint is made.

24 On reassembly, tighten the joint fasteners securely; if a wire terminal is being refitted, use serrated washers between the terminal and the bodyshell to ensure a clean and secure connection. When the connection is remade, prevent the onset of corrosion in the future by applying a coat of petroleum jelly or silicone-based grease or by spraying on (at

regular intervals) a proprietary ignition sealer or a water-dispersant lubricant.

3 Fuses and relays – general information

Fuses

1 Fuses are designed to break a circuit when a predetermined current is reached, in order to protect the components and wiring which could be damaged by excessive current flow. Any excessive current flow will be due to a fault in the circuit, usually a short-circuit (see Section 2).

2 The main fuses are located in the fusebox in the engine compartment, whilst other are located under the passengers side of the facia, and on the left-hand side of the luggage

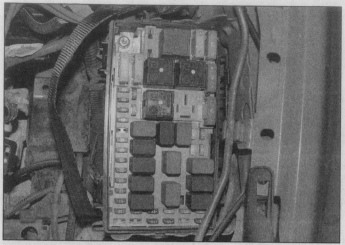

3.2a Engine compartment fusebox

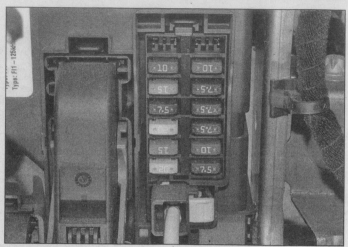

3.2b Fusebox under the passengers side of the facia

3.2c Luggage compartment fusebox (side panel removed for clarity)

3.3 Undo the screws and remove the cover over the passengers side facia fusebox

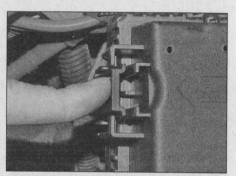

3.4 Depress the clips and open the engine compartment fusebox cover

compartment (see illustrations). The fuse allocations are given on the underside of the fusebox cover.

3 To gain access to the facia fuses, open the passengers glovebox, unto the 2 screws and remove the cover (see illustration).

4 To access the fuses and circuit breakers are located in the fuse/relay box in the engine compartment; release the clips and lift off the cover to gain access, and behind the left-hand luggage compartment side panel (see illustrations).

5 A blown fuse can be recognised from its melted or broken wire (see illustration).

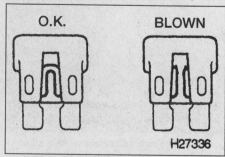

3.5 A blown fuse is recognised from its melted or broken wire

6 To remove a fuse, first ensure that the relevant circuit is switched off.

7 Using the plastic tool clipped to the main fusebox, pull the fuse from its location.

8 Spare fuses are provided in the main fusebox.

9 Before renewing a blown fuse, trace and rectify the cause, and always use a fuse of the correct rating (fuse ratings are specified on the inside of the fusebox cover panel). Never substitute a fuse of a higher rating, or make temporary repairs using wire or metal foil; more serious damage, or even fire, could result.

10 Note that the fuses are colour-coded as follows. Refer to the wiring diagrams for details of the fuse ratings used and the circuits protected.

Colour	Rating
Orange	5A
Red	10A
Blue	15A
Yellow	20A
Clear or White	25A
Green	30A

Relays

11 A relay is an electrically-operated switch, which is used for the following reasons:

a) A relay can switch a heavy current remotely from the circuit in which the current is flowing, therefore allowing the use of lighter-gauge wiring and switch contacts.

b) A relay can receive more than one control input, unlike a mechanical switch.

c) A relay can have a timer function – for example, the intermittent wiper relay.

12 The main and optional equipment relays are primarily located in the engine compartment fuse/relay box (see Fuses). Additional relays may be fitted, depending on model and specification and these are generally mounted adjacent to the component being controlled.

13 If a circuit or system controlled by a relay develops a fault, and the relay is suspect, operate the system. If the relay is functioning, it should be possible to hear it click as it is energised. If this is the case, the fault lies with the components or wiring of the system. If the relay is not being energised, then either the relay is not receiving a main supply or a switching voltage, or the relay itself is faulty. Testing is by the substitution of a known good unit, but

be careful – while some relays are identical in appearance and in operation, others look similar but perform different functions.

14 To remove a relay, first ensure that the relevant circuit is switched off. The relay can then simply be pulled out from the socket, and pushed back into position.

4 Electrical connectors – general information

1 Most electrical connections on these vehicles are made with multiwire plastic connectors. The mating halves of many connectors are secured with locking clips molded into the plastic connector shells. The mating halves of some large connectors, such as some of those under the instrument panel, are held together by a bolt through the center of the connector.

2 To separate a connector with locking clips, use a small screwdriver to pry the clips apart carefully, then separate the connector halves. Pull only on the shell, never pull on the wiring harness, as you may damage the individual wires and terminals inside the connectors. Look at the connector closely before trying to separate the halves. Often the locking clips are engaged in a way that is not immediately clear. Additionally, many connectors have more than one set of clips.

3 Each pair of connector terminals has a male half and a female half. When you look at the end view of a connector in a diagram, be sure to understand whether the view shows the harness side or the component side of the connector. Connector halves are mirror images of each other, and a terminal shown on the right side end-view of one half will be on the left side end-view of the other half.

4 It is often necessary to take circuit voltage measurements with a connector connected. Whenever possible, carefully insert a small straight pin (not your meter probe) into the rear of the connector shell to contact the terminal inside, then clip your meter lead to the pin. This kind of connection is called "backprobing." When inserting a test probe into a terminal, be careful not to distort the terminal opening. Doing so can lead to a poor connection and corrosion at that terminal later. Using the small straight pin instead of a meter probe results in less chance of deforming the terminal connector. "T" pins are a good choice as temporary meter connections. They allow for a larger surface area to attach the meter leads too.

Electrical connectors

5 Typical electrical connectors:

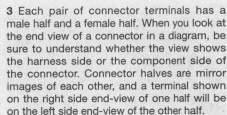
4.5a Most electrical connectors have a single release tab that you depress to release the connector

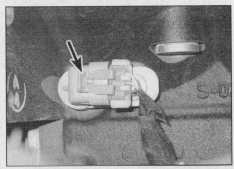
4.5b Some electrical connectors have a retaining tab which must be pried up to free the connector

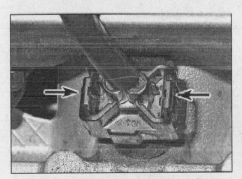
4.5c Some connectors have two release tabs that you must squeeze to release the connector

4.5d Some connectors use wire retainers that you squeeze to release the connector

4.5e Critical connectors often employ a sliding lock (1) that you must pull out before you can depress the release tab (2)

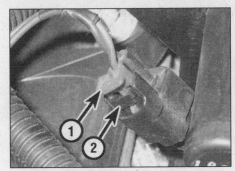
4.5f Here's another sliding-lock style connector, with the lock (1) and the release tab (2) on the side of the connector

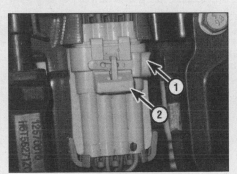
4.5g On some connectors the lock (1) must be pulled out to the side and removed before you can lift the release tab (2)

4.5h Some critical connectors, like the multi-pin connectors at the Electronic Control Module employ pivoting locks that must be flipped open

5.3 The mark should be visible in the window

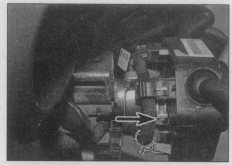

5.4a Slacken the clamp screw...

5.4b... and remove the steering column combination switch assembly

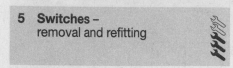

5 Switches – removal and refitting

Steering column combination switch assembly

Removal

1 Remove the steering wheel as described in Chapter 10 Section 12.

2 Remove the steering column shrouds as described in Chapter 11 Section 25.

3 Check the mark is visible in the airbag rotary contact unit window **(see illustration)**. This mark should be visible if the steering wheel was removed correctly (wheels straight-ahead). The contact unit it locked as the steering wheel is removed. Do not attempt to rotate the unit, or it will be damaged. Fiat insist that if the rotary contact unit has been rotated to the extent that the position of unit is unknown, the unit must be renewed.

4 Slacken the steering column combination switch assembly retaining clamp screw, release the clip, and slide the assembly from the column **(see illustrations)**. Disconnect the wiring plugs as the assembly is withdrawn.

Refitting

5 Refitting is a reversal of removal. If a new switch/rotary contact unit is being fitted, remove the locking tab securing the contact

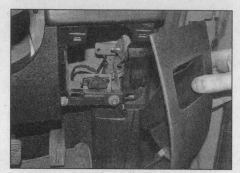

5.6 Pull the cover/storage compartment rearwards

unit. New units are supplied with the rotary contact unit pre-centred.

Facia switch panel

Grande Punto

Removal

6 Pull the drivers side facia storage compartment/cover rearwards, and remove it **(see illustration)**.

7 Reach up to behind the switch panel, move it slightly away from the steering column, and manoeuvre it from the facia **(see illustration)**. Disconnect the wiring plug as the panel is withdrawn.

Refitting

8 Refitting is a reversal of removal.

5.7 Move the switch panel to one side and manoeuvre it from the facia

Punto Evo/Punto 2012 MY

Removal

9 Open the drivers side facia storage compartment, reach through the aperture, and pull the facia panel/switch assembly rearwards to release the upper retaining clips **(see illustration)**.

10 Release the clips and detach the switch assembly from the facia panel **(see illustration)**. Disconnect the wiring plug as the assembly is withdrawn.

Refitting

11 Refitting is a reversal of removal.

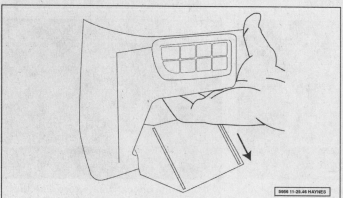

5.9 Pull the upper edge of the panel rearwards – LHD shown

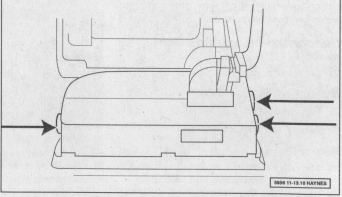

5.10 Release the clips and detach the switch assembly

5.13a Central switch/air vent panel retaining screws

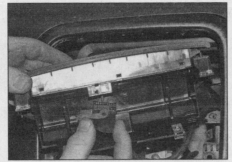

5.13b Lever over the locking catch and disconnect the wiring plug

5.14 Release the clips and detach the vent panel

Central switch panel

Grande Punto

Removal

12 Remove the facia audio support frame as described in Section 11 Section 25.

13 Undo the 3 screws underneath the switch panel, then manoeuvre the switch panel/vent assembly from the facia, releasing the upper clips **(see illustrations)**. Disconnect the wiring plugs as the assembly is withdrawn.

14 If necessary, unclip the vent panel, then undo the screws and detach the switch panel **(see illustration)**.

Refitting

15 Refitting is a reversal of removal.

Punto Evo/Punto 2012 MY

Removal

16 Remove the instrument panel centre frame as described in Chapter 11 Section 25.

17 Undo the retaining screws, and detach the switch panel from the centre frame **(see illustration)**.

Refitting

18 Refitting is a reversal of removal

Stop-light switch

19 Refer to Chapter 9 Section 14.

Horn switch

20 The horn switch is intergal with the drivers airbag assembly. If a faulty, the complete assembly must be replaced.

Handbrake-on warning light switch

21 Refer to Chapter 9 Section 18.

Reversing light switch

22 Refer to Chapter 7 Section 7.

Steering wheel switches

Removal

23 Remove the drivers airbag as described in Section 20.

24 Release the clips and pull the switches from the steering wheel. Disconnect the wiring plugs as the switches are withdrawn.

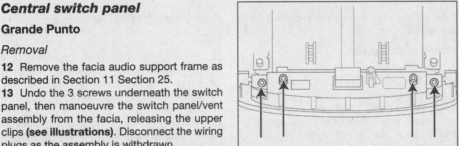
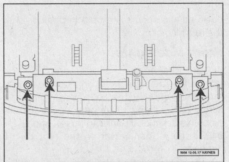

5.17 Undo the switch panel retaining screws

Refitting

25 Refitting is a reversal of removal.

Ignition switch

26 Remove the steering column shrouds as described in Chapter 11 Section 25.

27 Disconnect the wiring plug, undo the screw and remove the ignition switch.

28 Refitting is the reversal of removal.

Electric window/mirror switches

29 Using a blunt, flat-bladed tool, carefully prise the switch assembly from the door trim panel **(see illustration)**. Disconnect the wiring plug(s) as the panel is withdrawn.

30 Refitting is a reversal of removal.

---

6 Bulbs (exterior lights) – renewal

General

1 Whenever a bulb is renewed, note the following points:

a) *Disconnect the battery negative lead as described in Chapter 5A Section 4 before starting work.*

b) *Remember that if the light has just been in use, the bulb may be extremely hot.*

c) *Always check the bulb contacts and holder, ensuring that there is clean metal-to metal contact between the bulb and the socket contacts. Clean off any corrosion or dirt before fitting a new bulb.*

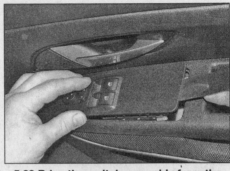

5.29 Prise the switch assembly from the door trim panel

d) *Wherever bayonet-type bulbs are fitted, ensure that the live contact(s) bear firmly against the bulb contact.*

e) *Always ensure that the new bulb is of the correct rating and that it is completely clean before fitting it; this applies particularly to headlight/foglight bulbs (see below).*

f) *With quartz halogen bulbs (headlights and similar applications), use a tissue or clean cloth when handling the bulb; do not touch the bulb glass with the fingers. Even small quantities of grease from the fingers will cause blackening and premature failure. If a bulb is accidentally touched, clean it with methylated spirit and a clean rag.*

Headlight

2 Open the bonnet, and if removing the left-hand headlight bulb on Grande Punto models, release the clip and pull the screenwash reservoir filler neck upwards from place **(see illustration)**.

6.2 Pull the screenwash reservoir filler neck from the retaining clip

6.3 Pull the rubber cap from the rear of the headlight

6.4 Pull the wiring plug from the bulb

6.5 Move the retaining clip to one side and fold it down

3 Pull the rubber cap from the rear of the headlight (see illustration).
4 Disconnect the wiring plug from the rear of the bulb (see illustration).
5 Release the retaining spring clip and remove the bulb from the headlight unit (see illustration).
6 When handling the new bulb, use a tissue or clean cloth to avoid touching the glass with the fingers; moisture and grease from the skin can cause blackening and rapid failure of this type of bulb. If the glass is accidentally touched, wipe it clean using methylated spirit. Avoid knocking or shaking the bulb as this may weaken the filament.
7 Install the new bulb, using a reversal of the removal procedure. Ensure that its locating tabs are correctly located in the light unit

cut-outs and secure the bulb in position with the retaining clip.

Front side lights

8 Open the bonnet, and if removing the left-hand side light bulb on Grande Punto models, release the clip and pull the screenwash reservoir filler neck upwards from place, as described earlier in this Section.
9 Pull the rubber cap from the rear of the headlight.
10 Squeeze together the clips and pull the side light bulbholder from the reflector (see illustration).
11 Pull the capless bulb from the bulbholder (see illustration).
12 Install the new bulb using a reversal of the removal procedure.

Front directional indicator

Grande Punto

13 Open the bonnet, and if removing the left-hand directional indicator bulb, release the clip and pull the screenwash reservoir filler neck upwards from place, as described earlier in this Section.
14 Rotate the bulbholder anti-clockwise a little, and withdraw it from the rear of the headlight (see illustration).
15 Push the bulb in slightly, rotate it anti-clockwise a little, and pull the bayonet-fitting indicator bulb from the holder.
16 Install a new bulb using a reversal of the removal procedure.

Punto Evo/Punto 2012 MY

17 Turn the steering wheel so the relevant roadwheel point to the inside of the vehicle.
18 Undo the 2 retaining screws and remove the access cover from the front section of the wheelarch liner (see illustration).
19 Working through the aperture, rotate the bulbholder anti-clockwise and pull it from the rear of the light unit (see illustration).
20 Press-in and rotate the bulb anti-clockwise a little to remove it from the bulbholder.
21 Install a new bulb using a reversal of the removal procedure.

Side repeater

22 Gently push the side repeater lens towards the rear of the vehicle, pull out the

6.10 Pull the side light bulbholder from place

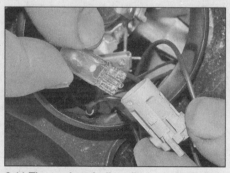

6.11 The capless bulb pulls from the holder

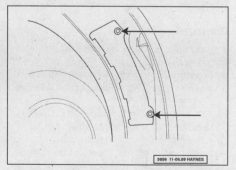

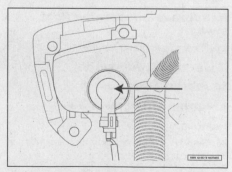

6.14 Front directional indicator bulb and holder

6.18 Undo the screws and remove the access cover

6.19 Rotate the bulbholder anti-clockwise

6.22 Push the lens rearwards, and pull out the front edge

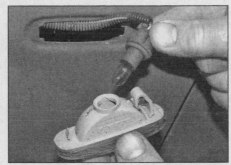

6.23 Rotate the bulbholder anti-clockwise

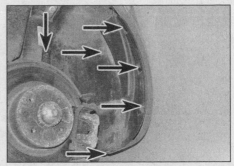

6.27 Front wheelarch section fasteners

front edge, and detach it from the wing panel (see illustration).

23 Rotate the bulbholder anti-clockwise a little, and pull it from the lens (see illustration).

24 Pull the capless bulb from the holder.

25 Install a new bulb using a reversal of the removal procedure.

Front foglight

Grande Punto

26 Raise the front of the vehicle and support it securely on axle stands as described in 'Vehicle jacking and support'.

27 Undo the screws/nut securely the front section of the front wheelarch liner (see illustration).

28 Pull the wheelarch liner rearwards a little, and disconnect the wiring plug from the rear of the foglight (see illustration)

29 Rotate the cover at the rear of the foglight anti-clockwise and remove it (see illustration).

30 Disconnect the wiring plug from the rear of the bulb, move the retaining spring to the side, and pull the bulb from the reflector (see illustration).

31 When handling the new bulb, use a tissue or clean cloth to avoid touching the glass with the fingers; moisture and grease from the skin can cause blackening and rapid failure of this type of bulb. If the glass is accidentally touched, wipe it clean using methylated spirit. Avoid knocking or shaking the bulb as this may weaken the filament.

32 Install the new bulb, using a reversal of the removal procedure. Ensure the cut-out in the bulb flange aligns with the reflector correctly.

Punto Evo/Punto 2012 MY

33 Remove the front fog light as described in Section 8.

34 Rotate the bulbholder anti-clockwise and pull it from the light unit (see illustration). Note that the bulb is integral with the holder.

35 When handling the new bulb, use a tissue or clean cloth to avoid touching the glass with the fingers; moisture and grease from the skin can cause blackening and rapid failure of this type of bulb. If the glass is accidentally touched, wipe it clean using methylated spirit. Avoid knocking or shaking the bulb as this may weaken the filament.

36 Install a new bulb using a reversal of the removal procedure.

Rear light assembly

37 Remove the rear light assembly as described in Section 8.

Grande Punto

38 Undo the 2 retaining screws, and detach the bulbholder from the light assembly (see illustration).

39 Press-in and twist the relevant bulb, and remove it from the holder.

40 Install the new bulb, using a reversal of the removal procedure.

Punto Evo/Punto 2012 MY

41 Release the 4 clips and detach

6.28 Pull the wiring plugs from the rear of the foglight

6.29 Rotate the cover anti-clockwise

6.30 Move the retaining clip to one side and withdraw the bulb

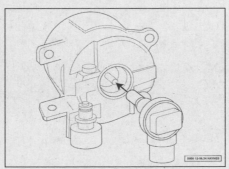

6.34 Rotate the fog light bulbholder anti-clockwise

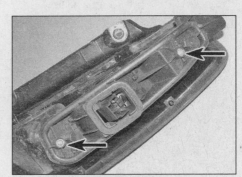

6.38 Bulbholder retaining screws – Grande Punto

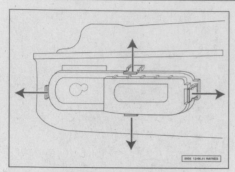

6.41 Release the clips and detach the bulbholder assembly

6.45a Rotate the rear fog/reversing light bulbholder anti-clockwise – Grande Punto

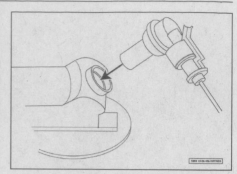

6.45b Rotate the bulbholder anti-clockwise – Punto EVO/2012

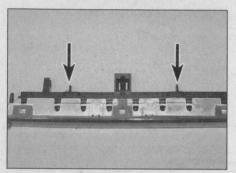

6.57 Bulbholder retaining clips

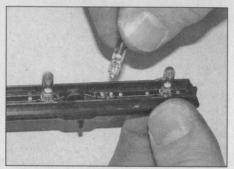

6.58 Pull the capless bulbs from the holder

Punto Evo/Punto 2012 MY

54 Pull the capless bulb from the holder.
55 Install a new bulb using a reversal of the removal procedure.

High level stop light

56 Remove the high level brake light as described in Section 8.
57 Release the clips and detach the bulbholder assembly from the lens **(see illustration)**.
58 Pull the relevant bulb from the holder **(see illustration)**.
59 Install a new bulb, using a reversal of the removal procedure.

Number plate light

60 Gently press the clip sideways, and pull the edge from place.
61 Rotate the bulbholder anti-clockwise and pull it from the light unit.
62 Pull the capless bulb from the holder.
63 Install a new bulb, using a reversal of the removal procedure.

the bulbholder from the light unit **(see illustration)**.
42 Press-in and rotate the relevant bulb anti-clockwise a little, then pull it from the holder. Note that the side light in the centre of the light is an LED, and cannot be replaced. If the LED is faulty, the complete bulbholder must be replaced.
43 Install a new bulb using a reversal of removal procedure.

Rear fog light

44 Raise the rear of the vehicle and support it securely on axle stands, as described in 'Vehicle jacking and support'.
45 Working underneath, rotate the bulbholder anti-clockwise and detach it from the light unit **(see illustrations)**.

Grande Punto

46 Press-in and rotate the bulb anti-clockwise to remove it from the holder.

47 Install the new bulb, using a reversal of the removal procedure.

Punto Evo/Punto 2012 MY

48 Pull the capless bulb from the holder.
49 Install a new bulb using a reversal of the removal procedure.

Reversing light

50 Raise the rear of the vehicle and support it securely on axle stands, as described in 'Vehicle jacking and support'.
51 Working underneath, rotate the bulbholder anti-clockwise and detach it from the light unit **(see illustrations 6.45a and 6.45b)**.

Grande Punto

52 Press-in and rotate the bulb anti-clockwise to remove it from the holder.
53 Install a new bulb, using a reversal of the removal procedure.

7 Bulbs (interior lights) – removal and refitting

Front courtesy lights
Version A

1 Use a screwdriver to release the clips at the rear, prise the light unit from the headlining, then open the access flap **(see illustrations)**.
2 Pull the relevant festoon type bulb from the contacts **(see illustration)**.

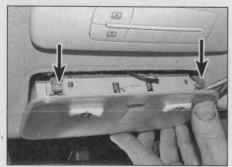

7.1a Release the clips, prise down the light unit...

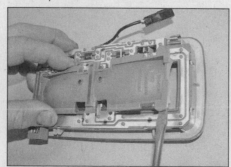

7.1b... and open the access flap

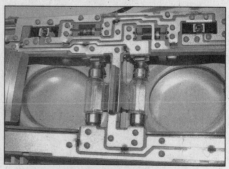

7.2 Pull the festoon bulb(s) from the contacts

7.4 Use a screwdriver to depress the clip each side

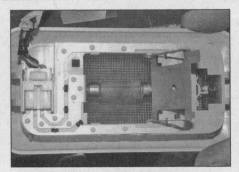

7.5 Slide open the flap and pull out the festoon bulb

7.8 Depress the clip at the end, and prise the light from place

3 Install the new bulb(s) and press the lens back into place.

Version B

4 Depress the clips each side and prise the centre courtesy light unit from place (see illustration).

5 Open the flap, and pull the festoon type bulb from the contacts (see illustration).

6 Install a new bulb, close the flap, and press the light unit back into place.

Luggage compartment light

7 Remove the rear parcel shelf.

8 Depress the clip and prise the light unit from place (see illustration).

9 Release the clips, open the protection and pull the capless bulb from the holder.

10 Install a new bulb using a reversal of the removal procedure.

8 Exterior light units – removal and refitting

Headlight

1 Remove the front bumper as described in Chapter 11 Section 6.

2 If removing the left-hand headlight on Grande Punto models, release the clip and pull the screenwash reservoir filler neck upwards from place (see illustration 6.2).

3 Disconnect the wiring plug from the rear of the headlight (see illustration).

4 Undo the 3 retaining bolts, release the tab and remove the headlight (see illustrations).

5 Refitting is a reversal of removal. On completion, it is advisable to have the headlight beam alignment checked with reference to Section 9.

Side repeater light

6 The side repeater light is removed during the bulb replacement procedure. Refer to Section 6.

Rear light cluster

7 Open the tailgate, undo the 2 retaining bolts, and manoeuvre the rear light cluster rearwards from place (see illustrations). Note how the locating pins engage with the holes in the vehicle body.

8 Disconnect the wiring plug as the light cluster is withdrawn.

9 Refitting is a reversal of removal.

High-level brake light

10 Open the tailgate, and prise the rubber grommets to access the high-level brake light retaining clips (see illustration).

11 Release the retaining clips, lower the

8.3 Slide out the clip and pull the wiring plug from the rear of the headlight

8.4a Undo the 2 lower bolts...

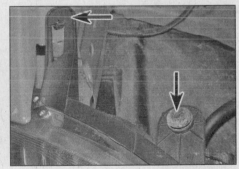

8.4b... the upper bolt, and lift the tab

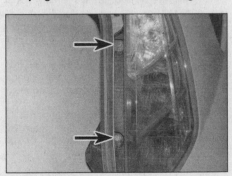

8.7a Undo the screws at the inner edge of the rear light cluster

8.7b Pull the light cluster rearwards to release the locating pins

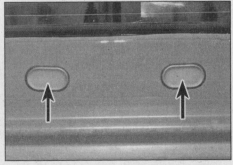

8.10 Prise out the rubber grommets

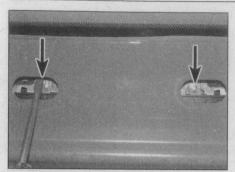

8.11a Depress the clips, and prise the light from the tailgate

8.11b Disconnect the washer hose and wiring plug

8.15 The fog light adjustment screw is accessed from beneath

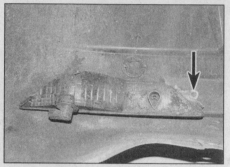

8.17 Undo the screw and remove the rear fog/reversing light

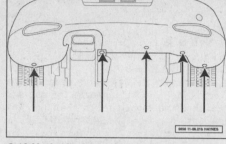

8.19 Undo the bumper fasteners below the fog or reversing light

tailgate, and manoeuvre the high-level brake light from place (see illustrations). Disconnect the wiring plug and washer hose as the light unit is withdrawn.

12 Refitting is a reversal of removal.

Front fog light

13 Remove the front bumper as described in Chapter 11 Section 6.

14 Undo the 3 screws, and manoeuvre the fog light forwards from the bumper. Disconnect the wiring plug as the fog light is withdrawn.

15 Refitting is a reversal of removal. Note that the aim of the fog light can be adjusted, by removing the rubber cap in the lower part of the front bumper, and rotating the adjustment screw (see illustration).

Rear fog light/Reversing light

16 Raise the rear of the vehicle and support it securely on axle stands, as described in 'Vehicle jacking and support'.

Grande Punto

17 Working underneath, disconnect the wiring plug, undo the retaining screw, and remove the light unit (see illustration).

18 Refitting is a reversal of removal.

Punto Evo/Punto 2012 MY

19 Undo the rear bumper lower fasteners beneath the fog light or reversing light (see illustration).

20 Disconnect the wiring plug, undo the 2 retaining screws, and move the rear fog light or reversing light.

21 Refitting is a reversal of removal.

9 Headlight beam adjustment – general information

1 Accurate adjustment of the headlight beam is only possible using optical beam setting equipment and this work should therefore be carried out by a Fiat dealer or suitably-equipped workshop.

2 For reference, the headlights can be adjusted by rotating the adjuster screws on the top of the headlight unit (see illustration).

3 All models have an electrically-operated headlight beam adjustment system which is controlled through the switch in the facia. On these models ensure that the switch is set to the off position before adjusting the headlight aim. Note that the headlight aim motor cannot be renewed separately from the headlight.

10 Instrument panel – removal and refitting

Removal

1 Disconnect the battery negative lead as described in Chapter 5A Section 4.

2 Fully lower and extend the steering wheel/column.

Grande Punto

3 Unclip the upper steering column shroud gaiter from the base of the instrument panel (see illustration).

4 Undo the 4 retaining bolts and remove the instrument panel surround trim (see illustrations).

5 Undo the 2 screws at the upper edge, pull the instrument panel rearwards and disengage the lower lugs (see illustrations). Disconnect the wiring plug as the panel is withdrawn.

6 No further dismantling of the panel is recommended. The panel is illuminated by non-replaceable LEDs.

Punto Evo/Punto 2012 MY

7 Undo the 2 retaining screws, and pull the instrument panel cover trim rearwards to release the retaining clips (see illustration).

9.2 Headlight beam adjustment screws

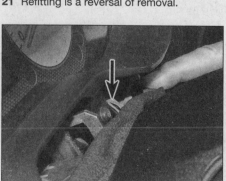

10.3 Pull the upper shroud gaiter rearwards from the panel to release the clips

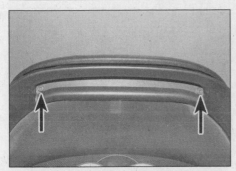

10.4a Undo the screws at the top of the instrument panel surround...

10.4b... and the screws below...

10.4c... and manoeuvre the panel surround rearwards

10.5a Instrument panel retaining screws

10.5b Lever over the catch and disconnect the wiring plug

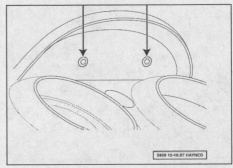

10.7 Instrument panel cover trim retaining screws

8 Unclip the column trim from the lower edge of the instrument panel (see illustration 10.3).
9 Undo the 4 retaining screws, and manoeuvre the instrument panel rearwards from position. Disconnect the wiring plug as the panel is withdrawn.
10 No further dismantling of the panel is recommended. The panel is illuminated by non-replaceable LEDs.

Refitting

11 Refitting is a reversal of removal. If a new instrument panel is fitted, the data stored in the body computer may need to be transferred to the new panel using Fiat diagnostic equipment (Examiner or equivalent). Entrust this task to a Fiat dealer or suitably equipped repairer.

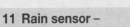

11 Rain sensor –
removal and refitting

Removal

1 Unclip the covers from the upper section, and lower section of the mirror base.
2 Slide the mirror assembly upwards from the windscreen mounting.
3 Disconnect the rain sensor wiring plug.
4 Release the retaining clips and remove the sensor. Avoid bare skin contact with the face of the sensor.

Refitting

5 Ensure both the sensor face and windscreen surfaces are clean and dry.
6 Position the sensor on the windscreen, and secure it with the retaining clips.
7 The remainder of refitting is a reversal of removal.

12 Horns – removal and refitting

Removal

1 Remove the front bumper as described in Chapter 11 Section 6.
2 Disconnect the wiring plug, undo the retaining bolt/nut and remove the horn(s) (see illustration).

12.2 Horn retaining bolt

Refitting

8 Refitting is a reversal of removal.

10 Wiper arm
removal and refitting

Removal

1 Operate the wiper motor, then switch if off so that the wiper arm returns to the at-rest/parked position.

Windscreen wiper arms

2 Prise off the wiper arm spindle nut cover, then slacken and remove the spindle nut (see illustration).
3 Lift the blade off the glass, and pull the wiper arm off its spindle. If necessary, the

13.2 Prise off the cover and undo the spindle nut

13.3 If necessary, use a puller to release the arm from the spindle

13.4 Lift up the cover to access the spindle nut

13.5 Special wiper arm pullers are available

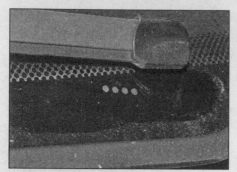

13.6a Front windscreen wiper blade alignment marks

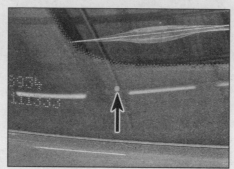

13.6b Tailgate screen wiper blade alignment mark

4 Remove the tailgate lower trim panel as described in Chapter 11 Section 23.
5 Disconnect the wiper motor wiring plug.
6 Drill out the 3 special rivets and remove the rear wiper motor (see illustration).

Refitting

7 Refitting is a reversal of removal.

15 Windscreen/tailgate washer system components – removal and refitting

arm can be carefully removed using a suitable puller (see illustration). If both windscreen wiper arms are removed, note their locations, as different arms are fitted to the driver's and passenger's sides.

Tailgate wiper arm

4 Lift up the spindle cover, then slacken and remove the spindle nut (see illustration).
5 Lift the blade from the glass, and pull the wiper arm from the spindle. If necessary, the arm can be removed using a suitable puller (see illustration).

Refitting

6 Refit the wiper arms to the spindles, aligning the blades to the reference marks on the windscreen (see illustrations). Tighten the retaining nuts securely.

14 Windscreen wiper motor and linkage – removal and refitting

Removal

Windscreen wiper motor assembly

1 Remove the windscreen scuttle panel as described in Chapter 11 Section 20, then unclip the panel from the bulkhead (see illustration).
2 Undo the retaining bolts, and manoeuvre the wiper motor assembly from place (see illustration). Disconnect the wiring plug as it becomes accessible.

Rear wiper motor

3 Remove the rear wiper arm as described in Section 13.

Washer reservoir

Removal

1 Open the bonnet, release the clip and pull the washer reservoir filler neck upwards from place (see illustration 6.2). Recover the seal.
2 Remove the front bumper as described in Chapter 11 Section 6.
3 Pull the washer pump from the reservoir. There's no need to disconnect the pipes/wiring. Be prepared for fluid spillage.
4 Unclip the washer hoses and wiring from the reservoir.
5 Release the 3 fasteners, and manoeuvre the washer reservoir from place.

Refitting

6 Refitting is a reversal of removal.

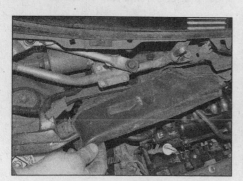

14.1 Unclip the panel from the bulkhead

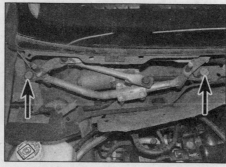

14.2 Undo the bolts and manoeuvre the wiper motor/linkage assembly from place

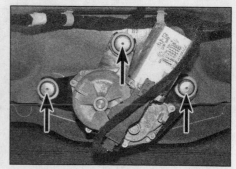

14.6 The rear wiper motor is secured by 3 special rivets

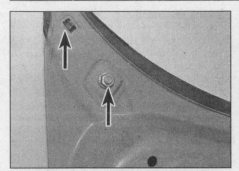

15.15a Undo the nut, release the clip...

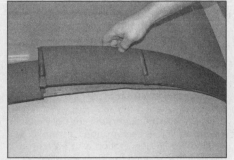

15.15b... and prise up the decorative trim

15.16 Squeeze together the clips and remove the windscreen washer jet

Windscreen/tailgate washer pump – removal and refitting

Removal

7 On Punto Evo/Punto 2012 MY vehicles, undo the 2 screws, and remove the access panel from the left-hand front wheel arch liner.

8 On all models, undo the screws/nut and pull back the front section of the left-hand front wheel arch liner.

9 Disconnect the wiring plug from the pump.

10 Disconnect the hoses from the pump.

11 Pull the pump from the reservoir. Be prepared for fluid spillage.

12 Check the condition of the sealing grommet, and renew if necessary. Note that the single pump provides fluid for the windscreen and tailgate screen.

Refitting

13 Refitting is a reversal of removal.

Jets

Removal

Windscreen washer jets

14 Open the bonnet, and disconnect the relevant washer hose from the 3-way connector.

15 Undo the retaining nut, release the clip, close the bonnet, then prise up the retaining clips and remove the left-, or right-hand decorative trim **(see illustrations)**.

16 Disconnect the washer hose, squeeze together the retaining clips, and remove the jet(s) from the bonnet **(see illustration)**.

Tailgate screen jet

17 Remove the high-level brake light as described in Section 8.

18 Unclip the high-level brake light lens cover.

19 Release the clips and detach the jet from the light assembly.

Refitting

20 Refitting is a reversal of removal. No adjustment of the jets is possible.

---

16 Infotainment units – removal and refitting

Caution: Do not bend the fibre optic cables at a radius of sharper than 25 mm.

Facia Radio/Audio unit

Removal

1 Disconnect the battery negative lead as described in Chapter 5A Section 4.

2 Insert the special extraction tools supplied with the vehicle into the holes on either side of the audio unit. Press them home until the internal clips can be felt to release **(see illustration)**. Note that if the original extraction tools are not available, new ones can be obtained from motor accessory outlets.

3 Pull the unit from the facia, then disconnect the aerial lead and wiring connector from the rear of the unit **(see illustration)**.

Refitting

4 Refitting is a reversal of removal, ensuring that the wiring is correctly routed behind the unit.

Bluetooth control unit

Removal

5 Disconnect the battery negative lead as described in Chapter 5A Section 4.

6 Remove the glovebox as described in Chapter 11 Section 25.

7 Undo the retaining screws, and manoeuvre the control unit from the glovebox aperture **(see illustration)**. Disconnect the wiring plugs as the unit is withdrawn.

Refitting

8 Refitting is a reversal of removal, noting the following points:

a) The control unit must be refitted, and the battery reconnected for at least 5 minutes before the ignition is turned on.

b) If a new control unit is fitted, the data stored in the body computer may need to be transferred to the new unit using Fiat diagnostic equipment (Examiner or equivalent). Entrust this task to a Fiat dealer or suitably equipped repairer.

Aerial

Note: *This is a complex task requiring patience and dexterity to accomplish without damage to the headlining.*

Removal

9 Remove the headlining as described in Chapter 11 Section 23.

16.2 Insert the special tools into the holes and pull the unit from the facia

16.3 Disconnect the wiring from the rear of the unit

16.7 Bluetooth control unit

10 Disconnect the aerial wiring plug.
11 Undo the nut, recover the split-washer, and remove the aerial from the vehicle roof.

Refitting

12 Refitting is a reversal of removal.

17 Speakers – removal and refitting

Note: *The following procedure descriptions apply to various vehicle specification levels. Therefore, the actual fitment of components will vary greatly.*
Caution: Do not bend the fibre optic cables at a radius of sharper than 25 mm.

Door speakers

1 Remove the door inner trim panel as described in Chapter 11 Section 13.

Main speaker

2 Disconnect the speaker wiring plug.
3 Drill out the 3 rivets and remove the speaker **(see illustration)**.
4 Remove any residue of the old rivets from the door.
5 Refitting is a reversal of removal, using new rivets.

Tweeter

6 Release the clips and detach the tweeter from the door inner trim panel.
7 Refitting is a reversal of removal.

Side panel speaker (3-door models)

8 Remove the rear side panel as described in Chapter 11 Section 23.
9 Disconnect the speaker wiring plug.
10 Drill out the rivets and remove the speaker **(see illustration)**.
11 Refitting is a reversal, using new rivets.

Rear sub-woofer

12 Open the tailgate.
13 Undo the 3 retaining bolts, and manoeuvre the sub-woofer from place. Disconnect the wiring plug as the unit is withdrawn.
14 Refitting is a reversal of removal.

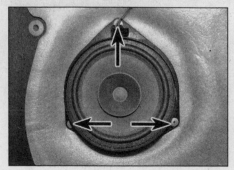

17.3 Main door speaker is secured by 3 rivets

18 Anti-theft system and engine immobiliser – general information

1 All models in the range are equipped as standard with a central locking system incorporating an electronic engine immobiliser function.
2 The electronic engine immobiliser is operated by a transponder fitted to the ignition key, in conjunction with an analogue module fitted around the ignition switch.
3 When the ignition key is inserted in the switch and turned to the ignition 'on' position, the control module sends a preprogrammed recognition code signal to the module on the ignition switch. If the recognition code signal matches that of the transponder on the ignition key, an unlocking request signal is sent to the engine management ECU allowing the engine to be started. If the ignition key signal is not recognised, the engine management system remains immobilised.
4 When the ignition is switched off, a locking signal is sent to the ECU and the engine is immobilised until the unlocking request signal is again received.
5 If a fault develops with the system, have the body control computer interrogated using Fiat diagnostic equipment (Examiner or equivalent).

19 Airbag system – general information, precautions and system de-activation

General information

1 A driver's airbag, passengers airbag, side air bags, and side window air bags are fitted as standard on all models, with a drivers side lower knee airbag available as optional equipment on most models. The driver's airbag is located in the steering wheel centre pad and the passenger's airbag is located above the glovebox in the facia. The side airbags are located in the front seat backs, and the side window airbags are located in the roof headlining on both sides of the car.
2 The airbag and seat belt pyrotechnic safety

17.10 Side panel speaker – 3-door models

systems are armed only when the ignition is switched on, however, a reserve power source maintains a power supply to the systems in the event of a break in the main electrical supply. The airbags are activated by crash sensors, and controlled by an electronic control unit located under the centre of the facia. The side airbags and side window airbags are activated by severe side impact and operate in conjunction with the main system. The pyrotechnic seat belt pretensioners operate independently of the main system.
3 The airbags are inflated by a gas generator, which forces the bag out from its location in the steering wheel, facia, seat back frame or roof headlining.

Precautions

⚠️ *Warning: The following precautions must be observed when working on vehicles equipped with an airbag system, to prevent the possibility of personal injury. Many of the precautions are equally applicable to the pyrotechnic seat belt pretensioners and should be similarly observed.*

General

4 The following precautions must be observed when carrying out work on a vehicle equipped with an airbag:
a) Do not disconnect the battery with the engine running.
b) Before carrying out any work in the vicinity of the airbag, removal of any of the airbag components, or any welding work on the vehicle, de-activate the system as described in the following sub-Section.
c) Do not attempt to test any of the airbag system circuits using test meters or any other test equipment.
*d) If the airbag warning light comes on, or any fault in the system is suspected, consult a Fiat dealer without delay. **Do not** attempt to carry out fault diagnosis, or any dismantling of the components.*

When handling an airbag

a) Transport the airbag by itself, bag upward.
b) Do not put your arms around the airbag.
c) Do not drop the airbag or expose it to impacts.
d) Do not attempt to dismantle the airbag unit.
e) Do not connect any form of electrical equipment to any part of the airbag circuit.

When storing an airbag

a) Store the unit in a cupboard with the airbag upward.
b) Do not expose the airbag to temperatures above 80ºC.
c) Do not expose the airbag to flames.
d) Do not attempt to dispose of the airbag – consult a Fiat dealer.
e) Never refit an airbag which is known to be faulty or damaged.

De-activation

5 The system must be de-activated before carrying out any work on the airbag components or surrounding area:

a) *Switch on the ignition and check the operation of the airbag warning light on the instrument panel. The light should illuminate when the ignition is switched on, then extinguish.*

b) *Switch off the ignition.*

c) *Remove the ignition key.*

d) *Switch off all electrical equipment.*

e) *Disconnect the battery negative lead as described in Chapter 5A Section 4.*

f) *Insulate the battery negative terminal and the end of the battery negative lead to prevent any possibility of contact.*

g) *Wait at least 10 minutes before carrying out any further work.*

Activation

6 To activate the system on completion of any work, proceed as follows:

a) *Ensure that there are no occupants in the vehicle, and that there are no loose objects around the vicinity of the steering wheel/ facia.*

b) *Ensure that the ignition is switched off, then reconnect the battery negative lead.*

c) *Open the drivers door and switch on the ignition, without reaching in front of the steering wheel. Check that the airbag warning light illuminates briefly then extinguishes.*

d) *Switch off the ignition.*

e) *If the airbag warning light does not operate correctly, consult a Fiat dealer before driving the vehicle.*

20 Airbag system components – removal and refitting

Caution: Refer to the warnings in the previous Section before carrying out the following operations.

1 Disconnect the battery negative lead as described in Chapter 5A Section 4.

Steering wheel airbag

Removal

2 Ensure the front wheels are in the straight-ahead position.

3 Insert the Fiat special tools (No. 1871 007 600) into the holes each side of the steering wheel boss **(see illustration)**. In the absence of these tools, use a flat-bladed screwdriver.

4 Press the tools into the steering wheel, releasing the springs which secure the airbag **(see illustration)**. The airbag will be felt to 'give' when the springs are released.

5 Move the airbag away from the steering wheel, squeeze together the clips and disconnect the wiring plugs **(see illustration)**.

6 If the airbag unit is to be stored for any length of time, refer to the storage precautions given in Section 19.

Refitting

7 Refitting is a reversal of removal, noting the following points:

a) *Do not strike the airbag unit, or expose it to impacts during refitting.*

b) *On completion of refitting, activate the airbag system as described in Section 19.*

Passengers airbag

Removal

8 Remove the passengers glovebox as described in Chapter 11 Section 25.

9 Undo the screws and remove the document holder/control unit from the glovebox aperture **(see illustration)**.

10 Disconnect the wiring plugs from the passengers airbag **(see illustration)**.

11 Undo the retaining bolt, and manoeuvre the airbag from position **(see illustration)**.

12 If the airbag unit is to be stored for any length of time, refer to the storage precautions given in Section 19.

Refitting

13 Refitting is a reversal of removal, noting the following points:

a) *Do not strike the airbag unit, or expose it to impacts during refitting.*

b) *Tighten the airbag retaining bolt to the specified torque.*

c) *On completion, activate the airbag system as described in Section 19.*

20.3 Insert a flat-bladed screwdriver into the hole each side of the steering wheel boss...

20.4... to release the spring clip each side

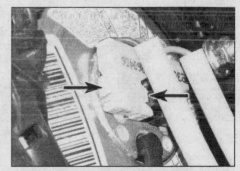

20.5 Squeeze together the clips and disconnect the wiring plugs

20.9 Remove the document holder or control unit as applicable

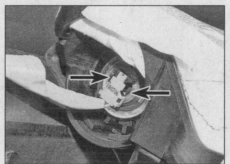

20.10 Squeeze together the clips and disconnect the wiring plug from each end of the airbag

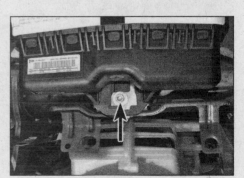

20.11 Passengers airbag retaining bolt

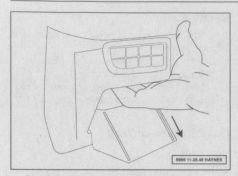

20.16 Pull the upper edge of the panel rearwards – LHD shown

Front seat airbags

14 Removal of the seat airbags requires the seat upholstery to be removed. This is a complex task, requiring patience and experience. Consequently, we recommend this is entrusted to a Fiat dealer or specialist.

Headlining airbags

15 On each side of the passenger cabin, a window airbag is fitted. The airbag runs from the lower part of the windscreen pillar to the C-pillar. To remove the airbag, the entire headlining must be removed. This task is outside the scope of the DIY'er, and therefore we recommend that the task be entrusted to a Fiat dealer or specialist.

Knee airbag

Removal

16 Open the drivers side facia storage compartment, then pull the upper edge of the facia panel rearwards to release the clips **(see illustration)**. Disconnect the wiring plugs as the panel is withdrawn.

17 Undo the 3 retaining bolts and release the knee airbag from position. Disconnect the wiring plugs as the airbag is withdrawn.

Refitting

18 Refitting is a reversal of removal, noting the following points:

a) *Do not strike the airbag, or expose it to impacts during refitting.*

b) *Tighten the airbag retaining bolts to the specified torque.*

c) *On completion, activate the airbag system as described in Section 19.*

Airbag control unit

Removal

19 Remove the centre console as described in Chapter 11 Section 24.

20 Unclip and remove the rear air ducts **(see illustration)**.

21 Where fitted, unclip the cover from above the control unit.

22 Disconnect the wiring plugs, undo the 3 retaining nuts, and remove the control unit **(see illustration)**.

Refitting

23 Refitting is a reversal of removal, tightening the retaining nuts to their specified torque.

Impact sensors

Front sensors

24 Remove the front bumper as described in Chapter 11 Section 6.

25 Move the horn and wiring to one side, then undo the bolts and remove the front wing/headlamp housing crossmember **(see illustration)**.

20.20 Unclip the rear air ducts

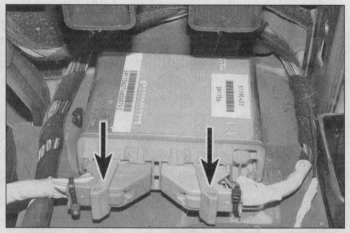

20.22 Lever over the catches and disconnect the control unit wiring plugs

20.25 The front wing/headlamp housing crossmember is secured by 4 bolts – left-hand bolts arrowed

20.26 Undo the bolt and remove the front sensor

20.29 Centre sensor beneath the console

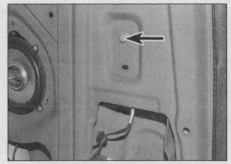

20.32a Undo the retaining bolt...

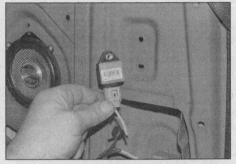

20.32b... and withdraw the sensor

26 Undo the retaining bolt, and remove the sensor. Recover the spacer, and disconnect the wiring plug as the sensor is withdrawn **(see illustration)**.
27 Refitting is a reversal of removal, tightening the sensor retaining bolt to the specified torque.

Centre sensor

28 Remove the centre console as describe in Chapter 11 Section 24.
29 Undo the retaining nuts and manoeuvre the sensor from place **(see illustration)**. Disconnect the wiring plug as the sensor is withdrawn.
30 Refitting is a reversal of removal, noting the arrow on the sensor must point to the front.

Side sensors

3-door models

31 Remove the relevant rear side panel as described in Chapter 11 Section 23.
32 Undo the retaining bolt, and remove the sensor **(see illustrations)**. Disconnect the wiring plug as the sensor is withdrawn.
33 Refitting is a reversal of removal, tightening the sensor retaining bolts to the specified torque.

5-door models

34 Remove the lower B-pillar trim panel as described in Chapter 11 Section 23.
35 Undo the retaining bolt, and remove the sensor. Disconnect the wiring plug as the sensor is withdrawn.
36 Refitting is a reversal of removal, tightening the sensor retaining bolt to the specified torque.

Rotary contact unit (clockspring)

37 The rotary contact unit is integral with the steering column combination switch assembly. Refer to Section 5.

21 Parking obstacle detection system – general information and component renewal

General information

1 Available as an option, the parking assistance system is an ultrasonic parking aid. The system uses sensors in the rear bumpers to transmit a signal which then bounces off any objects in range behind the car. The sensors receive the reflected signal, and the control unit can then calculate the distance of the object from the car. The system works at speeds up to 9 mph. The resulting distance information is conveyed to the driver by audio signal.
2 There are four sensors in the rear bumper. The control unit is located behind the left-hand side of the luggage compartment. The audio warning unit is are located in the instrument panel.

Electronic control module

Removal

3 Working in the luggage compartment, undo the 2 retaining screws and lower the control unit from the underside of the left-hand parcel shelf support.
4 Disconnect the control unit wiring plugs.

Refitting

5 Refitting is a reversal of removal.

Ultrasonic sensors

Removal

6 Remove the rear bumper as described in Chapter 11 Section 6.
7 Disconnect the wiring plug from the sensors.
8 Spread apart the retaining clips and withdraw the sensors from the bumper.

Refitting

9 Refitting is a reversal of removal.

22 Body computer – removal and refitting

Removal

1 Remove the passengers side glovebox as described in Chapter 11 Section 25.
2 Drill out the rivet, undo the bolts and remove the anti-tamper shield.
3 Note their fitted positions, then disconnect the various wiring plugs from the rear face of the body computer.
4 Undo the 3 retaining bolts, and manoeuvre the body computer from place. Disconnect the wiring plugs on the front face of the unit as they become accessible.

Refitting

5 Refitting is a reversal of removal.

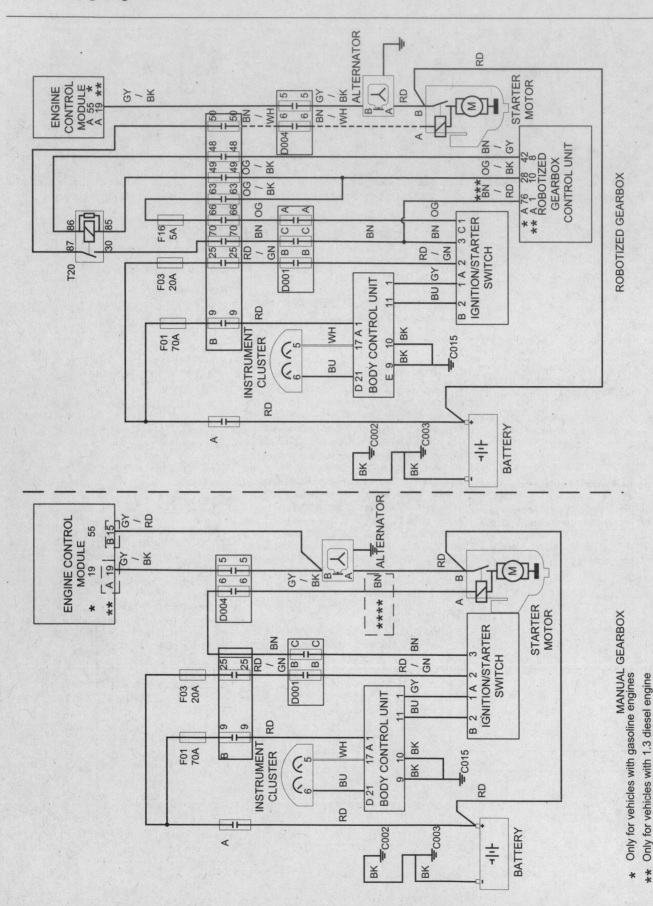

Starting and Charging from 10.08

* Only for vehicles with gasoline engines

** Only for vehicles with 1.3 diesel engine

*** For vehicles with 1.3 diesel engine the wire color is BN

****The wire color can be BN/WH according to equipment

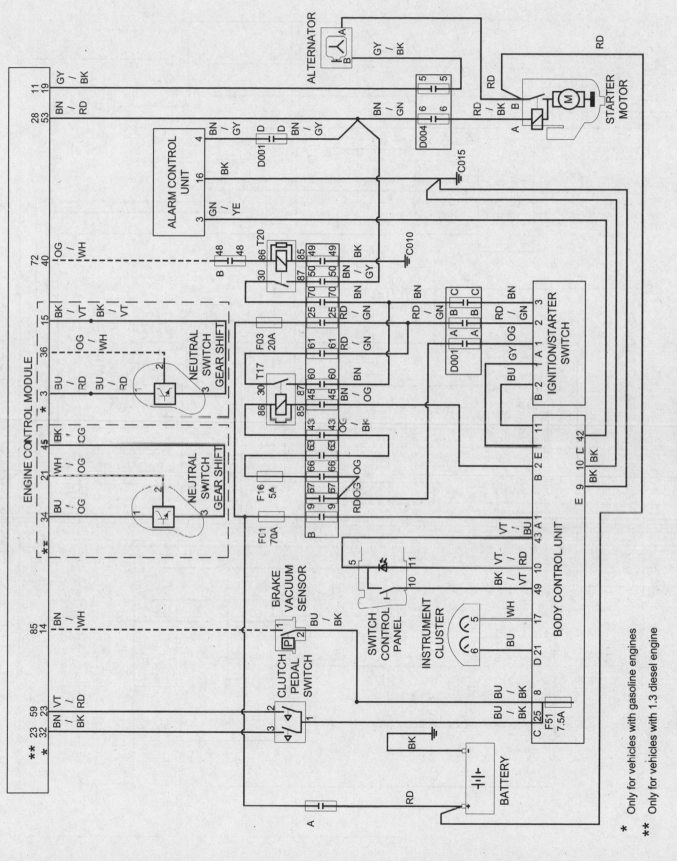

Starting and Charging Start&Stop euro 5

*   Only for vehicles with gasoline engines

**   Only for vehicles with 1.3 diesel engine

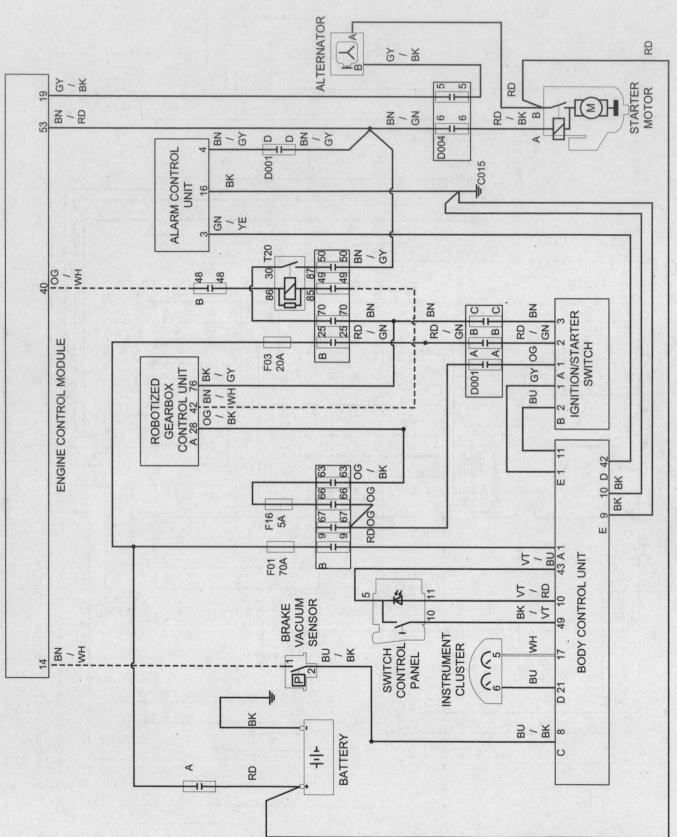

Starting and Charging Start&Stop euro 5 robotized

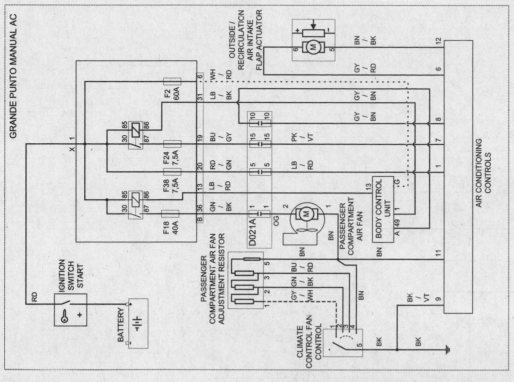

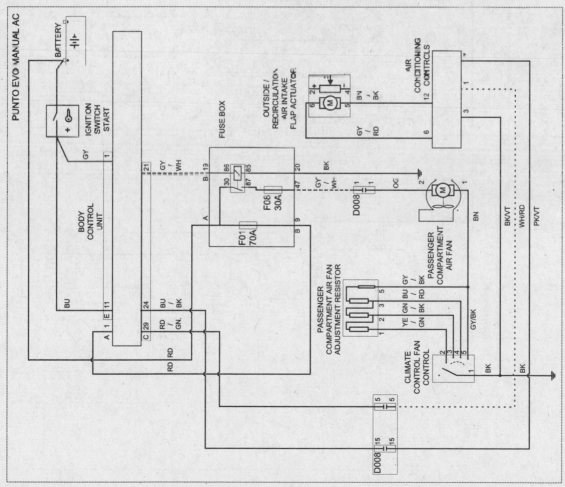

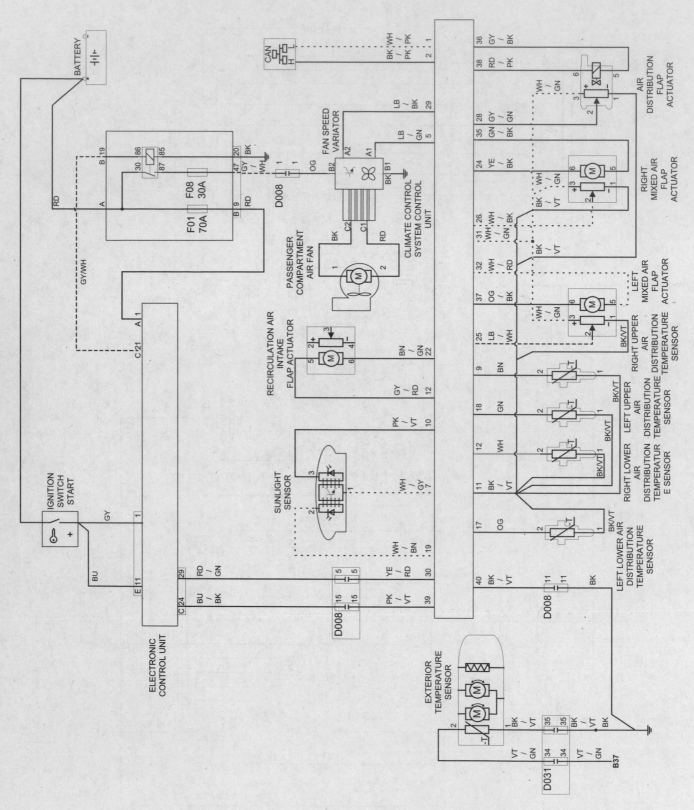

AC Automatic

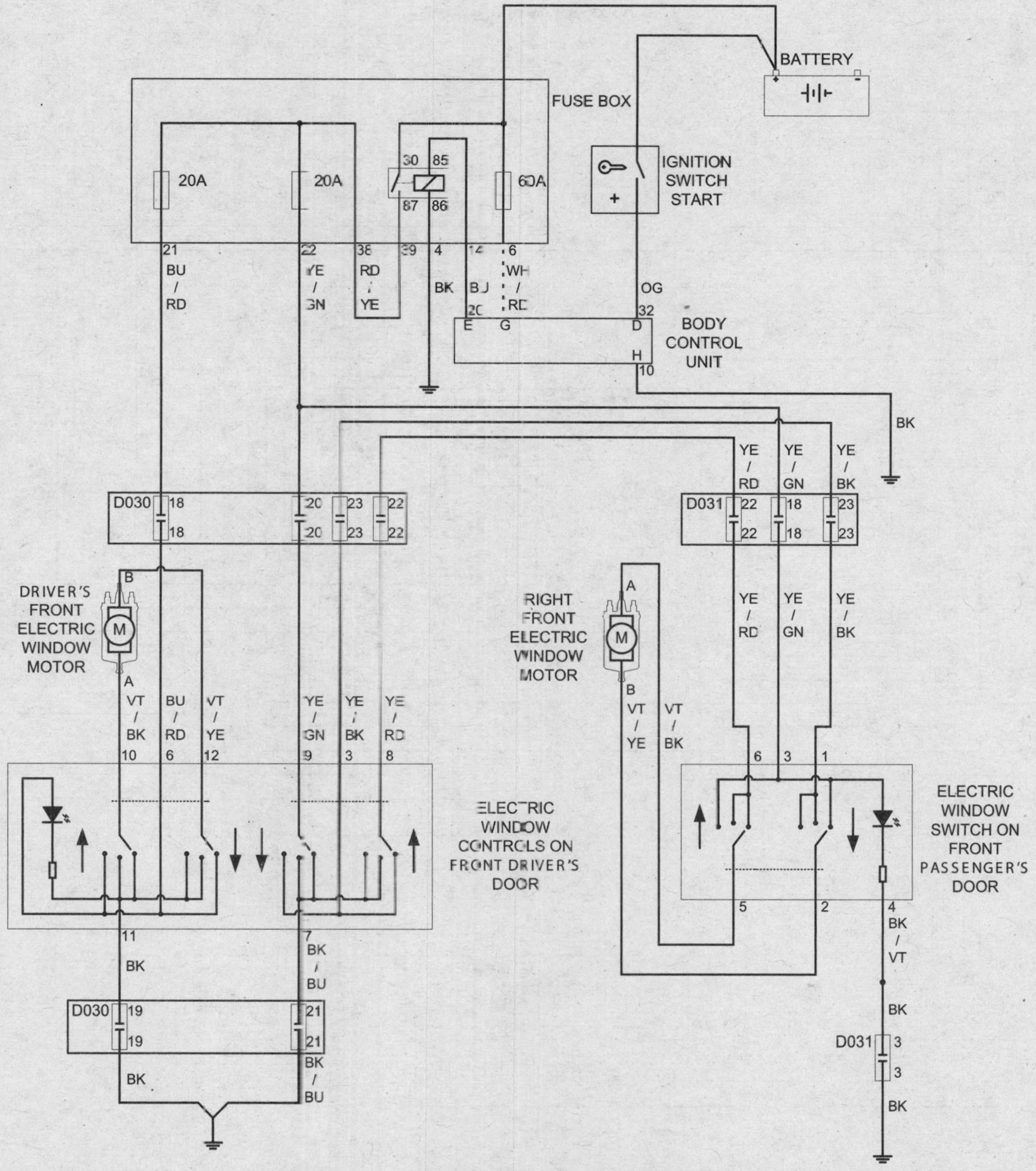

BATTERY

IGNITION SWITCH START

FUSE BOX

BODY CONTROL UNIT

60A

20A

20A

BK

OG

32

D

E

G

H

10

6

WH / RD

4

BK / BJ

20

BK / YE

30 85

87 86

3E

RD / YE

22

YE / GN

21

BU / RD

23 23
YE BK

18 18
YE GN

22 22
YE RD

D031

YE / BK

YE / GN

YE / RD

A   M   B

VT VT BK
YE YE

RIGHT FRONT ELECTRIC WINDOW MOTOR

ELECTRIC WINDOW SWITCH ON FRONT PASSENGER'S DOOR

1

3

6

2

5

4 BK VT

BK

3 3

D031

BK

22 22

23 23

20 20

D030

18 18

YE / RD
8

YE / BK
3

YE / GN
9

VT / YE
12

BU / RD
6

VT / BK
10

B   M   A

VT BU VT
BK RD BK
YE

DRIVER'S FRONT ELECTRIC WINDOW MOTOR

ELECTRIC WINDOW CONTROLS ON FRONT DRIVER'S DOOR

7 BK / BU

21 21
BK BU

11 BK

19 19
D030

BK

Power Windows for 3 doors

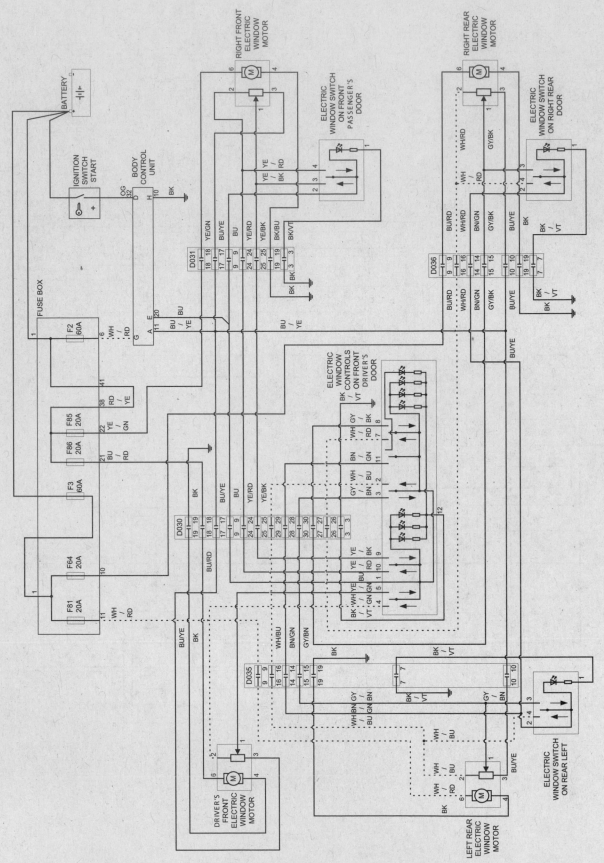

Power Windows for 5 doors

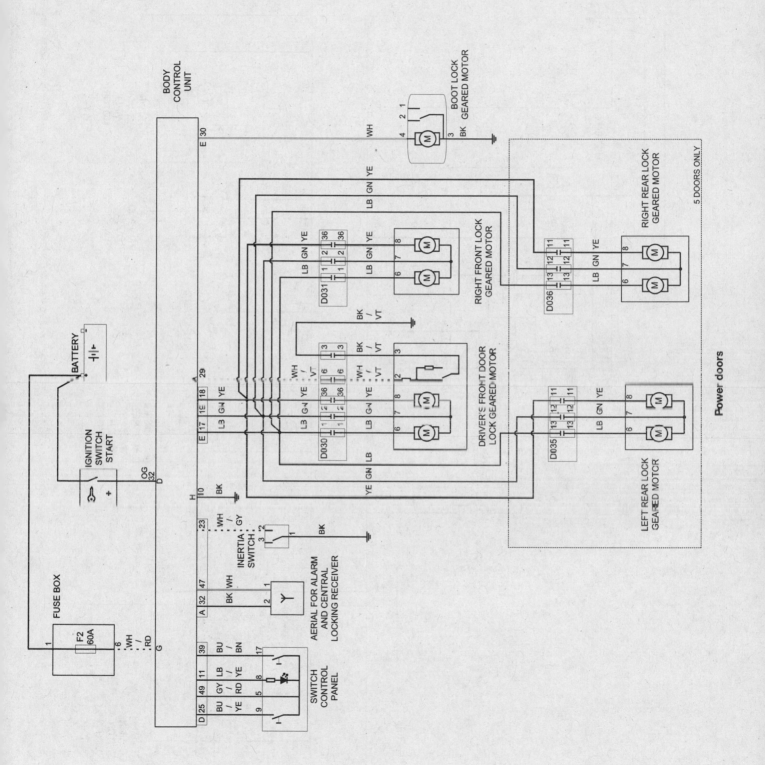

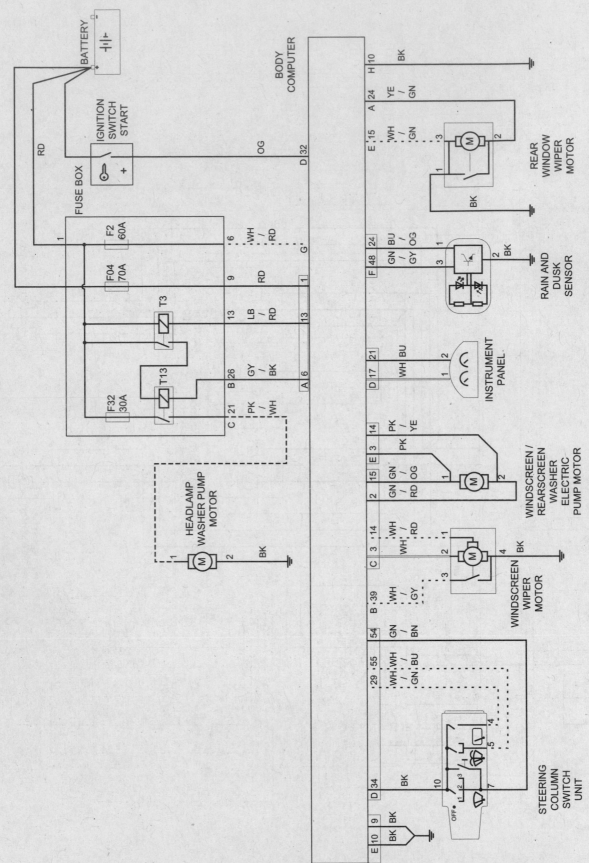

Wiper and washer

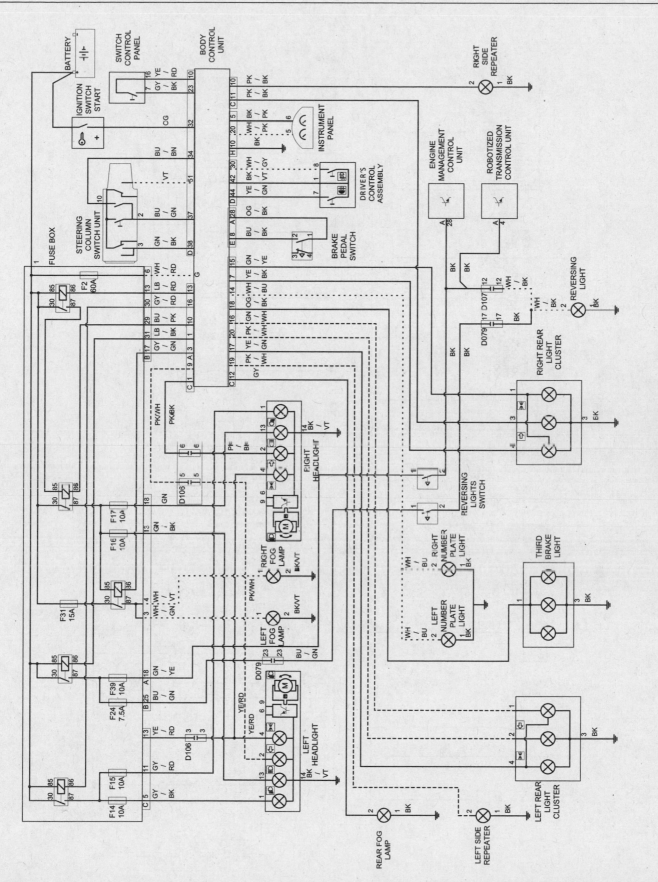

Exterior lights

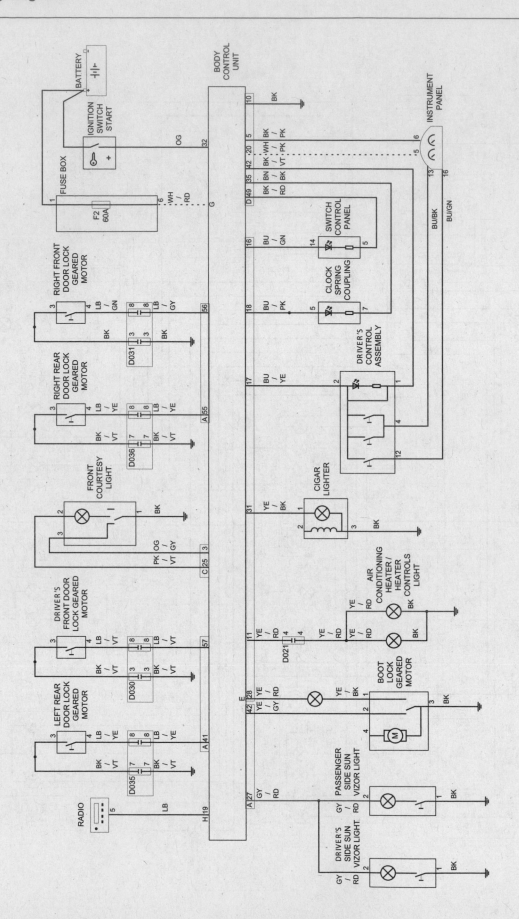

Interior lights

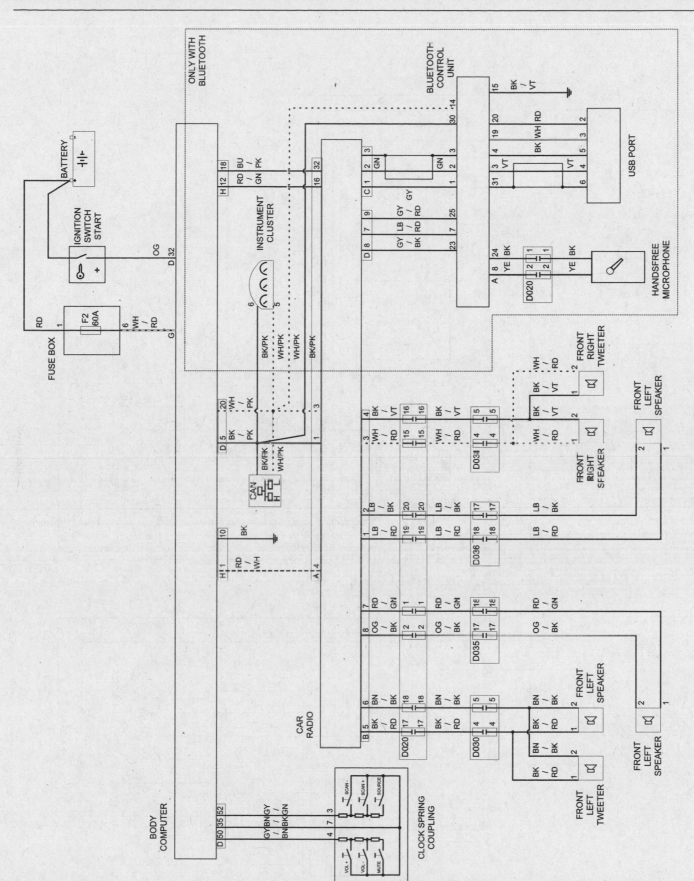

Radio, basic with handsfree

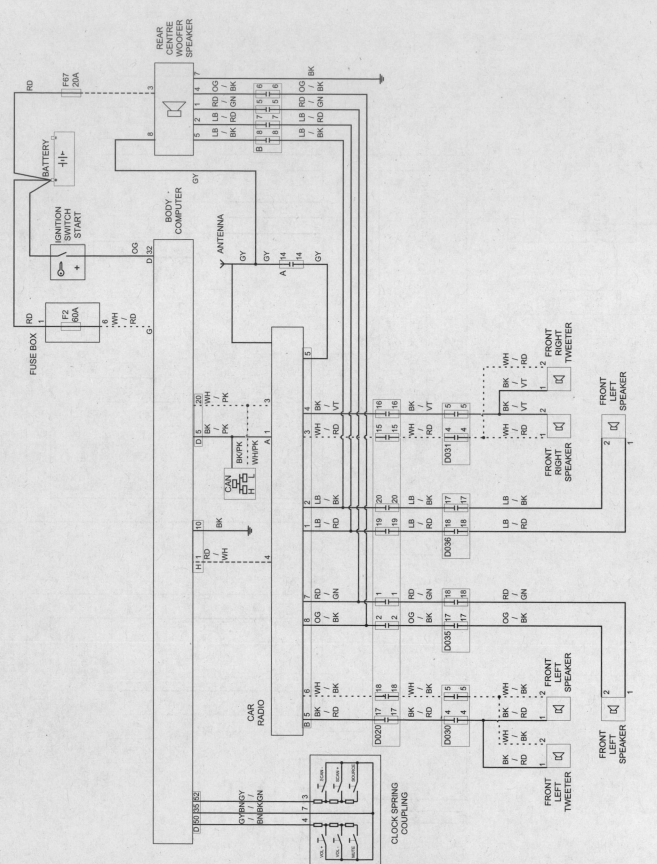

Radio hi-fi

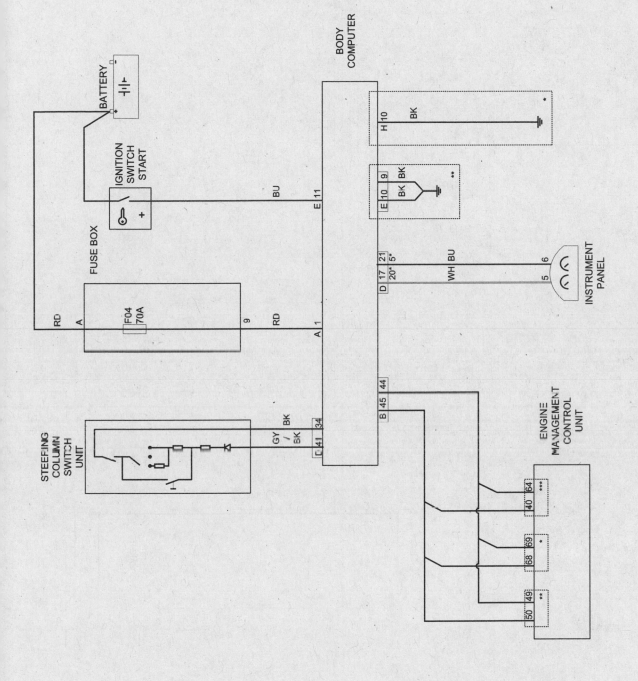

Cruise control

* - ONLY FOR 1.3 ENGINE
** - ONLY FOR 1.2 AND 1.4 ENGINE
*** - ONLY FOR 1.2 ENGINE

Reference REF•1

Dimensions and weights . . . . **REF•1**
Fuel economy. . . . . **REF•2**
Conversion factors . . . . **REF•6**
Vehicle jacking and support . . . . **REF•7**
Buying spare parts . . . . **REF•7**
General repair procedures . . . . **REF•8**

Vehicle identification . . . . **REF•9**
Tools and working facilities . . . . **REF•10**
MOT test checks . . . . **REF•12**
Fault finding . . . . **REF•16**
Index. . . . . **REF•22**

Dimensions and weights

Note: *All figures are approximate, and may vary according to model. Refer to manufacturer's data for exact figures.*

Dimensions

Overall length:
   Grande Punto . . . . 4030 mm
   Punto Evo/Punto 2012 MY . . . . 4065 mm
Overall width (excluding mirrors) . . . . 1687 mm
Overall height . . . . 1490 mm
Wheelbase . . . . 2510 mm

Weights

Unladen (fuel tank 90% full) . . . . 1015 to 1075 kg
Gross vehicle weight . . . . 1495 to 1635 kg
Maximum load on roof:
   Grande Punto . . . . 75 kg
   Punto Evo/Punto 2012 MY . . . . 50 kg

Fuel economy

Although depreciation is still the biggest part of the cost of motoring for most car owners, the cost of fuel is more immediately noticeable. These pages give some tips on how to get the best fuel economy.

Working it out

Manufacturer's figures

Car manufacturers are required by law to provide fuel consumption information on all new vehicles sold. These 'official' figures are obtained by simulating various driving conditions on a rolling road or a test track. Real life conditions are different, so the fuel consumption actually achieved may not bear much resemblance to the quoted figures.

How to calculate it

Many cars now have trip computers which will

display fuel consumption, both instantaneous and average. Refer to the owner's handbook for details of how to use these.

To calculate consumption yourself (and maybe to check that the trip computer is accurate), proceed as follows.

1. Fill up with fuel and note the mileage, or zero the trip recorder.
2. Drive as usual until you need to fill up again.
3. Note the amount of fuel required to refill the tank, and the mileage covered since the previous fill-up.
4. Divide the mileage by the amount of fuel used to obtain the consumption figure.

For example:

    Mileage at first fill-up (a) = 27,903
    Mileage at second fill-up (b) = 28,346
    Mileage covered (b - a) = 443
    Fuel required at second fill-up = 48.6 litres

The half-completed changeover to metric units in the UK means that we buy our fuel

in litres, measure distances in miles and talk about fuel consumption in miles per gallon. There are two ways round this: the first is to convert the litres to gallons before doing the calculation (by dividing by 4.546, or see Table 1). So in the example:

    48.6 litres ÷ 4.546 = 10.69 gallons
    443 miles ÷ 10.69 gallons = 41.4 mpg

The second way is to calculate the consumption in miles per litre, then multiply that figure by 4.546 (or see Table 2).

So in the example, fuel consumption is:

    443 miles ÷ 48.6 litres = 9.1 mpl
    9.1 mpl x 4.546 = 41.4 mpg

The rest of Europe expresses fuel consumption in litres of fuel required to travel 100 km (l/100 km). For interest, the conversions are given in Table 3. In practice it doesn't matter what units you use, provided you know what your normal consumption is and can spot if it's getting better or worse.

Table 1: conversion of litres to Imperial gallons

litres	1	2	3	4	5	10	20	30	40	50	60	70
gallons	0.22	0.44	0.66	0.88	1.10	2.24	4.49	6.73	8.98	11.22	13.47	15.71

Table 2: conversion of miles per litre to miles per gallon

miles per litre	5	6	7	8	9	10	11	12	13	14
miles per gallon	23	27	32	36	41	46	50	55	59	64

Table 3: conversion of litres per 100 km to miles per gallon

litres per 100 km	4	4.5	5	5.5	6	6.5	7	8	9	10
miles per gallon	71	63	56	51	47	43	40	35	31	28

Maintenance

A well-maintained car uses less fuel and creates less pollution. In particular:

Filters

Change air and fuel filters at the specified intervals.

Oil

Use a good quality oil of the lowest viscosity specified by the vehicle manufacturer (see *Lubricants and fluids*). Check the level often and be careful not to overfill.

Spark plugs

When applicable, renew at the specified intervals.

Tyres

Check tyre pressures regularly. Under-inflated tyres have an increased rolling resistance. It is generally safe to use the higher pressures specified for full load conditions even when not fully laden, but keep an eye on the centre band of tread for signs of wear due to over-inflation.

When buying new tyres, consider the 'fuel saving' models which most manufacturers include in their ranges.

Driving style

Acceleration

Acceleration uses more fuel than driving at a steady speed. The best technique with modern cars is to accelerate reasonably briskly to the desired speed, changing up through the gears as soon as possible without making the engine labour.

Air conditioning

Air conditioning absorbs quite a bit of energy from the engine – typically 3 kW (4 hp) or so. The effect on fuel consumption is at its worst in slow traffic. Switch it off when not required.

Anticipation

Drive smoothly and try to read the traffic flow so as to avoid unnecessary acceleration and braking.

Automatic transmission

When accelerating in an automatic, avoid depressing the throttle so far as to make the transmission hold onto lower gears at higher speeds. Don't use the 'Sport' setting, if applicable.

When stationary with the engine running, select 'N' or 'P'. When moving, keep your left foot away from the brake.

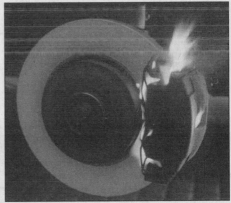

Braking

Braking converts the car's energy of motion into heat – essentially, it is wasted. Obviously some braking is always going to be necessary, but with good anticipation it is surprising how much can be avoided, especially on routes that you know well.

Carshare

Consider sharing lifts to work or to the shops. Even once a week will make a difference.

Electrical loads

Electricity is 'fuel' too; the alternator which charges the battery does so by converting some of the engine's energy of motion into electrical energy. The more electrical accessories are in use, the greater the load on the alternator. Switch off big consumers like the heated rear window when not required.

Freewheeling

Freewheeling (coasting) in neutral with the engine switched off is dangerous. The effort required to operate power-assisted brakes and steering increases when the engine is not running, with a potential lack of control in emergency situations.

In any case, modern fuel injection systems automatically cut off the engine's fuel supply on the overrun (moving and in gear, but with the accelerator pedal released).

Gadgets

Bolt-on devices claiming to save fuel have been around for nearly as long as the motor car itself. Those which worked were rapidly adopted as standard equipment by the vehicle manufacturers. Others worked only in certain situations, or saved fuel only at the expense of unacceptable effects on performance, driveability or the life of engine components.

The most effective fuel saving gadget is the driver's right foot.

Journey planning

Combine (eg) a trip to the supermarket with a visit to the recycling centre and the DIY store, rather than making separate journeys.

When possible choose a travelling time outside rush hours.

Load

The more heavily a car is laden, the greater the energy required to accelerate it to a given speed. Remove heavy items which you don't need to carry.

One load which is often overlooked is the contents of the fuel tank. A tankful of fuel (55 litres / 12 gallons) weighs 45 kg (100 lb) or so. Just half filling it may be worthwhile.

Lost?

At the risk of stating the obvious, if you're going somewhere new, have details of the route to hand. There's not much point in achieving record mpg if you also go miles out of your way.

Parking

If possible, carry out any reversing or turning manoeuvres when you arrive at a parking space so that you can drive straight out when you leave. Manoeuvering when the engine is cold uses a lot more fuel.

Driving around looking for free on-street parking may cost more in fuel than buying a car park ticket.

Premium fuel

Most major oil companies (and some supermarkets) have premium grades of fuel which are several pence a litre dearer than the standard grades. Reports vary, but the consensus seems to be that if these fuels improve economy at all, they do not do so by enough to justify their extra cost.

Roof rack

When loading a roof rack, try to produce a wedge shape with the narrow end at the front. Any cover should be securely fastened – if it flaps it's creating turbulence and absorbing energy.

Remove roof racks and boxes when not in use – they increase air resistance and can create a surprising amount of noise.

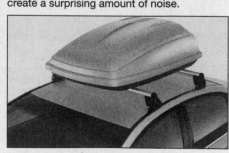

Short journeys

The engine is at its least efficient, and wear is highest, during the first few miles after a cold start. Consider walking, cycling or using public transport.

Speed

The engine is at its most efficient when running at a steady speed and load at the rpm where it develops maximum torque. (You can find this figure in the car's handbook.) For most cars this corresponds to between 55 and 65 mph in top gear.

Above the optimum cruising speed, fuel consumption starts to rise quite sharply. A car travelling at 80 mph will typically be using 30% more fuel than at 60 mph.

Supermarket fuel

It may be cheap but is it any good? In the UK all supermarket fuel must meet the relevant British Standard. The major oil companies will say that their branded fuels have better additive packages which may stop carbon and other deposits building up. A reasonable compromise might be to use one tank of branded fuel to three or four from the supermarket.

Switch off when stationary

Switch off the engine if you look like being stationary for more than 30 seconds or so. This is good for the environment as well as for your pocket. Be aware though that frequent restarts are hard on the battery and the starter motor.

Windows

Driving with the windows open increases air turbulence around the vehicle. Closing the windows promotes smooth airflow and

reduced resistance. The faster you go, the more significant this is.

And finally...

Driving techniques associated with good fuel economy tend to involve moderate acceleration and low top speeds. Be considerate to the needs of other road users who may need to make brisker progress; even if you do not agree with them this is not an excuse to be obstructive.

Safety must always take precedence over economy, whether it is a question of accelerating hard to complete an overtaking manoeuvre, killing your speed when confronted with a potential hazard or switching the lights on when it starts to get dark.

Conversion factors

Length (distance)

Inches (in)	x 25.4	= Millimetres (mm)	x 0.0394	=	Inches (in)
Feet (ft)	x 0.305	= Metres (m)	x 3.281	=	Feet (ft)
Miles	x 1.609	= Kilometres (km)	x 0.621	=	Miles

Volume (capacity)

Cubic inches (cu in; in³)	x 16.387	= Cubic centimetres (cc; cm³)	x 0.061	=	Cubic inches (cu in; in³)
Imperial pints (Imp pt)	x 0.568	= Litres (l)	x 1.76	=	Imperial pints (Imp pt)
Imperial quarts (Imp qt)	x 1.137	= Litres (l)	x 0.88	=	Imperial quarts (Imp qt)
Imperial quarts (Imp qt)	x 1.201	= US quarts (US qt)	x 0.833	=	Imperial quarts (Imp qt)
US quarts (US qt)	x 0.946	= Litres (l)	x 1.057	=	US quarts (US qt)
Imperial gallons (Imp gal)	x 4.546	= Litres (l)	x 0.22	=	Imperial gallons (Imp gal)
Imperial gallons (Imp gal)	x 1.201	= US gallons (US gal)	x 0.833	=	Imperial gallons (Imp gal)
US gallons (US gal)	x 3.785	= Litres (l)	x 0.264	=	US gallons (US gal)

Mass (weight)

Ounces (oz)	x 28.35	= Grams (g)	x 0.035	=	Ounces (oz)
Pounds (lb)	x 0.454	= Kilograms (kg)	x 2.205	=	Pounds (lb)

Force

Ounces-force (ozf; oz)	x 0.278	= Newtons (N)	x 3.6	=	Ounces-force (ozf; oz)
Pounds-force (lbf; lb)	x 4.448	= Newtons (N)	x 0.225	=	Pounds-force (lbf; lb)
Newtons (N)	x 0.1	= Kilograms-force (kgf; kg)	x 9.81	=	Newtons (N)

Pressure

Pounds-force per square inch (psi; lbf/in²; lb/in²)	x 0.070	= Kilograms-force per square centimetre (kgf/cm²; kg/cm²)	x 14.223	=	Pounds-force per square inch (psi; lbf/in²; lb/in²)
Pounds-force per square inch (psi; lbf/in²; lb/in²)	x 0.068	= Atmospheres (atm)	x 14.696	=	Pounds-force per square inch (psi; lbf/in²; lb/in²)
Pounds-force per square inch (psi; lbf/in²; lb/in²)	x 0.069	= Bars	x 14.5	=	Pounds-force per square inch (psi; lbf/in²; lb/in²)
Pounds-force per square inch (psi; lbf/in²; lb/in²)	x 6.895	= Kilopascals (kPa)	x 0.145	=	Pounds-force per square inch (psi; lbf/in²; lb/in²)
Kilopascals (kPa)	x 0.01	= Kilograms-force per square centimetre (kgf/cm²; kg/cm²)	x 98.1	=	Kilopascals (kPa)
Millibar (mbar)	x 100	= Pascals (Pa)	x 0.01	=	Millibar (mbar)
Millibar (mbar)	x 0.0145	= Pounds-force per square inch (psi; lbf/in²; lb/in²)	x 68.947	=	Millibar (mbar)
Millibar (mbar)	x 0.75	= Millimetres of mercury (mmHg)	x 1.333	=	Millibar (mbar)
Millibar (mbar)	x 0.401	= Inches of water (inH₂O)	x 2.491	=	Millibar (mbar)
Millimetres of mercury (mmHg)	x 0.535	= Inches of water (inH₂O)	x 1.868	=	Millimetres of mercury (mmHg)
Inches of water (inH₂O)	x 0.036	= Pounds-force per square inch (psi; lbf/in²; lb/in²)	x 27.68	=	Inches of water (inH₂O)

Torque (moment of force)

Pounds-force inches (lbf in; lb in)	x 1.152	= Kilograms-force centimetre (kgf cm; kg cm)	x 0.868	=	Pounds-force inches (lbf in; lb in)
Pounds-force inches (lbf in; lb in)	x 0.113	= Newton metres (Nm)	x 8.85	=	Pounds-force inches (lbf in; lb in)
Pounds-force inches (lbf in; lb in)	x 0.083	= Pounds-force feet (lbf ft; lb ft)	x 12	=	Pounds-force inches (lbf in; lb in)
Pounds-force feet (lbf ft; lb ft)	x 0.138	= Kilograms-force metres (kgf m; kg m)	x 7.233	=	Pounds-force feet (lbf ft; lb ft)
Pounds-force feet (lbf ft; lb ft)	x 1.356	= Newton metres (Nm)	x 0.738	=	Pounds-force feet (lbf ft; lb ft)
Newton metres (Nm)	x 0.102	= Kilograms-force metres (kgf m; kg m)	x 9.804	=	Newton metres (Nm)

Power

Horsepower (hp)	x 745.7	= Watts (W)	x 0.0013	=	Horsepower (hp)

Velocity (speed)

Miles per hour (miles/hr; mph)	x 1.609	= Kilometres per hour (km/hr; kph)	x 0.621	=	Miles per hour (miles/hr; mph)

Fuel consumption*

Miles per gallon, Imperial (mpg)	x 0.354	= Kilometres per litre (km/l)	x 2.825	=	Miles per gallon, Imperial (mpg)
Miles per gallon, US (mpg)	x 0.425	= Kilometres per litre (km/l)	x 2.352	=	Miles per gallon, US (mpg)

Temperature

Degrees Fahrenheit = (°C x 1.8) + 32   Degrees Celsius (Degrees Centigrade; °C) = (°F - 32) x 0.56

It is common practice to convert from miles per gallon (mpg) to litres/100 kilometres (l/100km), where mpg x l/100 km = 282

The jack supplied with the vehicle tool kit should only be used for changing the roadwheels – see "Wheel changing" at the front of this manual. When carrying out any other kind of work, raise the vehicle using a hydraulic trolley jack, and always supplement the jack with axle stands positioned under the vehicle jacking points.

When using a trolley jack or axle stands, always position the jack head or axle stand head under, or adjacent to one of the relevant wheel changing jacking points under the sills. Use a block of wood between the jack or axle stand and the sill (see illustration).

Do not attempt to jack the vehicle under the sump, final drive unit, or any of the suspension components.

Never work under, around, or near a raised vehicle, unless it is adequately supported in at least two places.

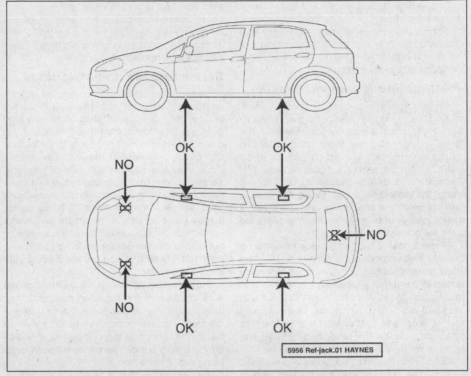

5956 Ref-jack.01 HAYNES

Reinforced jacking points are located at the front and rear of the sills each side of the car

Buying spare parts

Spare parts are available from many sources, including maker's appointed garages, accessory shops, and motor factors. To be sure of obtaining the correct parts, it will sometimes be necessary to quote the vehicle identification number. If possible, it can also be useful to take the old parts along for positive identification. Items such as starter motors and alternators may be available under a service exchange scheme – any parts returned should be clean.

Our advice regarding spare parts is as follows.

Officially appointed garages

This is the best source of parts which are peculiar to your car, and which are not otherwise generally available (eg, badges, interior trim, certain body panels, etc). It is also the only place at which you should buy parts if the vehicle is still under warranty.

Accessory shops

These are very good places to buy materials and components needed for the maintenance of your car (oil, air and fuel filters, light bulbs, drivebelts, greases, brake pads, touch-up paint, etc). Components of this nature sold by a reputable shop are of the same standard as those used by the car manufacturer.

Besides components, these shops also sell tools and general accessories, usually have convenient opening hours, charge lower prices, and can often be found close to home. Some accessory shops have parts counters where components needed for almost any repair job can be purchased or ordered.

Motor factors

Good factors will stock all the more important components which wear out comparatively quickly, and can sometimes supply individual components needed for the overhaul of a larger assembly (eg, brake seals and hydraulic parts, bearing shells, pistons, valves). They may also handle work such as cylinder block reboring, crankshaft regrinding, etc.

Tyre and exhaust specialists

These outlets may be independent, or members of a local or national chain. They frequently offer competitive prices when compared with a main dealer or local garage, but it will pay to obtain several quotes before making a decision. When researching prices, also ask what 'extras' may be added – for instance fitting a new valve and balancing the wheel are both commonly charged on top of the price of a new tyre.

Other sources

Beware of parts or materials obtained from market stalls, car boot sales, internet auction sites or similar outlets. Such items are not invariably sub-standard, but there is little chance of compensation if they do prove unsatisfactory. In the case of safety-critical components such as brake pads, there is the risk not only of financial loss, but also of an accident causing injury or death

Second-hand components or assemblies obtained from a car breaker can be a good buy in some circumstances, but this sort of purchase is best made by the experienced DIY mechanic.

Whenever servicing, repair or overhaul work is carried out on the car or its components, observe the following procedures and instructions. This will assist in carrying out the operation efficiently and to a professional standard of workmanship.

Joint mating faces and gaskets

When separating components at their mating faces, never insert screwdrivers or similar implements into the joint between the faces in order to prise them apart. This can cause severe damage which results in oil leaks, coolant leaks, etc upon reassembly. Separation is usually achieved by tapping along the joint with a soft-faced hammer in order to break the seal. However, note that this method may not be suitable where dowels are used for component location.

Where a gasket is used between the mating faces of two components, a new one must be fitted on reassembly; fit it dry unless otherwise stated in the repair procedure. Make sure that the mating faces are clean and dry, with all traces of old gasket removed. When cleaning a joint face, use a tool which is unlikely to score or damage the face, and remove any burrs or nicks with an oilstone or fine file.

Make sure that tapped holes are cleaned with a pipe cleaner, and keep them free of jointing compound, if this is being used, unless specifically instructed otherwise.

Ensure that all orifices, channels or pipes are clear, and blow through them, preferably using compressed air.

Oil seals

Oil seals can be removed by levering them out with a wide flat-bladed screwdriver or similar implement. Alternatively, a number of self-tapping screws may be screwed into the seal, and these used as a purchase for pliers or some similar device in order to pull the seal free.

Whenever an oil seal is removed from its working location, either individually or as part of an assembly, it should be renewed.

The very fine sealing lip of the seal is easily damaged, and will not seal if the surface it contacts is not completely clean and free from scratches, nicks or grooves. If the original sealing surface of the component cannot be restored, and the manufacturer has not made provision for slight relocation of the seal relative to the sealing surface, the component should be renewed.

Protect the lips of the seal from any surface which may damage them in the course of fitting. Use tape or a conical sleeve where possible. Where indicated, lubricate the seal lips with oil before fitting and, on dual-lipped seals, fill the space between the lips with grease.

Unless otherwise stated, oil seals must be fitted with their sealing lips toward the lubricant to be sealed.

Use a tubular drift or block of wood of the appropriate size to install the seal and, if the seal housing is shouldered, drive the seal down to the shoulder. If the seal housing is unshouldered, the seal should be fitted with its face flush with the housing top face (unless otherwise instructed).

Screw threads and fastenings

Seized nuts, bolts and screws are quite a common occurrence where corrosion has set in, and the use of penetrating oil or releasing fluid will often overcome this problem if the offending item is soaked for a while before attempting to release it. The use of an impact driver may also provide a means of releasing such stubborn fastening devices, when used in conjunction with the appropriate screwdriver bit or socket. If none of these methods works, it may be necessary to resort to the careful application of heat, or the use of a hacksaw or nut splitter device. Before resorting to extreme methods, check that you are not dealing with a left-hand thread!

Studs are usually removed by locking two nuts together on the threaded part, and then using a spanner on the lower nut to unscrew the stud. Studs or bolts which have broken off below the surface of the component in which they are mounted can sometimes be removed using a stud extractor.

Always ensure that a blind tapped hole is completely free from oil, grease, water or other fluid before installing the bolt or stud. Failure to do this could cause the housing to crack due to the hydraulic action of the bolt or stud as it is screwed in.

For some screw fastenings, notably cylinder head bolts or nuts, torque wrench settings are no longer specified for the latter stages of tightening, "angle-tightening" being called up instead. Typically, a fairly low torque wrench setting will be applied to the bolts/nuts in the correct sequence, followed by one or more stages of tightening through specified angles.

When checking or retightening a nut or bolt to a specified torque setting, slacken the nut or bolt by a quarter of a turn, and then retighten to the specified setting. However, this should not be attempted where angular tightening has been used.

Locknuts, locktabs and washers

Any fastening which will rotate against a component or housing during tightening should always have a washer between it and the relevant component or housing.

Spring or split washers should always be renewed when they are used to lock a critical component such as a big-end bearing retaining bolt or nut. Locktabs which are folded over to retain a nut or bolt should always be renewed.

Self-locking nuts can be re-used in non-critical areas, providing resistance can be felt when the locking portion passes over the bolt or stud thread. However, it should be noted that self-locking stiffnuts tend to lose their effectiveness after long periods of use, and should then be renewed as a matter of course.

Split pins must always be replaced with new ones of the correct size for the hole.

When thread-locking compound is found on the threads of a fastener which is to be re-used, it should be cleaned off with a wire brush and solvent, and fresh compound applied on reassembly.

Special tools

Some repair procedures in this manual entail the use of special tools such as a press, two or three-legged pullers, spring compressors, etc. Wherever possible, suitable readily-available alternatives to the manufacturer's special tools are described, and are shown in use. In some instances, where no alternative is possible, it has been necessary to resort to the use of a manufacturer's tool, and this has been done for reasons of safety as well as the efficient completion of the repair operation. Unless you are highly-skilled and have a thorough understanding of the procedures described, never attempt to bypass the use of any special tool when the procedure described specifies its use. Not only is there a very great risk of personal injury, but expensive damage could be caused to the components involved.

Environmental considerations

When disposing of used engine oil, brake fluid, antifreeze, etc, give due consideration to any detrimental environmental effects. Do not, for instance, pour any of the above liquids down drains into the general sewage system, or onto the ground to soak away. Many local council refuse tips provide a facility for waste oil disposal, as do some garages. You can find your nearest disposal point by calling the Environment Agency on 08708 506 506 or by visiting www.oilbankline.org.uk.

Note: It is illegal and anti-social to dump oil down the drain. To find the location of your local oil recycling bank, call 08708 506 506 or visit www.oilbankline.org.uk.

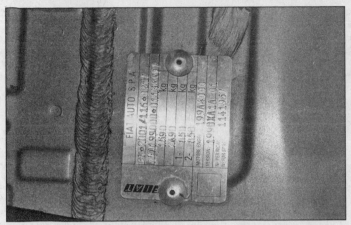

Vehicle identification plate in the luggage compartment

VIN plate on the right-hand front floor panel

Modifications are a continuing and unpublicised process in vehicle manufacture, quite apart from major model changes. Spare parts manuals and lists are compiled upon a numerical basis, the individual vehicle identification numbers being essential to correct identification of the component concerned.

When ordering spare parts, always give as much information as possible. Quote the car model, year of manufacture, body and engine numbers as appropriate.

The vehicle identification plate is situated at the left-hand side of the luggage compartment floor **(see illustration)**. It gives the VIN (vehicle identification number), vehicle weight information, engine type, bodywork version and spare parts number. The bodywork paint identification plate is located on the left-hand tailgate pillar, and gives the paint manufacturer, colour name, Fiat colour code, and respray/touch-up colour code. The VIN is repeated on a plate attached to the right-hand front floor panel, adjacent to the front seat **(see illustration)**.

The engine number is stamped on the front of the cylinder block **(see illustration)**.

The engine number is on the front of the cylinder block (exhaust manifold remove for clarity)

Introduction

A selection of good tools is a fundamental requirement for anyone contemplating the maintenance and repair of a motor vehicle. For the owner who does not possess any, their purchase will prove a considerable expense, offsetting some of the savings made by doing-it-yourself. However, provided that the tools purchased meet the relevant national safety standards and are of good quality, they will last for many years and prove an extremely worthwhile investment.

To help the average owner to decide which tools are needed to carry out the various tasks detailed in this manual, we have compiled three lists of tools under the following headings: *Maintenance and minor repair, Repair and overhaul*, and *Special*. Newcomers to practical mechanics should start off with the *Maintenance and minor repair* tool kit, and confine themselves to the simpler jobs around the vehicle. Then, as confidence and experience grow, more difficult tasks can be undertaken, with extra tools being purchased as, and when, they are needed. In this way, a *Maintenance and minor repair* tool kit can be built up into a *Repair and overhaul* tool kit over a considerable period of time, without any major cash outlays. The experienced do-it-yourselfer will have a tool kit good enough for most repair and overhaul procedures, and will add tools from the *Special* category when it is felt that the expense is justified by the amount of use to which these tools will be put.

Maintenance and minor repair tool kit

The tools given in this list should be considered as a minimum requirement if routine maintenance, servicing and minor repair operations are to be undertaken. We recommend the purchase of combination spanners (ring one end, open-ended the other); although more expensive than open-ended ones, they do give the advantages of both types of spanner.

☐ *Combination spanners:*
Metric - 8 to 19 mm inclusive
☐ *Adjustable spanner - 35 mm jaw (approx.)*
☐ *Spark plug spanner (with rubber insert) - petrol models*
☐ *Spark plug gap adjustment tool - petrol models*
☐ *Set of feeler gauges*
☐ *Brake bleed nipple spanner*
☐ *Screwdrivers:*
Flat blade - 100 mm long x 6 mm dia
Cross blade - 100 mm long x 6 mm dia
Torx - various sizes (not all vehicles)
☐ *Combination pliers*
☐ *Hacksaw (junior)*
☐ *Tyre pump*
☐ *Tyre pressure gauge*
☐ *Oil can*
☐ *Oil filter removal tool (if applicable)*
☐ *Fine emery cloth*
☐ *Wire brush (small)*
☐ *Funnel (medium size)*
☐ *Sump drain plug key (not all vehicles)*

Repair and overhaul tool kit

These tools are virtually essential for anyone undertaking any major repairs to a motor vehicle, and are additional to those given in the *Maintenance and minor repair* list. Included in this list is a comprehensive set of sockets. Although these are expensive, they will be found invaluable as they are so versatile - particularly if various drives are included in the set. We recommend the half-inch square-drive type, as this can be used with most proprietary torque wrenches.

The tools in this list will sometimes need to be supplemented by tools from the *Special* list:

☐ *Sockets to cover range in previous list (including Torx sockets)*
☐ *Reversible ratchet drive (for use with sockets)*
☐ *Extension piece, 250 mm (for use with sockets)*
☐ *Universal joint (for use with sockets)*
☐ *Flexible handle or sliding T "breaker bar" (for use with sockets)*
☐ *Torque wrench (for use with sockets)*
☐ *Self-locking grips*
☐ *Ball pein hammer*
☐ *Soft-faced mallet (plastic or rubber)*
☐ *Screwdrivers:*
Flat blade - long & sturdy, short (chubby), and narrow (electrician's) types
Cross blade – long & sturdy, and short (chubby) types
☐ *Pliers:*
Long-nosed
Side cutters (electrician's)
Circlip (internal and external)
☐ *Cold chisel - 25 mm*
☐ *Scriber*
☐ *Scraper*
☐ *Centre-punch*
☐ *Pin punch*
☐ *Hacksaw*
☐ *Brake hose clamp*
☐ *Brake/clutch bleeding kit*
☐ *Selection of twist drills*
☐ *Steel rule/straight-edge*
☐ *Allen keys (inc. splined/Torx type)*
☐ *Selection of files*
☐ *Wire brush*
☐ *Axle stands*
☐ *Jack (strong trolley or hydraulic type)*
☐ *Light with extension lead*
☐ *Universal electrical multi-meter*

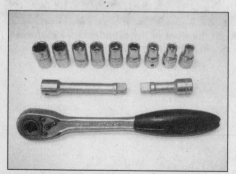

Sockets and reversible ratchet drive

Brake bleeding kit

Torx key, socket and bit

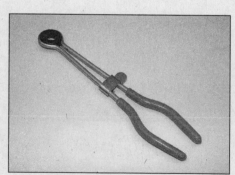

Hose clamp

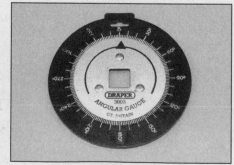

Angular-tightening gauge

Special tools

The tools in this list are those which are not used regularly, are expensive to buy, or which need to be used in accordance with their manufacturers' instructions. Unless relatively difficult mechanical jobs are undertaken frequently, it will not be economic to buy many of these tools. Where this is the case, you could consider clubbing together with friends (or joining a motorists' club) to make a joint purchase, or borrowing the tools against a deposit from a local garage or tool hire specialist.

The following list contains only those tools and instruments freely available to the public, and not those special tools produced by the vehicle manufacturer specifically for its dealer network. You will find occasional references to these manufacturers' special tools in the text of this manual. Generally, an alternative method of doing the job without the vehicle manufacturers' special tool is given. However, sometimes there is no alternative to using them. Where this is the case and the relevant tool cannot be bought or borrowed, you will have to entrust the work to a dealer.

☐ *Angular-tightening gauge*
☐ *Valve spring compressor*
☐ *Valve grinding tool*
☐ *Piston ring compressor*
☐ *Piston ring removal/installation tool*
☐ *Cylinder bore hone*
☐ *Balljoint separator*
☐ *Coil spring compressors (where applicable)*
☐ *Two/three-legged hub and bearing puller*
☐ *Impact screwdriver*
☐ *Micrometer and/or vernier calipers*
☐ *Dial gauge*
☐ *Tachometer*
☐ *Fault code reader*
☐ *Cylinder compression gauge*
☐ *Hand-operated vacuum pump and gauge*
☐ *Clutch plate alignment set*
☐ *Brake shoe steady spring cup removal tool*
☐ *Bush and bearing removal/installation set*
☐ *Stud extractors*
☐ *Tap and die set*
☐ *Lifting tackle*

Buying tools

Reputable motor accessory shops and superstores often offer excellent quality tools at discount prices, so it pays to shop around.

Remember, you don't have to buy the most expensive items on the shelf, but it is always advisable to steer clear of the very cheap tools. Beware of 'bargains' offered on market stalls, on-line or at car boot sales. There are plenty of good tools around at reasonable prices, but always aim to purchase items which meet the relevant national safety standards. If in doubt, ask the proprietor or manager of the shop for advice before making a purchase.

Care and maintenance of tools

Having purchased a reasonable tool kit, it is necessary to keep the tools in a clean and serviceable condition. After use, always wipe off any dirt, grease and metal particles using a clean, dry cloth, before putting the tools away. Never leave them lying around after they have been used. A simple tool rack on the garage or workshop wall for items such as screwdrivers and pliers is a good idea. Store all normal spanners and sockets in a metal box. Any measuring instruments, gauges, meters, etc, must be carefully stored where they cannot be damaged or become rusty.

Take a little care when tools are used. Hammer heads inevitably become marked, and screwdrivers lose the keen edge on their blades from time to time. A little timely attention with emery cloth or a file will soon restore items like this to a good finish.

Working facilities

Not to be forgotten when discussing tools is the workshop itself. If anything more than routine maintenance is to be carried out, a suitable working area becomes essential.

It is appreciated that many an owner-mechanic is forced by circumstances to remove an engine or similar item without the benefit of a garage or workshop. Having done this, any repairs should always be done under the cover of a roof.

Wherever possible, any dismantling should be done on a clean, flat workbench or table at a suitable working height.

Any workbench needs a vice; one with a jaw opening of 100 mm is suitable for most jobs. As mentioned previously, some clean dry storage space is also required for tools, as well as for any lubricants, cleaning fluids, touch-up paints etc, which become necessary.

Another item which may be required, and which has a much more general usage, is an electric drill with a chuck capacity of at least 8 mm. This, together with a good range of twist drills, is virtually essential for fitting accessories.

Last, but not least, always keep a supply of old newspapers and clean, lint-free rags available, and try to keep any working area as clean as possible.

Micrometers

Dial test indicator ("dial gauge")

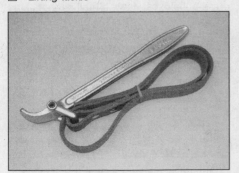
Oil filter removal tool (strap wrench type)

Compression tester

Bearing puller

This is a guide to getting your vehicle through the MOT test. Obviously it will not be possible to examine the vehicle to the same standard as the professional MOT tester. However, working through the following checks will enable you to identify any problem areas before submitting the vehicle for the test.

It has only been possible to summarise the test requirements here, based on the regulations in force at the time of printing. Test standards are becoming increasingly stringent, although there are some exemptions for older vehicles.

An assistant will be needed to help carry out some of these checks.

The checks have been sub-divided into four categories, as follows:

1 Checks carried out **FROM THE DRIVER'S SEAT**

2 Checks carried out **WITH THE VEHICLE ON THE GROUND**

3 Checks carried out **WITH THE VEHICLE RAISED AND THE WHEELS FREE TO TURN**

4 Checks carried out on **YOUR VEHICLE'S EXHAUST EMISSION SYSTEM**

---

1 Checks carried out **FROM THE DRIVER'S SEAT**

Handbrake (parking brake)

☐ Test the operation of the handbrake. Excessive travel (too many clicks) indicates incorrect brake or cable adjustment.
☐ Check that the handbrake cannot be released by tapping the lever sideways. Check the security of the lever mountings.

☐ If the parking brake is foot-operated, check that the pedal is secure and without excessive travel, and that the release mechanism operates correctly.
☐ Where applicable, test the operation of the electronic handbrake. The brake should engage and disengage without excessive delay. If the warning light does not extinguish when the brake is disengaged, this could indicate a fault which will need further investigation.

Footbrake

☐ Depress the brake pedal and check that it does not creep down to the floor, indicating a master cylinder fault. Release the pedal,

wait a few seconds, then depress it again. If the pedal travels nearly to the floor before firm resistance is felt, brake adjustment or repair is necessary. If the pedal feels spongy, there is air in the hydraulic system which must be removed by bleeding.

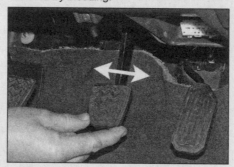

☐ Check that the brake pedal is secure and in good condition. Check also for signs of fluid leaks on the pedal, floor or carpets, which would indicate failed seals in the brake master cylinder.
☐ Check the servo unit (when applicable) by operating the brake pedal several times, then keeping the pedal depressed and starting the engine. As the engine starts, the pedal will move down slightly. If not, the vacuum hose or the servo itself may be faulty.

Steering wheel and column

☐ Examine the steering wheel for fractures or looseness of the hub, spokes or rim.
☐ Move the steering wheel from side to side and then up and down. Check that the steering wheel is not loose on the column, indicating wear or a loose retaining nut. Continue moving the steering wheel as before, but also turn it slightly from left to right.

☐ Check that the steering wheel is not loose on the column, and that there is no abnormal movement of the steering wheel, indicating wear in the column support bearings or couplings.
☐ Check that the ignition lock (where fitted) engages and disengages correctly.
☐ Steering column adjustment mechanisms (where fitted) must be able to lock the column securely in place with no play evident.

Windscreen, mirrors and sunvisor

☐ The windscreen must be free of cracks or other significant damage within the driver's field of view. (Small stone chips are acceptable.) Rear view mirrors must be secure, intact, and capable of being adjusted.

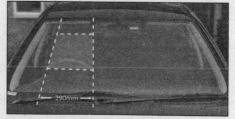

☐ The driver's sunvisor must be capable of being stored in the "up" position.

Seat belts and seats

Note: *The following checks are applicable to all seat belts, front and rear.*

☐ Examine the webbing of all the belts (including rear belts if fitted) for cuts, serious fraying or deterioration. Fasten and unfasten each belt to check the buckles. If applicable, check the retracting mechanism. Check the security of all seat belt mountings accessible from inside the vehicle, ensuring any height adjustable mountings lock securely in place.

☐ Seat belts with pre-tensioners, once activated, have a "flag" or similar showing on the seat belt stalk. This, in itself, is not a reason for test failure.

☐ The front seats themselves must be securely attached and the backrests must lock in the upright position.

Doors

☐ Both front doors must be able to be opened and closed from outside and inside, and must latch securely when closed.

Bonnet and boot/tailgate

☐ The bonnet and boot/tailgate must latch securely when closed.

2 Checks carried out WITH THE VEHICLE ON THE GROUND

Vehicle identification

☐ Number plates must be in good condition, secure and legible, with letters and numbers correctly spaced – spacing at (A) should be 33 mm and at (B) 11 mm. At the front, digits must be black on a white background and at the rear black on a yellow background. Other background designs (such as honeycomb) are not permitted.

☐ The VIN plate and/or homologation plate must be permanently displayed and legible.

Electrical equipment

☐ Switch on the ignition and check the operation of the horn.

☐ Check the windscreen washers and wipers, examining the wiper blades; renew damaged or perished blades. Also check the operation of the stop-lights.

☐ Check the operation of the sidelights and number plate lights. The lenses and reflectors must be secure, clean and undamaged.

☐ Check the operation and alignment of the headlights. The headlight reflectors must not be tarnished and the lenses must be undamaged.

☐ Switch on the ignition and check the operation of the direction indicators (including the instrument panel tell-tale) and the hazard warning lights. Operation of the sidelights and stop-lights must not affect the indicators - if it does, the cause is usually a bad earth at the rear light cluster. Indicators should flash at a rate of between 60 and 120 times per minute – faster or slower than this could indicate a fault with the flasher unit or a bad earth at one of the light units.

☐ Check the operation of the rear foglight(s), including the warning light on the instrument panel or in the switch.

☐ The warning lights must illuminate in accordance with the manufacturer's design. For most vehicles, the ABS and other warning lights should illuminate when the ignition is switched on, and (if the system is operating properly) extinguish after a few seconds. Refer to the owner's handbook.

Footbrake

☐ Examine the master cylinder, brake pipes and servo unit for leaks, loose mountings, corrosion or other damage. If ABS is fitted, this unit should also be examined for signs of leaks or corrosion.

☐ The fluid reservoir must be secure and the fluid level must be between the upper (A) and lower (B) markings.

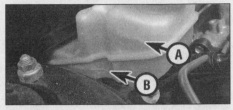

☐ Inspect both front brake flexible hoses for cracks or deterioration of the rubber. Turn the steering from lock to lock, and ensure that the hoses do not contact the wheel, tyre, or any part of the steering or suspension mechanism. With the brake pedal firmly depressed, check the hoses for bulges or leaks under pressure.

Steering and suspension

☐ Have your assistant turn the steering wheel from side to side slightly, up to the point where the steering gear just begins to transmit this movement to the roadwheels. Check for excessive free play between the steering wheel and the steering gear, indicating wear or insecurity of the steering column joints, the column-to-steering gear coupling, or the steering gear itself.

☐ Have your assistant turn the steering wheel more vigorously in each direction, so that the roadwheels just begin to turn. As this is done, examine all the steering joints, linkages, fittings and attachments. Renew any component that shows signs of wear or damage. On vehicles with power steering, check the security and condition of the steering pump, drivebelt and hoses.

☐ Check that the vehicle is standing level, and at approximately the correct ride height.

Shock absorbers

☐ Depress each corner of the vehicle in turn, then release it. The vehicle should rise and then settle in its normal position. If the vehicle continues to rise and fall, the shock absorber is defective. A shock absorber which has seized will also cause the vehicle to fail.

Exhaust system

☐ Start the engine. With your assistant holding a rag over the tailpipe, check the entire system for leaks. Repair or renew leaking sections.

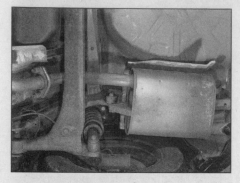

3 Checks carried out **WITH THE VEHICLE RAISED AND THE WHEELS FREE TO TURN**

Jack up the front and rear of the vehicle, and securely support it on axle stands. Position the stands clear of the suspension assemblies. Ensure that the wheels are clear of the ground and that the steering can be turned from lock to lock.

Steering mechanism

☐ Have your assistant turn the steering from lock to lock. Check that the steering turns smoothly, and that no part of the steering mechanism, including a wheel or tyre, fouls any brake hose or pipe or any part of the body structure.

☐ Examine the steering rack rubber gaiters for damage or insecurity of the retaining clips. If power steering is fitted, check for signs of damage or leakage of the fluid hoses, pipes or connections. Also check for excessive stiffness or binding of the steering, a missing split pin or locking device, or severe corrosion of the body structure within 30 cm of any steering component attachment point.

Front and rear suspension and wheel bearings

☐ Starting at the front right-hand side, grasp the roadwheel at the 3 o'clock and 9 o'clock positions and rock gently but firmly. Check for free play or insecurity at the wheel bearings, suspension balljoints, or suspension mount-ings, pivots and attachments.

☐ Now grasp the wheel at the 12 o'clock and 6 o'clock positions and repeat the previous inspection. Spin the wheel, and check for roughness or tightness of the front wheel bearing.

☐ If excess free play is suspected at a component pivot point, this can be confirmed by using a large screwdriver or similar tool and levering between the mounting and the component attachment. This will confirm whether the wear is in the pivot bush, its retaining bolt, or in the mounting itself (the bolt holes can often become elongated).

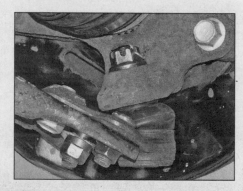

☐ Carry out all the above checks at the other front wheel, and then at both rear wheels.

Springs and shock absorbers

☐ Examine the suspension struts (when applicable) for serious fluid leakage, corrosion, or damage to the casing. Also check the security of the mounting points.

☐ If coil springs are fitted, check that the spring ends locate in their seats, and that the spring is not corroded, cracked or broken.

☐ If leaf springs are fitted, check that all leaves are intact, that the axle is securely attached to each spring, and that there is no deterioration of the spring eye mountings, bushes, and shackles.

☐ The same general checks apply to vehicles fitted with other suspension types, such as torsion bars, hydraulic displacer units, etc. Ensure that all mountings and attachments are secure, that there are no signs of excessive wear, corrosion or damage, and (on hydraulic types) that there are no fluid leaks or damaged pipes.

☐ Inspect the shock absorbers for signs of serious fluid leakage. Check for wear of the mounting bushes or attachments, or damage to the body of the unit.

Driveshafts (fwd vehicles only)

☐ Rotate each front wheel in turn and inspect the constant velocity joint gaiters for splits or damage. Also check that each driveshaft is straight and undamaged.

Braking system

☐ If possible without dismantling, check brake pad wear and disc condition. Ensure that the friction lining material has not worn excessively, (A) and that the discs are not fractured, pitted, scored or badly worn (B).

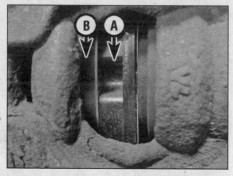

☐ Examine all the rigid brake pipes underneath the vehicle, and the flexible hose(s) at the rear. Look for corrosion, chafing or insecurity of the pipes, and for signs of bulging under pressure, chafing, splits or deterioration of the flexible hoses.

☐ Look for signs of fluid leaks at the brake calipers or on the brake backplates. Repair or renew leaking components.

☐ Slowly spin each wheel, while your assistant depresses and releases the footbrake. Ensure that each brake is operating and does not bind when the pedal is released.

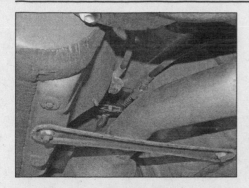

☐ Examine the handbrake mechanism, checking for frayed or broken cables, excessive corrosion, or wear or insecurity of the linkage. Check that the mechanism works on each relevant wheel, and releases fully, without binding.

☐ It is not possible to test brake efficiency without special equipment, but a road test can be carried out later to check that the vehicle pulls up in a straight line.

Fuel and exhaust systems

☐ Inspect the fuel tank (including the filler cap), fuel pipes, hoses and unions. All components must be secure and free from leaks. Locking fuel caps must lock securely and the key must be provided for the MOT test.

☐ Examine the exhaust system over its entire length, checking for any damaged, broken or missing mountings, security of the retaining clamps and rust or corrosion.

Wheels and tyres

☐ Examine the sidewalls and tread area of each tyre in turn. Check for cuts, tears, lumps, bulges, separation of the tread, and exposure of the ply or cord due to wear or damage. Check that the tyre bead is correctly seated on the wheel rim, that the valve is sound and properly seated, and that the wheel is not distorted or damaged.

☐ Check that the tyres are of the correct size for the vehicle, that they are of the same size and type on each axle, and that the pressures are correct.

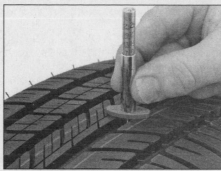

☐ Check the tyre tread depth. The legal minimum at the time of writing is 1.6 mm over the central three-quarters of the tread width. Abnormal tread wear may indicate incorrect front wheel alignment or wear in steering or suspension components.

☐ If the spare wheel is fitted externally or in a separate carrier beneath the vehicle, check that mountings are secure and free of excessive corrosion.

Body corrosion

☐ Check the condition of the entire vehicle structure for signs of corrosion in load-bearing areas. (These include chassis box sections, side sills, cross-members, pillars, and all suspension, steering, braking system and seat belt mountings and anchorages.) Any corrosion which has seriously reduced the thickness of a load-bearing area (or is within 30 cm of safety-related components such as steering or suspension) is likely to cause the vehicle to fail. In this case professional repairs are likely to be needed.

☐ Damage or corrosion which causes sharp or otherwise dangerous edges to be exposed will also cause the vehicle to fail.

Towbars

☐ Check the condition of mounting points (both beneath the vehicle and within boot/hatchback areas) for signs of corrosion, ensuring that all fixings are secure and not worn or damaged. There must be no excessive play in detachable tow ball arms or quick-release mechanisms.

4 Checks carried out on **YOUR VEHICLE'S EXHAUST EMISSION SYSTEM**

Petrol models

☐ The engine should be warmed up, and running well (ignition system in good order, air filter element clean, etc).

☐ Before testing, run the engine at around 2500 rpm for 20 seconds. Let the engine drop to idle, and watch for smoke from the exhaust. If the idle speed is too high, or if dense blue or black smoke emerges for more than 5 seconds, the vehicle will fail. Typically, blue smoke signifies oil burning (engine wear); black smoke means unburnt fuel (dirty air cleaner element, or other fuel system fault).

☐ An exhaust gas analyser for measuring carbon monoxide (CO) and hydrocarbons (HC) is now needed. If one cannot be hired or borrowed, have a local garage perform the check.

CO emissions (mixture)

☐ The MOT tester has access to the CO limits for all vehicles. The CO level is measured at idle speed, and at 'fast idle' (2500 to 3000 rpm). The following limits are given as a general guide:

At idle speed – Less than 0.5% CO
At 'fast idle' – Less than 0.3% CO
Lambda reading – 0.97 to 1.03

☐ If the CO level is too high, this may point to poor maintenance, a fuel injection system problem, faulty lambda (oxygen) sensor or catalytic converter. Try an injector cleaning treatment, and check the vehicle's ECU for fault codes.

HC emissions

☐ The MOT tester has access to HC limits for all vehicles. The HC level is measured at 'fast idle' (2500 to 3000 rpm). The following limits are given as a general guide:

At 'fast idle' – Less then 200 ppm

☐ Excessive HC emissions are typically caused by oil being burnt (worn engine), or by a blocked crankcase ventilation system ('breather'). If the engine oil is old and thin, an oil change may help. If the engine is running badly, check the vehicle's ECU for fault codes.

Diesel models

☐ The only emission test for diesel engines is measuring exhaust smoke density, using a calibrated smoke meter. The test involves accelerating the engine at least 3 times to its maximum unloaded speed.

Note: *On engines with a timing belt, it is VITAL that the belt is in good condition before the test is carried out.*

☐ With the engine warmed up, it is first purged by running at around 2500 rpm for 20 seconds. A governor check is then carried out, by slowly accelerating the engine to its maximum speed. After this, the smoke meter is connected, and the engine is accelerated quickly to maximum speed three times. If the smoke density is less than the limits given below, the vehicle will pass:

Non-turbo vehicles: 2.5m-1
Turbocharged vehicles: 3.0m-1

☐ If excess smoke is produced, try fitting a new air cleaner element, or using an injector cleaning treatment. If the engine is running badly, where applicable, check the vehicle's ECU for fault codes. Also check the vehicle's EGR system, where applicable. At high mileages, the injectors may require professional attention.

Engine

- [ ] Engine fails to rotate when attempting to start
- [ ] Engine rotates, but will not start
- [ ] Engine difficult to start when cold
- [ ] Engine difficult to start when hot
- [ ] Starter motor noisy or excessively rough in engagement
- [ ] Engine starts, but stops immediately
- [ ] Engine idles erratically
- [ ] Engine misfires at idle speed
- [ ] Engine misfires throughout the driving speed range
- [ ] Engine lacks power
- [ ] Engine backfires
- [ ] Oil pressure warning light illuminated with engine running
- [ ] Engine runs-on after switching off
- [ ] Tapping or rattling noises
- [ ] Knocking or thumping noises
- [ ] Pre-ignition (pinking) or knocking during acceleration or under load
- [ ] Whistling or wheezing noises

Cooling system

- [ ] Overheating
- [ ] Overcooling
- [ ] External coolant leakage
- [ ] Internal coolant leakage
- [ ] Corrosion

Fuel and exhaust systems

- [ ] Excessive fuel consumption
- [ ] Fuel leakage and/or fuel odour
- [ ] Excessive noise or fumes from the exhaust system

Clutch

- [ ] Pedal travels to the floor – no pressure or very little resistance
- [ ] Clutch fails to disengage (unable to select gears)
- [ ] Clutch slips (engine speed increases, with no increase in vehicle speed)
- [ ] Judder as clutch is engaged
- [ ] Noise when depressing or releasing clutch pedal

Manual transmission

- [ ] Noisy in neutral with the engine running
- [ ] Noisy in one particular gear
- [ ] Difficulty in engaging gears
- [ ] Jumps out of gear
- [ ] Vibration
- [ ] Lubricant leaks

Driveshafts

- [ ] Vibration when accelerating or decelerating
- [ ] Clicking or knocking noise on turns (at slow speed on full-lock)

Braking system

- [ ] Vehicle pull to one side under braking
- [ ] Noise (grinding or high-pitched squeal) when brakes applied
- [ ] Excessive brake pedal travel
- [ ] Brake pedal feels spongy when depressed
- [ ] Excessive brake pedal effort required to stop vehicle
- [ ] Judder felt through brake pedal or steering wheel when braking
- [ ] Pedal pulsates when braking hard
- [ ] Brakes binding

Steering and suspension

- [ ] Vehicle pulls to one side
- [ ] Wheel wobble and vibration
- [ ] Excessive pitching and/or rolling around corners, or during braking
- [ ] Wandering or general instablity
- [ ] Excessively stiff steering
- [ ] Excessive play in steering
- [ ] Lack of power assistance
- [ ] Tyre wear excessive

Electrical system

- [ ] Battery will not hold charge for more than a few days
- [ ] Ignition/no-charge warning light remains illuminated with the engine running
- [ ] Lights inoperative
- [ ] Fuel or temperature gauge inaccurate
- [ ] Horn operates continuously
- [ ] Horn inoperative
- [ ] Wipers fail to operate, or operate very slowly
- [ ] Wiper blades sweep over too large, or too small an area of glass
- [ ] Wiper blades fail to clean the glass effectively
- [ ] Screen or headlight washers inoperative, or unsatisfactory in operation
- [ ] Window glass moves only in one direction
- [ ] Window glass slow to move
- [ ] Window glass fails to move
- [ ] Central locking system inoperative, or unsatisfactory in operation.

Introduction

The vehicle owner who does his or her own maintenance according to the recommended service schedules should not have to use this section of the manual very often. Modern component reliability is such that, provided those items subject to wear or deterioration are inspected or renewed at the specified intervals, sudden failure is comparatively rare. Faults do not usually just happen as a result of sudden failure, but develop over a period of time. Major mechanical failures in particular are usually preceded by characteristic symptoms over hundreds or even thousands of miles. Those components which do occasionally fail without warning are often small and easily carried in the vehicle.

With any fault-finding, the first step is to decide where to begin investigations. Sometimes this is obvious, but on other occasions, a little detective work will be necessary. The owner who makes half a dozen haphazard adjustments or replacements may be successful in curing a fault (or its symptoms), but will be none the wiser if the fault recurs, and ultimately may have spent more time and money than was necessary.

A calm and logical approach will be found to be more satisfactory in the long run. Always take into account any warning signs or abnormalities that may have been noticed in the period preceding the fault – power loss, high or low gauge readings, unusual smells, etc – and remember that failure of components such as fuses or spark plugs may only be pointers to some underlying fault

The pages which follow provide an easy-reference guide to the more common problems which may occur during the operation of the vehicle. These problems and their possible causes are grouped under headings denoting various components or systems, such as Engine, Cooling system, etc. The Chapter and/or Section which deals with the problem is also shown in brackets. Whatever the fault, certain basic principles apply. These are as follows:

Verify the fault. This is simply a matter of being sure that you know what the symptoms are before starting work. This is particularly important if you are investigating a fault for someone else, who may not have described it very accurately.

Don't overlook the obvious. For example, if the vehicle won't start, is there fuel in the tank? (Don't take anyone else's word on this particular point, and don't trust the fuel gauge either!) If an electrical fault is indicated, look for loose or broken wires before digging out the test gear.

Cure the disease, not the symptom. Substituting a flat battery with a fully-charged one will get you off the hard shoulder, but if the underlying cause is not attended to, the new battery will go the same way. Similarly, changing oil-fouled spark plugs for a new set will get you moving again, but remember that the reason for the fouling (if it wasn't simply an incorrect grade of plug) will have to be established and corrected.

Don't take anything for granted. Particularly, don't forget that a 'new' component may itself be defective (especially if it's been rattling around in the boot for months), and don't leave components out of a fault diagnosis sequence just because they are new or recently-fitted. When you do finally diagnose a difficult fault, you'll probably realise that all the evidence was there from the start.

Engine

Engine fails to rotate when attempting to start

- ☐ · Battery terminal connections loose or corroded (Chapter 5A Section 4).
- ☐ Battery discharged or faulty (Chapter 5A Section 3).
- ☐ Broken, loose or disconnected wiring in the starting circuit (Chapter 12 Section 2).
- ☐ Defective starter solenoid or switch (Chapter 5A Section 2).
- ☐ Defective starter motor (Chapter 5A Section 8).
- ☐ Starter pinion or flywheel ring gear teeth loose or broken (Chapter 5A Section 9 and Chapter 2A Section 12 or Chapter 2B Section 12).
- ☐ Engine earth strap broken or disconnected (Chapter 12 Section 2).

Engine rotates, but will not start

- ☐ Fuel tank empty.
- ☐ Battery discharged (engine rotates slowly) (Chapter 5A Section 3).
- ☐ Battery terminals loose or corroded ('Weekly checks').
- ☐ Ignition components damp or damaged (Chapter 5B Section 2).
- ☐ Fuel injection system faulty (Chapter 4A Section 8).
- ☐ Worn or faulty spark plugs (Chapter 1 Section 17).
- ☐ Major mechanical failure (Chapter 2A or Chapter 2B).

Engine difficult to start when cold

- ☐ Battery discharged (Chapter 5A Section 3).
- ☐ Battery terminal connections loose or corroded ('Weekly checks').
- ☐ Worn or faulty spark plugs (Chapter 1 Section 17).
- ☐ Other ignition system fault (Chapter 5B Section 2 or Chapter 1 Section 18)Fuel injection system faulty (Chapter 4A Section 8).
- ☐ Low cylinder compressions (Chapter 2A Section 2 or Chapter 2B Section 2).

Engine difficult to start when hot

- ☐ Air filter element dirty or clogged (Chapter 1 Section 23).
- ☐ Fuel injection system faulty (Chapter 4A Section 8).
- ☐ Low cylinder compressions (Chapter 2A Section 2 or Chapter 2B Section 2).

Starter motor noisy or excessively rough in engagement

- ☐ Starter pinion or flywheel ring gear teeth loose or broken (Chapter 5A Section 7 and Chapter 2A Section 12 or Chapter 2B Section 12).
- ☐ Starter motor mounting bolts loose or missing (Chapter 5A Section 8).
- ☐ Starter motor internal components worn or damaged (Chapter 5A Section 9).

Engine starts, but stops immediately

- ☐ Blocked injector/fuel injection system fault (Chapter 4A).
- ☐ Loose or faulty electrical connections in the ignition circuit (Chapter 1 or Chapter 5B).
- ☐ Vacuum leak at the throttle body or intake manifold (Chapter 4A Section 9, 10, 11).
- ☐ Immobiliser fault – refer to a Fiat dealer or specialist.

Engine idles erratically

- ☐ Air filter element clogged (Chapter 1 Section 23).
- ☐ Uneven or low compressions (Chapter 2A Section 2 or Chapter 2B Section 2).
- ☐ Vacuum leak at throttle body, intake manifold or associated hoses (Chapter 4A Section 9, 10, 11).
- ☐ Camshaft lobes worn (Chapter 2A or 2B Section 10).
- ☐ Blocked injector/fuel injection system fault (Chapter 4A).
- ☐ Worn or faulty spark plugs (Chapter 1 Section 17).
- ☐ Timing belt incorrectly fitted/tensioned (Chapter 2A Section 5 or Chapter 2B Section 5).

Engine misfires at idle speed

- ☐ Faulty injectors/fuel injection system fault (Chapter 4A).
- ☐ Worn or faulty spark plugs (Chapter 1 Section 17).
- ☐ Vacuum leaks at the throttle body, intake manifold or associated hoses (Chapter 4A Section 9, 10, 11).
- ☐ Uneven or low compressions (Chapter 2A or 2B Section 2).
- ☐ Disconnected, leaking or perished crankcase ventilation hoses (Chapter 4B).

Engine (continued)

Engine misfires throughout the driving speed range

- ☐ Fuel pump faulty, or delivery pressure low (Chapter 4A Section 6).
- ☐ Fuel tank vent blocked, or fuel pipes restricted (Chapter 4A Section 7).
- ☐ Vacuum leak at the throttle body, intake manifold or associated hoses (Chapter 4A Section 9, 10, 11).
- ☐ Worn or faulty spark plugs (Chapter 1 Section 17).
- ☐ Faulty ignition coil (Chapter 5B Section 3).
- ☐ Fault injector/fuel injection system fault (Chapter 4A).
- ☐ Uneven or low compressions (Chapter 2A Section 2 or Chapter 2B Section 2).

Engine lacks power

- ☐ Timing belt incorrectly fitted (Chapter 2A Section 5 or Chapter 2B Section 5).
- ☐ Fuel pump faulty (Chapter 4A Section 6).
- ☐ Air filter blocked (Chapter 1 Section 23).
- ☐ Uneven or low compressions (Chapter 2A Section 2 or Chapter 2B Section 2).
- ☐ Faulty injectors/injection system fault (Chapter 4A).
- ☐ Brakes binding (Chapter 9).
- ☐ Clutch slipping (Chapter 6).
- ☐ Worn or faulty spark plugs (Chapter 1 Section 17).

Engine backfires

- ☐ Timing belt incorrectly fitted (Chapter 2A Section 5 or Chapter 2B Section 5).
- ☐ Vacuum leak at the throttle body, intake manifold or associated hoses (Chapter 4A Section 9, 10, 11).
- ☐ Blocked injector/fuel injection system fault (Chapter 4A).

Oil pressure warning light illuminated with engine running

- ☐ Low oil level, or incorrect oil grade ('Weekly checks').
- ☐ Faulty oil pressure sensor (Chapter 2A Section 16 or Chapter 2B Section 16).
- ☐ Worn engine bearings and/or oil pump (Chapter 2C).
- ☐ High engine operating temperature (Chapter 3).
- ☐ Oil pressure relief valve defective (Chapter 2A Section 15 or Chapter 2B Section 15).
- ☐ Oil pick up strainer clogged (Chapter 2A Section 15 or Chapter 2B Section 15).

Engine runs-on after switching off

- ☐ Excessive carbon build-up in engine (Chapter 2C).
- ☐ High engine operating temperature (Chapter 3).
- ☐ Fuel injection system fault (Chapter 4A).
- ☐ Incorrect oil level ('Weekly checks').

Tapping or rattling noises

- ☐ Worn valve gear or camshaft (Chapter 2A Section 10 or Chapter 2B Section 10).
- ☐ Ancillary component fault (coolant pump, alternator etc.) (Chapter 3 and Chapter 5A).

Knocking or thumping noises

- ☐ Worn big-end bearings (regular heavy knocking, perhaps more under load) (Chapter 2C).
- ☐ Worn main bearings (rumbling and knocking, perhaps less under load) (Chapter 2C).
- ☐ Piston slap (most noticeable when cold) (Chapter 2C).
- ☐ Ancillary component fault (coolant pump, alternator, etc.) (Chapter 3 and Chapter 5A).

Pre-ignition (pinking) or knocking during acceleration or under load

- ☐ Ignition timing incorrect/ignition system fault (Chapter 5B Section 2).
- ☐ Incorrect grade of spark plug (Chapter 1 Section 17).
- ☐ Vacuum leak at the throttle body, intake manifold or associated hoses (Chapter 4A Section 9, 10, 11).
- ☐ Excessive carbon build-up in the cylinder head (Chapter 2C Section 7).

Whistling or wheezing noises

- ☐ Leaking intake manifold or throttle body gasket (Chapter 4A Section 9, 10, 11).
- ☐ Leaking exhaust manifold or pipe-to-manifold joint (Chapter 4A).
- ☐ Leaking vacuum hose.

Cooling system

Overheating

- ☐ Insufficient coolant in the system ('Weekly checks').
- ☐ Thermostat faulty (Chapter 3 Section 4).
- ☐ Radiator core blocked, or grille restricted (Chapter 3 Section 3).
- ☐ Electric cooling fan faulty (Chapter 3 Section 5).
- ☐ Air lock in cooling system (Chapter 1 Section 29).
- ☐ Expansion tank pressure cap faulty (Chapter 1 Section 29).
- ☐ Engine coolant temperature sensor faulty (Chapter 3 Section 6).

Overcooling

- ☐ Thermostat faulty (Chapter 3 Section 4).
- ☐ Engine coolant temperature sensor faulty (Chapter 3 Section 6).

External coolant leakage

- ☐ Deteriorated or damaged hoses or hose clips (Chapter 3 Section 2).
- ☐ Radiator core or heater matrix leaking (Chapter 3 Section 8).
- ☐ Pressure cap faulty (Chapter 1 Section 29).
- ☐ Coolant pump leaking (Chapter 3 Section 7).
- ☐ Boiling due to overheating.
- ☐ Core plug leaking (Chapter 2C Section 11).

Internal coolant leakage

- ☐ Leaking cylinder head gasket (Chapter 2A Section 11 or Chapter 2B Section 11).
- ☐ Cracked cylinder head or cylinder block (Chapter 2C).

Corrosion

- ☐ Infrequent draining and flushing (Chapter 1 Section 29).
- ☐ Incorrect coolant mixture or inappropriate coolant type (Chapter 1 Section 29).

Fuel and exhaust systems

Excessive fuel consumption

- [ ] Air filter dirty or clogged (Chapter 1 Section 23).
- [ ] Faulty injector/fuel injection system fault (Chapter 4A).
- [ ] Brakes binding (Chapter 9).
- [ ] Tyres under-inflated ('Weekly checks').

Fuel leakage and/or fuel odour

- [ ] Damaged or corroded fuel tank, pipes or connections (Chapter 4A).

Excessive noise or fumes from the exhaust system

- [ ] Leaking exhaust system or manifold leaks (Chapter 4A).
- [ ] Leaking or corroded silencers or pipe (Chapter 4A Section 13).
- [ ] Broken mountings causing body or suspension contact (Chapter 4A Section 13).

Clutch

Pedal travels to the floor – no pressure or very little resistance

- [ ] Faulty master or slave cylinder (Chapter 6 Section 3 or Chapter 6 Section 4).
- [ ] Faulty hydraulic release system (Chapter 6).
- [ ] Broken clutch release bearing (Chapter 6 Section 6).
- [ ] Broken diaphragm spring in clutch pressure plate (Chapter 6 Section 5).

Clutch fails to disengage (unable to select gears)

- [ ] Faulty master or slave cylinder (Chapter 6 Section 3 or Chapter 6 Section 4).
- [ ] Faulty hydraulic hose.
- [ ] Clutch disc sticking on the gearbox input shaft splines (Chapter 6 Section 5).
- [ ] Clutch disc sticking on the flywheel or pressure plate (Chapter 6 Section 5).
- [ ] Faulty pressure plate assembly (Chapter 6 Section 5).
- [ ] Air in hydraulic system (Chapter 6 Section 2).

Clutch slips (engine speed increases, with no increase in vehicle speed)

- [ ] Faulty hydraulic release system (Chapter 6).
- [ ] Clutch disc linings excessively worn (Chapter 6 Section 5).

- [ ] Clutch disc lining contaminated with oil or grease (Chapter 6 Section 5).
- [ ] Faulty pressure plate or weak diaphragm spring (Chapter 6 Section 5).

Judder as clutch is engaged

- [ ] Clutch disc linings contaminated with oil or grease (Chapter 6 Section 5).
- [ ] Clutch disc linings excessively worn (Chapter 6 Section 5).
- [ ] Faulty or distorted pressure plate or diaphragm spring (Chapter 6 Section 5).
- [ ] Worn or loose engine or gearbox mountings (Chapter 2A Section 13 or Chapter 2B Section 13).
- [ ] Clutch disc or gearbox input shaft splines worn (Chapter 6 Section 5).

Noise when depressing or releasing clutch pedal

- [ ] Worn clutch release bearing (Chapter 6 Section 6).
- [ ] Worn or dry clutch pedal pivot.
- [ ] Faulty pressure plate assembly (Chapter 6 Section 5).
- [ ] Pressure plate diaphragm spring broken (Chapter 6 Section 5).

Manual transmission

Noisy in neutral with the engine running

- [ ] Input shaft bearings worn (noise apparent with clutch pedal released, but not when depressed) (Chapter 7 Section 6).
- [ ] *Clutch release bearings worn (noise apparent with clutch pedal depressed, possibly less when released (Chapter 6 Section 4).

Noisy in one particular gear

- [ ] Worn, damaged or chipped gear teeth (Chapter 7 Section 6).*

Difficulty in engaging gears

- [ ] Clutch faulty (Chapter 6).
- [ ] Clutch hydraulic hose faulty.
- [ ] Worn synchroniser units (Chapter 7 Section 6).*

Jumps out of gear

- [ ] Worn synchroniser units (Chapter 7 Section 6).
- [ ] *Worn selector forks (Chapter 7 Section 6).*

Vibration

- [ ] Lack of oil (Chapter 7 Section 2).
- [ ] Worn bearings (Chapter 7 Section 6).*

Lubricant leaks

- [ ] Leaking oil seal (Section).
- [ ] Leaking housing joint (Chapter 7 Section 6).
- [ ] *Leaking input shaft oil seal (Chapter 7).

Note: *Although the corrective action necessary to remedy the symptoms described in beyond the scope of the home mechanic, then above information should be helpful in isolating the cause of the condition, so that the owner can communicate clearly with a professional mechanic.*

Driveshafts

Vibration when accelerating or decelerating

- [ ] Worn constant velocity joint (Chapter 8 Section 2).
- [ ] Bent or distorted driveshaft (Chapter 8 Section 2).

Clicking or knocking noise on turns (at slow speed on full-lock)

- [ ] Lack of constant velocity joint lubricant, possible due to damaged gaiter (Chapter 8 Section 3).
- [ ] Worn constant velocity joint (Chapter 8 Section 3).

Braking system

Vehicle pull to one side under braking

- [ ] Worn, defective, damaged or contaminated brake pads/shoes on one side (Chapter 9 Section 4 or Chapter 9 Section 5 or Chapter 9 Section 11).
- [ ] Seized or partially seized front or rear brake caliper/wheel cylinder piston (Chapter 9 Section 8 or Chapter 9 Section 9 or Chapter 9 Section 12).
- [ ] A mixture of brake pad/shoe lining materials fitted between sides (Chapter 9 Section 4 or Chapter 9 Section 5 or Chapter 9 Section 11).
- [ ] Brake caliper mounting bolts loose (Chapter 9 Section 8 or Chapter 9 Section 9).
- [ ] Worn or damaged steering or suspension components (Chapter 10).

Noise (grinding or high-pitched squeal) when brakes applied

- [ ] Brake pad/shoe friction material worn down to metal backing (Chapter 9 Section 4 or Chapter 9 Section 5 or Chapter 9 Section 11).
- [ ] Excessive corrosion of brake disc/shoe – may be apparent after the vehicle has been standing for some time (Chapter 9 Section 6 or Chapter 9 Section 10).
- [ ] Foreign object (stone chipping, etc.) trapped between the brake disc and shield.

Excessive brake pedal travel

- [ ] Faulty master cylinder (Chapter 9 Section 13).
- [ ] Air in hydraulic system (Chapter 9 Section 2).
- [ ] Faulty vacuum servo unit (Section).

Brake pedal feels spongy when depressed

- [ ] Air in hydraulic system (Chapter 9 Section 2).
- [ ] Deteriorated flexible rubber brake hoses (Chapter 9 Section 3).
- [ ] Master cylinder mountings loose (Chapter 9 Section 13).
- [ ] Faulty master cylinder (Chapter 9 Section 13).

Excessive brake pedal effort required to stop vehicle

- [ ] Faulty vacuum servo unit (Section).
- [ ] Faulty servo unit check valve (Section).
- [ ] Disconnected, damaged or insecure brake servo vacuum hose (Chapter 9 Section 19).
- [ ] Faulty brake pipe or hose (Chapter 9 Section 3).
- [ ] Seized brake caliper/wheel cylinder (Chapter 9 Section 8 or Chapter 9 Section 9 or Chapter 9 Section 12).
- [ ] Brake pads/shoes incorrectly fitted (Chapter 9 Section 4, 5, 11).
- [ ] Incorrect grade of brake pads/shoes fitted (Chapter 9 Section 4, 5, 11).
- [ ] Brake pads/shoes contaminated (Chapter 9 Section 4, 5, 11).

Judder felt through brake pedal or steering wheel when braking

- [ ] Excessive run-out or distortion of brake disc/drum (Chapter 9 Section 6, 7, 10).
- [ ] Brake pad/shoe linings worn (Chapter 9 Section 4, 5, 11).
- [ ] Brake caliper mountings loose (Chapter 9 Section 8, 9).
- [ ] Wear in suspension or steering components or mountings (Chapter 10).

Pedal pulsates when braking hard

- [ ] Normal feature of ABS – no fault.

Brakes binding

- [ ] Seized brake caliper/wheel cylinder (Chapter 9 Section 8, 9, 12).
- [ ] Incorrectly adjusted parking brake (Chapter 9 Section 15).
- [ ] Faulty master cylinder (Chapter 9 Section 13).

Note: *Before assuming that a brake problem exists, make sure that the tyres are in good condition and correctly inflated, that the front wheel alignment is correct, and that the vehicle is not loaded with weight in an unequal manner.*

- [ ] Apart from checking the condition of all pipe and hose connections, any faults occurring on the anti-lock braking system should be referred to a Mercedes dealer or specialist for diagnosis.

Steering and suspension

Vehicle pulls to one side

- [ ] Defective tyre ('Weekly checks').
- [ ] Excessive wear in suspension or steering components (Chapter 1 Section 9).
- [ ] Incorrect front wheel alignment (Chapter 10 Section 18).
- [ ] Accident damage to steering or suspension components.

Wheel wobble and vibration

- [ ] Front roadwheels out of balance (vibration felt mainly through the steering wheel).
- [ ] Rear roadwheels out of balance (vibration felt mainly throughout the vehicle).
- [ ] Roadwheels damaged or distorted.
- [ ] Faulty or damaged tyre ('Weekly checks').
- [ ] Worn steering or suspension joints, bushes or components (Chapter 1 Section 9).
- [ ] Wheel bolts loose.

Excessive pitching and/or rolling around corners, or during braking

- [ ] Defective shock absorbers (Chapter 1 Section 9).
- [ ] Broken or weak coil spring and/or suspension components (Chapter 10).
- [ ] Worn or damaged anti-roll bar or mountings (Chapter 10 Section 8).

Wandering or general instablity

- [ ] Incorrect wheel alignment (Chapter 10 Section 18).
- [ ] Worn steering or suspension components (Chapter 1 Section 9).
- [ ] Roadwheels out of balance.
- [ ] Faulty or damaged tyre ('Weekly checks').
- [ ] Wheel bolts loose.
- [ ] Defective shock absorbers (Chapter 1 Section 9).

Excessively stiff steering

- [ ] Seized track rod end balljoint or suspension balljoint (Chapter 10).
- [ ] Broken or incorrectly adjusted auxiliary drivebelt (Chapter 1 Section 5).
- [ ] Incorrect front wheel alignment (Chapter 10 Section 18).
- [ ] Steering gear damaged (Chapter 10 Section 15).

Excessive play in steering

- [ ] Worn steering column universal joints (Chapter 10 Section 13).
- [ ] Worn steering track rod end balljoints (Chapter 10 Section 17).
- [ ] Worn steering gear (Chapter 10 Section 15).
- [ ] Worn steering or suspension joints, bushes or components (Chapter 10).

Lack of power assistance

- [ ] Faulty electronic power steering motor or control unit (Chapter 10 Section 14).

Steering and suspension (continued)

Tyre wear excessive

- [ ] Tyres under inflated (wear on both edges) ('Weekly checks').
- [ ] Incorrect camber or castor angles (wear on one edge) (Chapter 10 Section 18).
- [ ] Worn steering or suspension joints, bushes or components (Chapter 1 Section 9).

- [ ] Accident damage.
- [ ] Incorrect wheel alignment (feathered edges) (Chapter 10 Section 18).
- [ ] Tyres over-inflated (worn in centre of tread) ('Weekly checks').
- [ ] Worn shock absorbers (Chapter 10 Section 4).
- [ ] Tyres/wheel out of balance (tyres worn unevenly).
- [ ] Tyre/wheel damage ('Weekly checks').

Electrical system

Battery will not hold charge for more than a few days

- [ ] Battery defective internally (Chapter 5A Section 3).
- [ ] Battery terminal connections loose or corroded ('Weekly checks').
- [ ] Auxiliary drivebelt worn or incorrectly tensioned (Chapter 1 Section 5).
- [ ] Alternator not charging at correct output (Chapter 5A Section 5).
- [ ] Short circuit causing continual current drain (Chapter 12 Section 2).

Ignition/no-charge warning light remains illuminated with the engine running

- [ ] Auxiliary drivebelt broken, worn, or incorrectly adjusted (Chapter 1 Section 5).
- [ ] Internal fault in alternator or voltage regulator (Section).
- [ ] Broken, disconnected, or loose wiring in charging circuit (Chapter 12 Section 2).

Lights inoperative

- [ ] Blown bulb (Chapter 12 Section 6).
- [ ] Corrosion of bulbholder contacts (Chapter 12 Section 6).
- [ ] Blown fuse (Chapter 12 Section 3).
- [ ] Faulty relay (Chapter 12 Section 3).
- [ ] Broken, loose or disconnected wiring (Chapter 12 Section 2).
- [ ] Faulty switch (Chapter 12 Section 5).

Fuel or temperature gauge inaccurate

- [ ] Faulty fuel level sensor(s) (Chapter 4A Section 6).
- [ ] Faulty engine coolant temperature sensor (Chapter 3 Section 6).
- [ ] Faulty instrument cluster (Chapter 12 Section 10).

Horn operates continuously

- [ ] Horn contacts faulty (Chapter 12 Section 5).

Horn inoperative

- [ ] Horn switch contact faulty (Chapter 12 Section 5).
- [ ] Horn faulty (Chapter 12 Section 12).
- [ ] Fuse blown (Chapter 12 Section 3).

Wipers fail to operate, or operate very slowly

- [ ] Wiper blades stuck to screen, or seized linkage (Chapter 12 Section 14).
- [ ] Blown fuse (Chapter 12 Section 3).
- [ ] Faulty relay (Chapter 12 Section 3).
- [ ] Faulty wiper motor (Chapter 12 Section 14).

Wiper blades sweep over too large, or too small an area of glass

- [ ] Wiper arms incorrectly positioned on spindles (Chapter 12 Section 13).
- [ ] Excessive wear of wiper linkage (Chapter 12 Section 14).
- [ ] Wiper motor or linkage mountings loose (Chapter 12 Section 14).

Wiper blades fail to clean the glass effectively

- [ ] Wiper blade rubbers worn or perished ('Weekly checks').
- [ ] Wiper arms defective (Chapter 12 Section 13).
- [ ] Insufficient windscreen washer additive to adequately remove road film ('Weekly checks').

Screen or headlight washers inoperative, or unsatisfactory in operation

- [ ] Blocked washer jet (Chapter 12 Section 15).
- [ ] Disconnected, kinked or restricted fluid hose.
- [ ] Insufficient fluid in washer reservoir ('Weekly checks').
- [ ] Blown fuse (Chapter 12 Section 3).
- [ ] Faulty washer pump (Chapter 12 Section 15).
- [ ] Faulty switch (Chapter 12 Section 5).

Window glass moves only in one direction

- [ ] Faulty switch (Chapter 12 Section 5).

Window glass slow to move

- [ ] Regulator seized or damaged, or in need of lubrication (Chapter 11 Section 17).
- [ ] Door internal components or trim fouling regulator (Chapter 11 Section 13).
- [ ] Window guide rubber dirty or in need of lubrication (Silicone spray).
- [ ] Faulty motor (Chapter 11 Section 17).

Window glass fails to move

- [ ] Blown fuse (Chapter 12 Section 3).
- [ ] Broken or disconnected wiring or connections (Chapter 12 Section 2).
- [ ] Faulty motor (Chapter 11 Section 17).

Central locking system inoperative, or unsatisfactory in operation.

- [ ] Blown fuse (Chapter 12 Section 2).
- [ ] Broken or disconnected wiring or connectors (Chapter 12 Section 2).
- [ ] Faulty door/tailgate lock (Chapter 11 Section 9, 15).
- [ ] Faulty relay (Chapter 12 Section 3).

Note: *References throughout this index are in the form "Chapter number" • "Page number". So, for example, 2C•15 refers to page 15 of Chapter 2C.*

A

Accelerator pedal – 4A•3
Air bag system – 12•16, 12•17
Air cleaner assembly – 4A•3
Air conditioning system – 3•7, 3•8
Air filter – 1•12
Alternator – 5A•4
Anti-lock braking system (ABS) – 9•13, 9•14
Anti-theft system and engine immobiliser – 12•16
Antifreeze – 1•12, 1•14 (see also *Coolant*)
Auxiliary drivebelt – 1•7

B

Battery – 0•13, 5A•2, 5A•3
  tray – 5A•3
Body computer – 12•19
Body electrical systems – 12•1 et seq
Bodywork and fittings – 11•1 et seq
Bonnet – 11•6
  lock assembly – 11•6
  release cable – 11•6
Braking system – 9•1 et seq
  bleeding – 9•2
  caliper – 9•8, 9•9
  discs – 9•8
  drum – 9•9
  fault finding – REF•20
  fluid – 0•12, 1•12
  hydraulic pipes and hoses – 9•3
  master cylinder – 9•11
  pads – 1•8, 9•3, 9•6
  shoes – 9•9
Bulbs – 12•7, 12•10
Bumpers – 11•4

C

Camshaft and followers – 2A•8, 2B•10
Camshaft cover – 2A•6
Camshaft housing – 2B•8
Camshaft oil seal – 2A•7, 2B•8
Catalytic converter – 4B•2
Centre console – 11•18
Charging system – 5A•3

Clutch – 6•1 et seq
  assembly – 6•3
  bleeding – 6•1
  fault finding – REF•19
  fluid – 0•12
  master cylinder – 6•2
  release mechanism – 6•4
  slave cylinder – 6•3
Coil springs – 10•8
Compression test – 2A•3, 2B•3
Conversion factors – REF•6
Coolant – 0•12, 1•13 (see also *Antifreeze*)
Coolant pump – 3•4
Cooling, heating and ventilation systems – 3•1 et seq
  fault finding – REF•18
  hoses – 3•2
Crankshaft – 2C•7, 2C•9, 2C•11
  oil seals – 2A•7, 2B•8
Cylinder block/crankcase – 2C•8
Cylinder head – 2A•8, 2B•11, 2C•5, 2C•7
  and valves – 2C•6

D

Dimensions and weights – REF•1
DOHC (16-valve) 1.4L in-car repair procedures – 2B•1 et seq
Door – 11•8
  handle and lock – 11•8
  inner trim panel – 11•7
  window glass and regulator – 11•11
Driveshafts – 8•1 et seq
  gaiters – 1•8, 8•3
  fault finding – REF•19

E

Electric cooling fan – 3•4
Electrical system checks – 0•14
Electrical system fault finding – 12•2, REF•21
Emission control systems – 4B•1 et seq
Engine coolant temperature sensor (ECT) – 3•4
Engine fault finding – REF•17
Engine management system – 1•11
Engine mountings – 2A•9, 2B•13
Engine oil – 0•11, 1•6

Engine pressure warning light switch – 2A•12, 2B•15
Exhaust manifold – 4A•11
Exhaust system – 1•9, 4A•12
Exterior mirror – 11•11

F

Facia panels – 11•19
Fault finding – REF•16
  braking system – REF•20
  clutch – REF•19
  cooling system – REF•18
  driveshafts – REF•19
  electrical system – 12•2, REF•21
  engine – REF•17
  fuel and exhaust systems – REF•19
  manual transmission – REF•19
  steering and suspension – REF•20
Flywheel – 2A•9, 2B•12
Front anti-roll bar – 10•6
Front hub bearings – 10•3
Front hub carrier assembly – 10•2
Front subframe – 10•6
Front suspension lower arm – 10•5
  balljoint – 10•6
Front suspension strut – 10•4, 10•5
Fuel and exhaust systems – 4A•1 et seq
  fault finding – REF•19
Fuel economy – REF•2
Fuel injection components (DOHC 16v engines) – 4A•9
Fuel injection components (SOHC 8v engines) – 4A•7
Fuel injection system – 4A•7
Fuel pipes and fittings – 4A•4
Fuel pump and fuel level sensor unit – 4A•6
Fuel system depressurization – 4A•4
Fuel tank – 4A•7
Fuses and relays – 12•3

G

Gearbox oil – 7•2
Gearchange lever assembly – 7•3
Gearchange selector cables – 7•2
General engine removal and overhaul procedures – 2C•1 et seq

Note: *References throughout this index are in the form "Chapter number" • "Page number". So, for example, 2C•15 refers to page 15 of Chapter 2C.*

H

Handbrake – 1•9, 9•12
   cables – 9•12
   'on' warning light switch – 9•13
   lever – 9•13
Headlight beam adjustment – 12•12
Heater blower motor – 3•6
Heater matrix – 3•6
Heating and ventilation system – 3•5
Horns – 12•13
HT leads – 1•11

I

Ignition coils – 5B•2
Ignition switch and lock barrel – 5A•5
Ignition system – 5B•1 *et seq*
Ignition timing – 5B•3
Infotainment units – 12•15
Instrument panel – 12•12
Intake manifold – 4A•10
Interior trim – 11•16

J

Jump starting – 0•8

K

Knock sensor – 5B•3

L

Leaks – 0•7, 1•7
Light units – 12•11
Lubricants and fluids – 0•16

M

Main and big-end bearings – 2C•10
Manual gearbox – 7•1 *et seq*
   fault finding – REF•19
   oil – 1•13
MOT test checks – REF•12

O

Oil filter – 1•6
Oil pump and pick-up tube – 2A•10, 2B•14

P

Parking obstacle detection system – 12•19
Piston rings – 2C•10
Piston/connecting rod assembly –
   2C•7, 2C•9, 2C•12
Pollen filter – 1•11
Power steering electric motor – 10•10

R

Radiator – 3•2
Rain sensor – 12•13
Rear hub assembly – 10•7
Rear wheel cylinder – 9•11
Reversing light switch – 7•4
Routine maintenance and
   servicing – 1•1 *et seq*

S

Safety First – 0•5
Screen/headlight washer fluid – 0•10
Seats – 11•13
   belts – 11•14
Service indicator reset – 1•10
Shock absorber – 10•7
SOHC (8-valve) in-car repair
   procedures – 2A•1 *et seq*
Spark plugs – 1•10
Speakers – 12•16
Starter motor – 5A•5
Starting and charging systems –
   5A•1 *et seq*
Steering and suspension – 1•8
   fault finding – REF•20
Steering column – 10•9
Steering rack – 10•10
   rubber gaiters – 10•11

Steering wheel – 10•8

Steering wheel – 10•8
Stop-light switch – 9•12
Stub axle – 10•8
Sump – 2A•10, 2B•13
Sunroof – 11•13
Suspension and steering – 10•1 *et seq*
Switches – 12•6

T

Tailgate – 11•5
   lock components – 11•6
   strut – 11•5
Thermostat – 3•3
Timing belt – 1•13, 2A•4, 2B•5
   covers – 2A•4, 2B•4
   tensioner and sprockets – 2A•6, 2B•7
Towing – 0•7
Track rod end – 10•11
Tyres – 0•15, 0•16

V

Vacuum servo unit check valve – 9•13
Valve clearance – 1•10
Valve timings – 2A•3, 2B•3
Vehicle identification – REF•9
Vehicle jacking and support – REF•7

W

Wheel alignment and steering
   angles – 10•11
Wheel changing – 0•9
Windscreen and fixed window
   glass – 11•13
Windscreen wiper motor and
   linkage – 12•14
Windscreen/tailgate washer
   system – 12•14
Wiper arm – 12•13
Wiper blades – 0•14
Wiring diagrams – 12•20 *et seq*

Preserving Our Motoring Heritage

< The Model J Duesenberg Derham Tourster. Only eight of these magnificent cars were ever built – this is the only example to be found outside the United States of America

Almost every car you've ever loved, loathed or desired is gathered under one roof at the Haynes Motor Museum. Over 300 immaculately presented cars and motorbikes represent every aspect of our motoring heritage, from elegant reminders of bygone days, such as the superb Model J Duesenberg to curiosities like the bug-eyed BMW Isetta. There are also many old friends and flames. Perhaps you remember the 1959 Ford Popular that you did your courting in? The magnificent 'Red Collection' is a spectacle of classic sports cars including AC, Alfa Romeo, Austin Healey, Ferrari, Lamborghini, Maserati, MG, Riley, Porsche and Triumph.

A Perfect Day Out

Each and every vehicle at the Haynes Motor Museum has played its part in the history and culture of Motoring. Today, they make a wonderful spectacle and a great day out for all the family. Bring the kids, bring Mum and Dad, but above all bring your camera to capture those golden memories for ever. You will also find an impressive array of motoring memorabilia, a comfortable 70 seat video cinema and one of the most extensive transport book shops in Britain. The Pit Stop Cafe serves everything from a cup of tea to wholesome, home-made meals or, if you prefer, you can enjoy the large picnic area nestled in the beautiful rural surroundings of Somerset.

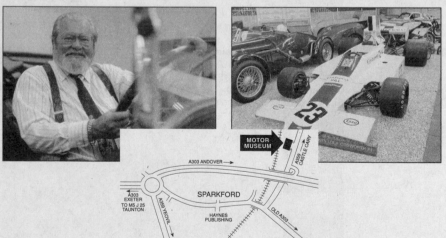

> John Haynes O.B.E., Founder and Chairman of the museum at the wheel of a Haynes Light 12.

< Graham Hill's Lola Cosworth Formula 1 car next to a 1934 Riley Sports.

The Museum is situated on the A359 Yeovil to Frome road at Sparkford, just off the A303 in Somerset. It is about 40 miles south of Bristol, and 25 minutes drive from the M5 intersection at Taunton.
Open 9.30am - 5.30pm (10.00am - 4.00pm Winter) 7 days a week, *except Christmas Day, Boxing Day and New Years Day*
Special rates available for schools, coach parties and outings Charitable Trust No. 292048